T0346717

Shared Reality

What Makes Us Strong and Tears Us Apart

E. TORY HIGGINS

OXFORD

UNIVERSITY PRESS

OXFORD
UNIVERSITY PRESS

Oxford University Press is a department of the University of Oxford. It furthers
the University's objective of excellence in research, scholarship, and education
by publishing worldwide. Oxford is a registered trade mark of Oxford University
Press in the UK and certain other countries.

Published in the United States of America by Oxford University Press
198 Madison Avenue, New York, NY 10016, United States of America.

Library of Congress Cataloging-in-Publication Data
Names: Higgins, E. Tory (Edward Tory), 1946– author.
Title: Shared reality : what makes us strong and tears us apart / E. Tory Higgins.
Description: New York : Oxford University Press, [2019]
Identifiers: LCCN 2018061051 | ISBN 9780190948054
Subjects: LCSH: Sharing. | Emotions.
Classification: LCC BF575.S48 H54 2019 | DDC 155.9/2—dc23
LC record available at https://lccn.loc.gov/2018061051

1 3 5 7 9 8 6 4 2

Printed by Sheridan Books, Inc., United States of America

Contents

Acknowledgments

This book would not have been written without the help and support of friends, family, colleagues, and teachers who contributed to its development in many different ways. It began with Wally Lambert at McGill University who introduced me to the wonders of how language, thought, and society impact one another. I now realize that Wally's groundbreaking approach to bilingual education was his recognition that learning another language was not so much about learning the grammar or syntax of the new language but, instead, was about wanting to share the feelings, thoughts, and concerns of that new language community. After graduating, I went to London School of Economics and Political Science where I studied with Norman Hotopf. Norman's version of language, thought, and society was a blend of his doctoral advisor, Bertrand Russell, and his postdoctoral advisor, Frederick Bartlett. Bartlett, especially, was a pioneer in studying shared reality by showing how information is modified when it is shared with others. As a doctoral student in the Department of Social Psychology at Columbia, I worked with Bob Krauss who was a groundbreaker in studying the development of communication. Inspired by his research, my doctoral dissertation examined developmental and social class differences in communication. It was my first research on language, thought, and society.

After leaving Columbia, I began working more on language and thought than language, thought, *and* society. It took me awhile to take seriously again the society part. But looking back, I recognize how much I was influenced by Wally, Norman, and Bob. I am very grateful to them.

I am also enormously grateful to Gerald Echterhoff. Gerald was a postdoctoral student with Bob Krauss when I returned to Columbia as a faculty member. I had just written a paper reviewing my previous work on communication where, for the first time, I referred to what was happening in my studies as communicators' creating a *shared reality* with their audience. Gerald asked me if I had done any new research testing this "shared reality" idea. I told him that I had not. He then asked me if I would be interested in working together on this idea. And, as they say, the rest is history. His contributions over more than a decade, along with his graduate students (especially René Kopietz), have been essential to understanding how shared reality works in interpersonal communication. Thanks, Gerald.

I am also enormously grateful to John Levine. Again, from the beginning, John was excited about the idea of shared reality. We had many wonderful conversations about the nature of shared reality. Not surprisingly, given John's historical contributions to the social psychology of groups, John taught me the importance of shared reality beyond just interpersonal communication to social groups more broadly. Fortunately, I had the opportunity to collaborate with him on this broader vision of shared reality. He has also made major contributions to my thinking about shared reality. Thanks, John.

There is one other person to whom I need to give special thanks—Maya Rossignac-Milon. I was very fortunate that several years ago Maya decided that she wanted to come to our Columbia graduate program specifically to collaborate on shared reality. Illustrating "It's a small world," Maya had worked with Donald Taylor at McGill University, and he and Wally Lambert were close colleagues and collaborators. Maya's burning issue has been the relation between shared reality and interpersonal relationships, including how partners experience "merged minds" when they establish a shared reality. I have learned a lot about shared reality over the years from my many conversations with Maya. Thanks, Maya.

I have learned about shared reality in many, many conversations with other students and colleagues—too many to mention them all. I do need to mention the following, however: James Cornwell, Becca Franks, Arie Kruglanski, Federica Pinelli, Bjarne Schmalbach, and Yaacov Trope. I am extremely grateful for the discussions that I have had with them. They have significantly influenced my thinking about shared reality.

This book also benefited greatly from those who provided exceptionally thoughtful and helpful comments and edits. I am extremely grateful to the following friends, family, and colleagues who read and commented on every chapter of the book: Kayla Higgins, Jennifer Jonas, Philip Kitcher, Arie Kruglanski, John Levine, Bill von Hippel, and Robin Wells. Their comments and edits improved the book enormously. I am also very grateful to those who gave me supportive and helpful feedback in the beginning and in the end of the process when I really needed such feedback: Gerald Echterhoff, Matthew Erdelyi, Ran Hassin, Holly Higgins, Harvey Hornstein, Nira Liberman, Maya Rossignac-Milon, Diane Ruble, Yaacov Trope, and Seymour Weingarten. I want to give a special thanks to John Levine who generously reread the entire book at the very end of the writing process because I knew he could make the "finished" book even better. And he did make the book better with his masterful edits. Thanks again, John.

I also want to give special thanks to Joan Bossert from Oxford University Press. Her strong support from the very beginning was critical to this book becoming a reality. I am especially grateful that she volunteered to act as my editor for the book. I feel very fortunate to have had her giving me the feedback I needed to write the kind of book that I wanted to write. I also want to thank Phil Velinov and production editor Sujitha at OUP for their contributions to making this book happen.

My daughter Kayla and my wife Robin are the bookends of my life. I could not have written this book without their support and their wisdom. I dedicate this book to them.

Introduction

"Wish you were here!" Most of us are familiar with this typical message on a picture postcard showing something like a beach at sunset. It first appeared on postcards at the end of the 19th century, and it quickly became ubiquitous. Why? Sometimes the message begins with "having a wonderful time" and then "wish you were here," suggesting that I wish you could also be having a wonderful time enjoying this beach at sunset. But I think there is more to it than that. In my own experience of "wish you were here," I wish that my partner or close friend was with me because *my* experience would be so much better, so much more wonderful. My experience doesn't seem quite real without sharing it with someone close to me. For my experience to be *really* real, I need my partner or friend to experience it with me. To be real, I need a *shared* reality. And this need of mine is only human. Indeed, it makes us human.

This book takes a different perspective on the age-old question of what makes us human. Historically, the answer to what makes us human, what makes us deal with the world in the ways we do, has been that we have a different kind of intelligence than other animals. A very different answer to what makes us human is provided in this book. Yes, humans have a different kind of intelligence than other animals, but we also have a different kind of *motivation*. The human motivation for shared reality—the motivation to share our feelings, thoughts, and concerns with others—is unique to humans. It is captured in "I wish you were here." When we are away from others close to us, we wish that we could share our experiences with them. When taking a walk with others, we point to something to draw our companion's attention to it, just to share what we find interesting. When talking to close friends, we tailor or adjust what we say about something to match their feelings and thoughts about it to have a shared reality with them. And when we do share our experiences with others, what is shared becomes more real. Indeed, the shared reality becomes *the* truth, the whole truth, and nothing but the truth, even when, as with our tailored messages, the truth is modified to create a shared reality.

Like human intelligence, human motivation is also special, and by "special," I mean remarkable. Humans are unique in wanting others to share their feelings, beliefs, and concerns. Like the sunset on the beach, we want to experience that what is relevant to us about the world—what objects, events, and issues are worthy of attention—is also relevant to others. And what we *share* with others is what we experience to be *real*. It is a *shared reality*. This book tells the story of this remarkable human motivation that defines who we are. It describes how this motivation makes us strong. It also describes how this motivation can tear us apart.

The story of our motivation to share reality with others is a story that we all need to know because this human motivation has *both* essential benefits and major costs for humans. On the upside, our motivation to create shared reality with others is critical for how we coordinate, cooperate, and relate to one another in our families, friendships, and communities. We even see this motivation in the behavior of human infants. They want to share with us what they find interesting and relevant by pointing to it and trying to get us to pay attention to it and appreciate that it is worthy of attention. They also look to us (i.e., check with us) to learn whether they should respond positively or negatively to some event or object. Historically, creating shared realities has been an essential part of the societies and cultures that humans have developed. It is the motivation for learning from others what they know that we do not and for teaching others what we know that they do not. It provides our basic connection to others and our feeling of belongingness with others. By creating shared realities with others, we come to know *the truth* about the world, that is, what is real about the world. Shared realities make the world meaningful to us. These benefits from shared reality are basic to who we are as humans.

Our motivation to share reality with others, however, also has major costs for humans. When we create shared realities with our fellow group members, these shared realities become the truth about what to feel and what to believe, and any other group to which we do not belong that has different feelings and beliefs about the world—whether it is a different ethnic group, religious group, or political group—is a group we distrust and even fear. They don't have "alternative facts" or simply a different viewpoint: They have false beliefs and dangerous feelings. We are right and they are wrong, and they must not be allowed to prevail in the marketplace of ideas. In this way, our motivation to create shared realities with in-group others but not out-group others leads to intergroup hatreds and conflicts from which millions of people have died. This major downside of shared reality is seen in current political conflicts that have poisoned public discourse and caused great suffering around the world.

Thus, our motivation to create shared reality with others not only reflects the best of us. It also reflects the worst of us. There is not a separate human motivation that is good and another that is bad. There is a singular motivation to share reality that has both upsides (helping in-group members) and downsides (attacking out-group members). Given this, it is important that we all know what exactly this motivation is and understand how it works and how it plays out in our everyday lives. The purpose of this book is to tell this story of the human motivation to create shared reality with others.

The shared reality story of human motivation is very different than the usual answer to the question, "What makes us human?" The usual answer highlights our intelligence, with our unique use of language often being cited as the prime example of our special superior intelligence. The different versions of this answer are typically some form of "Yay us!" After all, we're only human. When it comes to motivation, however, humans are not so sure that our motivations are superior to those of other species. Indeed, psychologists and other scientists have historically argued that our basic motives are the same as those of many other animals, including rats and pigeons. And, unlike our intelligence, we are not always proud of our motivation. We are not proud of aggression toward members of our own species, including killing innocent children. When this happens, you don't hear "Yay us!" Perhaps that's why we don't want to talk about motivation as what makes us human.

The potential downside of human motivation highlights another difference between the shared reality version of the story and the human intelligence version of the story. Discussions of how human intelligence differs from the intelligence of other animals typically emphasize the *advantages* we derive from our higher intelligence, such as our use of superior tools, our laws and ethical principles, our different forms of art, and our use of language. We even decided to distinguish our species from other species in the genus *"Homo"* (and other hominids) by calling ourselves "Homo *sapiens*"—Latin for "wise man."

But should it be our special intelligence that we emphasize when trying to understand what makes us human? That isn't clear. After all, it is not clear that when *Homo sapiens* and Neanderthals evolved from a common ancestor about half a million years ago, *Homo sapiens* were more intelligent than Neanderthals. It has been suggested that we might even have been less intelligent (considering brain size, for instance). Something other than intelligence, then, could have given us an advantage. And whatever that was—and I suggest that it could be the ways in which we create shared realities with others—it was the difference between our surviving as a species while all other hominids, including Neanderthals, did not. It was, and is, a critical part of who we are and why we survived. Rather than just our intelligence, our motivation to create shared realities with others was critical for how we cooperated and coordinated with each other in uniquely human ways. As we will see, infant human children in many ways are less intelligent than adult chimpanzees, but they want to share with others what they find relevant and interesting in the world in a way that chimpanzees do not.

In addition, if we are so intelligent and wise, and our intelligence and wisdom are such good things, why do we as members of different religious or political groups struggle simply to get along with each other or even listen to each other? Why do we as individuals suffer from so much depression and anxiety? What is the superior intelligence part of the human story *not* telling us about what it means to be human? And if there is something else, basic to who we are, that explains our downsides as well as our upsides, then we need to identify it and understand how it works. Only then can we do something to make our human lives better. And there *is* something else: our motivation to create shared realities with others. This motivation reflects the best of us and the worst of us. It has led to great cultural achievement and to great wars and to self-sacrifice to save the children of others and to self-sacrifice to *kill* the children of others (think suicide bombers).

When I say that the motivation to create shared realities with others is a critical part of the story of being human, I am arguing that it is a universal human motivation that underlies what we feel, what we believe, what we strive for, and how we relate to one another in ways that make us different from any other animal. And this shared reality story about being human, this motivational story, is not the same story as saying that humans have greater intelligence than other animals. Imagine that there are two animals from the same family sitting together and looking around. If they are animals that have arms and can make sounds, it does not take high intelligence for one of them to raise its arm and point at something it sees while uttering a sound to attract the attention of the other. Even six-month-old human infants do this. They notice something that they find interesting and then point to it while uttering something like "Ooh ooh!" It doesn't take an Einstein to do that. As far as intelligence goes, it's not that impressive. But here's the point. Other primates *don't* do that. They don't try to create joint attention to something just because they find it interesting. It's not that they can't do the pointing and utter something to draw attention to what they are looking at. It's just that they are not motivated to do that. Human infants want to share with another what they find interesting. For other primates, this simply doesn't matter. It is a difference in motivation, not a difference in intelligence.

What you might also have noticed about this example is that what human infants are doing here is not about language either. Uttering "Ooh ooh!" is not language. In fact, infants can and do get caretakers to look at what they find interesting without uttering anything at all, as when my infant daughter would grab my shirt and point excitedly at something while checking whether I was looking in the same direction. And when I did and then smiled, she would smile broadly. When human infants share their interest in things with others during the first year, it is part of a more general phase in which they share feelings with others, which includes learning from others what to feel positive about and what to feel negative about. It is the beginning of human children creating shared realities with others in ways that do not happen with other animals. It is so common among human infants that it can be taken for granted. No big deal. But it *is* a big deal because it makes us human and not some other animal. And it begins early on in children's development, well before symbolic development or other manifestations of higher intelligence.

One of my inspirations for writing this book is to tell the story of how children develop as humans by acquiring new forms of shared reality with others (Chapters 2 and 3). As infants grow (6–12 months), they begin to share feelings with their caretakers, such as sharing their excitement about something they see by pointing to it. Then as toddlers (18–24 months), they share social practices, such as sharing with others the eating practices of their community. Next, as older preschoolers (3–5 years), they share the goals and standards that their significant others have for them, such as sharing with their parents what they should try to achieve. In the final phase of shared reality development, school-aged children (9–13 years) learn social roles and coordinate their roles with others who are fulfilling complementary roles, such as sharing with other members of a sports team what is expected of those playing the different roles. Each of these new forms of shared reality has significant consequences for what children do and how they do it. Children benefit greatly from acquiring these new forms of shared reality, but there are potential costs as well—the trade-offs of being human.

In addition to the story of shared reality during childhood development, there is also the story of what happened in the evolution of our species. This story is important because it sheds light on where our motivation to create shared reality with others came from. For example, I discuss in Chapter 4 how our being bipedal contributed to our newborns being unusually weak at birth and how the exceptionally long period of dependency for human children could have created an evolutionary selection pressure on human children to share the feelings, thoughts, and concerns with their caretakers to receive the help they needed to survive.

How does the development of shared reality in humans play out in everyday life? This is the primary focus of the book. I will describe how shared reality impacts our being human, as revealed in *what we feel* (Chapter 5), *what we know* (Chapter 6), *our sense of self* (Chapter 7), *what we strive for and value* and *how we strive* (Chapters 8 and 9, respectively), *our attitudes and opinions* (Chapter 10), and *how we get along* (Chapter 11). I begin with how adults use interpersonal communication to create shared realities with others (Chapter 1). I begin with this part of the story because interpersonal communication is basic to how humans create shared reality with each other and because it clearly demonstrates how our shared realities, whether actually true or not, are treated as *the* truth. During our day-to-day interactions with others, we communicate to them about what is happening in the world, and when we do, we tailor or adjust what we say to them to match their feelings and thoughts about what is going on. Because we tailor what we say to our communication partners to create a shared reality with them, what we say is often distorted or biased. But it is *this* shared reality that is now treated as the truth. It becomes what we believe and what we remember. Our shared realities become the world we live in and know: *Sharing is believing*. And with tight networks of people talking just to each other, these shared realities are the DNA of our social bubbles.

PART I
THE EMERGENCE OF SHARED REALITY

1

Sharing Is Believing

You go to a party and meet a guy named Michael for the first time. During the party, you observe how Michael behaves. Later you are talking to a friend who you know is in the same club as Michael and so you mention that you met him for the first time at the party. Your friend says, "Oh . . . I don't really like Michael very much. What was your impression of him?" If you are like me—and most people—what you say next will be influenced by knowing that your friend has a negative impression of Michael. It is likely that what you say about Michael will move in the evaluative direction of your friend's feelings about him. This means characterizing Michael in a more negative manner than you would have otherwise. And that's what most of us would do. The question is: What do we later remember about how Michael *actually* behaved at the party? To answer this question, let's step back and consider what psychology tells us.

Seeing is believing. That's what we're told—and have been told for a very long time. It is a saying that goes back hundreds of years. It argues that only evidence that is physical or concrete can ever be truly convincing to us. Within social psychology, Leon Festinger, a father of modern social psychology, distinguished between *physical reality*, which is information about something in the world that is provided by our own physical experience of that thing, and *social reality*, which is information about something in the world that is provided by other people.[1]

Consistent with "seeing is believing," Festinger argued that physical reality trumps social reality. Social reality can matter, but only when the information from physical reality is unclear. Much of the time, our own observations would be our primary source of information. If we personally observed something, like Michael's behaviors at the party, then that is the truth about it. Only when we are uncertain about what we observed do we check with others about how we should characterize it. Yes, in trying to be polite on some topic or to be sensitive to someone's feelings on a topic, like our friend's impression of Michael, we might describe what happened differently to match that person's opinion on the topic. We might *say* something different depending on our audience. However, what we *really* believe remains unchanged. We saw what we saw, like Michael's behaviors at the party, and we believe what we saw regardless of what we said. After all, "seeing is believing." But what if that's *not* the case? What if what we *said*, rather than what we *saw*, turns out to matter—even when what we said does *not* match what we saw? What if there is a "saying-is-believing" effect rather than a "seeing-is-believing" effect?

I began my college education at McGill University in Sociology–Anthropology. My burning issue then was how language, thought, and society influence each other. I was a fan of Benjamin Lee Whorf's "linguistic relativity" idea (also called the Whorfian hypothesis) that the languages from different societies each shape the world view of the members of each language community. Simply put, the grammatical structure of the language you speak influences what you perceive and what you think.[2] Each of us lives in a world that our local language shapes for us.

From this Whorfian perspective, which is very different from the "seeing-is-believing" perspective, I experience a world that my language, English, creates for me rather than the world given to me by my senses. As a graduate student at Columbia University, I tried to test this idea by creating my own novel language with its own grammar that classified objects differently than English grammar. My research showed that participants could learn to classify objects differently after learning the new language. Unfortunately, after all my effort on this project, and despite the research being successful, I began to think that it did not mean much. It was like the participants were simply solving a problem I had given them. It wasn't changing what they knew or felt about something in the world.

When I left Columbia to begin my academic career at Princeton University, I began to think that it was the wrong aspect of language that had received attention regarding how language, thought, and society influence one another. Perhaps it wasn't language structure (syntax or grammar), or even language semantics (word or phrase meanings), that had the major impact in shaping our world views. Maybe what really mattered was language *use*, the particular ways that humans take action when we communicate to each other to achieve our goals—what has been called the *pragmatics* of language. The distinguished philosopher Ludwig Wittgenstein spoke of the "language game" to emphasize that words are used within a general framework of actions. In the 1950s, eminent sociologists in the area of symbolic interactionism, such as Erving Goffman and Harold Garfinkel, argued that interpersonal communication is a kind of game where the players follow the rules that are dictated by their communication roles.[3]

The roles in the communication game are the speaker role and the listener role, and participants in the communication game typically switch back and forth between these roles while always taking the other role into account as they play each role. It is not about language structure or syntax. It is about coordinated social interaction where there are shared roles and shared rules that are taken into account when making action choices to achieve some goal. Of special interest for the Michael example are the rules of the game that speakers (or writers) must follow.[4]

Rules for the Speaker Role

(1) Speakers should take into account the characteristics of their audience.

(2) Speakers should produce a message that is appropriate to their communicative intent or purpose.

(3) Speakers should convey the truth as they see it.

(4) Speakers should try to be understood (be coherent; be comprehensible).

(5) Speakers should give neither too much nor too little information.

(6) Speakers should be relevant (stick to the point).

(7) Speakers should produce a message that is appropriate to the context and circumstances.

In general, speakers do try to follow these rules when they communicate. When they do, what happens later? This was the question that interested me. When speakers follow the rules, what happens to them downstream? Is there a "seeing-is-believing" effect or a "saying-is-believing" effect? Note that if we have a "saying-is-believing" effect, it would not be what Whorf was talking about. It would not be that the syntax used by the speakers structured their thought. It would be language pragmatics rather than language syntax. It would be that speakers, following Speaker Rule #1, produce a message on a topic that takes into account the characteristics of their audience, such that the message based on the *same* information on the same topic would be *different* for audiences who had different characteristics. The speakers' messages would each be tailored to suit the specific characteristics of their particular audience, and, thus, the messages about the same information would be different for the different audiences. This is the case when we characterize Michael's behaviors more negatively than we would otherwise to suit our audience's negative impression of Michael.

But that's just the message you say. *Message, schmessage.* Given that all speakers saw exactly the *same* information, if speakers were later asked to recall the original information on the topic (exact "word-for-word" recall instructions), then, supposedly, a "seeing-is-believing" effect would be revealed. All speakers would basically remember the same information regardless of their following Speaker Rule #1 and tailoring their message toward the characteristics of their particular audience.

But, again, what if this is not the case? What if, instead, the speakers' own personal memory of the original information *was* influenced by what they said? What if their memory was biased away from the original information toward their audience-tailored message? This would reveal a "saying-is-believing" effect rather than a "seeing-is-believing" effect. And this effect on memory would not derive from Whorfian-like syntax. It would derive from communicators following the rules of their speaker role about how to use language when interacting with others (i.e., from pragmatics). It would be a Whorfian-*like* idea appearing in the form of pragmatic language use rather than in the form of syntax. As I once said years ago in a conference talk on this topic, it would represent a "*Whorf* in sheep's clothing."

The Golden Rule for Speakers

I decided to conduct a study to test for this "*Whorf* in sheep's clothing" when I arrived at Princeton. The topic was the evaluatively ambiguous behaviors of a person named Donald, such as the following ambiguous *persistent–stubborn* description of Donald: "Once Donnald makes up his mind to do something it is as good as done, no matter how long it might take or how difficult the going might be. Only rarely does he change his mind even when it might well be better if he did."[5]

The participants in the study were all assigned to the role of communicator, and they were asked to describe Donald's behaviors to an audience. In this role, they needed to follow Speaker Rule #1: *Speakers should take into account the characteristics of their audience.* In this case, the characteristic of their audience that communicators needed to take into account was the audience's attitude toward Donald—an audience who knew Donald from being in the same club at Princeton. The communicator participants learned that their audience either "kinda liked" Donald or "kinda disliked" Donald. Given this information about the audience's attitude toward Donald, did these Princeton students follow Speaker Rule #1?

Yes, they definitely did. They labeled Donald's behaviors with more positive than negative trait names when the audience "kinda liked" him (e.g., "persistent") and with more negative than positive trait names when the audience "kinda disliked" him (e.g., "stubborn"). And what we discovered from many studies over the next decades is that it is rare for people not to follow Speaker Rule #1. It could be called the *Golden Rule* for communicators.

Because communicators almost always follow the Golden Rule, they will bias their characterization of Donald's behaviors to match their audience's attitude toward Donald, which means they will fudge Speaker Rule #3: *Speakers should convey the truth as they see it*. But most of the time communicators are not aware of fudging Speaker Rule #3. They believe they followed that rule even when they changed what they said about Donald to match the audience's attitude toward him. This is because what they said to match the audience *became the truth* to them. It became the truth because they were motivated to create a shared reality with their audience through what they said in their message. That's what mattered.

What we found in this original study is that communicators follow the Golden Speaker Rule #1, which we call *audience tuning*. But this is not all that we found. We also found that, by so doing, the communicators' own subsequent memory and evaluations of the target person information became biased in the evaluative direction of their audience-tuned message. Moreover, these evaluative biasing effects on subsequent memory and attitudes did not weaken over time. If anything, they got stronger over time. It is as if their beliefs and feelings about the target person become what they *said* about him rather than what they *saw* (i.e., read) about him. What they said about Donald to evaluatively match their audience's attitude was what became the truth about Donald—it was a shared evaluation that they had created with the audience. Because of this, the communicators' memory of Donald's behaviors was reconstructed to fit this shared evaluation rather than to match what they had originally read about Donald's behaviors. It was not the actual truth about Donald's behaviors—*not* "seeing-is-believing." It was the truth created by tuning their message to their audience's attitude. This is why I called this effect "saying is believing."

What Causes the "Saying-Is-Believing" Effect?

The "saying-is-believing" effect is important because we follow Speaker Rule #1 all the time. And when we follow this rule in our everyday life, we treat our message as if it also followed Speaker Rule #3. That is, we treat our message as if it conveyed the *truth* on the topic. And, not surprisingly, this truth on the topic, our truth, then shows up in our memory and attitudes on the topic. What is happening is that we create a shared reality with our audience about the message topic—in this case, the target person Donald. And the shared reality makes this truth the whole truth and nothing but the truth; that is, we experience it as the *objective* truth.[6]

But how do we really know that this is what is going on, that creating a shared reality is what causes the "saying-is-believing" effect? Could it be something else that is happening? Actually, when I conducted my first study at Princeton I was thinking about a "*Whorf* in sheep's clothing," but I was not yet thinking about shared reality per se. As a social-cognitive psychologist at the time, I had a different mechanism in mind than shared reality. There was a substantial literature showing that how one labels an ambiguous figure influences how one later remembers it. For example, if there is an ambiguous figure that looks a little like eyeglasses and a little like an exercise dumbbell, then naming it either "eyeglasses" or "dumbbell" will cause distortions in memory reproductions in the direction of the name, such as the reproduction looking more like prototypic eyeglasses when it was named "eyeglasses."[7]

Indeed, at the same time that I was conducting research on the "saying-is-believing" effect, I was also conducting research on what happens to judgment and memory when someone earlier is unobtrusively exposed to a word: the effects of *verbal priming*. The research showed that when participants in an initial study were exposed to one or another word, such as either the word *persistent* or the word *stubborn*, then in a later (ostensibly "unrelated") study, their judgments and memory of a target's ambiguous behaviors were evaluatively biased toward the primed word. My research on the biasing effects of verbal priming used the same ambiguous Donald behaviors as my research on the "saying-is-believing" effect. And, notably, participants did not consciously remember the priming words from the initial "unrelated" study.[8] My verbal priming research, then, made me think of a different, cognitive mechanism as underlying the "saying-is-believing" effect.

From a strictly cognitive point of view, one could argue that the communicators in the "saying-is-believing" study would have two different mental representations for the information they had received about Donald's ambiguous behaviors. They would have a representation of the original information they had read about Donald's behaviors, and they would also have the message's evaluative labeling of that information. Given the known effect of labeling on memory, it was possible that the communicators' reconstruction of the original information was distorted toward the evaluative summary contained in the message. It would still be a "saying-is-believing" effect, but there would not be a shared reality mechanism underlying it. It would be a strictly cognitive mechanism—verbal priming.

For a long time I was satisfied with the "verbal priming" explanation for the "saying-is-believing" effect. And I might have remained so except for serendipity. I was asked to give a keynote address for an international conference on language, thought, and society—yes, my first love from college. I learned that there would be another keynote address at the conference, which would be given by Roger Brown who wrote the classic book, *Words and Things*.[9] This was a brilliant book among other brilliant work that he had written, and he was one of my heroes. Because he might hear my talk, I felt that I needed to do as good a job on my talk as possible. So I reread all of my research, and others' research, that had investigated the "saying-is-believing" effect. And I reread it with a critical eye, and, more important, with a fresh eye. In so doing, I became dissatisfied with the "verbal priming" explanation for the "saying-is-believing" effect. I thought more seriously about the "communication game" that I had studied years earlier.[10] What was the goal of the communicators? I decided that their goal was to create a shared reality with their audience about the target person. This new perspective was reflected in the title of my talk: *Achieving "Shared Reality" in the Communication Game: A Social Action That Creates Meaning*.[11]

From a cognitive perspective, what matters is that communicators produce, from audience tuning, an evaluatively biased message about the target person. That message would then bias reconstructive memory. From a shared reality perspective, however, it is not enough that communicators tune their message about the target person to match evaluatively the audience's attitude toward him or her. It is not only about the message itself. It is also about *why* communicators tune their message to match the audience's attitude. What was the goal of the audience tuning? Was it to create a shared reality with the audience or not? According to the shared reality perspective, for the audience-tuned message about Donald to be treated as the objective truth about Donald, it is necessary that the communication goal be to create a shared reality with the audience.

Because people's motivation to share reality with others is so strong, they typically tune their message toward an audience's attitude to create a shared reality with their audience about the topic at hand—in this case, what Donald is like as a person. But communicators can be motivated to tune their message toward their audience's attitude for other reasons as well. They might just want to be polite. They might have an ulterior or instrumental motive, like wanting to agree with their audience so that the audience will like them or to avoid conflict with their audience. They might take their audience's attitude as an opportunity to have fun by exaggerating what they say in the direction suggested by that attitude.

It doesn't matter from a cognitive perspective what the goal of the audience tuning might be. What matters is that the message representation is an evaluatively biased representation, and if it is, it should evaluatively bias memory. From a shared reality perspective, however, it *does* matter what the goal of the audience tuning is. What if the goal was not to create a shared reality with the audience? What if the goal of the audience tuning was simply for communicators to win a prize for successfully adapting their message to match the audience's attitude? If so, then the message would not be experienced as being the *truth* on the topic, and the "saying-is-believing" effect should be weakened or even eliminated. Thus, the cognitive perspective and the shared reality perspective make different predictions about what would happen when goals for audience tuning are introduced other than wanting to create a shared reality with the audience.

A study was designed to test directly the effects of audience tuning on memory when the goal of audience tuning is other than creating a shared reality with the audience.[12] It tested what happens when the goal of audience tuning, instead of being to create a shared reality with the audience, is strictly instrumental (ulterior incentive) or is just to have fun (entertainment). Participants in the instrumental condition learned that they could benefit from tuning their message toward their audience's attitude. They were told that those communicators who adapted their message to suit the perspective of their audience would be identified, and three among them would be randomly selected to receive a monetary reward equivalent to about $20 at the time of the study. Participants in the entertainment condition learned how they could have fun by tuning their message toward their audience's attitude. They were told that they should try their best to amuse their audience by exaggerating how much they adapted their message to their audience's attitude.

The communicators in the study were randomly assigned to either the instrumental goal, the entertainment goal, or the standard shared reality goal conditions. Importantly, for all of these goals, the communicators significantly tuned their message toward the attitude of their audience. The Golden Rule for speakers was followed in every condition. Indeed, not surprisingly, the communicators in the instrumental goal and entertainment goal conditions tuned toward their audience significantly *more* than the communicators in the shared reality goal condition; in other words, the messages were even more evaluatively biased. From a cognitive perspective, then, the audience-tuned messages should have an even greater effect on evaluatively biasing communicators' memory, an even greater "saying-is-believing" effect. But this is *not* what was found. In fact, in these conditions the "saying-is-believing" effect was *eliminated!* It was eliminated because the goal of the message tuning was not to create a shared reality with the audience and thus the message was not treated as being the truth. In contrast, in the standard shared reality goal condition where the message is treated at the truth, the usual "saying-is-believing" effect was found.

When "Saying Is Not Believing"

So even when communicators tune their message to suit their audience, a "saying-is-believing" effect is not necessarily found. It is not found when communicators do not have the goal of creating a shared reality with their audience. In the previous case, their goals were, instead, instrumental and entertainment goals. There are other reasons as well why communicators might not have the goal of creating a shared reality with their audience. The previously discussed studies all involved communicators producing a message for an audience who was a member of their own in-group.

What happens when the audience is a member of an *out-group* for the communicator?

In one study addressing this issue,[13] the communicators were students at the University of Cologne. Before the study, a pretest was conducted to determine which of several different groups the Cologne students would experience as an out-group, as indicated by their having low ratings of perceived similarity to them and low liking of them.[14] Based on this pretest, trainees from a nearby vocational school for hairdressers were selected as being an out-group audience for the Cologne communicator participants. In the in-group condition, the audience was as usual a student from the same university as the communicator (i.e., another Cologne student). All communicators were told that their audience presumably knew the target person quite well because the audience and the target person were volunteers in the same research project. As in previous studies, the communicators were also told that the audience "kinda liked" or "kinda disliked" the target person.

The study found that there was no difference between the in-group and out-group audience conditions in the extent to which communicators evaluatively tuned their message to match their audience's attitude toward the target person. For both the in-group audience and the out-group audience, communicators significantly tuned their message toward the audience. That is, presumably out of politeness, the communicators with an out-group audience still followed the Golden Rule for speakers.

This meant that the messages were evaluatively biased to the same extent in both conditions. Thus, from a cognitive perspective there should be a similar "saying-is-believing" effect on memory in both conditions. But this was *not* what was found. The usual "saying-is-believing" effect on memory was found for the in-group audience, but it was *eliminated* for the out-group audience.

Why was the "saying-is-believing" effect on memory eliminated in the out-group audience condition? The study included a measure of how much the communicators trusted the audience's judgment of others: "Do you think that [name of the audience] is a person whose judgment about other people one can trust?" Communicators trusted the audience's judgment of others significantly more when the audience was an in-group member than an out-group member. If your audience's judgment about others is not trustworthy, then you can't trust his or her attitude about the target person. And if you can't trust the audience's attitude about the target person, then you can't trust your message that you tuned to match this attitude. A message about the target person that is untrustworthy is a message that is not the truth about the target person. If the message about the target person is not the truth, then it is not relevant when recollecting the target person's behaviors.[15] This is why the "saying-is-believing" effect on memory was eliminated in the out-group audience condition. Indeed, an additional analysis showed that the memory bias depended on trust in the audience.

Subsequent research involving out-group audiences, such as German students communicating to a Turkish audience, found the same result as this study.[16] The communicators do evaluatively tune their message to match their out-group audience's attitude toward the target person, but their subsequent memory is not affected by their tuned message; that is, there is no "saying-is-believing" effect. This is an important lesson for how shared reality can work. When people consider a person to be a member of an out-group, they like the person less and trust the person less. The (unconscious) psychologic is something like the following:

I will tune my message toward this audience person because following Speaker Rule #1 is good manners and I am a polite person. But I do not want to create a shared reality with this person. My tuned message is *not* a shared reality with this person. Therefore, it is *not* the truth. Not being the truth, my message is not relevant for remembering the information I was given about the target person.[17]

This is a sad story about what it can mean to be human. When interacting with out-group members, we can behave politely toward them while all the time considering them to be irrelevant to us as either someone to connect with (the relational motive of shared reality) or someone to learn from (the epistemic motive of shared reality). With no shared reality being created, the interaction is treated as meaningless. It is as if the other person doesn't matter or doesn't *really* exist. Given our strong, natural motivation to create shared reality with other humans, not doing so when interacting with members of an out-group is like treating them as being nonhuman. We want to create a shared reality with members of our in-group but not with members of out-groups.

This is a form of *ethnocentrism*. The results of these "saying-is-believing" studies show that communicators tune their message to match the attitude of both in-group and out-group audiences, but their message only affects their memory—only is treated as *truthful*—when the audience is an in-group. These studies provide a new kind of evidence for how ethnocentrism functions. The elimination of a "saying-is-believing' effect with an out-group audience is an unconscious (implicit) measure of ethnocentrism. It measures not wanting a shared reality with the audience simply because that audience is an out-group member.

These studies also raise the question of what it means to treat other people with dignity. Is it enough to be "polite" when you talk to others? Is it enough to show "tolerance" by not arguing with others and tuning what you say to their attitude on a topic? You can do this, but if you are not motivated to find a shared reality with them, to question and explore where you might have feelings or beliefs in common, then you are treating them as if they don't really matter.

What does this all mean for the "saying-is-believing" effect? These out-group audience studies, like the studies where the goal of the audience tuning is not to create a shared reality with the audience, show that it is not always the case that communicators believe what they say. With out-group audiences and goals other than shared reality, the *saying* still happens (i.e., the communicators evaluatively tune their messages to the audience), but the *believing* does *not* happen (i.e., the communicators' memory of the target person's behaviors does not match the evaluative tone of their message). And this is because the communicators do not create a shared reality with their audience. For "saying-is-believing" to occur, a shared reality needs to occur. Thus, from the perspective of shared reality, the phenomenon is not really "saying-is-believing," any more than it is "seeing-is-believing." Instead, the phenomenon is "*sharing-is-believing.*"

There is an important implication of the phenomenon being "*sharing-is-believing*" rather than "saying-is-believing." It means that the experience of *sharing* should matter. Specifically, manipulations of the social experience could make the "sharing" appear where it did not exist before, which could make the "sharing-is-believing" effect appear where it did not appear before. Thus, it might be possible to find a way to make the message a *shared truth* between the communicator and the audience where it was not before—*even for an out-group audience.* In this way, an out-group audience could become someone whose feelings and beliefs *are* worthwhile, and the communicator's message that was tuned to that audience would now be worth believing. If so, then "sharing-is-believing" could now appear with an out-group audience. Let's see next how this can happen.

"Sharing-Is-Believing" with Out-Group Others

Let's consider again the out-group audience effects. The basic finding is that the "saying-is-believing" effect on memory does *not* occur when the audience is an out-group member despite the fact that the communicators did tune their message to match the attitude of that audience. How might the conditions of these studies be changed to produce the "saying-is-believing" effect by creating the "sharing-is-believing" effect? The answer is to change the *social* conditions in a way that changes the shared reality motives of the communicators. This could be done either by changing the social relationship between the communicator and the audience or by changing the perceived epistemic authority of the audience about the message topic (i.e., the target person).[18] There are studies that have examined the effect of each of these kinds of changes.

Changing the Relationship
between Communicator and Audience

The social situation in many of the standard "saying-is-believing" studies is rather impersonal. It involves three roles—the experimenter, the communicator, and the audience. The role of the communicator is to send a message about the target person's behaviors to the audience (without mentioning the target's name), and the audience's role is to identify whom the message is about—a referential communication task. In some studies, the experimenter also provided feedback to the communicator about whether the audience did or did not succeed in correctly identifying the target person.

In this social situation, the only relationship between the communicator and the audience was the group membership information provided by the experimenter, which signaled that the audience was either an in-group member for the communicator or an out-group member for the communicator. What would happen if, instead, there was more of a person-to-person social relationship between the communicator and the audience? What if the communicator felt that the audience was not just playing a particular role in a referential communication task but was a team *partner*?

This was the social situation that was created in a new version of the out-group audience study.[19] The basic study paradigm was the same as described earlier with German communicators sending a message about a German target person to a Turkish audience who knew the target person and apparently kind of liked or kind of disliked him. As in the previous studies, the communicators evaluatively tuned their message about the target person in the direction of their audience's attitude. A few minutes after sending their message, all communicators received feedback that, based on their message, the audience had successfully identified the target person. The social nature of this success feedback was manipulated, however. In one condition, the success feedback was given impersonally by the experimenter, as in previous studies. In the new condition, the success feedback was given personally by the audience who greeted the communicator using a chat window and told the communicator that he or she had identified the target person from the communicator's message.

In the standard condition where the success feedback was impersonally given by the experimenter, the same result was found as in previous studies with an out-group audience: There was no "saying-is-believing" effect. However, in the new condition where the success feedback was personally given by the audience, the "saying-is-believing" effect now *appeared!* The *epistemic* truth of the message was the same in the two feedback conditions given that communicators were told in both cases that the message was successful. What was different between the two feedback conditions was the *relationship* between the communicator and the audience. In the new audience feedback condition, the feedback was personal and expressed success as a team—"*We* did it!" Because the communication situation now involved a personal relationship, communicators had a stronger social relational motive to create a shared reality with their audience. This would be reflected in the "saying-is-believing" effect now appearing where it was absent before because now there was "sharing" to create "believing."[20]

Changing the Epistemic Authority of the Out-Group Audience

The out-group audience study just described demonstrates that a "saying-is-believing" effect can be made to appear where it was absent before by changing the social relationship between the communicator and the out-group audience—changing the *social relational motive*. What about changing the *epistemic motive*? Would that work? What would happen if the epistemic authority of the out-group audience about the message topic (i.e., about the target person) was changed?

This was tried in another recent study.[21] This out-group audience study used the same basic paradigm as the out-group studies that have been previously described. The one change was adding a new condition where the (male) *target* person was *Turkish* like the (male) Turkish audience rather than being German like the communicator. Thus, the out-group audience kind of liked or kind of disliked someone in his *own in-group* rather than someone in the communicator's in-group.

What should this experimental change in the target person's group membership do? It should increase the *epistemic authority* of the audience. The Turkish audience is not likely to have as much expertise as the German communicator in evaluating a German target person, but he is likely to have more expertise in evaluating another Turkish person. Given that another motive for creating a shared reality with someone is to establish the truth about something, the German communicators should be more motivated to share reality with the Turkish audience when his attitude is about another Turkish person. If so, then a "saying-is-believing" effect should now appear where, with a German target person, it was absent.

All the communicators were German, and the audience was always Turkish. In one condition, as in prior studies, the target person was German. In the new condition, the target person was Turkish. As usual, the communicators in both conditions evaluatively tuned their message to match the positive or negative attitude of their audience toward the target person. Despite this message tuning, when the target person was German, there was no "saying-is believing" memory effect, replicating prior out-group audience studies. However, when the target person was Turkish, the "saying-is believing" memory effect now *appeared* even though the audience was an out-group member! Additional data showed that this was because the communicators' epistemic trust in the audience's attitude about the target person was significantly greater when the target person was Turkish like the audience. What this shows is that it is possible to create a shared reality with an out-group member under conditions where the out-group member is an epistemic authority (i.e., an expert) on the topic of the communication exchange. Then, communicators who tune their message toward the attitude or opinion of the out-group audience will treat their message as being the truth on the topic—a "sharing-is believing" effect.

These studies show that relations to members of our out-groups, whether they be ethnic, religious, or political out-groups, are not hopeless. Yes, there is a general tendency just to follow the rules of politeness when interacting with them and otherwise treat the interaction as meaningless. Such default ethnocentrism is a problem. But these studies show that it is not insurmountable if the motives for creating a shared reality with them are introduced. One way is to experience them as a team partner with whom "we" can succeed on a task, thereby satisfying the relational motive of shared reality. Another way is experience them as an expert on our communication topic, thereby satisfying the epistemic motive of shared reality. In the current world of intergroup tensions, we need to develop these ways of creating shared realities with those outside of our own in-groups. We need to develop ways of *sharing* that can lead to shared *believing* about what problems are relevant, are worthy of our attention, and need to be addressed together.

How Audience Tuning to Create a Shared Reality Shapes Our Truth

What we have found in our shared reality research about the effects of audience-tuned messages on memory was not how memory was supposed to work. If you held constant the original information that you received about something *and* you held constant how that information was verbally encoded in a message, then extraneous matters like what is your relationship to the audience, what is the relationship of the audience to the topic of the message, and so on would have no bearing on your memory for the original information. It was "seeing-is-believing" and "saying-is-believing" that mattered. It was not "sharing-is-believing." Memory was *not* determined by shared reality mechanisms.

This is why the "suddenly appear" results that I have just described seemed like magic to me. Frankly, they still seem like magic to me. Except that this is actually how we function as humans. It is not going to happen with any other animal. Humans tune their messages to an audience to share the feelings, beliefs, and concerns that others have about things in the world. The tuned message then becomes the *truth* about the world—a truth that is shared with others. This has the benefit of strengthening our bond, our connectedness with others, and our sense of knowing what is real.

But shared truth need not *be* the truth. Let me repeat what is clearly illustrated by the original "saying-is-believing" studies themselves: The shared truth in these studies is a distortion of the behavioral evidence about the target person. The memory is aligned with a message that was biased toward the positive or negative attitude toward the target person. The memory is not an accurate recall of the original information about the target person. It is an evaluatively biased *distortion* of that information. And in everyday life we use tuned messages to create shared realities on all kinds of topics that don't have the evidence to support what is said in the message, including cases, like religious beliefs, where the evidence must be taken on faith. No other animal *creates its own truth* by *tuning* messages to match the audience's feelings, beliefs, and concerns. They do not ignore the physical evidence to create a shared reality. Our "sharing-is-believing" creates our own world—for better and worse.

Just to be clear, how we humans create truth from message tuning is *not* a story about how humans have language whereas other animals do not. It is not a story about human language. Yes, the communications in our studies involve the use of language. But the different conditions in the studies that I have reviewed all involve the use of language. Indeed, the language being used in the messages in most of our studies do *not* vary within each of the different conditions (e.g., within the condition where the audience "kinda likes" Donald). That is, the message tuning *as language* is the *same* within each of the different conditions. If the phenomenon were about language, there would be the same effect on memory in the condition where the communicators tuned their message toward the audience's positive attitude about the target person, and there would be the same effect on memory in the condition where they tuned their message toward the audience's negative attitude. But clearly this is *not* the case as evident by all the different results within each of these conditions depending on changes in the *shared reality* conditions. The effects on memory, on what we know and believe, including our evaluative beliefs, are about shared reality with the audience and not about the language of the message per se. The story that matters is not Whorf's linguistic relativity. The story that matters is the human motivation to create shared reality with others.

What we have learned is that the "seeing-is-believing" adage is incorrect. And even the alternative "saying-is-believing" idea is inadequate. Instead, what we have learned is "*sharing-is-believing*." And we experience the effects of "sharing-is-believing" all the time. Sharing-is-believing makes us stronger by creating relationships with others where we feel and think about things in the same way and remember what happened in the world in the same way. This strengthens our connections with others and enhances our trust in others. By making sense of the world and giving meaning to the world, it also allows us to experience what we know about the world as being the objective truth about the world.[22] All of this gives us confidence when dealing with the world around us.

That's the good news: how shared reality makes us strong. But "sharing-is-believing" can, and often does, tear us apart. Recently, politics—in the United States and around the world—has been dominated by this powerful variable. Increasingly, people talk to just members of their in-group—the "political bubble." And this in-group can be created from chatrooms and tweets where those communicating live far away from each another. Face-to-face communication within a local community, which used to limit the size of a radical group, is no longer necessary. Even a person with a very radical idea (e.g., the earth is flat) can find someone else to verify it by communicating across the Internet. And then only those who share this reality become part of the group communicating to one another. This distorts each in-group's understanding and memory of what is happening in the world while making any alternative to their shared reality seem strange or deceptive or even dangerous.

And, if just to be polite, you do tune your message on some issue when talking to a member of the "other" political party, this will have no effect on your feelings or beliefs about the issue. For change to happen, a shared reality needs to be created, which, as we have seen, requires that epistemic and relational motives be fulfilled.[23] If you do not trust or like the "other" with whom you are communicating, then your tuning toward their attitude on some issue will not impact your feelings or beliefs about the issue. We remain in our separate political bubbles, in our alternative truths. This effect of "sharing-is-believing" is tearing us apart.

I have described in this chapter the process by which shared reality emerges, or does not emerge, during interpersonal communication. It is time to look at how shared reality emerges during childhood development. Shared reality does not occur all at once but develops through different phases. Which kind of shared reality emerges at different childhood phases tells us a lot about what makes us human. The next two chapters tell that story.

Notes

1. See Festinger (1950, 1954).
2. See Whorf (1956). See also Sapir (1928).
3. See Garfinkel (1967), Goffman (1959), and Wittgenstein (1953).
4. See, for example, Austin (1962), Grice (1971, 1975), Gumperz and Hymes (1972), Rommetveit (1974), and van Dijk (1977). For an early review of how people follow these rules, see Higgins (1981a).
5. See Higgins and Rholes (1978).
6. For further elaboration on this movement from subjective to objective truth as a function of creating a shared reality, see Hardin and Higgins (1996).
7. This is an example from a classic study by Carmichael, Hogan, and Walter (1932).
8. See Higgins, Rholes, and Jones (1977). For a general review of early priming and accessibility effects, see Higgins (1996). For more recent discussions of priming effects, see the edited volume by Molden (2014).
9. See Brown (1958b).
10. See Higgins (1981).
11. See Higgins (1992).
12. See Echterhoff, Higgins, Kopietz, and Groll (2008).
13. See Echterhoff, Higgins, and Groll (2005).
14. Relatively low liking of and perceived similarity to a group's members is a standard indicator of perceiving another group to be an out-group (see Deaux, 1996).
15. For a discussion of the relation between truth and relevance, and the relation between relevance and what is accessible for remembering, see Eitam and Higgins (2010).
16. See Echterhoff et al. (2008).
17. For those readers who are familiar with cognitive dissonance theory (Festinger, 1957), you might think that a cognitive dissonance mechanism might contribute to the results I have discussed. Evidence that this is unlikely is discussed in Echterhoff et al. (2008). In this particular case, if communicators bias their message to match the audience's attitude toward the target person, this bias (dissonant cognition) is even more problematic when done for an out-group audience whom you don't like and don't trust. Therefore, the pressure to validate the message, and thereby produce a "saying-is-believing" message, should be even greater for an out-group than an in-group audience.
18. For a fuller discussion of the epistemic authority of the in-group, see Kruglanski et al. (2005).
19. See Echterhoff, Kopietz, and Higgins (2013).
20. It is important to note that the difference between the two success feedback conditions was not due to a difference in mood or a difference in general perception of similarity to the outgroup as a category. The communicators were asked how much they were in a good mood or a bad mood, and there was no difference between the two success feedback conditions. They were also asked how similar they felt they were to Turks in general or Germans in general, and again there was no difference

between the two success feedback conditions. Thus, the new audience success feed-back condition did not make them feel better or reduce their general perception of similarity to Turks. What it did was create a more personal relationship with this Turkish audience individual, which motivated wanting a shared reality with him.

21. See Echterhoff et al. (2017).
22. See Echterhoff, Higgins, and Levine (2009), and Hardin and Higgins (1996).
23. See also Echterhoff and Schmalbach (2018).

2

Childhood Development of Shared Reality

Infants and Toddlers

Almost 20 years after getting my PhD at Columbia, I returned to be a professor in the department. It felt more than a little awkward, especially interacting with faculty members who had been my teachers and mentors and were now my colleagues. Fortunately, I was not alone. I had with me my wife and my infant daughter. When my wife went back to work at Bell Labs in New Jersey, I was the primary caregiver during the daytime. I am grateful for this because my daughter, Kayla, taught me more about infants than I would have learned otherwise. In particular, Kayla taught me how human infants share the world with their caregivers.

Infants' cognitive growth during their first year of life is impressive. But it is their motivation to share their experience of the world that I find amazing. And with Kayla, it is what I most enjoyed about being with her. We went outside to the park in front of our home, and, with her sitting on my lap, we would mostly just look around. Usually there was something that caught her attention, like a bird on a branch, and she would point to it and get me to pay attention to it. When she did so, I had this wonderful experience of her trying to share the world with me. She was the one who was initiating the sharing. She experienced this event as being worthy of attention, and she was communicating that to me. When I then paid close attention to what she was pointing at and maintained my attention, *we* experienced that event as being relevant. Together, we experienced *shared relevance*. Magic time for humans.

How humans create shared realities with others is not found in other animal species. It is an evolution that is distinct to *Homo sapiens*. And once we became *Homo sapiens*, the ways in which humans created shared realities with others continued to change and evolve. Today we share our feelings and beliefs about what is happening in our lives and in the world around us with hundreds and even thousands of others through Internet media like email, Facebook, and Twitter.

These are the evolutionary and historical stories of how creating shared realities with others made us and makes us human—stories I discuss in Chapter 4. As interesting and important as these stories are, however, they are not the only story of human development of shared reality. What I find equally fascinating are the changes in shared reality that happen in today's world as our children develop. Beginning in infancy, children pass through different phases of development when new modes of sharing reality emerge that change how they relate to others around them. Each new shared reality mode changes the lives of children, and those lucky enough to be with them when it happens. This and the next chapter tell that story of the child development of shared reality.

What I will be describing in the next two chapters concerns phenomena in childhood development that have been reported in the cognitive, social-cognitive, socio-emotional, and clinical literatures. Generally speaking, these different literatures have treated the phenomena I describe as being separate—each associated with a specific kind of development studied by a particular subdiscipline of child development. I believe, however, that these phenomena are not separate but, instead, reflect different modes of sharing reality with others. At each phase there emerges for the first time a particular mode of shared reality that is reflected in various phenomena across the subdisciplines. I discuss what appears to be different phenomena within a single conceptual umbrella—changes in children's shared realities with others.

I will describe four phases of childhood development in which significantly new modes of shared reality appear. Each new mode has essential benefits for children, such as improving their relationships with close others like family members. However, each new mode also has potential costs, such as undermining relations with members of groups who have different shared realities than their group (out-groups). In this chapter, I describe how the shared realities of children change during the first two phases of childhood and how these changes affect both children's self-regulation and their social relationships—for better *and* worse.

The Emergence of New Shared Realities During Childhood

I believe that the *shared feelings* that emerge when children are in the second half of their first year (6–12 months) is when children begin to create a shared reality with others. I am not suggesting, however, that there is nothing happening before then that contributes to the development of shared reality. After all, human babies are human from birth, and, thus, they are likely to show early on their potential for creating shared realities with others. Thus, I begin this chapter by describing what might contribute early on to the development of shared reality—the early childhood precursors of shared reality.

Precursors of Shared Reality in Early Childhood Development

As a species, humans have some distinctive physical characteristics.[1] The relatively large amount of white that there is in the eyes of humans compared to other primates makes it easier to follow the eye gaze of another person. Because of this, infants are able to detect the direction of an adult's visual gaze when it occurs within their visual field.[2] This facilitates coordinating attention. It also provides feedback for the success or failure of this coordination.

Another distinctive human characteristic is that human babies are born well before full brain development. This is important because it means that they need to be taken care of longer than babies of other animals. Human babies require very close caregiver–child connections for several months. Fortunately, they are also born with, or acquire early, several predispositions that help them learn about people, such as finding of special interest human faces, voices, and movements.[3] In addition, because human adults live longer than other primates, there is often an older adult present who can provide additional care (the "grandmother" effect). These human characteristics increase the emphasis on close and coordinated interactions between children and their caregivers, which is a precursor of creating shared reality with others.

With respect to the social connectedness of shared reality, it is also worth noting that infants readily imitate the action of another person,[4] while showing a definite preference for familiar people, such as their mother, father, older siblings, or frequent caregiver. They often cry when the familiar person leaves the room. The impact of social familiarity on interaction preference even extends beyond the caretaking network. There is evidence, for example, that infants will reach for a particular toy more when it is offered by a native speaker of their language than when the same toy is offered by a foreign-accented speaker.[5]

All of these human characteristics could have contributed to the emergence of the motivation to share the feelings and interests of others. The well-known developmental psychologist, Jerome Bruner, emphasized the importance of imitation in children learning to communicate with others.[6] As just mentioned, young infants will copy and imitate what an adult does, and slightly older infants (by nine months) will copy even novel actions, such as combining two objects to make a rattle.[7] And it need not be an exact imitation but, instead, an action that takes into account the intention underlying the desired effect. [8] Although not constituting shared reality per se, such imitation would be a precursor to shared reality.

When considering precursors to sharing reality, perhaps the closest is the face-to-face turn-taking interactions that infants have with others, especially their caregiver. Infants just a few months old will engage in complementary turn taking, such as behaving more passively when an adult is more active and behaving more actively when an adult is more passive.[9] This is not imitation because the infant is producing a complementary response rather than the same response. The infants are being responsive rather than copying. Similarly, infants will take turns with an adult in expressing feelings in a way that goes beyond just copying what the adult does, such as expressing happiness vocally after an adult expressed happiness facially.[10]

One other development during infancy also supports the emergence of the first shared reality phase of shared feelings. It is a cognitive-developmental change that George Herbert Mead, the eminent sociologist and philosopher, first noted almost a century ago.[11] Specifically, infants can *anticipate* how another person, such as their mother or father, will respond to something. This ability allows infants to anticipate that what they are paying attention to their mother or father would pay attention to if they pointed to it. Clearly, this ability would support the first phase of shared reality development—shared feelings that includes the shared relevance I experienced with Kayla.[12]

Shared Feelings

Shared feelings as the first phase of shared reality development occurs around 6 to 12 months of age. During this period children begin to point at something that attracts their attention and urge others to attend to the same thing. This phenomenon was originally called *joint attention*. However, I believe that there is more happening than just joint attention. I believe this because, as I mentioned earlier, I experienced such pointing interactions with my daughter Kayla when she was an older infant, and it was clear to me that she was not simply trying to get me to look at what she was seeing but wanted me to share her excitement about it.

Notably, Kayla was *not* trying to get me to give her what she was pointing to—she was not asking me to climb up the tree and capture the bird for her. Her pointing was not instrumental in this sense but was informing me that there was something up in the tree that was worth looking at. This illustrates the recognized difference between pointing as a request to another person to do something (a protoimperative gesture) versus pointing as a *comment* to another person about something in the world (a protodeclarative gesture).[13] Kayla's pointing was a comment on the bird being worthy of my attention—trying to create shared relevance with me.

Some researchers would call this account of my daughter's pointing a "rich" interpretation (i.e., overly speculative) because I have no direct evidence of the motive underlying Kayla's pointing. However, other observers of such events give a similar interpretation of such pointing, describing it as sharing interest with a communicative partner, or as affective sharing.[14] For example, the distinguished developmental psychologist Inge Bretherton says that during this phase infants' affective and gestural communications seem intended "to attract and direct the addressee's attention to topics of mutual interest."[15] Similarly, when comparing human infants' pointing to the gestures of other primates, the eminent developmental and comparative psychologist Michael Tomasello and his colleagues propose taking a deeply social view on such pointing gestures. They argue that the pointing gestures of human infants involve uniquely human skills and motivations for sharing attitudes and interests, that they reflect a uniquely human motive "to simply share experience with others."[16]

Tomasello and his colleagues also provide an excellent example of how infants' intrinsic motivation for sharing interest in something underlies such pointing gestures.[17] In a study with one-year-old infants, an object (i.e., a toy, a light, a puppet) appeared through an opening in a screen and then moved. When the infants pointed to it, an experimenter immediately reacted by either looking back and forth between the infant's face and the event while talking excitedly about what was going on in the event (joint attention), looking just at the infant's face (face), looking just at the event (event), or looking at neither the infant nor the event (ignore). Across subsequent trials, it was the infants who were in the joint attention condition, compared to the other conditions, who pointed more and more often as if the joint attention and joint interest was creating a connection between the child and the experimenter, thereby increasing their motivation to create a shared reality with the experimenter.

There is also evidence that infants will make an effort to share what it is that an adult finds interesting. In one study,[18] for example, adult caregivers with their 12-month-old infants turned their head to gaze at something and then uttered the sound "Oh!" with an excited facial expression. In one condition, they gazed at something behind a barrier or within a box that the infant could not see (infant cannot see condition). In the other condition, they gazed at something in front of the barrier or box that the infant could see (infant can see condition). The infants were more likely in the "infant cannot see" condition than the "infant can see" condition to crawl over to look at what the caregiver was excited about. By so doing, they could share in the excitement. And, good news, they did get the chance to play with the hidden toy once they crawled over to look at it.

Pointing to or gazing at something interesting is not the only way that children and adults create a shared interest in something. Another way is by sharing an object they are playing with, such as exchanging a toy with another infant. Such sharing also creates another person's interest in something that the child finds interesting.[19]

I should note that shared interest in something does not necessarily mean having the same evaluative reaction to it.[20] For shared reality to occur, it is enough that a child shares with a caretaker that something is worthy of their attention—to share that this thing is *of interest*. Together, they share its relevance. The experience of *shared relevance* is enough for shared reality. When Kayla pointed to the bird on the branch, I verified that I also thought it was relevant by paying close attention to the bird and maintaining my attention. Together, we experienced that we were watching the same thing and treating it as worthy of attention. That was enough. We did not need, in addition, to have the same evaluative reaction to it. Indeed, there were times when we did not even know how each other was evaluatively reacting to what we were watching together. In such times it was enough to quietly watch it together and experience each other giving it our attention.[21]

Of course, Kayla and I could have the same evaluative reaction to what we were watching together. In this particular case, for example, Kayla smiled while looking at the colorful bird on the branch, looked over at me and saw that I was also smiling while looking at it, and then Kayla smiled even more broadly. What this adds is a shared evaluative reaction to an object or event (in this case, positive).

Adding shared evaluation is important. In this first phase of shared reality development, it is important for children to learn to share either positive or negative reactions to particular objects and events. Consider another time when Kayla and I experienced shared relevance. A big dog, off its leash, was walking toward us, and we were both paying close attention to it. We had shared relevance about this big dog, but in this case Kayla clearly wanted more than just shared relevance. She wanted to know whether I felt positive or negative about it, liked it or disliked it, and she looked to me for guidance. How was I reacting to this big dog walking toward us?

By around the end of their first year, children can recognize that an adult's emotional display is about a particular object or activity.[22] They develop the ability to learn what the valence of an object or activity is by reading an adult's positive or negative facial or vocal expression when reacting to it.[23] When the expression is negative, for example, they will avoid that object or activity. In classic research on infants' responses to caregivers' feedback, infants crawl across a raised platform with a pattern on it until they arrive at a transparent (but solid) Plexiglass surface that creates the appearance of a deep cliff. On the other side of this surface is their mother. Do they continue crawling toward their mother across this surface? They are less likely to cross when their mother's emotional facial expression is negative than when it is positive.[24]

Infants in this way learn to share adults' positive or negative feelings about different objects, called "social referencing" by developmental psychologists. Because shared reality relates to epistemic motivation, to wanting to make sense of the world and learn how it works, it is also notable that infants are more responsive to the emotional signals of adults regarding objects when the children's own initial emotional reaction to an object is ambiguous than when they have a clear positive or negative reaction.[25] Infants even seem to recognize who is the epistemic expert in a particular situation. Typically, they will look at their mother, if she is present, to check how they should react to something. But there is evidence that in a laboratory setting, when confronted with a novel toy object introduced by the experimenter that is slowly approaching them on the table, they will direct their looks to the experimenter in the room rather than to their mother. It is as if the child considered the experimenter to be the local "expert."[26] This is really quite impressive for an infant.

There is evidence, then, that around the end of the first year, infants communicate with pointing gestures to create shared interest or relevance in an object or event, and they learn how to evaluatively react to different objects and events (positive vs. negative) from observing adults' emotional reactions to them. It is why I refer to this phase as "shared feelings."[27] More generally, this first phase is a period when children increasingly coordinate their expressive actions in a way that matches their surrounding circumstances.[28] There is evidence, for example, that older infants display concern when another person is in distress and will even try to comfort a distressed person.[29] Such comforting, in particular, could be interpreted as infants tuning their socio-emotional response to coordinate with the feeling state of another.

The importance to infants of shared feelings is also evident in their preference for others who share how they feel about something over those who do not. In a study that illustrates this especially well, infants' preference for either graham crackers or green beans was determined at the beginning of the study.[30] Then two rabbit puppets expressed their preference between these two foods. One rabbit puppet preferred the same food as the infant (shared food preference), whereas the other puppet preferred the other food. Then two dog puppets behaved in a way that either helped or harmed the rabbit puppet with the shared preference or the rabbit puppet with the different preference. Which of these two dog puppets did the infants prefer? Which would you prefer? This was measured by showing the infants the helper and harmer dog puppets and seeing which puppet the infant reached for. The study found that 9-month-old infants, and especially 14-month-old infants, were more likely to choose the dog puppet that was nice to the rabbit puppet who had a shared food preference with them.

Even in infancy, then, children are displaying a remarkable kind of shared reality with others. What are the epistemic and social relational consequences of the emergence of shared feelings in infancy? To begin with, children and their caregivers are sharing what each finds interesting about the world. These child interactions with responsive caregivers[31] make an important contribution to children because they learn what their caregivers consider to be significant in the world around them. The caregivers indicate what they, as representatives of their cultural community, consider to be worthy of notice. They also decide when to signal to the child that what the child has pointed out is, indeed, worthy of notice and worthy of shared interest. As adults, caretakers are epistemic authorities for children. Their views on the world are treated as evidence about what is real.[32]

Even at this young age, then, shared reality interactions with those around them are teaching the child about what is and is not considered to be significant, what does and does not *matter*. Knowing what matters to others is a major benefit for children as they become members of their cultural community. But there is also a potential downside to this socialization. When there is *no* shared interest, as when a caregiver is unresponsive to what they are pointing at, children could begin to filter out events as no longer being relevant that they otherwise would have found interesting. Thus, there could be a narrowing of what in the world is worth paying attention to and feeling wonder about. Dads, for example, could share with their sons the relevance of large construction equipment more than they do with their daughters. In addition, a caregiver could signal that something *is* relevant, like how people are dressed, that contribute to in-group versus out-group distinctions. And this can happen because of the power of shared reality.

Notably, shared feelings are not just about sharing knowledge with others about what does and does not matter in the world (epistemic). As illustrated in the previously discussed study on choosing the dog puppet that is nice to the rabbit puppet with shared preferences, shared feelings can also be important for interpersonal relations. Learning to share what adults like and what they dislike allows the child to get along better with other members of the community. As the renowned social psychologist Fritz Heider pointed out many decades ago in his balance theory, people like and feel connected to others who have similar preferences to their own.[33]

This effect of shared feelings on interpersonal liking and connectedness greatly benefits children and the people around them by bringing them together. It makes those relationships stronger. But, once again, it has potential costs. What one community finds interesting or not interesting, prefers or not prefers, finds positive or negative, is not necessarily shared by a different community. What one community finds relevant and likes, another community might find irrelevant or silly or weird or even disgusting. Thus, even as early as the phase of shared feelings, there is the potential for prejudicial in-group/out-group comparisons.

There are other potential downsides of shared feelings that should be mentioned. When caregivers interact with infants, they can communicate to a child, "This is what I find to be interesting, and it is what *I* find interesting that matters and not what *you* find interesting." Caregivers could consistently *fail to verify* the child's interest in things, communicating regularly that they do *not* share what the child finds relevant and interesting. The good news from the research is that the frequency of maternal affirmations of children (i.e., social verifications) increases during infancy. However, even at the end of the phase of shared feelings there are significant differences among mothers in how frequently they affirm their children's bids for attention.[34] This means that some infants are at risk for a low frequency of maternal affirmations. Given the importance of shared relevance and shared feelings for infants, this can be a serious downside to being human for these unfortunate infants. These infants can lose the sense that their reactions to the world matter—that they matter.

Parents who consistently fail to affirm what their children find interesting is one kind of poor parenting. Another kind of poor parenting is teaching children to treat something as more relevant, more important, than it deserves, including teaching them to respond more positively to something or more negatively to something than they should. As one example, teaching a child to be highly vigilant around insects, even harmless insects like cellar spiders (aka daddy longlegs), silverfish, or millipedes, can create a dysfunctional shared phobia that can be passed down from generation to generation.

One final note: Shared relevance is a dimension and is not restricted to just shared *high* relevance. Children can also learn that something is *not* worthy of attention—shared *irrelevance*. They can share the feeling that something is not important, not worthy of their attention or effort to engage, such as the members of an out-group.[35] In extreme cases, shared irrelevance over time can create a group of young people who agree with each other that what their community values, what it wants them to do, is not worth doing. Together, they resent and resist being told to strive to achieve what they find irrelevant—what they find meaningless. This *shared irrelevance* can be a strong motivational force. On the one hand, it can motivate them to disengage (e.g., widespread political apathy). On the other hand, it can motivate them to rebel and look for something else. The solution need not be to join a terrorist group, but it is one possible solution.[36] And if it is their only solution, they could seize it together.

Shared Practices

Among the cognitive-developmental psychologists of the 20th century, perhaps the two greatest were Jean Piaget and Lev Vygotsky. Although they did not agree on everything, they did agree that the most significant change during childhood development is the symbolic development that occurs around 18 to 24 months, especially as it relates to the development of language.[37] For Piaget and Vygotsky, as well as many recent cognitive-developmental theorists, *this* development among toddlers is critical because it transforms how children *think*—the *cognitive* transformation that makes us human.

But is the transformation that occurs around 18 to 24 months simply a cognitive transformation? Even with respect to communication, is the story just a cognitive-development story? I believe that at least as important to our ability to communicate is the *motivational* developments that occur in early development—new modes of creating shared realities with others. And, as we have just seen, this has already begun prior to the symbolic development that occurs during 18 to 24 months. It has already begun when shared feelings appear in infancy. The cognitive transformation that is emphasized most is the development of language—the development of a language system of multiword utterances and the syntax and grammar underlying it. I especially disagree with this emphasis on language development as being what makes us human. There are a few points I wish to make about this.

The first point is that the infants who demonstrate shared feelings are not even using *single* words yet, never mind language, but they are *already* sharing reality with others. The second point is that when single-word utterances do appear, which is *before* language-related multiword utterances appear around 18 to 24 months, these single-word utterances are *signals* rather than *symbols*, and it is the shared realities that are involved in symbol use that is critical for later communication development. Finally, when children do use single-word utterances as symbols, they matter because they are *shared practices* rather than because they are a cognitive ability per se. Moreover, using single-word symbols is *not* the only shared practice that children learn during this phase. Thus, there is a lot of shared reality development happening well before children use the multiword utterances that constitute the grammar and syntax of language. What makes us human is a shared reality story, not a language story. I will now develop this argument more fully.

To appreciate the significance for shared reality, and thereby for communication, of the emergence of symbolic single-word utterances, one must appreciate that the single-word utterances that children use before this phase are signals and not symbols. Children's early single-word signals are used instrumentally, like motor gestures, to make something happen. They are equivalent to a pet dog scratching the door to be let outdoors. For children's use of words, it might be "juice," as a request for juice, or "up" (often accompanied by arms lifted up), as a request to be picked up. The words are used as requests or demands. According to the animal communication expert Herbert Terrace, this is also the case for the hand gestures of the great apes (chimpanzees, gorillas) who have been taught sign language by human trainers.[38]

But then something important happens with human children. Around 18 to 24 months, there is a qualitative change in how they use single words— a change that does not occur with other primates. Children don't just use single-word utterances to recruit help from another person to get what they want (i.e., words as protoimperatives). As Terrace puts it, children now use single-word utterances to name things (tacts) and not just to demand things (mands): "Tacts are not followed by primary reinforcement. Their sole function is to share knowledge with another person for its own sake."[39]

The qualitative difference between children's *symbolic* single-word utterances versus *signal* single-word utterances is evident in what happens after the symbolic words emerge—children's vocabulary explodes. This is the well-known *naming period* phenomenon. During this period, children excitedly point to objects asking someone older to tell them their names.[40] Before the shift from word signals to word symbols, children learn a couple of new words a week. Afterwards, they learn *5 new words a day*[41]—a phenomenal 35 new words a week.

The discovery that "everything has a name"[42] is momentous for children. The distinguished psychologist William Stern was apparently the first to describe this discovery. He noted that around 18 to 24 months of age children first realize that each object has its permanent symbol, a sound pattern that identifies it.[43] Hellen Keller, who was both deaf and blind as a child, provides one of the most compelling descriptions of this discovery of symbolic names in her classic book, *The Miracle Worker*.[44] She tells how she initially used her fingers to spell out words, such as the word "d-o-l-l" or the word "h-a-t," the way she was taught by her teacher, Anne Sullivan (the miracle worker). She experienced this as simple imitation—making her fingers go the way her teacher used her fingers to spell out the letters of a word in Hellen's hand. This went on for several weeks. One day her teacher took her out on a walk. Someone was drawing water, and she placed Helen's hand under the spout. While the water was streaming over one of Helen's hands, her teacher spelled "w-a-t-e-r" into the other hand, first slowly and then quickly. "I stood still, my whole attention fixed upon the motions of her fingers . . . and somehow the mystery of language was revealed to me. I knew then that 'w-a-t-e-r' meant the wonderful cool something that was flowing over my hand. That living word awakened my soul, gave it light, hope, joy, set it free!"[45]

With this discovery of her first symbolic word, Helen Keller says that her life was transformed. Notably, it is not grammar, syntax, or the use of multiword utterances that is her story. Instead, it is recognizing that a symbolic vehicle, in her case the fingers spelling "w-a-t-e-r," referred to something else.

As Piaget and Vygotsky, as well as other cognitive-developmental psychologists, emphasize, symbols *are* special developmentally from a mental representation viewpoint. But what has been overlooked is that symbols are *also* special developmentally from a shared reality viewpoint. During the naming period, children point to an object so that someone older will tell them which verbal sound pattern refers to that type of object. In this "original word game," as Roger Brown called it in his classic book, *Words and Things*,[46] they also check with others which objects are included and excluded as referents of a name (i.e., verbal sound category). The fact that they do so indicates that they recognize that this older person has knowledge about which names refer to which object categories—knowledge that the children do not have but want to have.

As Paul Harris points out in his important book, *Trusting What You're Told: How Children Learn from Others*,[47] the fact that toddlers ask others questions about what the name of some object is means that they can conceive of an object having a name even though they do not know what the name is, and they believe that the person they question *can*, and *will*, tell them what the name is. They recognize that other people have knowledge that they do not yet have and they can acquire this knowledge. By asking for and then retaining this knowledge for names, they create a shared reality with others about how communication with words works. It is a shared reality about *the practice of communicating with words* in interpersonal interactions, as both encoders of words and decoders of words. As

Harris tells us, toddlers' questioning of others to learn the names of things represents an information-gathering strategy that is distinct to humans and is used even before these children can use words properly to ask questions.

Toddlers' using single-word labels in the same way as those around them is an important example of the shared practices that emerge during this phase. There is a study that nicely illustrates the impact of labels on toddlers.[48] Two-year-olds were given a hybrid object that mostly looked like a key but could also be used as a spoon, together with photographs of a cereal bowl and a car. They were asked to demonstrate the function of the hybrid object. When the key-looking hybrid was not labeled, the children demonstrated its function to start the car. But when it was unexpectedly labeled as a "spoon," the children demonstrated its function to eat from the cereal bowl. Thus, these two-year-olds accepted the shared practice suggested by the adult's label. The study also found that the two-year-olds who most often accepted the unexpected label for the hybrid object were also the children who had the largest vocabulary. This suggests that children who trust that they can learn the right shared practice from adults, such as the right label to use for an object, acquire shared reality labels more quickly.

In this regard, it is interesting that older toddlers (24 months old) at least are sensitive to feedback from others—social cues of assent or dissent—about what is the *real* name for some object. For example, in one study two experimenters sat next to each other, opposite from the participant toddler.[49] A pair of novel toys were held up one at a time, and one experimenter gave first one toy a novel name (e.g., "modi") and then the other toy the *same* novel name ("modi"). The second experimenter, while looking at the child, gave a head gesture for one toy that indicated agreement with the first experimenter's claim of name but gave a head gesture for the other toy that indicated disagreement with the first experimenter that the name was correct for that toy. The children had to select one of the two objects as the answer to the question, "Which one is the modi?" The two-year-olds chose the toy receiving the second experimenter's assent more than the toy receiving the dissent. Thus, the second experimenter broke the ambiguous tie to create a shared reality with the toddler.

Before leaving this symbolic naming part of the shared practices story, I want to emphasize how impressive such single-word utterances are for communicating shared realities with others. Consider the following exchange of a child and her mother that a friend kindly shared with me:

CHILD NAOMI (IN CAR SEAT, POINTS AT STE JUSTINE HOSPITAL AS WE DRIVE PAST): Hostipal! Mommy works hostipal!

ADULT: Yes. That's the hospital where Mommy works.

NAOMI: Mommy walks work hostipal purple backpack.

ADULT: Mommy walks to the hospital each morning to go to work and wears her purple backpack.

NAOMI: Mommy purple backpack walks work hostipal. Mommy works office in hostipal. Mommy walks work office in hostipal. Mommy walks work purple backpack office in hostipal. Mommy.

I want to highlight that you don't need to know Naomi to understand what she is talking about even when her grammar is way off: "Mommy walks work purple backpack office in hostipal." Naomi does not need grammar to be understood. Human children as young as two years old use strings of single words to communicate very effectively—without grammar. And why is this? Because they are motivated to share symbolic communication practices with others. And, because of this motivation, toddlers during this phase do eventually learn grammar quite quickly. But, as illustrated in the previous example, they do *learn* it from exposure and instruction. Toddlers' multiple-word utterance don't begin with grammatically correct sentences. What they do begin with is the motivation to learn how to use symbolic vehicles, words, as a shared practice. And their caretakers typically know what they are talking about—despite the lack of grammar—and *then* they calmly repeat their message in a revised manner to *teach* them grammar.

And, notably, even for adults, it need not be about grammar per se. When one thinks about a fictional character who stands for wisdom, for a mentor worth learning from, for many people no character is greater than Yoda from *Star Wars*. One of his classic lines is "No. Try not. Do . . . or do not. There is no try." This message does not work because of grammar. It works because of ideas that Yoda wants to share with us about taking action, and we can understand what is being communicated without the need for grammar per se. For example, that last part of what he said could have been "No try there is," and it would have been just as effective. What makes us human is not our use of grammar. With only strings of single symbolic words, we humans would have been completely different than any other animal. What matters is our motivation to share practices. And, yes, our use of shared symbolic vehicles (e.g., art)—not just words—happens to be one of our most effective shared practices, one of our most effective *shared tools*.

The use of grammar when communicating with one another is an especially effective way of creating new shared realities. Grammar serves our motivation to create shared realities with others, which is likely why it evolved.

I recognize that children learning language in the sense of syntax and grammar is a very important part of their development, but it is *not* what makes us human. It is *not* the key to what makes our communication so different from other animals. What makes our communication different is our motivated shared practice of using symbolic word utterances to refer to mental concepts. What also needs to be highlighted is that the development of symbolic single word utterances, as important as it is, is not the only new shared reality learning that happens during the phase of *shared practices.* This phase is also the time for toddlers to learn other social practices and social routines from their guided participation in community activities[50]—what Barbara Rogoff, an expert in the development of cultural learning, describes as the "routine ways of doing things in any community's approach to living."[51] This includes eating routines, dressing routines, bathing routines, as well as the toilet routines famously described in Sigmund Freud's "anal period."[52]

According to Erik Erikson, a psychodynamic pioneer in studying the stages of socio-emotional development, success in learning such routines contributes to children experiencing "autonomy," whereas failure contributes to children experiencing "shame."[53] Although children's experience of self-evaluative shame from failing to meet internal standards occurs in the next phase of shared self-guides, toddlers can be teased and shamed by others as indirect forms of social control when they fail to act in the appropriate way.[54]

When learning these social routines, toddlers want to be independent, do things right, and be in control—the classic "terrible twos" where the exclamations "Me do it!" and "No!" rule. Although this childhood phase is, in fact, not always so terrible, independence and control do matter to toddlers. And toddlers are being asked to control themselves; they are being asked to "stand on their own two feet." Importantly, caregivers typically structure the learning settings and activities to support and scaffold what the children need to learn and deal with.[55]

What each child is being asked to do depends on what his or her family (or community) says should be done, and because this varies considerably across cultures,[56] what exactly needs to be done is basically arbitrary. It is arbitrary like the communication practice of which particular word sound category is used to refer to the four-legged animal that barks and tries to lick you (the word sound category "dog" if the child happens to be in an English-speaking community). Children learn their family's eating practices, dressing practices, and so on, just as they learn the practice of symbolic word usage when communicating. Children learn "This is how we do it."

What is remarkable about toddlers is how motivated they are to learn and follow shared practices even when these practices have features that don't make sense to them. Indeed, there is evidence that this motivation can be strong enough that children will perform a task in the manner they observed someone else perform it despite there being a better, alternative way to get the job done—the case of *overimitation*. In one study,[57] for example, 12-month-old, 18-month old, and 24-month-old children observed how an adult opened three different boxes, each containing a desirable toy, by using a particular object to open each box. The children could then try to attain the toy by copying how the adult model opened each box with the object, or they could ignore how the model opened each box and simply open it without using the object, which was more straightforward.

The 12-month-olds cared more about the outcome than the modeled means or practice. They simply, and easily, used their hands to try to open the box rather than using the object that the model used. In contrast, the 18-month-olds and, especially, the 24-month-olds used the modeled object to try to open the box even though it would have been easier to just use their hands. Indeed, some 24-month-olds persisted in copying the model's practice even when doing so failed to open the box.

The 18-month-olds and 24-month-olds could easily have done what the 12-month-old children did and open the box using their hands. In fact, one might imagine they would be even more likely to use this straightforward strategy. But they did not. What mattered to them was to learn and imitate the practice that they had observed, even if they didn't understand the point of doing it that way. This clearly demonstrates how important shared practices are to them.

Moreover, sometimes there is, in fact, a good reason for a shared practice, and it is functional to imitate the practice even if you don't know why it is sensible to do so. This is how wise practices can be handed down from generation to generation despite many, if not most, individuals not knowing why it is a *wise* practice. Significantly there is evidence that chimpanzees act more like the 12-month-old children in this regard. They don't imitate a model's behavior if there is a simpler way to get what they want.[58] And this could be a disadvantage for passing on a wise practice if the chimpanzee observer does not understand the wisdom of the practice and sees a simpler way to do something.[59]

Thus, being willing to share a practice despite not understanding why it is a shared practice can have major benefits for humans. But I cannot complete this discussion of overimitation without mentioning that it also has its potential downsides. Not all shared practices are *wise* practices. Because a practice was wise when it began does not mean that it is wise now. It is possible to improve a practice or abandon it all together for something better. Remember that some of the 24-month-olds persisted in copying what the model did even when they did not succeed in opening the box to get the toy inside. This is problematic. Simply following a shared practice because it is a shared practice, without reconsidering its functionality, can be a problem. Once again, overimitation can have costs as well as benefits.

By the way, overimitation provides another example of how shared relevance can differ from shared feelings. It is likely that the 24-month-olds who persisted in copying the model even when they were failing to open the box and get the toy inside were not feeling good about this shared practice. Indeed, more generally, there can be shared practices that some people do not enjoy, such as daily religious practices like saying prayers at night. But they do so nonetheless because they share the belief that the practice is worth doing. In other words, group members can experience the shared relevance of a practice even if they have neutral or even negative feelings about it.

Thus, toddlers are motivated to create a shared reality with significant others, especially with adult authorities, regarding how to carry out particular activities—shared practices. This includes participating in new shared practices necessary for coordinated play, such as working together with someone on a play activity where success requires that each perform a different function (e.g., one person pushes up a cylinder with an object and holds it in place until the other person retrieves the object).[60] It is also during this phase that toddlers engage with others in a more coordinated turn-taking manner, such as waiting their turn to vocalize during conversations and timing what they do to be responsive to what's happening with their partner.[61] From a shared reality perspective, then, the cognitive-developmental, social-cognitive developmental, and socio-emotional development changes that occur during this phase are describing the same basic developmental change—the emergence of shared practices.

One additional activity that emerges during this period should also be mentioned—pretend play.[62] Around two years of age, children begin to use props to play out an imaginary activity, such as imagining that a teddy bear is wet and then using a piece of paper as a make-believe towel.[63] The props function like symbolic words. They are arbitrary symbolic vehicles that refer to a mental category. Children use these symbolic props to carry out everyday shared practices, such as drying an object that is wet. This allows children to practice a shared routine without needing the normal conditions associated with that routine, which is beneficial for them.[64]

The developmental changes that occur when shared practices emerge have, once again, both benefits and potential costs for children. When children use symbolic word utterances, for example, the sound pattern category (the lexical name), the object category, and the symbolic relation between them are *all* shared realities. What earlier research has emphasized about this change is its epistemic significance—how it affects thought. This includes the classic Whorfian hypothesis that thought is shaped by language.[65] The significance of this development for social relationships has received much less attention, although Vygotsky, for example, did point out, "Signs and words serve children first and foremost as a means of social contact with other people."[66]

When we use symbolic utterances—even when we are alone—we are relating to others, experiencing shared realities with others, and experiencing our affiliation with others. Thus, the phase of shared practices reflects an important change in how children are connected to others. Indeed, this change in our connection to others from the emergence of symbolic single-word utterances is in some ways more profound than Whorf's hypothesis. More profound because, rather than only affecting thought, the shared reality of symbolic words impacts with whom you feel connected and share the world—*whose knowledge about the world matters.*

The epistemic and social relationship effects of symbolic single-word utterances are highlighted by the uniquely human behavior of incorporating words when using tools.[67] Infants will use a spoon to eat and also to bang to make noise or get attention. A spoon is just a particular object in the world that can be used in multiple ways. But once a spoon is called a "spoon" in the phase of shared practices, there begins the encoding and decoding of the word "spoon" as shared communication practices. This has the benefit of adults communicating to children, "This is how we do it," with children learning the role of the spoon in the eating practice—the "right way" of using a spoon. But there is a potential downside as well. Associating particular words with specific objects could inhibit creative use of objects. Consider the spoon example again. When the name for this object, "spoon," comes to mind it activates a particular practice or use for that object (i.e., eating), rather than alternative uses such as taking the cap off a jar or making noise. It is interesting in this regard that young bilingual children who learn early on that there is more than one right way to name the same object are also more creative.[68]

As just noted, sharing verbal practices with others, like calling a spoon "spoon" in an English-speaking community, connects toddlers with others in their community, and this is clearly beneficial to children and to society. However, by connecting more closely to those who share reality about the symbolic utterances, distance can also be created from those who do not share this reality.[69] Even something as minor as saying English words with a foreign accent—a slight variation in the word-sound-pattern shared practice—can be viewed with suspicion. There is evidence that it is important to young children that others use language in the same way that they do.

In one study, accent versus accuracy were pitted against each other.[70] Native English-speaking young children observed two adults suggest different novel names for each of different novel objects. Both adults spoke in English, but one speaker had a native English accent and the other had a foreign accent. The first finding was that all the children preferred the novel name that was suggested by the native-accented speaker. This is evidence for the power of a shared practice even when it only concerns a variation in a word sound pattern.

The next part of the study pitted accent against accuracy. Now the two speakers gave names for *familiar* objects, and, in one condition, the native speaker always gave the *incorrect* name and the foreign-accented speaker always gave the correct name. Following this speaker "accuracy" manipulation, once again the two adult speakers gave novel names for novel objects. The four- and five-year-old children now chose the novel name for a new novel object suggested by the accurate foreign-accented speaker rather than the inaccurate native speaker. However, the younger children did not! This finding suggests that, for them, speaking in the right *way* was the shared practice that mattered most.

More generally, shared practices—shared knowledge of how things should be done—has the benefit to the in-group community of accepting one another when they perform the shared practice. But they also have the potential cost of out-group members being rejected because they do things differently. In addition, the potential in the phase of shared practices for creating prejudicial in-group/out-group comparisons can develop later into moral ideological disputes. As one example, shared eating practices could develop into becoming for or against vegetarianism or becoming for or against Hindu or kosher Jewish eating practices. Shared practices are shared beliefs to which children become committed and this is true of moral ideologies as well. Thus, the emergence of shared practices has the potential downside of initiating the growth of the type of perceived in-group/out-group differences that become ideological differences later. Ideological differences need not lead to conflict, but they often do. And, when that happens, they can become the worst kinds of conflict.

Notes

1. See Suddendorf (2013).
2. Butterworth and Jarrett (1991).
3. Flavell (1999).
4. Legerstee (1991).
5. Kinzler, Dupoux, and Spelke (2007)
6. Bruner (1983, among other works by Bruner).
7. Suddendorf (2013).
8. Gergely, Bekkering, and Király (2002).
9. Trevarthen (1979).
10. Stern (1985).
11. Mead (1934). See also Case (1985) for a mental representational account of this development.
12. I need to make clear what I am and am not saying about the development of shared reality in childhood. I am saying that during each phase a new mode of shared reality emerges and that this new shared reality has significant consequences for children's self-regulation and interpersonal relationships. There is a qualitative change in how children interact with and get along with others. I am not claiming that the changes appear suddenly or that there is nothing happening before they occur. The emergence of each phases has precursors, including cognitive and social-cognitive developments, as well as changes in the social lives of children (e.g., going to school for the first time). My position is simply that the sequence of shared reality modes that emerge is ordered such that Phase 1 occurs before Phase 2, Phase 2 before Phase

3, and so on, without skipping a phase. In addition, although I suggest typical age ranges in which a new phase occurs, for any particular child it could occur earlier or later than the range I mention, especially for later phases that can vary across cultures and across historical periods. I must also emphasize that the changes I describe are not all that is happening during childhood development. Clearly, there are other major cognitive, social-cognitive, and socio-emotional changes that occur during childhood, as well as maturational and biological changes. Because the story of shared reality developmental story is just part of what happens during childhood development, the age ranges that I describe for shared reality development have gaps that are filled with these other kinds of developmental changes. These other changes include changes that support the emergence of a new shared reality mode (i.e., other precursors). This book, however, is about the shared reality contribution to being human. Other childhood developments are obviously important, but developments in shared reality also matter and I believe that they have received insufficient emphasis in the literature.

13. See Bates, Camaioni, and Volterra (1975).
14. See, for example, Liszkowski (2005, 2018), Saarni, Campos, Camras, and Witherington (2006), Suddendorf (2013), and Tomasello, Carpenter, Call, Behne, and Moll (2005).
15. See Bretherton (1991, p. 24).
16. See Tomasello, Carpenter, and Liszkowski (2007, p. 9). For a recent review of the evidence that the ability for shared reference is firmly established around 12 months of age, see Liszkowski (2018).
17. See Liszkowski, Carpenter, Henning, Striano, and Tomasello (2004).
18. See Carpenter, Nagel, and Tomasello (1998).
19. See Eisenberg, Fabes, and Spinrad (2006) and Hay and Rheingold (1983).
20. Note that something can be interesting either because it is liked (attractive) or because it is disliked (repulsive). Two people can share that something is interesting while having opposite emotional reactions to it. For a classic discussion of what it means to find something "interesting," see Mandler (1975).
21. Later on in this chapter I will discuss the other end of the shared relevance dimension—shared irrelevance. This can also produce a shared reality when people experience that they agree that something is *not* worthy of attention.
22. See Carpenter et al. (1998) and Moses, Baldwin, Rosicky, and Tidball (2001).
23. See, for example, Mumme, Fernald, and Herrera (1996).
24. See Sorce, Emde, Campos, and Klinnert (1985) and Mumme and Fernald (2003).
25. See Kim and Kwack (2011).
26. See Stenberg (2009).
27. I believe that the term *feeling* is appropriate because Saarni et al. (2006) describe a "feeling" as the registration that an event *matters*, which is true of finding something interesting and learning what is positive and what is negative, and they discuss how feelings can be generated through perceiving the vocal, facial, or gestural expressions of others, which is precisely what infants do.
28. See Saarni (2000).

29. See Eisenberg and Fabes (1998); Zahn-Waxler, Radke-Yarrow, Wagner, and Chapman (1992).
30. See Hamlin, Mahajan, Liberman, and Wynn (2013).
31. See the "good enough parent" described by Winnicott (1965); see also Harter (1999).
32. See Kruglanski et al. (2005).
33. See Heider (1958).
34. See Tamis-LeMonda, Bornstein, and Baumwell (2001).
35. I am grateful to Maya Rossignac-Milon for highlighting the importance of shared irrelevance. High school athletes, for example, can share the belief that playing sports is relevant whereas studying is irrelevant or not worth the effort to engage. We also discussed the fact that, given shared relevance is a dimension, it is possible to have shared relevance at other positions along the dimension, such as two people agreeing that something has moderate relevance (neither high nor low). As with other dimensions, however, it is possible that shared high relevance or shared irrelevance has greater motivational force than moderate relevance.
36. With his colleagues, Arie Kruglanski, a world renowned expert on the psychology of terrorism, has examined the motivational force of the quest for a life of meaning and importance—the quest for significance—in recruiting young people to become terrorists. The good news is that it is possible to *deradicalize* terrorists by making them feel that a nonterrorist life can be significant, that is, by transforming traditional community values from their previous condition of shared irrelevance to a new condition of shared relevance. See Kruglanski et al. (2013) and Kruglanski et al. (2014).
37. See Piaget (1926, 1951/1962) and Vygotsky (1962).
38. See Terrace (2005).
39. See Terrace (2005, p. 99).
40. See Chouinard (2007).
41. See Nelson (2005).
42. See Brown (1958).
43. See Stern (1914). Vygotsky (1962) agreed with Stern that this turning point is observable from children asking for the name of objects and the subsequent sharp increase in children's vocabulary, and he agrees that this is a decisive turning point in the child's linguistic, cultural, and intellectual development.
44. See Keller (1902).
45. See Keller (1902, p. 23).
46. See Brown (1958b).
47. See Harris (2012).
48. See Jaswal and Markman (2007).
49. Fusaro and Harris (2013).
50. See Rogoff (2003), Rossano (2012), Thompson (2006), and Whiting and Whiting (1975).
51. Rogoff (2003, p. 3).
52. See Freud (1937).
53. Erikson (1963).

54. See Rogoff (2003).
55. See Rogoff (1990) and Saarni (2000).
56. See Rogoff (2003) and Rogoff, Paradise, Mejia Arauz, Correa-Chavez, and Angelillo (2003).
57. See Nielsen (2006). See also Gergely et al. (2002).
58. See Horner and Whiten (2005).
59. For discussions of other potential benefits of overimitation, see Lyons, Young, and Keil (2007), Nielsen (2006), and Whiten, McGuigan, Marshall-Pescini, and Hopper (2009).
60. See Warneken, Chen, and Tomasello (2006) and Warneken and Tomasello (2007).
61. See Dix, Cheng, and Day (2009) and Rutter and Durkin (1987); see also Eckerman, Davis, and Didow (1989).
62. See, for example, Harris (2000), Harris and Kavanaugh (1993), and Piaget (1951/1962).
63. See Harris (2000).
64. See Harris (2000).
65. Whorf (1956).
66. See Vygotsky (1978, p. 28).
67. See Vygotsky (1978).
68. See Leikin (2012).
69. See Spelke (2013).
70. See Corriveau, Kinzler, and Harris (2013).

3

Childhood Development of Shared Reality

Preschoolers and Schoolers

How children create shared realities with their close others can be surprising. Years ago I had a conversation with a friend who told me that he was concerned about his son who had set very tough standards for himself and was very self-critical when he failed to meet them. He said that he was surprised about this because he and his wife had been very careful not to set standards too high for their son or to criticize him if he did not perform well. Being clinically trained, he then paused, looked at me, and said, " Yay, I know what you are thinking—that I just *think* that I did that, when in fact I demanded a lot from my son and was critical of him." I replied that, in fact, I did believe him. But then I asked him whether he was demanding of himself and critical of himself when he performed below his own high standards. He was taken aback. He had not considered before that his son had observed *him* as a model of self-regulation and had identified and accepted his father's high standard of self-evaluation for himself. After all, he loved his father and wanted to be like him—classic identification and another way that children can create a shared reality with their parents.

What is clear from the last chapter is that young children are highly motivated to create shared realities with their close others. It is also clear that creating these shared realities can have costs as well as benefits for the children, such as my friend's son becoming self-critical like his father was self-critical. These emerging shared realities are essential for children to become fully part of the human community, but they also have downsides that need to be recognized. In this chapter I will describe the next two phases of the development of shared reality—*shared self-guides* and *shared coordinated roles*. Once these two shared realities have emerged, children are no longer just children. Indeed, historically, and still today in some parts of the world, children are now expected to take on adult responsibilities and are no longer treated as children. Thus, these next two phases of childhood development are very important to the story of what makes us human.

Shared Self-Guides

From a historical perspective, it is interesting that the classic cognitive-developmental literature and the socio-emotional developmental literature have differed in whether what happens in the 18- to 24-month period versus what happens in the three- to five-year period is the more important part of the human development story. In the classic cognitive-developmental literature, the emergence of symbolic processes and language in the 18- to 24-month period has been considered to be the most important development. In contrast, in the classic socio-emotional literature, and especially the psychodynamic literature, what happens in the three- to five-year period has been considered to be the most important development because this is when children adopt significant others' goals and standards for their own self-regulation and self-evaluation.

This latter emphasis on children's sharing significant other's goals and standards for them began, as did so much in the history of socio-emotional psychology, with what Sigmund Freud had to say about human development. Freud described how the development of the superego (or conscience) in the three- to five-year period changes children's self-regulation forever by their identifying with (accepting) significant others' goals and standards for themselves.[1] During this period children develop a shared reality with significant others about what kind of person to be—shared realities about what goals to pursue and standards to follow.[2] This self-regulatory process has been referred to as "identification"[3] and as "internalization"[4] in the developmental literature.[5]

Although "identification" and "internalization" are sometimes used interchangeably, they are different kinds of shared self-guides. This is well illustrated by what happened to my friend and his son. My friend told me that he and his wife were careful not to communicate to their son what type of person they wanted him to be. They did not want him to internalize high standards that could lead to self-criticism whenever he failed to meet them. But his son, instead, identified with my friend—wanted to be like his father—and thus accepted as his own standards for himself the standards that my friend had for himself. This is identification rather than internalization. These are two different kinds of shared self-guides, but in both cases children are accepting a parent's goals or standards for their own self-regulation. What my friend's story highlights is how motivated three- to five-year-olds are to create a shared reality with their significant others.

If one route for creating strong self-guides is not offered (internalization), they can take another route (identification).

The self-regulatory process of pursuing goals and following standards that take others' desires or expectations for them into account is clearly related to Freud's concept of the superego because children's superego would represent their understanding of what significant others believe they ought to do (conscience). But preschoolers understanding of what their parents (or other significant others) want or expect them to do is not restricted to what their parents believe they *ought* to do. It also includes their parents' hopes and aspirations for them.[6] Importantly, preschoolers acquire these self-guides not only from feedback and direct instruction from their caregivers but also from observing how a significant other responds to others, including how mommy or daddy responds positively or negatively to the behavior of their older sibling or a positive or negative comment from their parents about a playmate of the child (i.e., observational learning).[7]

What is central to shared self-guides is that significant others provide standards of good behavior or performance that the child accepts and uses for self-regulation without the need for external control or surveillance by others. Specifically, children follow a standard even when there is no one observing what they do who will reward or punish them for doing it and there is no one in the immediate situation who is asking or telling them to do it. In a longitudinal study that nicely illustrates this, a composite measure of "internalization" or "conscience" was created by combining the results of two tasks given to preschoolers.[8] In one task, the child was in a room where there were attractive toys on a shelf, but the child's mother told the child that playing with these toys was off limits. Then the mother left the child alone in the room while the child performed a dull task. Whether the child followed the prohibition standard was observed without the child knowing.

In the other "conscience" task, the child played a throwing game with Velcro-covered balls and was told that he or she would receive a prize for each ball that stuck to the target. The rules for the game, such as the child having to stay far away from the target, as well as face away from it, made it practically impossible to succeed and win a prize. Again, the experimenter left the child alone, allowing the child to cheat (or not) unobserved.

The study found that the children's demonstration of "conscience" on these two tasks was predicted by how well they had performed, a year earlier, on a task that required their suppressing a dominant response to follow an instruction, which on the "conscience" tasks meant suppressing the desire to play with the attractive toys or stick a ball on the target to win a prize to follow the rules. This study illustrates that preschoolers can resist temptation and follow rules they have been given *even when they are alone* (i.e., without needing to be watched).

Another way to measure whether preschoolers will accept and follow rules is to observe whether they follow rules *in the absence of pressure to do so*. A study that illustrates that preschoolers can do so tested whether children follow the rule of sharing with others without direct social pressure from others to do so. The study involved children playing with attractive toys in the presence of an experimenter-manipulated puppet. Children younger than four years old tended not to share their toys with the puppet unless the puppet expressed its desire for the toys or made an explicit request for the toys. In contrast, four-year-old children shared their toys more spontaneously without needing these forms of direct social pressure.[9]

Preschoolers, then, self-regulate in terms of others' standards for them that they have accepted (i.e., shared self-guides) without needing external social pressure or control. These shared self-guides influence what they choose to do or not to do. In addition, by accepting these self-guides in their own self-regulation, they experience positive and negative feelings, respectively, when they succeed or fail to meet them. There is evidence of a shift, for example, between two and four years of age in children's self-evaluative responses, such as a dramatic increase in pouts or frowns after failure and smiling after winning. This developmental shift has been interpreted as an increase in children's self-evaluations that no longer depend simply on how they expect adults to react to their performance.[10] These positive and negative feelings from self-evaluation include feelings such as pride and shame or guilt,[11] even in the absence of observation or feedback from an adult. Indeed, it has been argued that children's experiences of these *moral* emotions stem from children evaluating themselves in relation to standards of what kind of person they want to be or should be, and around three years of age these standards are internally represented social standards.[12]

What is the difference between "shared practices" and "shared self-guides" as social norms? This is an important question for understanding the development of norms in general and moral development in particular. Shared reality is always *about* something. So what are the norms about for shared practices versus shared self-guides? For shared practices, the norms are about the practices, the activities themselves. They are not about the children themselves or about their significant others. *The norms are about how the activities are done*. The shared practices are about how eating is done or how dressing is done or how using words is done by all members of the community.[13]

In contrast, for shared self-guides, the norms are about the goals and standards that the child needs to pursue that relate that particular child to a particular significant other. *The norms are about a particular child in relation to a particular significant other*. The children, literally and figuratively, look up to their significant others. Their status and power is above them. This is why Freud's term, the *super*ego, is so apt for what is happening with shared self-guides. Children look up to their significant others and want their guidance about how to get along in the world and what to become. A child's self-guides, as normative guidance, come from his or her significant others and they are about that child.[14]

This difference between shared practices and shared self-guides as norms is similar to the distinction between *descriptive* norms and *injunctive* norms.[15] The norms related to shared practices *describe* how people in the community usually do the activities. The norms of related to shared self-guides *prescribe* what a specific child should do to meet the goals and standards for that child that are held by his or her significant others. And this difference also constitutes a moral development difference. Children's success or failure to perform shared practices constitutes behavior that is *correct* or *incorrect*. In contrast, children's success or failure to perform shared self-guides constitutes behavior that is *right* or *wrong*. Both kinds of norms strongly motivate behavior, and success or failure to meet them has significant affective consequences. Nonetheless, they are different. Those poor preschoolers with their shared self-guides now have to deal with adults—and their older siblings as well—making a *moral* issue out of their mistakes and errors. Oh, for the good old days, just a year or so ago, when a mistake was just an incorrect error and not a moral failing.

Given its implications for self-regulation and self-evaluation, this general socio-emotional part of the emergence of shared self-guides is very important. But there is also an important social-cognitive developmental change during this phase that contributes to these socio-emotional changes and needs to be highlighted. Children from three to five years of age can for the first time coordinate two separate systems of relations, such as coordinating observable responses like another person's behavior with unobservable responses like this other person's feeling or belief that produced the behavior.[16] This cognitive capacity underlies their ability to make inferences about the expectations and preferences that their parents have in relation to their own behaviors.[17] In particular, children can now understand that another person wants them and expects them to behave in particular ways and that how this person responds to them depends on what this person wants and expects of them[18]—this person's goals or standards for them. Preschoolers accept these goals and standards of others for themselves and use them in their self-regulation and self-evaluation—transforming them to shared self-guides. And, notably, this change in inferring and responding to the inner states of others—others' feelings, beliefs, and concerns—is also evident in changes in how children play with their peers. Cooperative play with peers emerges between 20 and 24 months of age and increases between 24 and 28 months of age,[19] but only around three years of age does children's cooperative play involve sharing desires, intentions, and goals[20].

There is another important social-cognitive change that occurs during this phase. Katherine Nelson, a renowned expert on children's development of "self" knowledge, notes that two-year-old children have a limited sense of their self in the past or the future. Even their play concerns "what is or can be, not with what was and what may yet be."[21] But by four or five years of age, children become aware of themselves as individuals with a past and a future.[22] The development of a narrative self contributes to the emergence of a cultural self. Children begin to consider the possibility that things as they are might instead be some other way.[23] This matters because it means that children can now self-regulate in relation to shared goals and standards not only in terms of who they *are* in the present but also who they could *become* in the future.[24]

What this means is that children cannot just rest on their laurels. As toddlers, it was enough to carry out the shared practices, but now the preschoolers need to continue to improve, especially for shared self-guides that are aspirations for the future. As the early psychology pioneer James Mark Baldwin put it, "it is not I, but I am to become it. Here is my ideal self, my final pattern, my 'ought' set before me."[25] In his classic book *Becoming*,[26] Gordon Allport suggested that it is because children during this phase are self-regulating in relation to what others want them to *become* that they develop a stable sense of self-identity and long-range goals that provide directions for striving.

And this is not all that is happening during the phase of shared self-guides. There is yet another well-known change that occurs that is typically discussed under the phrase, "theory of mind" (TOM). Some of what I have already discussed is related to this literature. However, the emphasis in this literature is not on the development of shared realities per se. Indeed, perhaps the best known example of the development of TOM from three to five years of age would appear to involve children's ability to recognize a *non*shared reality. This is the famous "false belief" test.

In the classic version of the false belief test,[27] a character named Maxi had put his chocolate somewhere and then left, and while he was away his mother moved it to a different location. The child participants in the study are asked where Maxi will look for the chocolate when he returns. Generally speaking, children under three years of age say that Maxi will look where his mother put the chocolate, where it is now. Children around four years of age usually say that Maxi will look where he originally put his chocolate, even though they know that this is not where the chocolate actually is now. These older children are said to have passed the false belief test.

The test is called "false belief" because Maxi's belief about where the chocolate is located is false and different from the children's belief about where the chocolate actually is now. This TOM shift as a function of age is an interesting phenomenon.[28] And, as I said, it appears to illustrate a *non*shared reality that develops in preschoolers because it is often described as the ability to understand that others have beliefs, desires, and intentions that are *different* from one's own.[29] But I would like to offer a somewhat different interpretation of what is happening in studies like the Maxi study—an interpretation that involves a shared reality rather than a nonshared reality.

It is true that the children and the character Maxi have different beliefs about the location of the chocolate. And children cannot just assume that what they know and what Maxi knows about the world is the same. It is different than shared practices because it is fine for two-year-olds to assume that others share the practice of using particular words for particular object categories, that they share basic eating practices, and so on. In their family and local community, others probably *do* share those practices. But children will fail the false belief test if they simply assume that "what I know, you know."

What are preschoolers doing to pass this test? I propose that they are creating a particular kind of shared reality. Specifically, they are sharing reality with Maxi about where they would look for the chocolate *if they were in his situation*—what I years ago called "situational role-taking"[30]: "If I were in Maxi's shoes, I would look for the chocolate where Maxi put it because he doesn't know it was moved."

According to this proposal, the TOM change among preschoolers *does* involve a shared reality change after all—it involves the ability to share with another person the same course of action for getting the chocolate in *the same knowledge situation*. *Guide* in its most general sense means something that directs or influences the course of action to a particular end.[31] Here, the children are assuming that in the same knowledge situation what would guide their behavior and what would guide Maxi's behavior are the same. This constitutes another kind of self-guide regulation because the children are guided by what they would do *if* they were in the target's situation—"What would *I* do with the *same* knowledge as Maxi?" It is not the truth about where the chocolate really is, but it is the truth about what you and Maxi would do in the same knowledge situation—*a shared self-guide*.

Importantly, to pass this test children do not have to consider what they would do in Maxi's situation if they thought that Maxi and they were very different kinds of persons who would react differently even in the same situation. If they thought that they and Maxi would not behave the same way even in the same situation, then they would have to inhibit what they would do in that situation and consider instead how Maxi—a very different person than them—would behave in that situation. That would be a much more challenging task. It is the "individual role-taking" of seeing the world through the eyes of others in the same situation, where *their* eyes are different than *your* eyes, rather than just putting yourself in their shoes and assuming that you would both react in the same way.[32] Individual role-taking is the kind of nonegocentrism that the literature has shown does not develop until later.[33] But this TOM task only requires situational role-taking, and situational role-taking involves shared self-guides.

I should also note that there is an intriguing positive relation between children's engagement in make-believe play, such as role play or having an imaginary friend, and the TOM development among preschoolers.[34] Again, make-believe play, such as pretending to be a pirate who has found a treasure that other pirates might steal away, does not require the kind of nonegocentrism that is involved in individual role-taking. But it does require situational role-taking, such as imagining what you would do if you were in the pirate's situation. Like TOM, this involves shared self-guides, which could be why there is a positive relation between them.

Situational role-taking can also be involved in children sharing their toys with others because children can put themselves in another child's situation of not having the toy they are playing with and know that in that child's situation they would want to be given a chance to play with the toy. If so, then one would expect TOM to be positively related to children sharing their toy with another child without needing a direct expression of desire for the toy or a direct request for it. In fact, this is the case.[35]

I should emphasize that although both shared practices and shared self-guides involve shared guidance, the nature of that guidance is different. The guidance in shared practices involves children learning from others how food utensils, word sounds, and so on should be used by them as members of their community. The guidance in shared self-guides involves children learning from others what goals they should pursue and what standards they should use in their personal self-regulation. Preschoolers understand that other people want them to behave in particular ways and that others' responses to them depend on whether or not their behavior matches these others' goals and standards for them (i.e., self-guide mediation). By using others' viewpoints for their own self-regulation and self-evaluation, children acquire *shared* self-guides. This has the benefit that children can plan their behaviors to match these shared self-guides, which gives them an enhanced subjective sense of self-control. And to the extent that significant others' responses to a child *are* based on their goals and standards for that child, children's new ability to infer those goals and standards increases the likelihood that they will be effective in self-regulation. This would be a major benefit from this shared reality phase.

In addition, by sharing significant others' self-guides for them, children are treating some goals and standards as more *relevant* for them than others. Having shared relevance regarding which goals and standards are important allows children to have priorities in goals and standards. There are many possible goals and standards that could guide children's self-regulation. Generally speaking, it makes children stronger in self-regulation to select among the many different options and establish priorities. In this way, having shared relevance for which goals and standards matter most— shared self-guides—can be a major benefit for children.

In terms of mechanisms of social influence, there is a major difference between social regulation based on compliance and social regulation based on shared self-guides: the difference between your behaving in certain ways because these behaviors are instrumental for attaining rewards and avoiding punishments from others versus behaving in certain ways because the behaviors match values and standards for how you should behave that you have accepted.[36] As noted by Anna Freud, Sigmund Freud's daughter and a pioneer in developmental psychopathology, when children reach the latter phase, their self-control no longer depends on the anticipation of suffering that may be inflicted by outside agents.[37] A permanent institution has now been set up that embodies others' wishes and requirements. This shift in social influence benefits society because children will better control how they behave in ways that match what society wants without the need for direct surveillance. It also benefits children's sense of self-determination because they experience their choices of how to behave as being more intrinsically motivated (what they want to do) than extrinsically motivated (what they have to do).[38]

The shared self-guides that preschoolers acquire change children's motivational and emotional lives because they begin to use those self-guides as goals to pursue and as standards to evaluate their success or failure in attaining those goals. If their monitoring system perceives a discrepancy between their actual self and a self-guide, they can take action to reduce it. They can also plan action taking potential discrepancies into account, thereby using prospective self-evaluation in the service of current self-regulation.[39] They can situationally role-take, which can help them understand how others would feel if they were to behave toward them in a prosocial or antisocial manner and thereby better internally control their actions toward others. Such improvement in self-regulation could benefit children by contributing to the decline in aggression that occurs during this period.[40]

These are all significant self-regulatory benefits for children from the emergence of shared self-guides, along with the benefit mentioned earlier from the shared relevance of shared self-guides setting priorities regarding which goals and standards are important to pursue and meet. But there are potential costs as well, including epistemic costs. When planning, you choose among the options that you know and have established as being relevant. The problem is that children's shared goals and standards may become the only accessible and salient options to them because they have been established as the relevant goals and standards, and relevance underlies accessibility and salience.[41] Because of the shared relevance of the shared goals and standards, other possible options may not even be considered, even when another option could be a better fit for a child, such as a young girl building things versus dressing up. And this potential downside continues so that teenagers plan to have careers that their parents want them to have rather than what fits their interests or skills. Shared self-guides can be so strong that children don't even *know* what else they might choose.

With respect to emotions that preschoolers experience when they fail to meet standards, there is also evidence that preschoolers who violate moral standards manifest guilt reactions about their standard violation.[42] Indeed, as a major downside of shared self-guides, depression involving excessive guilt has been observed in preschoolers.[43] With respect to trade-offs, it is also worth noting that it is children with *more* secure attachments who are more likely to share moral standards and establish them as being more relevant.[44] This makes sense because children with more secure attachments would have stronger social relational motives and thus would be more motivated to create shared relevance and shared reality with others. The trade-off from this is that although these securely attached children, with their stronger shared moral standards and stronger self-guides in general, will benefit from being more likely to fulfill the moral standards and attain their shared goals, they will also suffer more when they fail to do so.[45]

The trade-offs from shared self-guides having high shared relevance provides a clear example of how shared reality can both make us strong and tear us apart. The high shared relevance of our shared self-guides—for both children and adults—makes us stronger because the relevance gives us priorities in our goals and standards and the sharing means that others support our self-regulatory efforts. But the high shared relevance of our shared self-guides can also tear us apart because failures to meet our goals and standards are experienced as failures in our own eyes and (we believe) in the eyes of others. Such failures can produce intense emotional suffering in a way that other animals do not experience. Moreover, as we develop, we can have different shared self-guides with different significant others, such as parents versus close peers or even mother versus father, and this can produce conflict in shared relevance that results in confusion and motivational uncertainty.[46]

Shared Coordinated Roles

I still remember vividly what preschoolers look like when they are playing soccer (European football). They look like bees swarming around the ball, but instead of trying to sting the ball they are trying to kick the ball. To say it is disorganized is an understatement because not only do you not know whether a player's position on the team is offense or defense, you don't even know which team the player is on. They simply try to kick the ball and direction hardly matters. Developmental psychologists call this "associative" play, which is interaction without organization that looks like every child for himself or herself, and it is distinguished from "cooperative play" where everyone has a role in coordinated teamwork.[47]

After observing this rather amazing, and frankly amusing, phenomenon for one season, I volunteered to coach girls soccer in the West Side League of New York City (with a background playing high school soccer for several years). I coached for two years when the girls were seven and eight years of age. It gave me a great opportunity to observe the emergence of shared coordinated roles. My first goal as a coach was to pull the players apart on the field to make it possible to distinguish the roles of offense and defense and, perhaps most important, to make it possible for the players to pass to one another. It wasn't until the second year of our team that the players began to take the others' roles and positions on the field into account. How exciting it was when the players finally understood, for example, that there was a role of center forward and that position needed to take into account where the right and left forwards were positioned on the field to give them a leading pass *and* the right and left forwards needed to position themselves *away* from the center forward in order to receive a leading pass. Watching the development of my team over the two years was very special because it left an indelible sense of the significance of the emergence of shared coordinated roles in childhood.

When does this emergence of shared coordinated roles happen in childhood? Admittedly, I am not sure exactly. It could depend on the child and on the activity. Without question, deciding the age parameters for this last "schooler" phase of shared reality development was more difficult than the previous phases. From a neuroscience development perspective, there is a transition around 10 years of age that marks an important change point in amygdala–cortical functional connectivity.[48] From a socio-cultural development perspective, important changes occur as soon as children begin schooling, which typically would be around six years of age.

Formal schooling is a new social-life phase for children that, for most of them, exposes them to a much greater variety of adult authorities and peers than ever before.[49] As Eric Erikson states, "school seems to be a culture all by itself."[50] The schooling that some children receive is not formal schooling but is more like an apprenticeship or helping out adults with their activities and thereby learning from doing. In cultures where children early on *participate* in adult activities with family members and learn productive roles, such as farm families, rather than *preparing* to become adults like children who attend a formal school, this phase of shared coordinated roles could occur even earlier.[51]

Given all these possibilities described in the literature, finding a precise demarcation period for shared coordinated roles is difficult. Indeed, illustrating historically the difficulty of demarcating this phase, Freud's proposed "latency period" lasts from about five years of age to puberty, and Mead was not clear about when the "generalized other" stage actually appeared. What I believe is that this phase of shared coordinated roles emerges when schooling begins, whether the schooling is formal or informal, and this shared reality is qualitatively distinct from the shared reality change that emerged in the earlier phase of shared self-guides. Moreover, the shared reality change that emerges with shared coordinated roles really matters for becoming a human adult. The end of this phase, which is generally around 13 years of age (and perhaps a little earlier or a little later), spells the end of childhood. What children have in place by the end of this phase is the shared reality motivation to cooperate with others in group activities that require the coordination of multiple roles, with the group member in each role understanding what is expected of them and the members performing the other roles.

Shared cooperative activity, or teamwork, has the essential characteristics of mutual responsiveness. It involves coordinated plans of action and intentions that require understanding the complementary roles.[52] Such shared cooperative activity has also been highlighted as critical to the development of humans as a distinct species, including our unique ethical concerns.[53] It is our ability to work together in groups of strangers (i.e., nonrelatives) that distinguishes us as a species, and we can do so by organizing ourselves into coordinated and complementary roles.[54] It is during this phase that such shared coordinated roles emerge.

Yes, preschoolers have shared goals and standards with their significant others. But this is quite different from the sharing of teamwork and complementary roles that occurs with schooling. Most especially different is its *impersonal* nature. The shared self-guides apply to a child's own personal self-regulation and self-evaluation. The shared self-guides are what the children's own significant others want for them as particular individuals. With shared coordinated roles, the rules and norms demanded by a specific activity apply to anyone engaging in that activity and to anyone who enacts a specific activity-related role. Children learn that what is relevant is not them as individuals but as role players coordinating with other role players where everyone shares knowledge about the complementary roles.

With respect to children following rules, Piaget said children's codification of rules occurs around 11 to 12 years of age. He says that such rules "constitute a well-marked social reality" that is "independent of individuals."[55] It is not about you; it is about the role. Someone else can substitute for you, take over the role you are performing. Returning to the soccer example, the role of center forward is not restricted to a particular player. It is a role that can be performed by different players. Indeed, this was the case for my soccer team. If the player who usually performed the role of center forward was sick for one game, the team did not lose the position of center forward. Another player took over this role. In addition, different players were given the opportunity to play center forward during a game just to allow them to practice the role in an actual game.

Moreover, most group activities, like soccer, involve multiple roles, and each role player must understand how each of the other roles work to coordinate with them effectively. The player in the role of center forward needs to coordinate with the players in the roles of left forward and right forward, and the players in these latter roles need to coordinate with the player in the role of center forward. Without taking the other roles into account, the player in each role will not be passing appropriately. Important characteristics of groups are that the members work interdependently for some shared purpose and the members have specialized, differentiated roles within the group as they work together to pursue their collective purpose.[56] This kind of group organization with coordinated roles emerges in schoolers.

The difference between schoolers and preschoolers in the way that they relate to others while engaged in an activity is precisely the distinction that was made by Mead when distinguishing *play* versus *game*.[57] He says that in play a child takes the role of a particular significant other and in relation to self: "Daddy, I will be you and you will be me." In contrast, a game is not a particular other. It is a *generalized other*, and the expectations for each role are the same for all those who enact the role. Moreover, the role cannot be enacted alone but must take into account the other roles in the game. As Mead says, "the attitudes of the other players which the participant assumes organize into a sort of unit, and it is that organization which controls the response of the individual."[58] And later he says, "That which makes society possible is such common responses, such organized attitudes."[59] In a game there is an organization of interrelated roles, and it is to the organization as a whole that the child belongs. Notably, Piaget also says that although children's play around 4 years of age can involve different roles, between 7 and 11 years of age there is an ever increasing *coordination* of roles, as well as *games* with rules.[60]

Children live in a very different social world when shared coordinated roles emerge. Preschoolers pursue goals in the service of meeting shared self-guides that concern them in particular as an individual person. They experience the standards and objectives that they have accepted and incorporated as being what significant others want them, individually, to become. The expectations of others that they try to meet are about them in particular, and the others are typically particular significant others. When shared coordinated roles emerge, strangers are now telling them what is expected of anyone occupying the role they are performing—not them in particular. And, to make a social entity thrive (e.g., a work team, a sports team, a school club), they must coordinate their role-relevant behavior with what others are expected to do in their roles.

For schoolers, the objectives and standards are no longer associated with significant others, but instead, as Mead said, are associated with the generalized other. It is not you that matters; it is the larger entity, which now controls your behavior. It is the organization that controls your response. The eminent developmental psychopathologist Harry Stack Sullivan believed that it is in early adolescence when true collaboration originates, in the sense of collaboration implying mutuality.[61] This represents a dramatic shift in socially regulated self-regulation. We share teamwork and coordinated roles with equals.[62]

The paradigmatic case of shared coordinated roles is communication between two persons who take turns being in the speaker role and the listener role while participating in the "communication game," where *game* refers to purposeful social interaction involving interdependent roles and conventional rules.[63] Schoolers become better over time in tailoring their message to suit the inner states (e.g., attitudes, knowledge) of their communication partner. Early on, schoolers can still assume more common knowledge with their communication partner than is justified. In my own research on communication development, for example, I found that, compared to 13-year-olds, even children as old as 9 years were relatively poor at fully taking into account that they had knowledge that another person might not have.

Although they understood that a stranger in their town would not know something like how to get from A to B, they could still make the mistake of trying to inform a stranger by using the names of the local landmarks, such as the name of a church, which a stranger would not know.[64]

With the emergence of shared coordinated roles, there is a sharp improvement in children's conversational skills, and they begin to function in a manner more comparable to adults. There is evidence, for example, that compared to children in Grade 2 whose conversations were brief or aborted 55% of the time, the conversations of Grade 5 children (about 10 years of age) were brief or aborted only 15% of the time. And on a measure of conversational turn-taking that distinguished between turns that were related to what had just been said versus unrelated, 40% were unrelated for Grade 2 children compared to only 15% being unrelated for Grade 5 children. Notably, this research found that the conversations of the Grade 5 children on these measures were quite comparable to those of adults.[65]

A classic study by Sam Glucksberg and Bob Krauss, pioneers in the experimental study of communication development, illustrates the development of schoolers' effective coordination between speakers and listeners.[66] The speakers had to tell a listener how to stack a set of colored blocks on a peg. After the speaker's message, the listeners gave feedback that they did not understand which block the speaker meant. Whereas speakers in kindergarten tended to respond with silence or simply repeat what they had said before, fifth-graders either provided a new description or modified their earlier description, which was like what adult speakers did.

Notably, the development during this phase is more about learning how to cooperate in coordinated game roles than it is about language development per se. The kindergartners had the language capacity to say what the older children said when they provided a new description or modified their earlier description. From a language capacity perspective, the kindergarteners could have said what the older speakers said, but they didn't. They simply weren't motivated to change their original message because they assumed that if they knew their message referred to the correct block, then their audience would know as well (egocentrism). They had not yet reached the shared reality phase of fulfilling the expectations of the speaker role, which includes taking the knowledge of the listener into account and recognizing that this knowledge could be *different* than their knowledge. And, finally, it should be emphasized that communication is about fulfilling *roles* during this phase. There is a significant difference between schoolers enacting the communication roles of speaker and listener, as compared to toddlers being encoders and decoders of symbolic utterances.[67]

During the phase of shared coordinated roles, the source of prescriptive norms broadens from significant other to the generalized other where the normative expectations for a child involves roles, such as the roles of speaker and listener, that are the same for anyone enacting the role— the same basic standards for all. This change is also reflected in a broadening of descriptive norms for self-evaluation during this phase. Although preschoolers compare their current possessions with other individuals who belong to their group, such as comparing how much candy they have (self–other ingroup comparisons), schoolers begin to make more complex comparisons involving, for example, group-level comparisons involving the in-group and out-groups.[68] Schoolers also begin to rank their own performance and that of others along dimensions of competence using standards that apply to everyone[69]—once again, the same standard for everyone.

There is also a change in how schoolers perceive authority. Authority is now seen as a shared, consensual hierarchical relation between parties that is adopted (for varying lengths of time) because it confers benefits for the group. Rather than obeying an authority because that person is an older significant other, obedience is now experienced as being in the service of cooperation and coordination, and it is a shared, consensual relation among more or less equal members of the group.[70] Because the coordination is for the common good, the peer authorities (e.g., captain of a team) also believe that they should listen to their subordinates (i.e., the other team members) who are responsible for other roles in the group. Importantly, authority for peer groups rests on the consent of the governed.[71] Children can exercise mutual control from regarding each other as equals. Everyone in society shares an equal responsibility to obey the rules, and respect for them develops from recognizing their social regulation function, particularly their organizational function like division of labor.

Significantly, these changes in how children relate to one another are also reflected in changes in friendships. From preschoolers to schoolers, there is a shift from friendship being about doing something *with* another child, like doing some play activity together, to friendship being about doing something *for* another child, such as trying to help them out with their problems or having them help you out with your problems.[72] It is like games where there is cooperation and coordinated roles to serve each other's interests and assist one another. There is a change in what is expected from a close friend. The role of close friend is different. It includes sharing secrets and concerns with one another that allows each child to help out the other more effectively. Because children now share their problems and their secrets, close peer friendships can become more intimate, and their partner tries to help them with their problems.[73] Because the collaboration and coordination is between equals, it can have a unique kind of intimacy, a new kind of shared teamwork where each partner wants to help the other partner achieve his or her interests. In comparison, the prior parent–child relationships are quite unequal in this regard. Given that so much of schoolers' activities are impersonal, having a close friend with this kind of intimacy is a blessing. It can be a special benefit of this phase of development.

As with the other phase changes, the phase of shared coordinated roles also involves cognitive and social-cognitive developmental change. By this phase, children are capable of coordinating values along two distinct dimensions,[74] as reflected in Piaget's concept of decentration—the ability to consider and relate two separate dimensions at a time, such as both length and width. When comparing their performance to that of another child, for example, children can now consider simultaneously the difference in actors' outcomes and the difference in actors' effort (e.g., better outcome with same effort), which makes ability inferences possible.[75] By relating two dimensions as a time, children can recognize not only that they perform better (or worse) than their peers on some activity but also that this activity is more (or less) worthwhile than most other activities. Being "good" or "bad" at something also acquires new significance because it is perceived to be a stable disposition (i.e., not just a performance failure or success). There are now shared realities about *character traits* and abilities, which are not present before.[76]

These cognitive and social-cognitive changes are important for the role learning that occurs during this phase. In their classic chapter on role theory, Ted Sarbin and Vernon Allen point out that role learning is difficult. Not only must one learn the expectations for a specific role but also the expectations for its complementary roles: "Learning a role adequately requires the learning of the entire role set."[77] It also requires that children tune each time to the specific role set member with whom they are currently interacting. Thus, role enactment with a role set partner involves coordinating the expectations associated with the child's role with those of the current complementary role partner. This would occur during this phase and not before.[78]

By the end of the phase of shared coordinated roles, schoolers move out of the last stage of childhood. There will, of course, be more developments in shared reality—more developments in the complexity of adult-like shared reality—but the child has now taken another major step by having shared teamwork and shared coordinated roles. Children are more prepared now to engage in adult-related activities, including participating in organized activities and taking on leadership roles in those activities.

Erik Erikson, the pioneering child clinician, provided an early proposal about the potential trade-offs that can arise from this phase of shared reality change when he called it the "Industry vs. Inferiority" age. As he notes, while children seem all set for "entrance into life," the life being entered is some form of schooling (formal or informal; preparatory or participatory) where personal goals must be "tamed and harnessed to the laws of *impersonal* things." [79] Erikson considers this phase to be the most decisive socially because "industry involves doing things beside and with others, a first sense of division of labor."[80] If all goes well, then, the child becomes a team player who does his or her part to help the team succeed—*industry*. If it does not go well, the child can feel inadequate as a team member compared to his or her peers—*inferiority*. In addition, the child may become a conformist from the pressure to conform, such as conforming to traditional gender-role stereotypes.[81]

There is an important difference between preschoolers' shared reality and schoolers' shared reality that needs to be highlighted. For preschoolers, the shared reality is with significant others, especially parents but other close persons as well. Shared reality is based on the interactions and close relationships with significant others, and the target of the interaction is the child as an individual. These shared realities with significant others continue throughout life, with new significant others entering into our lives, such as romantic partners. But what emerges with schoolers' shared coordinated roles is an additional shared reality with group norms and social rules. It involves enacting social roles that are defined with respect to anyone carrying out the role. It is more impersonal and general. Children are evaluated by strangers in terms of general standards that apply to everyone rather than shared self-guides for them as a specific person. Indeed, because of this, there can be a conflict between personal self-guides and group norms, a conflict related to the self-regulatory problem that Erving

Goffman, the eminent sociologist, called "role distance."[82] From an epistemic perspective, enacting roles within a larger organizational unit can also limit children's thinking to only what is relevant to the role to only those truths that are contained in their role and its complementary roles. This is a downside of the new phase of shared coordinated roles.

The change to self-regulation in relation to goals and standards of the generalized other rather than just the goals and standards of the child's significant others has an additional downside. The goals and standards set for preschoolers by others, and which they accept for their own self-regulation, are not always in their best interest. What if it would be better for a child to have different or additional goals and standards? Although it is difficult for preschoolers to change a shared reality with a significant other because significant others typically have more power than the child, there is still some possibility of negotiation or co-construction of goals and standards for the child because significant others usually have the child's interests at heart (at least in today's world). In contrast, the generalized other of schoolers' shared coordinated roles does not have a particular child's interests at heart. It has the organizational activity's interests at heart (or the interests of the players of that activity). If children don't like the goals and standards of the generalized other in relation to some activity, it is extremely difficult, if not impossible, for them to do anything about it. They would need to create a new consensus among the players, including authorities on the activity who have no personal relationship with them. How do you deal with a generalized other. What does it do to children's sense of control effectiveness when they need to manage a generalized other?

Not only can the generalized other have different goals and standards for children than their own goals and standards for themselves, but also different groups can have different goals and standards for them. Children can experience having different roles or selves in different relationships (e.g., group of friends vs. best friend).[83] Children's teachers can have one viewpoint on the rules and roles they want the children to follow and perform while their peers have a very different viewpoint.

There are both benefits and potential costs for schoolers from their exposure to a wide array of different viewpoints. By learning to understand and share a wide variety of viewpoints, children can improve their social perspective-taking skills, which has been found to relate positively to prosocial behavior.[84] On the other hand, self-regulatory conflicts can also occur. Early adolescent girls, for example, can experience a conflict between their parents' wanting them to make schoolwork and household duties their top priorities while their friends want them to make their social life together their top priority. This can create inner conflict for children that makes successful self-regulation difficult and produces uncertainty and confusion.[85] And there is evidence that early adolescence is a period of uncertainty and identity confusion.[86]

Because children need to take into account general roles, norms, and rules that apply to everyone, they are also likely to be concerned over being criticized by others, even strangers. There is a "pressure to conform."[87] Trade-offs during this phase can be seen between the benefit of children being able to balance their own needs with the needs of others when participating in group activities, while also being concerned with how others evaluate them in relation to group norms and standards, such as becoming very concerned about what they wear and how they look.

By the way, the fact that by the end of the phase of shared coordinated roles children move out of the last stage of childhood can be difficult for children. Yes, if all goes well, they can take pride in their industry—in their ability to coordinate with others as equals. But, like Peter Pan, children can prefer to remain in a "never-ending childhood." When children have been treated as special by their significant others, it can be difficult to enter the impersonal phase of shared coordinated roles and be treated as just enacting a role like anyone else enacting that role. I noticed this with my daughter Kayla when she entered Grade 6 (middle school). I realized that she was sad because she understood that she was losing her childhood. Indeed, at Christmas she continued to express a belief in Santa Claus, despite her close cousin and friends telling her there was no Santa Claus. She may have recognized the advantage of receiving Santa Claus presents, but I believe that it was her way to hold onto her childhood a little longer.

There is another kind of trade-off for schoolers that relates to the change mentioned earlier from conceptualizing people in terms of physical features or behaviors to conceptualizing them in terms of dispositional abilities and traits. This includes self-evaluation. On the one hand, children can now represent their own repeated successes as reflecting their ability to meet others' expectations for them, creating a new kind of feeling of self-confidence. On the flip side, they can also represent their repeated failures as reflecting their inability to meet others' expectations for them, which makes them vulnerable to a new kind of helplessness feeling.[88] Combining this with increased concerns with how others evaluate you in relation to group norms and standards, this can be a difficult time for children. Indeed, feelings of social anxiety and experiences of peer rejection typically intensify during this phase. In addition, the increased use in self-evaluation of normative social comparisons (i.e., shared standards) contributes to a decline in positive self-evaluations during this phase.[89]

A recent study provides a striking illustration of the motivational significance of the shared worldviews during this phase.[90] The study found that 6- to 11-year-old children will attribute prosocial behaviors to those who share their ideological beliefs but not those who share just their shared preferences (like shared interests) or shared facts (like what is the name of something). Where does this effect of shared ideological beliefs on prosocial judgments come from?

One possibility suggested by the researchers is that religious beliefs have a stronger connection to good and bad behaviors than other beliefs. From a shared reality perspective, it is also possible that ideologies, such as religious beliefs, relate to objectives and standards for the community that extend beyond just individual goal pursuits. They concern what a good member of the ideological group should do and believe and how they should interact with one another. They coordinate the members in terms of a collective interest and not just personal interests. If a person shares your ideological beliefs, that person is a good member of the group. It would make sense that a good member of *your* group would be a good person—hence, the attribution of prosocial behaviors.

Such in-group positive judgments of fellow group members would benefit both the individual members and the group as a whole: It would make them stronger. But, once again, it would also have the potential downside of yielding less positive judgments about those who do *not* share the ideological beliefs—yet another source of in-group/out-group bias. Thus, like the other developmental phases, the emergence of shared coordinated roles has upsides and downsides. The upside is essential for large groups of humans to work together in complex organizations—to create "civilizations." The downside can and does create conflicts between groups that have different shared realities—the "clash of civilizations." *With the emergence of shared coordinated roles, humans can function at our most and least civilized.*

By the way, contemporary societies do not take what happens to children during the phase of shared coordinated roles seriously enough. By the end of this phase, they are no longer children. In the distant past, hundreds of years ago, they were not treated like children. But now they are. From an historical perspective, it is relatively recently that we have created new social life phases where these young people are treated as if they were still children, with labels like "juvenile," "adolescent," and even "college *kid*." But they are not children, and they would like to be treated as the young adults that they have become by the end of the phase of shared coordinated roles. If we don't treat them that way, then they are open to joining other groups that will take them seriously, treat them as adults—like street gangs and ISIS.

I have now discussed the emergence of shared reality in childhood development. In the last chapter of this section, I will move back in time—way back in time—to describe how shared reality emerged in humans as a species. This is the story of how shared reality evolved in humans, the roots of human shared reality.

Notes

1. See Freud (1923/1961).
2. See Higgins (1989a, 1991).
3. See, for example, Harter (1999, 2006) and Moretti and Higgins (1999).
4. See, for example, Kochanska, Murray, Jacques, Koenig, and Vandegeest (1996) and Stipek, Recchia, and McClintic (1992).
5. "Internalization" in the sense of children having *internal* representations of others' goals and standards for them, which they accept as their own, should not be confused with "internalization" in the sense of children self-regulating in relation to their own personal standpoint that is experienced as distinct from the standpoint of others. Self-evaluation that distinguishes the child's own personal perspective from the perspective of another person does not occur until after Phase 3 (see Harter, 1999, 2006). See also the discussion of Deci and Ryan (1985, 2000) about internalization being a developmental continuum, and the proposal by Lewis (2007) for using the term *incorporation* for the identification process. The term *interiorization* has also been used in the literature as an alternative to *identification*.
6. See Higgins (1987, 1989a, 1991) for the distinction between self-regulatory guides (goals and standards) that are oughts versus ideals. It should be noted that preschoolers need not distinguish between what is an ought versus what is an ideal for them to internalize both. Their parents know the difference between what is an ought and what is an ideal, as do older children, but preschoolers are likely to treat both as goals to pursue and standards to follow, without appreciating the difference between them.
7. See Bandura (1986) and Lewis (2003).
8. See Kochanska and Knaack (2003).

9. See Wu and Su (2014). See also Svetlova, Nichols, and Brownell (2010).
10. See Stipek et al. (1992).
11. See Kochanska, Casey, and Fukumoto (1995), Lewis (1995), Lewis, Alessandri, and Sullivan (1992), Mascolo and Fischer (1995), and Stipek (1995).
12. See, for example, Lagattuta and Thompson (2007). See also Hart and Matsuba (2007) and Stipek (1995).
13. This does *not* mean that there are no personal consequences of failing to meet Phase 2 norms. As I mentioned in Chapter 1, toddlers in Phase 2 can suffer from being teased and shamed by others when they fail to follow shared practices (i.e., fail to act in the normative, appropriate way).
14. I should also note that Piaget (1932/1965, pp. 61–62) describes the "egocentric" child of Phase 3 as being constrained by adults, looking up to adults, and looking upon rules as being sacred. He also says that because the children and their significant others are not equal, there is no genuinely mutual interaction, which contributes to the children remaining shut up in their own ego.
15. For a discussion of this distinction, see Cialdini (2003) and Cialdini, Reno, and Kallgren (1990).
16. This development is described in Case's (1985) neo-Piagetian model of cognitive development.
17. See Shantz (1983).
18. See Fischer and Watson (1981).
19. See, for example, Eckerman, Davis, and Didow (1989) and Eckerman and Whitehead (1999).
20. See, for example, Brownell, Nichols, and Svetlova (2005) and Howes (1988).
21. See Nelson (2005, p. 130).
22. See Nelson (1992) and Gopnik and Graf (1988).
23. See Nelson (2003, 2005).
24. See Higgins (2005).
25. See Baldwin (1897, p. 36).
26. Allport (1955).
27. See Wimmer and Perner (1983).
28. For discussions of its nature and significance, see Flavell (2004) and Wellman, Cross, and Watson (2001).
29. It should be noted that aspects of TOM development may occur in Phase 2. For highly thoughtful reviews of the development of TOM, see Baillargeon, Scott, and He (2010) and Wellman (2014).
30. See Higgins (1981b).
31. See "Guide" (1989).
32. See Higgins (1981b).
33. See, for example, Selman and Byrne (1974).
34. See Harris (2000) and Schwebel, Rosen, and Singer (1999).
35. See Wu and Su (2014).
36. See Hoffman and Saltzstein (1967) and Kelman (1958).
37. See Freud (1937).

38. See Deci & Ryan (1985, 2000).
39. See Bandura (1986), Carver and Scheier (2008), and Higgins (1989b, 1991).
40. See Dodge, Coie, and Lynam (2006) and Eisenberg and Fabes (1999).
41. See Eitam and Higgins (2010).
42. See, for example, Kochanska et al. (1995).
43. See Luby (2010).
44. See Kochanska, Aksan, Knaack, and Rhines (2004).
45. See Higgins (1989a, 1991) and Neuman, Higgins, and Vookles (1992).
46. See Van Hook and Higgins (1988).
47. See Parten (1932).
48. See Gabard-Durnam et al. (2014).
49. See for example, Erikson (1950/1963), Higgins and Parsons (1983), Pianta, Rimm-Kaufman, and Cox (1999), and Saarni (2000).
50. See Erikson (1950/1963, p. 259).
51. See Rogoff (2003) and Rogoff, Paradise, Mejia Arauz, Correa-Chavez, and Angelillo (2003).
52. See Bratman (1992).
53. See, for example, Kitcher (2011), Suddendorf (2013), and Tomasello (2014).
54. See Harari (2015).
55. See Piaget (1943/1965, p. 24).
56. See Hackman and Katz (2010).
57. See Mead (1934).
58. See Mead (1934, p. 154).
59. See Mead (1934, p. 161).
60. Piaget (1951/1962).
61. This statement about Sullivan comes from Loevinger (1976, p. 73).
62. For a discussion of self-regulation in groups, see Levine, Alexander, and Hansen (2010).
63. For a discussion of the communication game, see Higgins (1981a).
64. See Higgins (1977). For a fuller discussion and review of communication development, see also Glucksberg, Krauss, and Higgins (1975). It should be noted that these children did understand that there was something that they knew that the stranger did not know, like how to get from A to B, and thus they passed the TOM test. But in their message to inform the stranger they made the mistake of using local names that the stranger would not know. And, by the way, this can also happen with adults talking about local matters like giving directions, as I am sure that you, like I, have experienced more than once (e.g., ". . . and then take a right at the courthouse").
65. See Dorval and Eckerman (1984).
66. See Glucksberg and Krauss (1967).
67. See Higgins (1981) for a description of the normative expectations or rules associated with the roles of speaker and listener.
68. See Levine and Moreland (1986) for analyses of outcome comparisons in group contexts.
69. See, for example, Ruble (1983).

70. See, for example, Damon (1977) and Kohlberg (1969).
71. See Damon (1977).
72. See, for example, Damon (1977), Selman (1980), and Youniss (1980).
73. See Berndt (1983), Sullivan (1953), and Watson and Valtin (1997).
74. See Case (1985), Fischer (1980), and Piaget (1970).
75. See Higgins (1991) and Ruble (1983).
76. See Rholes and Ruble (1984) and Ruble and Rholes (1981).
77. See Sarbin and Allen (1968, p. 546).
78. This developmental analysis is based on Robbie Case's brilliant neo-Piagetian work on the different phases of children's cognitive development (Case, 1985, 1992).
79. See Erikson (1950/1963, p. 258; emphasis added).
80. See Erikson (1950/1963, p. 260).
81. See Hill and Lynch (1983).
82. See Goffman (1961).
83. See Harter (1999).
84. See Eisenberg, Fabes, and Spinrad (2006) and Fabes, Carlo, Kupanoff, and Laible (1999).
85. See Harter (1986), Harter (1999), Higgins (1991), Loevinger (1976), and Van Hook and Higgins (1988).
86. See, for example, Blos (1961), Erikson (1963), and Fischer and Lamborn (1989).
87. See Hill and Lynch (1983).
88. See, for example, Dweck and Elliott (1983), Rholes, Blackman, Jordan, and Walters (1980), and Ruble and Rholes (1981).
89. See Harter (2006).
90. See Heiphetz, Spelke, and Banaji (2014).

4

The Roots of Human Shared Reality

How special are we! Not, "*How* special are we?" (question) but "How special are *we*!" (exclamation), spoken with *attitude*. Humans think we are special. We look around at what the world looks like and declare, "No other animal is like us!" Then the only question becomes, "Why exactly are we *so* special?"

Perhaps the strongest statement of how special we are was given in the Renaissance in the form of the *scala naturae*, the *Chain of Being*, which was a conception of the natural order of things (shown in the following text). It shows the hierarchy of all things, the God-given great chain of being. Humans are placed above all other earthly creatures or living things. Humans are just below angels. Humans are *not* animals.

Notably, there was also a parallel natural order or ranking of the qualities of being human. The equivalent of God here is our *intelligence*. Our intelligence is in "God's own image." And next down at the level of angels, is our rationality, our ability to think and make choices. Of course, our rationality also requires our intelligence, and thus what we are being told here, as usual, is that what makes humans special is our intelligence.

Well, it won't surprise you that I am not a fan of this depiction of what makes us human. I believe that what makes us human is not just about the kind of intelligence we each possess but is at least as much about our particular kind of interpersonal motivation—our motivation to create shared realities with others.[1] To know what it means to be human, we need to know about this motivation. The purpose of this book is to discuss and describe this motivation in all its marvelous forms, and the previous chapters have done so with respect to the different kinds of shared reality that emerge during human childhood development and the process of shared reality creation in human communication. The purpose of this chapter is to discuss and describe the evolutionary roots for these marvelous forms of shared reality.

A (Very) Brief History of (Human) Time

Where to begin this story? I should start by noting that common chimpanzees (chimps) and bonobos, who are equally humanity's closest living relatives, had a common ancestor with humans about six million years ago. We did not evolve from them and they did not evolve from us. And they and we evolved quite differently during the next six million years. That is one time marker but not where I will begin the story. The next time marker is around 2.5 million years ago when the genus *Homo* evolved (early *Homo*), and particularly *Homo erectus* around 1.8 million years ago.[2] I will begin the story with *Homo erectus*. The next time marker is around 200,000 years ago when *Homo sapiens* (archaic) evolved, followed by modern sapiens (*Homo sapiens sapiens*). The second, and most significant, part of my story will be about modern sapiens, in the 30,000- to 50,000-year period. Then the story jumps to the Agricultural Revolution around 10,000 years ago, the period when great civilizations emerged, which is the last part of my story about shared reality evolution.

Like the book as a whole, my concern in this chapter is with our human motivation to create shared realities with others. That is the evolution story I want to discuss. Thus, I am not suggesting that this motivation does not exist in some form in other current animal species (e.g., great apes), or that it did not exist in other hominids in the genus *Homo* (e.g., Neanderthals). Indeed, regarding the latter issue, I am quite confident that it *did* exist among our *Homo erectus* ancestors (even prior to Neanderthals), as I discuss in the following text.

Shared Reality Development in the Evolution of *Homo Erectus*

Richard Wrangman, in his fascinating and insightful book, *Catching Fire: How Cooking Made Us Human*, argues, "We humans are the cooking apes, the creatures of the flame."[3] He proposes that the way that our ancestors *Homo erectus* learned to use fire to prepare and cook food, as well as to keep warm, give light, and ward off predators at night, transformed who we are, including biologically. He describes evidence from archaeological sites of *Homo erectus* groups controlling fire about 400,000 years ago and even earlier. But the most convincing evidence that *Homo erectus* groups were cooking food are the changes that happened to their anatomy over time.[4]

As Wrangham puts it,

> animals are superbly adapted to their diets, and over evolutionary time the tight fit between food and anatomy is driven by food rather than by the animal's characteristics. . . . Horses do not eat grass because they happen to have the right kind of teeth and guts for doing so; they have tall teeth and long guts because they are adapted to eating grass. Humans do not eat cooked food because we have the right kind of teeth and guts; rather, we have small teeth and short guts as a result of adapting to a cooked diet.[5]

When did our ancestors become adapted to the cooked food that they were eating on a regular basis? Wrangham argues that the anatomical evidence suggests that it was in the evolution from early *Homo* to *Homo erectus*. Compared to early *Homo*, *Homo erectus* showed a major decrease in tooth size, increase in body size, a smaller gut, and a much larger brain (over 40% increase in cranial capacity). All of these changes are consistent with a switch to eating cooked rather than raw food. Regarding the much larger brain, bigger brains need more energy and the better digestion from cooking food has the benefit of increasing energy.[6]

Another interesting anatomical shift was changes in the shoulder, arm, and trunk that made *Homo erectus* less good at climbing than *early Homo*. The speculation is that they no longer needed to sleep above ground because their control of fire gave them two advantages. The light from the fire allowed them to see dangerous predators (think saber-toothed cats, lions, leopards, hyenas) and potentially harmful nonpredators (think elephants, rhinoceroses), and the burning fire scared these animals away. Importantly, the noncooking functions of fire could also have contributed to significant changes in the social interactions and relationships among our ancestors—changes that set the stage for new modes of shared reality to develop.

One very significant change is that just the firelight itself allowed the day to be extended. With the firelight, the group could engage in additional social activities that did not interfere with what the group needed to do during the daytime.[7] By sitting together around the fire, not only to eat but also to gain warmth, light, and protection, there was the opportunity for new kinds of face-to-face interactions that could support creating shared realities together. I wonder what the topic was at these first fireside chats?

Well, thanks to the research of Polly Wiessner on the Ju/'hoansi Bushmen, we have some idea at least of what one group of hunter-gatherers talked about at fireside chats, even if we cannot generalize backwards a million years given the changes that occurred in communication practices. The important finding from Wiessner's work is that day talk and firelight talk among the Ju/'hoansi Bushmen are not the same.[8] Day talk is practical talk on daily matters, like talk on economic matters. In contrast, firelight talk includes stories, told particularly by older people. By listening to these stories, group members learned about the broader cultural institutions that support cooperation and trust within the group, such as marriage practices. Firelight stories create shared realities about what matters to the group (i.e., shared relevance), shared feelings, and the institutions (i.e., shared practices) that allow the group members to work together effectively. Wiessner notes that even today we enjoy telling stories around the fire.

The use of fire to cook produced another change that might not seem at first to be especially significant, but could be very significant indeed.[9] Who does the cooking now that fire makes it possible? Given that the men went out hunting each day and the women stayed around home to forage and take care of the children, it is not surprising that it was the women who ended up doing the cooking. This turned out to really matter. Preparing the meal and cooking the meal is not only a lot of work, it also requires a lot of different skills. These skills need to be learned, and they need to be taught by females to females. This not only creates a new social role—the important role of cook—but it also constitutes a clear *sexual division of labor*. Males learned from males how to hunt, and females learned from females how to cook (and forage and mother).

This division of labor allowed both males and females to become more expert in their particular roles. It involved functional cooperation and coordination—shared coordinated roles. And it also involved others' expectations about the responsibilities associated with a role. A "married" man expected his "wife" to have the meal cooked on time. It was not just about the individual. It was about the role.

Notably, the effect of controlling fires and cooking food extended beyond this new and significant sexual division of labor. Eating the food cooked by the fires meant that there needed to be broader social coordination as well. The fire needed to be tended, and the food was often shared beyond just the immediate nuclear family. In the preparation of the food, the females could cooperate and help one another. It has been suggested that such activities ended individual self-sufficiency and began community mealtimes. New social practices and social norms developed for how to eat food and how to share food.[10]

Wrangham is not alone in believing that the shift to *Homo erectus* is very significant in human evolution. In his thoughtful and scholarly book, *The Secret of Our Success: How Culture is Driving Evolution, Domesticating Our Species, and Making Us Smarter*, Joseph Henrich argues that it is about two million years ago that our ancestors *crossed the Rubicon*—that is, there was no turning back on the momentous change when cultural evolution became the primary driver of evolution.[11] What mattered now for our ancestors was what other individuals knew that they did not know—*what they could learn from them*. What supported learning from others would be favored by evolution, with there being a selection pressure for making humans especially adept culture learners.[12]

Henrich makes the important point that by being motivated to learn from others what *they* have discovered or figured out, communities over time can steadily improve practices, ways of doing things, that enhance their chances of survival in their local environment—*cumulative learning*. And, importantly, these practices and technologies can, over generations, become sufficiently complex that an individual starting from scratch would be highly unlikely to invent them on his or her own. Thus, when we find evidence that a community had developed complex practices and tools, it is evidence that individuals within that community *shared* their knowledge with others. Not only were individuals motivated to learn from one another, they were also likely to have been motivated to teach one another. Such findings are evidence for shared reality motivation.

Because complex tools and practices cannot be simply reinvented from scratch by individuals, it was possible for a community of our ancestors to lose important knowledge about how to do something, to lose previously shared knowledge. For example, the technology and know-how involved to make bows and arrows is very complicated, and it can be completely lost if the experts are no longer available to learn from. This has happened several times to different communities. There is evidence that even the know-how for starting a fire can be lost to a community.[13]

There is an especially compelling example from the Polar Inuit of how the loss of key knowledge can happen to a community.[14] The Polar Inuit live surrounded by ice in a very far north region of Greenland. It is believed that an epidemic in the 1820s killed many members of their community.

But, worst of all, the oldest members of their community were hit especially hard. With their death, critical knowledge was lost, including how to make bows and arrows as well as kayaks. Without kayaks, they could not travel to other Inuit communities to relearn the knowledge they had lost. Without knowing how to make bows and arrows (shown in the following picture), they could no longer hunt caribou in late summer and fall—a loss of a major source of meat. For decades the population declined. Illustrating the importance of social learning, when they finally made contact with another group of travelling Inuit, who knew how to build kayaks, the Polar Inuit quickly learned how to make kayaks and other things again (in new versions). Their population then increased.

Two Copper Inuit archers in Minto Inlet, N.W.T. by George Hubert Wilkins, 1916
Canadian Museum of History, 51166 LS

Let me say a little more about the Inuit bow shown in the picture to illustrate the point that making this bow is not something that will happen from scratch by some "genius" individual if all prior knowledge (and bows) are lost. The difficulty is that a caribou's hide is tough and they have to be killed from a distance. It takes a lot of bow power to accomplish this. Fine you say, just build a really big and strong bow. But the Polar Inuit live surrounded by ice. They don't have the trees to make a really big and strong bow (as was done by other communities who did have such trees). They had to find a solution using the driftwood, horn, and antlers that were available to them. They had to make short bows and find a way to increase their power without breaking. Ultimately they ended up with a bow like that in the picture that was wider near the center, recurved at the end to form a backward C shape, and had a woven web of sinew lashed to the back to increase tension strength.[15]

Social learning is critical to make the kind of bow that was used by the Polar Inuits. More generally, evidence of complex practices and technologies is evidence of social learning, of shared reality. As described earlier, there is such evidence for *Homo erectus* from the evidence of their cooking food. But learning how to cook food is not all that was learned by *Homo erectus* communities that involved the kind of expertise that is learned from others and accumulates across generations.

As just one example, *Homo erectus* communities made large stone tools that required impressive skills in quarrying the stone slabs used to make the tools, including slabs large enough to probably require levers, which then had to be transported (sometimes long distances). The next challenge was to craft the tool itself, such as an hand axe, which itself involved multiple steps. The last step in this process, called "knapping," involves repeatedly striking a stone with a tool (a hard hammer or a soft hammer) to remove material to create a desired final shape, which is itself quite technical and difficult to learn. Those making the tools needed to know how different kinds of stones would break when struck by a particular kind of hammer.[16] Over time the techniques for toolmaking became increasingly difficult and complex. The teacher–student relation of social learning—shared reality—was needed to make it happen.

In his illuminating book, *The Gap: The Science of What Separates Us from Other Animals*, Thomas Suddendorf makes another interesting point about the tools made in *Homo erectus* communities.[17] They were made in a standardized fashion over many years. Suddendorf concludes from this that members of such communities were both able *and* motivated to learn from others what was needed to make the tools. Their toolmaking became *social traditions* that they practiced—shared practices. Knowing the science (and art) of toolmaking was a shared reality.

There is one final feature of *Homo erectus* communities that should be highlighted. There is evidence suggesting that people in *Homo erectus* communities lived longer than those in early *Homo* communities. This could also be significant. By living longer, mothers can help out parenting their children's children, which would increase children's exposure to adults from whom they can learn—the "grandmother effect."[18] More generally, both the male and female elders in the community are now living longer and they are the knowledgeable experts—where the expression "Older is wiser" came from—who can best teach the children. This is another advantage of *Homo erectus* over early *Homo* in the development of beneficial shared realties.

Shared Reality Development in the Evolution of *Homo Sapiens*

So how about us—we *Homo sapiens* or *Homo sapiens sapiens*? What happened in our historical evolutionary development that made us who we are today regarding shared reality motivation that is more than, or different from, the *Homo erectus* story? *Homo sapiens* (archaic) evolved around 200,000 years ago. But I want to focus on the later *Homo sapiens* who lived around 30,000 to 50,000 years ago (roughly the Upper Paleolithic, Late Stone Age)—modern sapiens. By this time they were much like us today (or at least like human hunter-gatherers today), which must be, of course, why we call them *Homo sapiens sapiens*, the wisest of wise humans. Just like us.

From all accounts, modern sapien communities *were* impressive in their knowledge, abilities, and aesthetics.[19] What these communities now had were boats, fishing equipment (e.g., fish hooks), ropes, bows and arrows, knife blades, sewing needles, oil lamps, engraving tools, jewelry (using sea shells and ivory beads), art (including cave paintings), and religious rituals (including burials). They lived in organized settlements. They had substantial leisure time. They had music. Oh, did I mention language? They had language. Who could ask for anything more?

Speaking of the art, the cave painting shown in the following picture is from the Chauvet Cave (replica of original) at the Ardéche gorge in France. It is believed to have been created from 30-40,000 years ago. The ivory figurine sculpture of a mammoth shown in the subsequent picture is from the Vogelherd Cave in southwestern Germany. It is believed to have been created about 35,000 years ago.

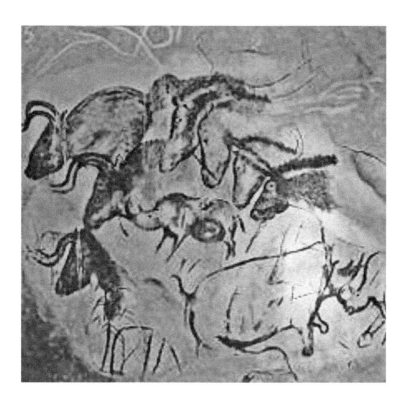

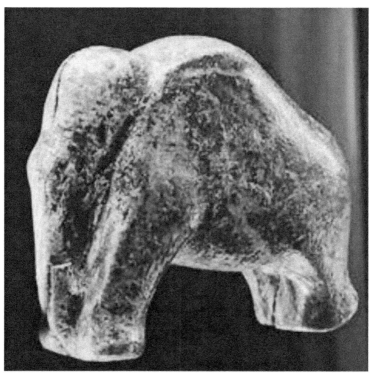

Remarkable works of art. And then there are other works of art like the ivory figurine from the Stedel Cave in Germany (thought to be 30,000 to 40,000 years old) where the body of the figure is human but the head is leonine (lion or lioness), which is a representation of something that does not even exist. Such artistic productions are happening in a period when modern sapiens are also adorning themselves with jewelry and are practicing ritual burials of the dead, with increasing use of red ochre in the ritual as a shared practice. There is evidence that they had music because flute-like bone pipes have been found. And animal skin drums may have been used in rituals because they have been found in the graves of shamans.

That gives you some idea about the School of Fine Arts in the modern sapiens communities. How about the School of Science and Engineering? Well, the boat was a great invention. Not only does a boat help out in fishing, but it also creates an entirely new form of travel, and, for some ventures, it is the only way to get from where you are to somewhere else that is separated by a long stretch of open water. Scientists are very impressed, for example, with modern sapiens' feat of boating from Asia to Australia. And it *is* impressive given the many miles of open water between Australia and the nearest part of Asia.[20] In addition, they invented the bow and arrow. The bow and arrow are very difficult to manufacture—or even to imagine for that matter. The bow and arrow are also an important invention because they change hunting dramatically (a safe distance to kill the prey) and change war (a safe distance to kill the enemy). And it is precisely because the bow and arrow are so difficult to manufacture and as a shared practice require experts to teach others the necessary skills that, as mentioned earlier, it is possible to lose the skills to manufacture them.

The modern sapien communities also built tools to manufacture products, such as tools for drilling and piercing, and, perhaps especially important, eyed needles that could be used to sew clothes. They created stone fat-burning lamps that could be carried by hand, which meant that fire could be moved from place to place safely, including at times and places that would normally have been dark. This broadened the range of activities that individuals could perform, including creating and viewing the wondrous art at the Chauvet Cave.[21]

Finally, I should mention that, in the School of Business, the modern sapien communities engaged in long-distance trade and exchange.[22] This is evident, for example, from seashells that came from the Mediterranean and the Atlantic being found at 30,000-year-old modern sapien sites that were inland and far away. Management also improved. Habitations and hunting stations became more complex with separate spaces for different functions, such as cooking food, butchering food, and sleeping.[23]

So what should we make of all this? This issue is hotly debated, and, given that I am not an expert on evolution or biology, I don't want to offer strong opinions on evolutionary issues, such as whether there was a Big Bang genetic event in human history. But I can't resist saying something about one debate. There are those who look at these changes in modern sapien communities and conclude that they provide clear evidence for the birth of human language. And they conclude this because they *assume* that nothing this dramatic in the advance of human culture could happen without language. And one example of this is that impressive boat ride from Asia to Australia that I mentioned earlier. What would you conclude about that long boat ride over open water? Think about it for a while.

I think many of us would conclude that given that this challenge occurred over 40,000 years ago (and some argue even earlier), the boat manufacturers (those who built the boat) and the crew (those in charge of the water travel itself) must have been experts in what they were doing. In addition, the trip itself would need to be planned carefully (e.g., taking route and weather conditions into account), and, all together, they would need to organize themselves well, coordinate well, and cooperate well.

Would you conclude that this is basically a story about language?[24] Is it likely that these boaters could communicate with words? Yes, and I will discuss why later. But that does not mean that this is basically a story about language per se, nor that language is critical to make this trip happen. To me, what is critical to make this trip happen is that humans create shared realities with one another, with word use being one useful tool to accomplish this, but not the only tool. The fact that communities have complex technologies that single individuals could not invent on their own does not mean that they must have language. If it did, then we should conclude that *Homo erectus* had language, and this is not the claim. There are ways of communicating that do not require language. This includes teaching and observing how others work together. What is critical for organization and cooperation is having shared coordinated roles, where different individuals have different assigned roles in a coordinated activity and are *motivated* to cooperate together for a common purpose.

Let's leave the case of traveling to Australia by boat and consider now more generally what can happen when people travel long distances.

I mentioned earlier that there is evidence that modern sapiens engaged in long distance trade. What should we conclude from this? That having language was critical? In his wonderful book, *Sapiens: A Brief History of Humankind*, Yuval Harari concludes instead that modern sapiens must have *trusted strangers*. He states: "The fact is that no animal other than Sapiens engages in trade, and all the Sapiens trade networks about which we have detailed evidence were based on fictions. Trade cannot exist without trust, and it is very difficult to trust strangers."[25]

Harari argues that trusting strangers requires agreement between you and the stranger about some common entity, such as sharing beliefs nowadays about the dollar and the Federal Reserve Bank. By the way, only a very small percentage of US dollars in circulation are actually backed by gold. What backs the dollar is trust in promises. According to Harari, what backed trade in tribal societies was the trust established from having a common god, mythical ancestor, or totem animal. That is, trade needs trust and trust needs the creation of shared realities with others. It is a story about shared reality rather than a story about language per se. Beyond trade, Harari makes the more general point that large settlements where there are cooperative interactions among nonfamily members and even strangers requires such shared beliefs in *fictions* like tribal spirits.

To illustrate how humans are motivated to create shared realities even when they are fictional, let me briefly describe the research by Muzafer Sherif, a social psychology pioneer, on the development of social norms in groups. The study works like this. Three men make judgments about the movement of a light. To begin with, each person sits alone in a completely dark room. A light comes on and, after a short time, apparently moves. Each of the three men is instructed to press a key as soon as he sees the light move and then report, as accurately as possible, the distance that the light moved (in inches). Each of them makes many judgments. For each of them, a range and a norm of distance judgments is established over time. In addition, the range and norm—whether the distance the light moved was short, long, or medium—is typically different for the three men. Each of them has their own particular norm.

Now the three men get together as a group and make judgments about the movement of the same light. One at a time, in whatever order they wish, they take turns in making their judgments aloud. Again, many judgments are made, and in the beginning the judgments are quite different, like the difference between their judgments when they were making their judgments alone. Over time, however, their judgments begin to become more and more similar—*converging* toward a *group norm* about how much the light is moving. They now function like a group seeing things the same way rather than as individuals who each have their own personal opinion. Together, they have created a shared reality about the movement of the light.

But here's the thing. The light, in fact, was *stationary*. It actually *never* moved. It was the observers' saccadic eye movements in the completely dark room that made the stationary light appear to move.[26] The shared reality that each group created was a fiction. Despite this, the group members followed this shared reality later even when they again made judgments alone. They treated this fiction as the truth about the light's movement. Consistent with Harari's point, creating shared realities with others is just something that modern sapiens do.

And our normative fictions are not restricted to how the world works. For example, we have normative fictions about what is and is not beautiful. Consider body adornments or decorations for instance. Some people nowadays think tattoos are beautiful despite there being other people who think they are hideous. What matters is that someone has a body decoration that they feel good about and know others that feel the same way about it, others who verify their feeling about it—a shared reality about an aesthetic fiction. And it has been suggested that body decorations as a common shared practice began with modern sapiens.[27]

By the way, if language did begin with modern sapiens, it would have begun along with creating other shared fictions like which body adornments are beautiful. It would have begun with symbolic single-word utterances. A symbolic single-word utterance like the sound pattern for "dog" (or "chien") does not actually have anything to do with dogs. The sound pattern you hear is not what you hear when you interact with a dog. Dogs don't make sounds like the sound pattern for the word *dog*. It is a fiction, a shared reality, that "dog" is *the* name for that particular category of animal (that we mentally represent). But all that matters in the English-speaking community is that we agree, that we have the common fiction, that the sound pattern for the word "dog" refers to (or names) this particular category of animal.

Notably, this is all separate from the grammar or syntax that is language proper. As I discussed in Chapter 1, humans can communicate quite well by stringing together single word utterances (even when the word string violates grammar).[28] It does not require using the kind of language that linguists like Noam Chomsky talk about. What does it require? It requires an animal that is motivated to create shared realities with others even when these realities are fictional. And it is likely that modern sapiens were such an animal given their burial rites and their trade with strangers and, perhaps most important, their art. Cave paintings are symbolic expressions and include depictions of fictional creatures, including some that look half human and half animal, like the half human-half leonine sculpture figurine from the Stedel Cave.

These activities of modern sapiens suggest that these communities could also have symbolic single-word utterances, which could then be strung together to share information about past or future events. With a string of single symbolic signs our ancestors could have communicated *excitedly*: "river . . . lion . . . saw [pause] here . . . come [pause] run . . . me . . . you." Who needs grammar? Such strings of single symbolic signs strung together, combined with hand gestures and facial expressions, might even be enough for whatever communication was needed to make that boat trip to Australia eventually happen. Chomsky-like language proper is not critical to make that trip happen.

I should make one other point about symbolic single-word utterances. They are, indeed, a special kind of shared practice. They are special because they are symbolic fictions. But not just this. They are also special because they represent arbitrary rules that individuals cannot just alter on their own. Stone cutters could follow traditional methods and forms when making objects, but they could also try something a little new that they think is more effective. If the revised product they make as individuals works well, that's all fine and good. Maybe others will go along and share this new technique or maybe they won't. It doesn't matter. You can continue to do it your new way.

In contrast, you cannot just make up a new sound pattern for the object category dog. Well, you can, but it won't be successful in communication. If others don't go along and share the new sound pattern with you as the new name for dog, then communication fails. There are strict rules about this, and it is all about the shared fictions. People who can do this can create other strict rules about social coordination involving religious norms and norms of governing that organize community members. Indeed, there is evidence that modern sapiens had relatively large and well-organized communities.[29] All of this would create a significant change in what it means to be human—a major change that has been called the "Upper Paleolithic Revolution."[30]

I would like to end this section by considering body adornment again. In the 1950s there was a major archaeological discovery of an Upper Paleolithic settlement in Sungir Russia. It included a burial site about 30,000 years old containing a tomb with a young boy (about 12 or 13 years old) and a young girl (about 9 or 10 years old). They were each covered with thousands of ivory beads (over 10,000 altogether). According to Harari, it would take an experienced artisan over three years to fashion this many beads. What could these children have actually accomplished to deserve that kind of burial? Harari makes the intriguing suggestion that only cultural beliefs (i.e., shared realities) could justify this extravagance.[31] This could be some shared beliefs about the children's association to revered others (e.g., children of high status parents, incarnations of dead spirits, ritual sacrifices for a leader). This would be additional evidence, then, of shared beliefs (and shared values) within a modern sapien community that creates a fiction; in this case, that these children and these adornments belong together (like that barking, tail-wagging animal belongs with the word sound pattern "dog").

Shared Reality in the Agricultural Revolution and Development of Civilization

There is good reason to use the term *revolution* when talking about what happened in modern sapien communities in the Upper Paleolithic period around 30,000 to 50,000 years ago. There were many significant developments in that period that impacted how humans created shared realities with others. Indeed, it is not clear whether subsequent changes, as dramatic as they seem to be in many respects, such as the contrast between the everyday life of contemporary city dwellers and the life of hunter-gatherers, actually constitute a qualitative change in shared reality development. In this regard, I should note that our Upper Paleolithic ancestors are called *Homo sapiens sapiens*, just like us today.

That said, a lot happened in the lives of *Homo sapiens sapiens* in the last 30,000 years. For one thing, around 13,000 years ago we became the last surviving human species. Neanderthals had already become extinct around 30,000 years ago. This certainly would have made us feel very special by the time of *scala naturae* in the Middle Ages—look at us, so different from any other animal! And, then, around 10,000 years ago, the Agricultural

Revolution began and, with it, great civilizations and empires, along with written language to boast about them. Obviously, I can't describe everything that happened in the Agricultural Revolution, but I do need to say something about this period as it relates to shared reality.

The Agricultural Revolution is about domestication and civilization. Charles Darwin described how humans, through selection, changed plants and animals in the *domestication* process, making them different from their wild ancestors. He distinguished the more general process of natural selection from human's conscious breeding of plants and animals to directly select for desirable traits.[32] Domesticating particular plants and animals has the advantage of securing a more predictable supply of them, as well as creating those traits in them that are most desired by humans, such as selected animals becoming tamer and more docile (i.e., less wild).

One of the consequences of such domestication was more frequent and predictable food surpluses. This, in turn, made it possible for humans to live together in greater numbers—in larger and larger villages, then towns, and then cities. Although there were some large settled communities before domestication began, domestication greatly increased the human phenomenon of large groups of people living together. However, food surpluses from domestication are not, in themselves, enough for large groups of people to live together effectively. To keep things in order, daily face-to-face interactions and close personal relationships are not enough. What can coordinate all these people and make them cooperate with one another? You guessed it—shared realities.

As Harari puts it, people invented stories about great gods as shared myths to build "astounding networks of mass cooperation, unlike any other ever seen on earth."[33] We discussed earlier how it is likely that modern humans had some religious beliefs. But the shared religious belief systems (and socio-political belief systems) were quite different during the Agricultural Revolution. In his groundbreaking book, *The Ethical Project*, the philosopher Philip Kitcher similarly argues that when 1,000 or more people live together and they need to avoid conflicts and deal with strangers, a system of agreed-upon rules must be established, and it is especially advantageous to social order if people share the belief (myth) that those rules are "*god-given*."[34]

How is it advantageous? If a community is small enough, then group members can more easily observe what each other is doing, report what each is doing to others (gossip), and then punish anyone who breaks a rule, including shunning that person. Simply put, compliance from surveillance can be enough. But this is not going to work with a large population of strangers. Who is going to see and know that someone secretly broke a rule? I can't watch everyone, and you can't watch everyone. But hold it. What if there were some superhuman being, or set of superhuman beings, who could see and know everything that each of us did? Such superhuman beings could then enforce the rules and punish anyone who stepped out of line. But who are these superhuman beings? Hmm . . . why don't we get together and invent them, which is what we did and called them *gods*.[35]

This was a very effective shared reality for instilling cooperation and coordination among humans. And we didn't stop there in the Agricultural Revolution. We developed civilizations, which are complex societies that have social stratification and cultural elites. What the elites did to institute control over the large populations was to create formal codes of law about how members of the community should behave, taking into account that, naturally, the laws would differ a little (or a lot) depending on your class and/or your gender. But that's not all that they did. They created one more highly significant shared reality. The code of laws, the leader presenting the code, or both were *god-given*.

My personal favorite of how this works is the Code of Hammurabi. Hammurabi was the King of Babylon who reigned from 1792 to 1750 BCE (about 4,000 years ago). His code consisted of 282 laws and standards that provided many different kinds of rules, including how to conduct commercial interactions and what fines to set for different kinds of infractions.[36] For example, it stipulated that if a "superior" man (there were superiors, commoners, and slaves) blinded the eye of another superior man, then his eye should also be blinded. Remember "an eye for an eye?" Another law, which my daughter would dislike, was that children were the property of their parents. This meant that if I killed someone else's daughter, then my daughter, not me, would be killed.

The rules are quite fascinating (and sometimes disturbing), but that is not all to the story. Where did Hammurabi get this code of laws and standards? Yes, you guessed it. They were god-given to him. Hammurabi humbly states the following:

I am Hammurabi, noble king. I have not been careless or negligent toward humankind, granted to my care by the god Enlil, and with whose shepherding the god Marduk charged me.[37]

Hammurabi is making the point that by giving us (we citizens of Babylon) these laws and standards, he is just following the orders of the gods (god Enlil and god Marduk). And if I, Hammurabi, the King of Babylon, am willing to follow the orders of these gods, then you too should follow these orders that I am passing down to you. All very nicely hierarchical, very clear, and thousands of years before *scala naturae*.

Speaking of Babylonia, Kitcher tell us that there was a Babylonian wisdom culture dating back before 2,700 years ago that told their communities how to live a "moral" life.[38] One text stated, "Do not return evil to your adversary / Requite with kindness the one who does evil to you." Sound familiar? The Golden Rule several thousand years ago. More generally, what is happening in the Agricultural Revolution is that shared realities about how to live the "good" life in an ethical sense is emerging in explicitly written statements. By being written, they can be shared more easily and broadly across space and time. As Kitcher would say, the "ethical project" had already begun with modern sapiens, but having written codes *and* the endorsement of gods in the Agricultural Revolution ratcheted things up substantially.

It should also be noted that the "good" ethical life does not refer just to following rules and injunctive norms. It is not just about shared duties and responsibilities (oughts). It is also about shared aspirations and shared standards of excellence (ideals).[39] There is division of labor according to individuals' skills and talents, such as the ability to be a scribe (think law codes) or an accountant (think taxes). Religious myths impact role fulfillment as well because they provide the shared belief that the all-seeing, all-knowing gods appreciate those who fulfill their societal roles well. As Kitcher states it, "the myth that divine approval descends on those who fit themselves to their station and discharge its duties with energy is a valuable extension of the idea of unseen enforcement."[40] This includes not only maintaining your role responsibilities (oughts), but also developing your talents, improving your skills to carry out your role at higher and higher levels of excellence (ideals).

I like Henrich's label for these kinds of changes in the Agricultural Revolution—"self-domestication." Humans' new motto in the Agricultural Revolution could be: "If you're wild, you're not civilized." Plants are not allowed to be wild (think weeds). Animals are not allowed to be wild (think beasts). And humans are certainly not allowed to be wild (think primitives or barbarians). We all need to be civilized. And if this requires that we introduce *taxation* to make civilization happen, to pay for our really big buildings, and the luxurious lives of the cultural elite, which apparently we did from the historical record, then so be it. What really matters is that we are civilized.

Being "civilized" has always been considered a good thing to be. Simply check the dictionary or thesaurus for its meanings and connotations: to bring people to a more advanced stage of social, cultural, and moral development; to be polite, gracious, and well-mannered; or to be accomplished, enlightened, and refined. Compare this to the meanings and connotations of being "uncivilized": to be uneducated, ignorant, and backwards or to be unintelligent, boorish, crude, and vulgar. Which would you choose to be? That was quick and easy. And it makes clear why we want to be civilized. And the more civilized, the better. Given that, what could be better than being a member of a "great" civilization? And, if this is the case, then the Agricultural Revolution was a wonderful thing to happen to humans because only in this period did "great" civilizations appear across the world, including the thousands-of-years-old civilizations of the ancient Chinese (Han China), ancient Egyptians, Babylonians, Harappans, Macedonians, Mayans, and Mesopotamians (in alphabetical order to avoid insulting anyone).

But "self-domestication" doesn't really sound so good. Who exactly was domesticating whom? Taking Hammurabi as an example, it was the cultural elite at the top, with their priests, who were domesticating others within the community. They were doing the "civilizing." The shared reality was that some members of the community were superior to other members from birth, and this was even captured in the written laws by distinguishing between "superior" and "commoners." Being superior beats being common.

Such hierarchical divisions were shared realities and they impacted the everyday lives of people. A more recent example would be the traditional caste system in India, with the highest caste living a very different life than the lowest caste. And then there are those who are not even recognized as being part of a caste—the out-of-caste, outcasts, variously labeled untouchables, Harijans, and Dalits. In brief, for the majority of the community members in "great" civilizations, there were clearly downsides from the shared realities that existed.

Harari makes the point that being a community member in a civilization (being "civilized)" is not a bargain for most people. It would be better to be a hunter-gatherer. This is because civilizations are complex communities that need division of labor with multiple recognized roles and the rules to coordinate them—shared realities. He makes the troubling point: "Unfortunately, complex human societies seem to require imagined hierarchies and unjust discrimination. . . . Scholars know of no large society that has been able to dispense with discrimination altogether. Time and again people have created order in their societies by classifying the population into imagined categories."[41] The new shared realities ushered in by the Agricultural Revolution—our becoming civilized—created a new kind of social discrimination for humans. A major downside indeed.

This is not the only downside of the shared realities associated with civilization and domestication. They have not only changed how humans relate to one another. They have changed how humans relate to other animals. And this matters because we have become responsible for the survival of many animal species. What we do has a major impact on other animals. As hunter-gatherers, we lived together with other animals dealing with many of the same demands and pressures as them. In this sense, we naturally experienced shared relevance with other animals. This could have contributed to the connectedness that hunter-gatherers are said to have had with other animals. But when we began to domesticate other animals, our relation to animals changed radically. We lost the connectedness with other animals that we once had. This is especially clear for animals who rely on us to care for them, which includes not only our pets but also our farm animals and zoo animals. In the time of the hunter-gatherers, the animals took care of themselves. They didn't need us to survive. Now many animals, and entire animal species, need us to survive. How can we relate to them that they can be more effective and survive? How can *we* be more effective by learning from them, letting *them* teach *us* about the world?

Good parenting is not the answer. Animals in zoos and homes, even after they are fully mature, are often treated like children being nurtured by us, with us being their surrogate parents. This is a caring and even loving relationship, but it is an unequal relationship. It is parent-to-child rather than adult-to-adult. To be effective, mature animals need to be treated as the adults they are—not as wild things, but as adults of their particular animal species, like the adults we are of our human species. How can we create more of an adult-to-adult relationship with other animals? You got it, by creating shared realities with them. And how can we create shared realities with them? We can begin with shared relevance.

We have all heard about "horse whisperers." We recognize that they have a special gift. What is this gift? It is the gift of listening to the inner state of the horse, by carefully studying its expressions and movements (the body language), and responding appropriately. Horse whisperers signal to the horse that what matters to the horse also matters to them. And over time this builds trust. The horse and the whisperer become partners.

Creating a relationship with an animal as a "whisperer" is not restricted to horses as partners. It can be done with many other animals. Dogs are an obvious example because dogs are highly responsive to human social cues.[42] Although most humans who have pet dogs love and care for their dog, this does not make them dog whisperers. Indeed, even among professional dog trainers who know much more than most of us about how to train dogs, only some are dog whisperers. Among dog trainers, the highest level of human–dog relationship is called an "adult–adult relationship." This is when both the dog and the trainer behave as adult individuals, in contrast to having an adult–child relationship where the trainer takes on the adult role and the dog is given the child role.

What does this adult–adult relationship between dog and trainer look like?[43] A dog and its trainer approach another dog. The trainer's dog wants to play with this other dog. But it first looks at the trainer to check how the trainer is reacting to this other dog. Is my trainer, my partner, having a positive or a negative reaction to this other dog? If positive, then approach. If negative, then avoid. Importantly, the reverse situation also occurs, where the trainer checks the reaction of his or her dog to a new dog that is approaching them. Is my dog, my partner, having a positive or a negative reaction to this other dog? If positive, then approach. If negative, then avoid. This is an equal, adult–adult relationship where the trainer and the dog as partners learn from each other how to react to a third party. They may not begin with the same emotional reaction to the third party, but they share the relevance of the third party from the beginning. And, then, they converge on how to react to the third party.

This is an example of a dog whisperer. It illustrates how shared relevance can be created with an animal that builds connectedness and trust.[44] For example, if your dog stops and looks at something or sniffs at something and then checks back with you, you can make eye contact and then pay attention to what he or she is looking at or sniffing at. You can signal that what your dog is treating as being worthy of attention is worthy of your attention too. You create a moment of shared relevance with your dog.[45] It is these moments of shared relevance that we need to experience with other animals. We need to reconnect with them in this way for their sake and for our own sake. We need to overcome the downside of domestication that came with civilization.

A Closing Comment on the Roots of Human Shared Reality: Why Did It Happen?

In this chapter, I have (very briefly) described the emergence of different kinds of shared realities in the communities of our ancestors. I began with what happened during the *Homo erectus* period over a million years ago when learning from others how to make tools and, especially, how to use fire—for warmth, light, protection, and, especially, cooking—played a big role in creating shared realities with others, including shared role coordination such as sexual division of labor. I then skipped all the way to the Upper Paleolithic period of modern sapiens (*Homo sapiens sapiens*) when all sorts of new shared practices and shared beliefs emerged from engaging in such amazing activities as boating, sewing, painting, trading, and burying. Prior to there being formal institutions of higher education (tens of thousands of years prior), there was the functional equivalent of Schools of Fine Arts, Science and Engineering, and Business. There was a lot to learn, and humans needed to be first-rate teachers and first-rate students and work together to create the exciting new shared realities. Who wants to play the flute or learn archery? It was a great time to be human.

And then, about 10,000 years ago, we got serious. No more "wild thing." *Domesticated* was in; *wild* was out. We domesticated plants such as wheat and animals such as goats. We domesticated ourselves, including developing religions with rules for how we should carry out our everyday lives. When you develop shared realities about what it means to be a good *moral* person, wild is out. Not nearly as much fun. Oh, and did I mention taxes? And discrimination based on shared realities about hierarchical social categories? As I keep saying, never forget the downsides of our never-ending motivation to create shared realities with others.

This is a highly significant story of how different kinds of shared realities emerged in human evolution. But you may have noticed that I did not say anything about why this is the *human* (or *Homo*) story, and particularly the *Homo sapiens sapiens* story, rather than the great ape story. What is it about us that led to this story? Well, of course, I can only speculate about this, which is all that anyone can do at this point. And, because it is very speculative, I have left it to the end of this chapter. The one thing I feel strongly about is *not* saying that all of this happened because we are more special than other animals. But there must be something different about us. What is different?

You know that I am not going to answer that it is our superior intelligence or our ability to talk in grammatical sentences. You know that my answer is going to have something to do with our motivation to create shared realities with others. And you are right on both counts. My answer, in brief, is this: *Our weakness made us strong.*

An important difference between us and other animals is how long after birth we remain weak and dependent on others. To begin, thanks in part to our being bipedal, our females must give birth to a nonfully developed baby for that baby to get through the birth canal. Let's face it, human newborns are pretty pathetic. They can't even hold their head up high, which, of course, they should do given how special they are for being next to angels. Compared to other animals, they start weak and stay weak for years. The childhood of humans is significantly longer than other animals. Consider chimpanzees which are our closest relative. Compared to us, chimpanzees (and other nonhuman primates) have a faster postnatal maturation rate and a younger age at first reproduction (several years before humans). There is also some recent evidence (from how long it takes to grow teeth) that even Neanderthals matured faster than humans,[46] which also means it is not just about being bipedal.

So why does it matter that human children mature slowly? It matters because their immaturity (weakness) makes them dependent on mature others *for a long time.* For many years, they can't survive without help. This could have created an evolutionary selection pressure for human children to figure out what motivates the mature others in their species to help them to stay alive. And what motivates these mature others is their feelings, beliefs, values, and concerns—their inner states. Human children want to share these inner states to interact effectively with these mature others and get the help they desperately need—the human motivation to share reality with others.[47]

My speculation, then, is that human children's weakness during a long childhood of dependency made them stronger by resulting in a motivation to create shared realities with others. It is some new version of "What doesn't kill you makes you stronger." I should also add that our longer childhood, our growing up slowly, may be related to our longer life, our aging more slowly than many other animals. If so, then this would give us another shared reality advantage—having older members of our family and community around to teach us.

It would be nice to just end this discussion here, with "Our weakness made us strong." But I can't because this would suggest that the emergence of our motivation to create shared realities with others, and all the different ways that we do so, is simply a good news story. By now, you know it is not. It is also a bad news story. Part of the bad news is that creating shared reality with others makes us emotionally suffer from failures to meet others' goals and standards for us that we have accepted as our own. Another part of the bad news is that creating shared reality with some groups and not with other groups leads to conflicts and hatreds between groups that have different shared beliefs. This is a very serious downside of shared reality motivation. Indeed, it threatens the survival of our species.

I have just described very briefly how humans developed from an evolutionary perspective. In prior chapters, I described the different kinds of shared reality that emerge during child development, as well as the process by which shared reality emerges (or not) during interpersonal communication. It is time now to look more closely at how our motivation to create shared realities with others plays out throughout our everyday lives—how shared reality makes us human.

Notes

1. Years ago in a paper on self-consciousness, I said: "Perhaps what is unique about humans is not so much their use of language or tools or instruction per se, but rather their motivation to share reality with others about the past, present, and future. Perhaps this motivation can account not only for the development of self-consciousness, but also for humans' use of language, tools, instruction, and so on" (Higgins, 2005, p. 170).

2. I should note from the beginning that I am not an expert in human evolutionary biology, biological anthropology, or comparative psychology, and thus I am relying on experts in these areas for my descriptions. I am also not making any claims that dispute the basic conclusions of those scientific disciplines. Rather, my purpose is to relate what has been generally described in the literature to the development of the human motivation to create shared realities with others. It is *that* relation that I am speculating about.

3. See Wrangham (2009, p. 14).

4. I should note that *Homo erectus* was around for a very long time—over 1.5 million years. When I describe different activities as being carried out in *Homo erectus* communities, I am not suggesting that these activities necessarily occurred early on. They could have occurred later during the *Homo erectus* period. My only suggestion is that they occurred prior to the evolution of *Homo sapiens*, and thus there is evidence for humans creating shared realities with one another prior to their being *Homo sapiens*. To this extent, I disagree with those who suggest that nothing much of importance was happening in human societies that was distinctly human before *Homo sapiens*.

5. See Wrangham (2009, p. 89).

6. See Aiello and Wheeler (1995) and Wrangham (2009). See also Gibbons (2007).

7. See Wiessner (2014).

8. See Wiessner (2014).

9. See Wrangham (2009).

10. See review by Wrangham (2009, pp. 152–156).

11. Henrich (2016). For another excellent book on the role of culture in evolution, see Jablonka and Lamb (2005).

12. See Henrich (2016, pp. 57–58).

13. See Henrich (2016, pp. 228).

14. See Henrich (2016, pp. 211–212). See also Boyd, Richerson, and Henrich (2011). Also note that, by giving this example, I am not equating Polar Inuit communities, which are modern human communities, with *Homo erectus* communities. I am simply making a point about how technically difficult activities are too complex to be the result of some individual genius. They take know-how that must be learned from others. Indeed, there is no evidence of bows and arrows in *Homo erectus* communities.

15. For further discussion of this bow, see Boyd et al. (2011). For a description of the multistep, very complicated process of making an arrow, see Henrich (2016, p. 107).

16. See Henrich (2016) and Suddendorf (2013). For a discussion of increasing tool complexity, see also Perreault, Brantingham, Kuhn, Wurz, and Gao (2013) and Stout (2011).

17. See Suddendorf (2013).

18. See Hawkes (2003) and Suddendorf (2013).

19. Once again, I need to be clear what I am and am not claiming here. I am not suggesting that what I describe about modern sapien communities never appeared in earlier communities, but the evidence of its occurrence is much clearer for modern sapien communities than for earlier communities, and there is a clear contrast between them and *Homo erectus* communities.

20. See Holden (1998).

21. See De Beaune and White (1993).

22. See Harari (2015) and Howells (1997). See also Bar-Yosef (2002).

23. See Bar-Yosef (2002).

24. For a very thoughtful discussion of this issue, see Holden (1998).

25. See Harari (2015, p. 35–36).

26. See Sherif (1936).
27. See Bar-Yosef (2002).
28. See also Henrich (2016) on a related point.
29. See Howells (1997).
30. See Bar-Yosef (2002).
31. See Hatari (2015, p. 58).
32. See Darwin (1859, 1868).
33. See Harari (2015, p. 103).
34. Kitcher (2011).
35. I am indebted to Philip Kitcher for this insight (see Kitcher 2011).
36. See Roth (1977).
37. See Roth (1997, p. 133).
38. See Kitcher (2011, p. 119, fn 20).
39. See Cornwell and Higgins (2015) for a discussion of the difference between the ought-prevention focus and ideal-promotion focus ethical systems.
40. See Kitcher (2011, p. 128).
41. See Harari (2015), p. 173.
42. See Johnston, Byrne, and Santos (2018).
43. For this information about dog trainers and the following illustration of the adult–adult relationship between trainers and their dogs, I am very grateful to Valeria Viazmytynova, who comes from a family of dog trainers.
44. Our pets are the prime example of animals with whom we can have a better relationship through creating shared realities—becoming a dog whisperer, cat whisperer, bird whisperer, and so on. Admittedly, there are animals to whom we don't want to whisper, like animals that can harm us. But for animals who need our help to survive, including those that can harm us, we still need to understand and share what is relevant to them to help them. Finding shared relevance with them still matters. It still begins with shared relevance.
45. One thing that is of interest to dogs is the urine of other dogs. When they pay attention to it, you can signal that it is worthy of attention by stopping and waiting. You don't have to sniff it yourself. But, just to give sniffing a chance, you and your pet dog could both smell other things together, like the citrus or spicy pepper ingredients in the meal you are making. You can share the relevance of these ingredients. And your dog's reaction will tell you how strong the ingredient is because your dog has the better nose (over 100 million olfactory receptors compared to our 5 million or so). Just make sure to thank your dog for sharing these moments.
46. See Smith et al. (2010).
47. See Higgins and Pittman (2008).

PART II
HOW SHARED REALITY
MAKES US HUMAN

5

What We Feel

What matters to you? What do you find interesting? What do you like and dislike? What makes you happy or sad? At peace or nervous? What makes you feel proud or ashamed of yourself or feel respect or contempt for another? In countless ways, our feelings are a major part of our everyday life. And the shared realities that we create with others are central to what we feel. This chapter describes how and why this is so.

What Matters

Let's begin at the beginning. When you sense something happening, do you even pay attention to it? If something doesn't matter, if it is irrelevant, then you don't pay attention to it and don't feel anything about it. Thus, to understand how shared reality impacts what we feel, we need to begin with how shared reality affects what does and does not matter at the outset, how shared reality affects whether you experience something as being relevant or irrelevant.

You might think that whether something matters or not to people is "wired in," part of our human nature. Examples that come to mind are our natural fears of spiders, snakes, high places, death, and so on. But, actually, these fears are not natural. There are a couple of fears that we are born with—fear of falling and fear of loud noises—but that is it. Think of all the other fears we have, such as fear of public speaking, and it becomes obvious that our major fears are not something we are born with. This does not mean they don't tell us something important about what makes us human. They do. And they do because to be human is to create shared realities with others about what matters and how to feel about it, including what to fear.

I discussed in Chapter 2 how the interactions between infants and their caretakers communicate to children what is or is not worth paying attention to, what does and does not matter. Parents, for example, can point to something they find interesting and draw their child's attention toward it while vocally expressing excitement in what they are looking at: "Look! Look! There's a rabbit!!" The infant cannot understand the words yet but can understand that what they are both looking at is worth looking at: This thing matters. Infants can also see something that they find interesting and want their parent to look at it, too. They will point to it, make sounds of excitement, and try to get their parent to share their interest in it. But how their parent reacts will communicate whether this thing really does matter or not. If their parent looks at it and gets excited, then it matters. If their parent briefly looks at it and then turns away with no excitement, then it does not matter.

These interactions send clear messages to infants about what does and what does not matter in the world. It is the beginning of children becoming a member of their culture. Cultures anoint what matters through its members having these kinds of interactions with their infants. And what matters changes as cultures change. A particular kind of root, for example, might not matter until the invention of cooking by fire because the root is indigestible or even poisonous unless it is cooked.[1] Why would a parent want a child to share interest in something, especially given that it is just a root, if it has no function? But this would change once it is edible food.

The importance of shared attention for which objects and activities are prioritized has been noted in the literature.[2] There is evidence that babies are especially interested in objects that they and others attend to together.[3] Indeed, neuroscience research with nine-month-old infants has found that a neural correlate of attentional processes is enhanced when they engage in joint attention interaction with an adult, where the adult first gazes at the infant's face and then looks at an object, compared to a nonjoint attention interaction, where the adult just looks at the object.[4] There is also evidence that when people believe that another person is attending to something at the same time as them (vs. at a different time) and the other person is similar (vs. dissimilar) to them, then they will pay more attention to the details of what they are observing.[5] Attending simultaneously to something with a similar other person enhances the experience of sharing reality with this person, which, in turn, makes what is being observed matter more, including its details. When interacting partners perceive that they are attending to the same thing, it is prioritized, which results in its receiving broader and deeper processing.[6]

Sharing reality with others isn't only about identifying which objects or events in the world matter. It is also about which distinctions between things matter. Everyone knows the story about how English speakers have only one word for snow—"snow"—but Inuit-speaking Eskimos in northern Canada have 50 or more distinct words for snow. For example, there is "matsaaruti" for wet snow that can be used to ice the runners of a sleigh, "pukak" for salt-looking crystalline powder snow, and "aqilokoq" for snow that is softly falling.[7]

By the way, it was the famous anthropologist Franz Boas who caught the world's attention by mentioning that Eskimo Inuit had many different words for snow. This led some scholars to argue that it was the presence of so many words for snow that caused Inuit-speaking Eskimos to see distinctions among different kinds of snow that English speakers cannot see, which, in turn, was taken as support for Whorf's linguistic relativity hypothesis. But their many different words for snow didn't make Eskimos see different kinds of snow that they would otherwise have not seen. The distinctions among different kinds of snow were highly functional in the everyday life of Eskimos. The distinctions mattered. Because they mattered, different words were created to communicate about them. The different words followed the *relevance* of the distinctions and not the other way around. Even without the words, the distinctions would matter and would be pointed out by caretakers to young children independent of, and even prior to, the children learning the different names. Oh, and getting back to Franz Boas, he didn't make a big deal of the Inuit Eskimo having all these snow words. He was more interested in their folklore—and his learning to live entirely on seal meat, like they did.[8]

Although distinctions among objects or activities can matter and children can learn that they matter, without the need for caretakers to use different names for them, typically the distinctions *are* given different names, and this *does* contribute to creating shared realities. Indeed, the fact that some category of things has its own name signals to children that this category of things must matter. The distinct name makes the relevance of the category salient to children. And the fact that its name is different from the name of other categories of things helps to distinguish among different things that each matter. So naming does contribute in an important way to creating shared realities, to learning what matters.

Unfortunately, naming does something else as well. It communicates not only that this category of things matters and is different from other categories but also that other distinctions among different members of the same named category do *not* matter. Different bananas that vary in size and color, and even shape, are all called "banana" despite these variations, and this clearly communicates to children that these variations do not matter. Over time, children, and we, pay little attention to such variations. We might pay attention to color as a sign of ripeness, but that is about it. And this is a downside of becoming human because we stop appreciating the specialness of each particular instance of a category. When we were younger and pointing with excitement at some specific thing we were looking at, such as a particular robin, we could wonder at its specialness. And if a day later we saw another member of the same category, another robin, we could point with excitement again at this new thing and wonder at *its* specialness. But at some point we might hear, "Oh, yes, that's another robin," as if it is *just* another robin. No big deal. Not something really worth noting because there are lots of robins. What's special about this particular, specific robin can be lost.

There is an example of children learning from others which distinctions matter that has fascinated me for years: children's learning which word sound differences matter for distinguishing among words and which sound differences don't matter. Phonemes are perceptually distinct categories of speech sounds in a specific language that distinguish among different words, such as the phoneme sound categories /p/ and /b/ in the words p̲ad versus b̲ad, and /d/ and /t/ in the words ba̲d versus ba̲t. Variations in sounds *within* the phoneme category of one language will not be perceptually distinguished even though that same variation will be perceptually distinguished by speakers of another language if they are phonemes that distinguish between words in that language. For example, although /r/ and /l/ are distinct sound categories in English, they are not in Japanese.

Very young human infants can perceive and discriminate among all of the different speech sounds that are found across *all* human languages. They do not have a preference for the phonemes that are used in any particular language. But soon they begin to share the phoneme preference of those caretakers with whom they interact. There is evidence, for example, that even one-month-old English-speaking infants will pay more attention to differences near the boundary between /b/ and /p/ than to equal-sized differences within the /b/-category or within the /p/-category. By six months of age, infants stop paying attention to sound distinctions that are not phonemes in their language community. They no longer matter. By not being a shared reality, these sound distinctions have become so irrelevant that they no longer receive attention.[9]

Throughout childhood and afterwards, it is our interactions with significant others that create shared realities about what does and does not matter. However, there is increasingly another important source of social input about what matters—the media (e.g., newspapers and magazines, radio, television) and, perhaps especially nowadays, social media (e.g., Facebook, Twitter). Through the media, we not only hear opinions about what matters from experts, including self-proclaimed experts, but the very fact that something is discussed and commented on the media creates a shared reality that it must matter, it must be relevant. On Facebook we even see feedback about how many "likes" (i.e., thumbs up) a post received. The more thumbs up, the more it matters. And that's not all. It also tells us how we should feel about it. If there are lots of thumbs up, you too should like it. If there are lots of thumbs down, you should dislike it. And we don't even have to know personally the individuals who gave the thumbs up or the thumbs down.

Before ending this section, I need to say something about one object whose mattering really matters to each of us—our self. There are types of child–parent interactions (discussed more fully in Chapter 8) that send a message to children that they don't matter. One of these is abuse, and the other is neglect. Neglect may be the worst of all because the message to the child is that you don't even matter enough to expend the energy to abuse. This could explain why children will misbehave knowing that they will be punished so that, at least, someone will pay attention to them. If they receive punishment for something they did, it means that someone paid attention to what they did, which means that what they do matters. That is more important than the pain of punishment.

And it is not just children. Adults can also prefer negative attention to no attention: "Any attention is better than no attention." Dale Carnegie said: "A person's name is to that person, the sweetest, most important sound in any language." When someone uses your name they create a shared reality with you that this is *your* name and its use is in reference to you—*you* matter. We would prefer that someone says our name in a positive manner, but we prefer that it is said than never said at all.

What Is Positive or Negative

I also discussed in Chapter 2 how infants, by creating shared realities with their significant others, learn what to feel positive about and what to feel negative about, what to like and what to dislike. Children as young as 12 months can recognize that someone's emotional display is in response to a particular object or activity, and they learn whether to respond to that object or activity in a positive or negative manner by paying attention to such facial or vocal expressions.[10] The classic example mentioned earlier is an infant checking his or her mother's facial expression when choosing whether to cross an apparently deep cliff (with a solid but transparent surface) and stopping when the mother has a negative expression.[11]

A compelling example of how shared reality can determine whether to treat something as positive or negative is food preferences. In his excellent book, *The Secret of Our Success: How Culture Is Driving Human Evolution, Domesticating Our Species, and Making Us Smarter*, Joseph Henrich tells the tale of why chili peppers taste good.[12] He begins by making three points: (a) We are the only animal that puts spices in our food; (b) generally speaking, putting spices in our food contributes little or nothing nutritionally; and, my favorite, (c) in many spices, the active ingredients are actually *aversive* chemicals whose function is to keep unwanted things like insects or mammals away from the plants that produce the spices.

Bottom line: It is *not* natural to eat spices. But many of us love spicy food. Why? We learned to love spicy food from others whom we saw eat it and respond positively: "Mm-mm-mm, boy do I love chili peppers!" Why did we spice our food to begin with? Because they are effective against pathogens in our food, especially pathogens in meat, and our wise elders, at least tacitly, recognized this. And this shared practice matters, especially in hotter areas of the world—the same areas where spicing food is most common (think India, Indonesia, and Mexico).

Of course it is not just our food preferences that are shaped by our interactions with members of our family and community. It is our preferences in music, recreation activities, clothes, and so on. In addition, how shared reality impacts what we experience as positive and as negative is not limited to our observations of others' responses to different objects and activities, others' choice about what to do and what not to do. It also derives, importantly, from our shared self-guides and our shared social norms.

Let's begin with our shared self-guides. As I discussed in Chapter 3, preschoolers acquire shared self-guides (shared goals and standards) with their significant others around roughly 3-5 years-of-age. Later, schoolers acquire "generalized other" norms about social roles and social rules. But this does not mean that these older children, and adolescents and adults as well, do not continue to have shared self-guides with significant others in their lives, including with the post-childhood new significant others in their adolescent and adult lives, such as their mentors and romantic partners. They do. And these shared goals and standards have a significant impact on both what matters and what is experienced as positive and as negative.

First, individuals' shared goals and standards contribute significantly to whether an activity (or behavior) is relevant or irrelevant and, if relevant, how much it matters. If an activity is a means (i.e., is instrumental) to attaining a shared goal, to satisfying a shared standard, then that activity is relevant. The more important the goal and standard, the more that instrumental activity matters. The outcome of that activity will also matter more if the instrumental activity relates to a shared goal and standard.

Second, individuals' shared goals and standards contribute significantly to whether an activity (or behavior) is positive or negative. If an activity *supports* attaining a goal or satisfying a standard, then it will be experienced as positive. If it *impedes* fulfilling the goal or standard, then it will be experienced as negative.[13] Notably, what this means is that whether an activity is positive or negative is not just a function of its properties. It depends on its relation to a person's goal and standards. The activity could be painful, like mountain climbing in bad weather, but still be positive because it supports a person's goal to be the kind of mountain climber who can deal with bad conditions. A Muslim suicide bomber will experience blowing himself up as a positive activity if he believes that jihad means killing infidels and will make him a better Muslim. This also means that the same activity could be experienced as positive by one person and negative by another person depending on the goals and standards that each of them share with others. And, once again, how positive or negative the activity is experienced will depend on how important the shared goal and standard is.

It is not only the activity itself whose positivity or negativity is determined by its relation to shared goals and standards. The positivity or negativity of the *outcome* of the activity (or behavior) is also determined by its relation to shared goals and standards. Imagine that the activity is a student studying for and then taking an exam. The student gets a B on the exam.

Is that outcome a success or a failure, positive or negative? As we will see, it depends on the student's goals and standards, which are typically shared with their significant others, such as their parents or close friends.

The children of wealthy families attending Ivy League colleges in the 1900s had the goal and standard of getting C grades to be a "gentleman," in contrast to being a "grind" whose constant studying made them a boring person. Franklin Delano Roosevelt was successful in this by getting mostly Cs at Harvard. Getting a B on an exam would be a failure. It would mean he was a grind. Other students were grinds, but he was a gentleman. Interestingly, he did get Bs in courses on government; perhaps he had different goals and standards for that field. Of course, nowadays getting a B for many Ivy League students would also be experienced as a failure but for a very different reason than FDR. It would be a failure in relation to the goal and standard of getting an A and, for some students, getting straight As. And getting straight Cs nowadays would be experienced as a disaster for most students.

Self-guides that are shared with significant others function as reference points that determine what is experienced as positive or as negative. Social norms do so as well. Social norms involve the generalized other and apply to everyone, and they also function as reference points for what will be experienced as positive or as negative. When your behavior fulfills social norms that you embrace, it is experienced as positive. When your behavior breaks social norms, it is experienced as negative. Social norms differ from self-guides because they apply to everyone who is capable of fulfilling them (e.g., not newborns) whereas your self-guides are *your* self-guides. Other people are not expected to fulfill your self-guides, but they are expected, like you are, to fulfill social norms. This means that, unlike self-guides, social norms are used as reference points to evaluate not only your own behaviors and outcomes as positive or negative but also others' behaviors and outcomes.

As I previously noted, the use of a social norm as a reference point for evaluating another person's behavior as positive or as negative depends on believing that the other person is capable of fulfilling that social norm. It also depends on whether the other person is relevant to the shared reality underlying the social norm. Because social norms are *shared* realities, there are epistemic and social relational factors underlying them. If someone is a member of an out-group, they may not know what behavior is expected by the social norm. They may be capable of doing the behavior, but they don't know that this behavior is expected of them (low epistemic knowledge). In addition, an out-group member is not socially connected to the in-group (low relational bond). Thus, their behavior in relation to a social norm has low relevance compared to the behavior of an in-group member.

The irony of this is that a violation of an in-group social norm can be experienced more negatively when it is committed by an in-group member (high shared reality relevance) than an out-group member (low shared reality relevance). And this difference can be seen even with young children. In one study,[14] three-year-old children were introduced to two hand puppets where one puppet, Max, had a native accent like the children and wore a bracelet with the same color as them, and the other puppet, Henri, had a foreign French accent and wore a bracelet with a different color than them. The children became acquainted with Max before Henri appeared.

The adult experimenter, who was a member of the participant children's in-group, performed a task in a particular way and said to the participant child, "We do it like this." The in-group or out-group puppet then performed the task incorrectly, and the participant children had the opportunity to protest. The three-year-old children were much more likely to protest when the in-group puppet violated the norms of how to play the game than when the out-group puppet violated the norms.

Thus, even preschoolers are more likely to tolerate a violation of a game norm when it is committed by an out-group outsider than when the same violation is committed by an in-group member. The norm violation is experienced as more negative when it is committed by someone with whom you have a shared reality because the violation has higher relevance. And it is not just young children. It is well-known that even a small deviation by a member of one's own group, whether it be a religious group or a political party, is more upsetting to people than the same violation by a member of an out-group: "He should know better!"[15]

Stanley Schachter's landmark research on emotion provides a classic example of how creating a shared reality with another person can determine the kind of feeling you experience.[16] The participants in one study were told that the purpose of the study was to test the effects on visual skills of a new vitamin called "Suproxin." The participants agreed to be injected with the vitamin. Rather than receiving a vitamin, the participants in one condition actually received epinephrine (adrenalin) that would cause them later to feel aroused. Before receiving the injection, the participants were given different information about how the injection would make them feel. Some of them were given accurate information about how the injection would make them feel. They were told that they might experience arousal side effects. The other participants were given inaccurate information about how the injection would make them feel. They were told either that the injection would have no side effects or that they might experience side effects from the injection that were very different from epinephrine arousal (e.g., feet might feel numb; parts of the body might itch).

After receiving the injection from the physician, the physician leaves and the experimenter enters with supposedly another participant in the study who is actually a confederate working for the experimenter. The experimenter asks them both to sit in the room to wait for the "Suproxin" vitamin to become active in the bloodstream. The experimenter leaves the room and the confederate, after introducing himself and chatting a bit, begins to behave in one of two ways. In the "Euphoria" condition, the confederate acts in different silly ways, such as folding up paper and throwing them like small basketballs into a wastebasket. In the "Anger" condition, the confederate makes irritated comments about the questions being asked in the questionnaires they were both given to fill out, such as what the average annual income of the participant's father is and which member of the participant's immediate family does not bathe or wash regularly.

The participants who received accurate information about the injection's side effects can explain their arousal as being due to the injection. But the participants who received inaccurate information about the injection's side effect cannot explain their arousal as being due to the injection. Thus, they need to find another explanation for their arousal, and they look to their current situation for an answer. If the participants create a shared reality with the confederate about the emotional nature of their situation (i.e., that it is either an euphoria-related or an anger-related situation), then they have an answer. Indeed, compared to the participants in the "informed" condition, the participants in the "misinformed" conditions were more likely to verbally or nonverbally express emotions that matched the confederate's euphoria-related or anger-related behaviors. They created a shared reality with the confederate about what to feel in this situation.

This research by Schachter on how people look to others to create a shared reality about what they are feeling was inspired by his earlier work on anxiety and social affiliation.[17] The participants in this research, who were all college females, entered a lab filled with laboratory equipment and met a serious-looking experimenter who was dressed in a white laboratory coat with a stethoscope in his pocket. He told them that they were there to serve as subjects in an experiment concerned with the effects of electric shock. In the "High Anxiety" condition, they were told that they would be hooked to the electrical-looking equipment and receive a series of electric shocks that "will be quite painful but, of course, they will do no permanent damage."[18] In the "Low Anxiety" condition, there was no electrical equipment in the room, and they were told that the very mild shocks would not be painful in any way and would feel more like a tickle or tingle. They were assured in this condition that they would enjoy the experiment.

The participants were then told that it would take about 10 minutes to get ready, so they would need to wait in a room for that period. They were given a choice about whether to wait in a room alone or together with other subjects. Whereas one third of the "Low Anxiety" participants chose to be together with others, almost two thirds of the "High Anxiety" participants chose to be together with others.

A follow-up study found that participants in the "High Anxiety" condition did not choose to be with other people simply for the comfort of being with others. If the other people were waiting for a meeting with their advisor, then the "High Anxiety" participants did not choose to be with them. They chose to be with others if those others were also waiting to be shocked. As Schachter said, they wanted to share their feeling with those in the same situation as them. He goes on to say that it is not true that "misery loves company." Instead, misery loves only *miserable* company. That's the company with whom they can create the shared reality of shared feelings.

What Kind of Positive and What Kind of Negative

People don't just have positive or negative reactions to what happens. They have specific kinds of positive reactions and specific kinds of negative reactions. Our shared realities with others are a major determinant of what kind of positive reaction and what kind of negative reaction we have to something that happens. For example, those infants who checked their mother's facial expression when choosing whether to cross the cliff and stopped when their mother had a negative expression did not experience just any negative reaction. These infants experienced the same particular negative emotion that their mother was expressing—fear. Not sadness. And, with a nod to Schachter, the participants with the angry confederate *did* behave in a negative irritated manner and not in a negative sad or fearful manner.

I have discussed how the self-guides that children share with their significant others can determine whether an activity or outcome is relevant or not, whether it is positive or not, and how positive or how negative it is. But that's not all. Self-guides can also determine *what kind of positive reaction* and *what kind of negative reaction* is experienced—even for the *same* objective event such as receiving a failing F grade on an exam. That's because self-guides are psychologically related to two distinct motivational systems—the *promotion* system that is concerned with advancing from the current state toward a better state and the *prevention* system that is concerned with maintaining a current satisfactory state against a worse state.[19]

I will discuss in more detail in later chapters the differences between the promotion and prevention systems. Here I will discuss enough about these two systems to understand why they produce different positive and different negative experiences. Let me briefly describe the two kinds of positive parent–child interactions and the two kinds of negative parent–child interactions that contribute to children acquiring a stronger promotion system or a stronger prevention system.

There are two different kinds of positivity that parents can create for their child when interacting with them. Each sends a particular message to the child about what the world is like. One kind of positive interaction creates a *presence of positive* psychological situation for the child, such as a father hugging his daughter after she gives him a drawing she made. This kind of interaction sends a *promotion* message to the child that the world is a place where nurturance and growth occurs. Children in this case represent and identify with their parents' goals and standards for them as being hopes for them. They acquire shared *ideal* self-guides.

A different kind of positive interaction creates an *absence of negative* psychological situation for the child, such as a mother stopping her son from putting his hand on a hot stove. This kind of interaction sends a *prevention* message to the child that the world is a place where you need to be careful and responsible to maintain safety and security. Children in this case represent and identify with their parents' goals and standards for them as being their responsibilities. They acquire shared *ought* self-guides.

Children also acquire ideal and ought self-guides from negative interactions with their parents. A promotion example of a negative psychological situation for a child would be a daughter having a pleasant meal with her mother and then spilling her food, and her mother responding by no longer smiling at her—the *absence of positive*. When parent–child presence-of-positive interactions are combined with such absence-of-positive interactions, they send promotion success and failure messages to the child that the world is a world of potential *gains* and possible *nongains*—progress is possible.

A prevention example of a negative psychological situation for a child would be a father yelling at his son after the son hit his younger brother—the *presence of negative*. When parent–child absence-of-negative interactions are combined with such presence-of-negative interactions, they send prevention success and failure messages to the child that the world consists of potential *nonlosses* and possible *losses*—things could go wrong.

These differences between shared promotion ideal self-guides and shared prevention ought self-guides produce different positive experiences and different negative experiences when people succeed or fail, respectively.[20] And this is true even when the success or failure is objectively the same. Take, for example, winning the Nobel Prize in Economics. How would you feel? Almost certainly positive. But what kind of positive? Most people I think would feel overjoyed. This makes sense because winning the Nobel Prize, even for a very talented person, is an ideal, something you hope might happen but mostly dream about. This means that it would be a promotion ideal, and success at attaining a promotion ideal makes you feel happy and joyful. Because this would be an extreme success, you would feel extremely joyful—overjoyed.

Although feeling overjoyed seems most likely, it is not the only possibility. What if some individuals believed that their significant others expected them to win the Nobel Prize? What if winning the Nobel Prize was something that, amazingly enough, members of their in-group simply did? That is, what if you believed that winning the Nobel Prize was your responsibility—a shared ought self-guide? Then when you succeeded you would not feel overjoyed. Instead, you would feel *relieved*. And this is precisely what a University of Chicago economist said when he won the Nobel Prize in Economics. He said he was relieved. After all, he was surrounded by close colleagues who had already won that prize. He felt it was his responsibility to win the prize as well. This clearly demonstrates how people can have different positive feelings from the same success depending on whether it is success in relation to shared promotion ideals or in relation to shared prevention oughts.

Just as positive feelings from success can be different in relation to promotion ideals versus prevention oughts, negative feelings from failure can also be different. When students receive a F on an exam, they are very likely to feel negative. But, once again, different students can have very different negative feelings depending on whether their course grades relate to promotion ideals or prevention oughts. If your course grades relate to promotion ideals, the grades you hope to achieve, then receiving a F on an exam will make you feel sad, disappointed, or despondent. In contrast, if your course grades relate to prevention oughts, the grades you believe are your responsibility to achieve, then receiving a F on an exam will make you feel nervous, worried, or on edge. The former dejection-related emotions are very different from the latter agitation-related emotions.

It should also be noted that the differences in positive experiences and negative experiences as a function of whether success or failure is in relation to promotion ideals or prevention oughts are not restricted to differences in emotional experiences. They also involve differences in other kinds of motivational experiences.[21] Success in relation to promotion ideals makes people feel more eager and enthusiastic. Motivational intensity increases (like the high intensity of joy). In contrast, success in relation to prevention oughts makes people feel *less* vigilant. Motivational intensity decreases (like the low intensity of feeling calm and relaxed). These are very different motivational experiences.

There are also very different motivational experiences from failure when it is in relation to promotion ideals versus prevention oughts. Failure in relation to promotion ideals makes people feel discouraged, less eager. Motivational intensity decreases (like the low intensity of feeling sad). In contrast, failure in relation to prevention oughts makes people feel *more* vigilant. Motivational intensity increases (like the high intensity of feeling nervous).

What this means is that our experiences of our successes and failures in life are very different depending on whether we are pursuing promotion ideals or prevention oughts. It is as if we lived in different worlds of experience. And these differences can even affect how we experience and respond to other people's feelings about their successes or failures. In one study, for example,[22] participants read transcripts about another person's distress from failing to meet a self-guide. The actual failure was the same: a recent incident of this shy person's persistent difficulty meeting new people. In one case, this target person described the failure as a failure to meet an ideal self-guide (a hope), reported feeling sad, and was described as having down-cast eyes and a low voice. In the other case, this target person described the failure as a failure to meet an ought self-guide, reported feeling anxious, and was described as fidgeting and having hurried speech.

The participants themselves were dealing with their own ideal self failures or their own ought self failures. Consistent with the previous discussion, after reading about the target's failure, the participants dealing with personal ideal self failures felt sadder and more discouraged whereas the participants dealing with personal ought self failures felt more afraid and agitated. But that is not all that happened. The participants were also asked how much, as they read the transcript, they felt compassion about the distress of the target person and whether the target person's emotional reaction was appropriate to his or her situation. When the target person's failure was the *same* kind of self-guide failure that participants' themselves were dealing with (i.e., an ideal failure for both themselves and the target or an ought failure for both themselves and the target), their compassion for the target was significantly higher, and they judged the target person's emotional reaction to be appropriate to the situation.

To put these findings in another way, when the target's failure was in relation to a self-guide (ideal vs. ought) that was *different* than the kind of self-guide failure that they were dealing with, the participants had less compassion for the target and judged the target's emotional reaction to be not appropriate to the situation. It is as if people dealing with ought self failures were to say to someone distressed from an ideal self failure, "I don't get it. Why are you sad? That doesn't make sense."

What I have discussed so far is how people's emotional and motivational experiences of their life and the life of others—what kind of positive experience and what kind of negative experience—depends on whether they are responding in relation to shared ideal self-guides or shared ought self-guides. There is a version of this that is especially fascinating—*emotional transference*. For Sigmund Freud,[23] transference was not only a clinical phenomenon where patients would respond to their therapist (typically male) in terms of their unconscious fantasies about a parent (typically their father). It was also an everyday life phenomenon where individuals have mental representations of their significant others that can impact how they respond to another person who reminds them (unconsciously) of a particular significant other and is then responded to as if this person *was* that significant other. Susan Andersen has conducted extensive and groundbreaking studies examining such transference in everyday life.[24]

When we meet someone who happens to resemble one of our significant others in some way, our mental representation of that particular significant other is activated. This can cause us to remember, feel about, and behave toward this new person as if he or she *was* our significant other.[25] Indeed, when participants' significant other possessed a particular characteristic, the participants report, with *high* confidence, that they saw this characteristic in the target person who superficially resembled that significant other, even though no such information about the target person was actually presented.[26]

But that is not all. When we meet someone who resembles a significant other, such as resembling our mother or father, our shared self-guides with that significant other are also activated. And if we happen to have failures in relation to those shared self-guides, we will suffer emotionally. Will the kind of suffering be different if our failures are in relation to shared ideal self-guides with that significant other versus shared ought self-guides with that significant other? This is the question that Andersen and her colleagues tested.

In the first session of one such study,[27] undergraduates described their father and mother. Notably, all participants described their parents as being important to them and loved by them. They also completed a measure of their ideal and ought self-guides to identify one set of participants who had failures from their shared ideal self-guides and another set who had failures from their shared ought self-guides. Two weeks later in a supposedly unrelated study, they were told they would meet a new person. To examine how their feelings *changed* after learning about the person they would meet, the participants' feelings were measured at the beginning of this second session and then received the description of the new person. For some participants, the description included personal characteristics that resembled one of their parents (the potential transference condition). In addition, for some of these participants, the new person resembled a parent whose ideal self-guides for them they were failing to meet whereas for others the new person resembled a parent whose ought self-guides for them they were failing to meet.

If transference occurred, when that new person resembled (vs. did not) a parent whom they loved and was important to them, participants should feel more positive toward that person and expect that this person would be more accepting of them. Indeed, both of these classic transference effects were found. In addition, and importantly, there was an increase in participants' dejected-related feelings when the new person activated their parent's ideals for them (which they were failing) and an increase in agitation-related feelings when the new person activated their parent's oughts for them (which they were failing).[28]

There is other evidence for this kind of transference effect on individuals' feelings. In one study, for example, participants were asked a variety of questions about different people they knew.[29] One question, for instance, asked how much their father would ideally want them to do well on an anagram task (strength of *father ideal* for them). Another question asked how much their father felt they had a duty or obligation to do well on an anagram task (strength of *father ought* for them). Before performing the actual anagram task, they worked on some practice items. While they were working, some participants were subliminally (unconsciously) primed with father-related words (e.g., father; dad). They then performed the anagram task. After completing the task, they received either success or failure feedback. Those whose fathers held a strong ideal for them felt cheerful after success feedback and dejected after failure feedback, whereas those whose fathers held a strong ought for them felt relaxed after success feedback and agitated after failure feedback.

These transference findings are remarkable—and troubling. In Andersen's research, participants expecting to meet a new person who resembled one of their own parents felt more positive toward, and more accepted by, this new person. Nonetheless, they still suffered prior to meeting the new person because the new person activated their parent with whom they shared self-guides that they were failing to meet. They suffered dejection-related feelings when those shared self-guides were ideals, and they suffered agitation-related feelings when those shared self-guides were oughts. This highlights a troubling human vulnerability from our shared realities. It is a vulnerability that can tear us apart in a way that does not exist in other animals. By having shared self-guides with a significant other, simply meeting (or even just expecting to meet) a new person who resembles that significant other can activate a failure to meet the self-guides shared with that significant other, thereby causing us to suffer. And it need not be a new person. A person can have a romantic relationship with a partner who resembles one of their parents, and this can cause suffering if the person is failing to meet self-guides that are shared with that parent—even if they are not failing to meet shared self-guide with the current partner.

When people accept the goals and standards that significant others have for them, they use them to guide their goal pursuits, and they use them as well to evaluate their own performance, their own successes and failures. But that is not all. Standards that we share with significant others can also be used to evaluate other objects and events, how we feel about things that we observe and engage with in the world. For example, what counts as a good or great movie, or a good or great hamburger, often depends on our shared standards with others. Moreover, individuals can have different significant others who have different standards, and how they evaluate something can depend on which significant other is salient (accessible) at the time of evaluation.

There is a study that nicely illustrates this.[30] The participants in the study were undergraduate women. The women believed that they were participating in two separate studies when actually the first study was used to manipulate whether the significant other that was activated (primed) was "two older family members" or "two friends on campus." The ostensible purpose of the first study was to investigate "visualization." The participants were told to picture in their minds various scenes, people, and situations that they would discuss later. The people they were asked to visualize were either the "two older family members" or the "two friends on campus."

In the ostensible second study, a female experimenter gave the participants some passages to read, supposedly to determine what made passages interesting or enjoyable. The key passage was second, and it was a sexually permissive fiction story describing a woman having a sexual dream about a man she found attractive. After reading this passage, the participants were asked how much they liked it. The study found that how much the female participants liked the *same* passage depended on which significant other had been activated earlier. They liked it less when the "two older family members" were activated than when the "two friends on campus" were activated, reflecting a difference in standards of sexual permissiveness.

Moral Evaluations and Feelings

The previous study relates to a very important kind of standard used to evaluate behaviors and events—moral standards. Humans take a moral perspective on both our goals to pursue and our means for pursuing them. Robert Merton, a giant figure in 20th century sociology, noted: "Every social group invariably couples its cultural objectives with regulations, rooted in the mores or institutions, of allowable procedures for moving toward these objectives."[31] The "cultural objectives" are our acceptable goals, and the "allowable procedures" are our acceptable means. We have shared realities about what are the proper goals to pursue and what are the proper ways to pursue them.

Humans care so much about doing things in a *proper* way that it influences our feelings about things even when what is considered "proper" is not actually a moral issue. For example, what Americans consider to be the proper way to use a fork is different from how the British (and Europeans) use a fork. Americans use a fork in their right hand with the prongs facing upward. The British use a fork in their left hand with the prongs facing downward. How the British use a fork doesn't feel right to Americans. How Americans use a fork feels *really* wrong to the British. Indeed, when Americans are using a fork and a knife together, they typically use the fork in their left hand while cutting and then *switch* to using the fork in their right hand when eating. The British keep the fork in their left hand when cutting *and* when eating. That makes sense to them. To them, it feels like the "proper" way to do it, the "right" way to do it! But let's not make a moral issue out of this—which is my point because we often do.

By the way, I have read that the reason for this difference between Americans and the British has to do with early American settlers being poor. They could not afford the luxury of everyone at the table having their own knife. Each family had to share a single knife. The knife was passed around and each person, when it was his or her turn with the knife, cut all of the meat on the plate. Then, with all of the meat cut, only the fork remained to eat the meat. Given that most Americans were right-handed, it was easier to use the fork with the right hand. Now that makes sense. And it all happened because they were poor. Yet another reason not to make a moral issue out of this.

Well, we shouldn't make a big deal, never mind a moral issue, out of different shared realities concerning practices that are or are not experienced as the "proper" or "right" way to do something. But we do nonetheless. Consider what happened in a study my colleagues and I conducted at Columbia.[32] The participants were asked to express their preference between a Columbia coffee mug and an inexpensive pen. We were only interested in those participants who made the same choice—overwhelmingly the coffee mug, as intended. We wanted this because we wanted to examine how much they valued the *same* object that they chose—the coffee mug—as a function of whether their decision was or was not made in the "right" way.

Before the participants actually made their choice, they were randomly assigned to two different conditions that varied in what was emphasized about the decision. In one condition, the *outcome* of the decision was emphasized with the title, "The BEST CHOICE!" and the instructions: "The *best choice* is the choice with the better consequences." In the other condition, the *process* of the decision was emphasized with the title the "Right Way." It began with the title, "Making Your Decision in the RIGHT WAY!" and the instructions: "You need to make your decision in the *right way.*"

In both conditions, the instructions ended the same way: "Think of the positive and negative consequences of choosing the mug. Think of the positive and negative consequences of choosing the pen. Please write down your thoughts on the lines below." Thus, the specific actions asked of the participants were the same in both conditions. What varied was whether the outcome or the process was emphasized—these specific actions are about the *best* outcome or they are about the *right* process.

After they had considered the two options and expressed their preference for the mug, they were actually given, to their surprise, the opportunity to buy the mug—paid for with their own money. To assess how much they really valued the mug, a standard experimental economics method was used. They were shown an envelope and told that it contained the price of the mug. If the price they offered for the mug was less than the amount in the envelope, they would not get the mug. However, if the price they offered was more than or equal to the amount in the envelope, they would get the mug *for the price they offered.* The study found that the participants in the *Right Way* condition offered substantially more money to buy the same chosen mug than participants in the *Best Choice* condition.

And this was not all. The participants were also asked how much they agreed with cultural maxims about the importance of pursuing goals in a proper way, such as "The end does not justify the means" and "What counts is not whether you win or lose, but how you play the game." If participants' greater liking of the mug in the *Right Way* condition is because they care about doing things in the proper way, then this effect should be stronger for those participants who believe that it is important to pursue goals in a proper way. Indeed, the greater money offered to buy the mug in the *Right*

Way condition than the *Best Choice* condition was significantly higher for participants who had stronger beliefs in the importance of pursuing goals in a proper way.[33]

These findings are intriguing because the decision-making process that was described as the *right way* to make the choice was a proper process, but it was not a *morally* proper process. We have found, however, that there is considerable slippage in what people treat as moral. We have found, for example, that if people "feel right" about a decision they make because the means they used to make it was a fit with their motivational orientation, such as using eager (vs. vigilant) means when you have a promotion (vs. prevention) goal orientation, then they experience their decision as being *morally* right—"If it feels right, it *is* right."[34]

In sum, there are many different ways that shared reality can influence how we feel. To begin with, shared reality can determine which objects or events or behaviors in the world are relevant to us, which matter and which don't. Among those that do matter, shared reality can determine whether we experience something as being positive or negative. It can also determine which kind of positive experience we have (e.g., joy vs. peace) and which kind of negative experience we have (sad vs. anxious).

Moreover, these different kinds of positive and negative experiences can occur simply from meeting someone who minimally resembles one of our significant others with whom we share promotion ideal self-guides or prevention ought self-guides. We can have different feelings about an object or event depending on which of our significant others is salient or accessible at the moment. Shared self-guides can also influence how much compassion we feel for the different kinds of distress that other people experience. Finally, shared standards can intensify how much something feels right or feels wrong—not only for issues that are actually moral issues but also for issues that are not.

In all of these ways, our shared realities with others have a profound and pervasive effect on our life experiences. And our feelings are just the beginning. Our shared realities also impact what we believe and what we know. This aspect of what makes us human is considered next.

Notes

1. For a fascinating discussion of the effect of cooking on what humans can eat, see Wrangham (2009).

2. For an excellent review, see Shteynberg (2015).
3. See Baron-Cohen (1995) and Bruner (1983).
4. See Striano, Reid, and Hoehl (2006).
5. See, for example, Shteynberg and Apfelbaum (2013) and Shteynberg et al. (2014).
6. See Shteynberg (2018).
7. See Robson (2013).
8. See Robson (2013).
9. For discussions of these phenomena, see Eimas, Siqueland, Jusczyk, and Vigorito (1971), Kuhl (1983), and Werker and Tees (1984).
10. See Carpenter, Nagell, and Tomasello (1998), Moses, Baldwin, Rosicky, and Tidball (2001), and Mumme, Fernald, and Herrera (1996).
11. See Sorce, Emde, Campos, and Klinnert (1985).
12. See Henrich (2016).
13. See Brendl and Higgins (1996).
14. See Schmidt, Rakoczy, and Tomasello (2012).
15. This can also occur with harsher evaluations of a poor performance of an in-group member versus an out-group member—called the "black sheep effect." See Marques and Yzerbyt (1988).
16. See Schachter (1964) and Schachter and Singer (1962).
17. See Schachter (1959).
18. See Schachter (1959, p. 13). What a line! A classic Schachter-style manipulation.
19. See, for example, Higgins (1997) and Higgins and Cornwell (2016).
20. For fuller discussions of these promotion and prevention differences in psychological situations and emotions, see Higgins (1987, 1989a, 1989b, 1991, 1997, 2001).
21. For fuller discussions of these promotion and prevention differences in motivation, see Higgins (1997, 1998b).
22. See Houston (1990).
23. See Freud (1912/1958).
24. See, for example, Andersen and Baum (1994), Andersen and Berk (1998), Andersen and Cole (1990), Andersen, Glassman, Chen, and Cole (1995), and Berk and Andersen (2000).
25. See Andersen and Chen (2002) and Andersen, Reznik, and Glassman (2005).
26. See Andersen et al. (1995), Andersen and Cole (1990), and Glassman and Andersen (1999).
27. See Reznik and Andersen (2007).
28. Notably, for each participant given a new person with characteristics resembling his or her own parent, another participant was given that same new person but the characteristics did not resemble the parent of that participant (yoked control). The study found that the increases in negative emotions were greater in the "resemble own parent" condition than in the "not resemble own parent" condition, even though the new person's characteristics were the same in both conditions. This indicates that the effects on participants' feelings were not due to just the content of the new person's characteristics. What mattered was that the new person resembled a participant's

parent and that parent had either ideals or oughts for them that the participant was failing to fulfill.

29. See Shah (2003).
30. See Baldwin and Holmes (1987).
31. See Merton (1957, p. 133). See also Rokeach (1973) and Schwartz (1992).
32. See Higgins, Camacho, Idson, Spiegel, and Scholer (2008).
33. James March, a major figure in organizational decision-making, has proposed that pursuing goals in an appropriate or proper way has its own relation to value creation, separate from just hedonic outcomes (rational instrumentality). The findings from these studies support his proposal (March 1994) in a novel manner by showing that the chosen object itself can increase in monetary value when the decision is made in a proper way.
34. See Camacho, Higgins, and Luger (2003).

6

What We Know

It's More Than Meets the Eye

In the 1964 US Supreme Court case of *Jacobellis vs. Ohio,* a judgment needed to be made on whether a particular motion picture was or was not hard-core pornography (i.e., obscene). In a famous judgment, Supreme Court Justice Potter Stewart wrote the following statement to explain why he believed that the material at issue was *not* obscene:

> I shall not today attempt further to define the kinds of material I understand to be embraced within that shorthand description [hard-core pornography], and perhaps I could never succeed in intelligibly doing so. But *I know it when I see it*, and the motion picture involved in this case is not that.

Potter Stewart's phrase—"I know it when I see it"—has become history. But he did not invent the idea behind the phrase. Many of us think that we know *what* something is, what category it belongs to, because it has certain properties, even when we cannot clearly define what exactly are those properties. We think that our judgment that something is or is not a member of a category is because of *its* properties. It is *not* about *us*. "I know that's a banana because it is yellow and has a crescent-moon shape." Yes, that is what we think. But we can be wrong because our belief about what something is can be more about *us* than about the properties of the thing we are looking at. And not us as just our personal opinion, but us as sharing a reality with others. When it comes to our judgments, there is more than meets the eye because what we believe has its roots in our shared realities with others.

Before continuing, read the following story about a student called Sue:

> *Sue and I are college students at Columbia. One day we arranged to meet in front of Low Memorial Library. It was very sunny that morning when*

I walked slowly up to the library. I could recognize Sue from far away because I saw her blue jacket. We decided to go to a nearby café as both of us like pastry a lot. Then I was quite surprised to see Professor Jones, our political science professor, approaching us on our way to the café. He stopped to talk to us and mentioned how high the quality of Sue's paper was. Sue did not show any particular reaction. Maybe she had a bit of a smile on her face.

Do you have any clear impression of what kind of person Sue is? Most people do not. The story was intended to be very vague about her personality, and, indeed, for most people the information *is* very vague. But in one study, there were some participants who, nonetheless, had a clear impression that Sue was *conceited*. If you are not one of those people, this will seem quite surprising because there is very little evidence, if any, to support that conclusion.

Why did these participants conclude that Sue was conceited? They were individuals for whom the concept of "conceited" was highly accessible before they even read the story about Sue. It was highly accessible for a couple of reasons. First, before even reading the story about Sue, these participants had been exposed unobtrusively to words related to "conceited" (recent *verbal priming* of the concept "conceited"). Second, before the study itself, a measure of the chronic accessibility of different trait concepts had found that the trait "conceited" was chronically accessible for these particular participants.[1] When "conceited" was a chronically accessible trait for participants *and* they had been recently primed with "conceited," then they had the clear impression that Sue was conceited, without their being aware that their impression of Sue was influenced by the *prior* accessibility for them of the concept "conceited." No one else had this impression. And why would they have this impression given the lack of evidence for such a conclusion from the actual information they had received about Sue? Poor Sue, a victim of the high accessibility of a shared trait concept.

I have argued elsewhere that there is a fundamental bias in human judgment that I call the "aboutness" principle.[2] Basically, it means that when we make judgments, such as what kind of person someone is based on his or her behavior, we think that the source of that judgment is the information we have regarding that person—the judgment is *about* that person's behaviors. If you were to challenge people's judgment as to why they think that person is a certain kind of person, they would justify their judgment by referring to how that person behaved. It does not occur to us that the source of our judgment about someone could have nothing to do with the information we have regarding that person's behavior but, instead, have something to do with *us*, such as a trait concept that happens to be chronically accessible to us, a trait concept that happened to be recently primed, or, in this case, both.

What this and other research shows is that a judgment can actually be *about* the person making the judgment rather than the properties of the target being judged—in this case, the accessibility of the socially shared meaning of "conceited." Why does this matter? It matters because, as I discussed in Chapter 2, the meaning of words derives from our shared realities with others. When children learn symbolic names for things, they are learning shared realities about which names refer to which categories or concepts about things in the world. Soon children learn not only the names for objects but also the names for traits to characterize people. Because of this, exposure to a name will activate the trait concept, which can then be used to characterize a person despite there being little evidence to justify its application to that person—like characterizing Sue as conceited.

This effect of shared reality on what we know is basic to what makes us human. It adds to what I discussed in Chapter 1 as "sharing is believing." There I described how our memory for behaviors and events—what we believe about them later—is greatly influenced by what we say about them to our communication partners when trying to create a shared reality with them. This is an important part of the story regarding how shared reality impacts what we know, or at least what we think we know. Notably, as illustrated by the results from the "sharing-is-believing" studies and the accessibility effect of shared trait names that I have just described, these shared realities can produce distortions in judgment and memory.

In contrast to Chapter 1, this chapter concerns shared reality effects of how we represent objects and events in the world prior to our communicating about them. Our concepts *themselves* are shared realities with others, and what we see or don't see or what we believe or don't believe depends on the concepts that derive from our shared realities with others. What you know when *you* see *it* is not so much about *it* as it is about *you*, where the *you* is your repertoire of concepts that you have acquired as shared realities with others. And this repertoire can be activated not only by you but also by others through what is said to you (whether you are conscious of it or not), as happens with verbal priming. I will consider such effects in more detail next.

What We Believe from Prior Activation of Socially Shared Meanings

The behavioral description of Sue—"Sue did not show any particular reaction. Maybe she had a bit of a smile on her face"—is vague in that there is little evidence from the information given for making any categorization at all regarding what kind of person Sue is. This is different from the passage about Donald that was used in the "sharing-is-believing" studies that I discussed in Chapter 1. In those studies, the original descriptions of Donald's behaviors were evaluatively ambiguous in that there was good evidence for making either of two evaluatively opposite categorizations regarding Donald's personality. Consider, for example, the following descriptions from the Donald passage:

> *Other than business engagements, Donald's contacts with people were rather limited. He felt he didn't really need to rely on anyone. Once Donald made up his mind to do something it was as good as done no matter how long it might take or how difficult the going might be. Only rarely did he change his mind even when it might well have been better if he had. By the way he acted one could readily guess that Donald was well aware of his ability to do many things well.*

What is your impression of Donald? Often people have a mixed impression. This would make sense because the descriptions are, in fact, evaluatively ambiguous. Moreover, you might disambiguate one part of the passage in a positive direction and another part in a negative direction. And different people have different impressions.

What about the description of Donald in the very last sentence? Read it again. It is possible that for this description most of you have the same impression—that Donald is conceited. If so, this could be because you have already been exposed to the word "conceited"—and the trait concept associated with it—several times in this chapter. *Conceited* has been verbally primed for you. But for those who participated in the beginning pilot studies that tested how individuals respond to Donald, approximately half had the impression that Donald was *confident* rather than conceited. The first and second sentence descriptions are evaluatively ambiguous between "independent" and "aloof," and the third and fourth sentence description is the evaluatively ambiguous "persistent" or "stubborn" description that you have seen before.

The evaluatively ambiguous descriptions of Donald were not used only in the "sharing-is-believing" studies. They were also used in other studies to investigate, like the Sue study, what happens when participants are unobtrusively exposed to trait words (verbal priming) as part of one study and then later, in a supposedly unrelated study, read about someone's behaviors and form an impression of that person. In the original study investigating such verbal priming, participants performed a first task in which they were primed with either positive trait concepts or negative trait concepts that could be used in a later second task to characterize the behavioral descriptions of Donald that they were given to read.[3] They were told that the purpose of the first task was to examine the effects of information processing on perception. They were told to name, as quickly as possible, the background color of 10 different slides. Before each slide appeared, they heard a word that they had to repeat after naming the color of the slide (ostensibly to make the task more difficult). Embedded among these 10 words were the words related to either the positive trait concepts (e.g., "confident," "independent," "persistent") or the negative trait concepts (e.g., "conceited," "aloof," "stubborn").

After completing this task, the participants were taken to a separate room where a different experimenter gave them instructions for a "verbal comprehension" task. As part of this task, they read the passage about Donald. They were asked to characterize the descriptions of Donald. About two weeks later, they returned and were asked to rate how desirable they considered Donald to be. The study found that the participants did not have a mixed impression of Donald. Instead, they characterized him either with positive traits or with negative traits depending on whether they had been exposed earlier in the first task to the positive trait words or the negative trait words, respectively.[4] In addition, the participants who had been exposed to negative (vs. positive) trait concepts and had characterized Donald negatively had a more negative attitude toward him two weeks later.

All of the participants in this study read the *same* information about Donald. One might expect that different participants would have different impressions of him, including many having a mixed impression of him. But given random assignment and the ambiguity of the information, one would not expect there to be systematic differences between two groups of participants in their impressions of Donald simply because of a minor difference in what happened to them in an earlier unrelated study that had *nothing* to do with Donald. And one would certainly not expect their attitudes toward Donald to be different two weeks later.

Yes, one would not expect it, but that *is* what happened. By simply activating different shared concepts for evaluatively characterizing people as an incidental part of a different study, participants' initial impressions of Donald in a subsequent study, and their attitudes toward him two weeks later, were significantly different. This was not good news for Donald in the condition where participants were incidentally exposed to negative trait terms in the first study prior to their reading about him in the second study. Poor Donald, another victim of high accessibility of shared trait concepts.

In the study just described, the exposure to the shared trait concepts occurred in a prior situation that was separate from the situation where individuals formed an impression of Donald. This was why the effect was so surprising because the prior exposure to the shared trait concepts was logically irrelevant to the information about Donald and should not have influenced how Donald was perceived. In everyday life, however, the exposure to shared trait concepts or other shared concepts is not always irrelevant to perceiving the target. The exposure often comes in the form of hearing someone else's belief about a target that is expressed in terms of shared concepts. If we create a shared reality with this other person, as we are typically motivated to do, then we will perceive the target in terms of this shared reality.

Harold Kelley, a pioneer in experimental social psychology, conducted a classic demonstration of this type of shared reality effect.[5] The target persons, who were unknown to the participants, were substitute teachers for different sections of a course because the regular instructor was out of town. The managers of the course took the opportunity of having substitute teachers to study how different classes react to different instructors. The students were given some written introductory information to read about their new instructor. The information was the same for all students in the class, except that (randomly) half of the students in the class read the label "rather cold" about the instructor whereas the other half read the label "very warm," as follows:

Mr____ is a graduate student in the Department of Economics and Social Science here at M I T. He has had three semesters of teaching experience in psychology at another college. This is his first semester teaching Ec 70. He is

26 years old, a veteran, and married. People who know him consider him to be a [rather cold] [very warm] person, industrious, critical, practical, and determined.

The students did not know that different students in the class received different labels. Nor did the actual instructors. The instructors led the class in a 20-minute discussion. Afterwards, the students were asked to give their honest impression of their instructor and were told that this was not a test of him nor would it affect his future. The students who received the "rather cold" label perceived their instructor as being more formal, less sociable, less humorous, and even *less humane* than the students who received the "very warm" label. In each case, the *same* instructor who led the *same* class discussion was perceived very differently as a function of prior labeling that had nothing to do with the actual instructor or the discussion. The students created different shared realities about their instructor from having been exposed earlier to different labels about him, prior to and separate from their actual class with him. Their impressions of him, supposedly based on their class with him, were dramatically different. This certainly illustrates a downside of our motivation to create shared realities with others. Once again, it is bad news for the poor instructors whose students received the "rather cold" label before ever meeting him—less humane!?

The downside of our creating shared realities with others through accepting what others say about something is not restricted to our forming false impressions of other people. It occurs for objects and events in general. And, again, the effects can be dramatic. Elizabeth Loftus was a pioneer in bringing attention to how human memory in general, and eyewitness testimony in particular, can be faulty and biased.[6] This can occur from several sources, but one source is witnesses creating a shared reality about an event they saw with an interviewer who asks them questions about it.

In a classic study on eyewitness testimony,[7] participants viewed different films depicting traffic accidents. After watching each film, the participants were asked to give an account of the accident they had just seen and then answered a set of specific questions that included a question about the speed of the vehicles involved in the collision: "About how fast were the cars going when they hit each other?" In addition to some participants being exposed to the word "hit," other participants were exposed to the following alternative words: "smashed," "collided," "bumped," and "contacted." The participants' judgment of how fast the cars were going was 31.8 mph for "contacted" versus 40.8 mph for "smashed," with the judgments for the other labels falling in between.

In a second study, the participants were shown a film about a multiple car accident and then were either asked about the speed of the cars in the accident with the word "smashed" or the word "hit" or were not asked about speed at all (the control condition). The participants returned a week later and, without seeing the film again, were asked, "Did you see any broken glass?" The participants answered "Yes" or "No." There was, in fact, *no* broken glass in the filmed accident. As would be expected given that there was no broken glass, only about 10% of the participants in the control and "hit" conditions said "Yes." But in the "smashed" condition, almost one third of the participants said "Yes," despite there being no glass at all in the film.

This second study shows how, when the word "smashed" is used by another person and individuals share this characterization of the accident as being about cars smashing, an event can be remembered as including something that did not happen—the presence of broken glass. Again, this is not good news. It is especially not good news when you realize that it is often police officers or reporters, who did not even observe the event first hand, who first question a witness about what the witness saw. If a police officer or a reporter wants a particular answer—and this certainly can happen— then they can use the question they ask to bias what the witness remembers about what happened.

I should add that such questioning can not only directly bias what witnesses remember but also bias what witnesses *say* to tailor their answer to the questioner audience, which introduces audience tuning and additional biasing from the "sharing-is-believing" effect discussed in Chapter 1. Quite a mess for the truth. And the truth matters because whether or not a defendant is convicted in a trial, or even becomes a defendant in the first place, can depend on what a witness says happened.

It is not just questioning that can produce shared reality memory errors. Construction of false memories from simple exposure to what others have to say about an event can also produce shared reality memory errors. In one study,[8] for example, two participants looked at a book containing color pictures that told a crime story: *While two men are playing snooker, a woman is seen stealing one of their wallets. When the men entered the snooker hall she was also seen at the entrance door.* This depicted information was the same for all participants. What differed was that half of the participants were shown this woman standing alone, without an accomplice, whereas the other half saw her with a man, an accomplice.

When the participants were asked questions about the entire story, they initially remembered correctly this piece of information—whether they had seen the woman with or without an accomplice. After a five-minute delay, dyads (or pairs) of participants, with one participant having seen an accomplice and the other *not* having seen an accomplice, were asked to describe, together, what happened as if they were describing it to a police officer, concentrating on the sequence of events and the actions of the different characters. They then answered questions about the story, including whether the woman did or did not have an accomplice. Despite the fact that the information the dyad saw was different regarding this issue, and this was evident from their earlier individual answers on this issue, the two converged in their memory (beliefs) about what happened. Instead of the dyads having no agreement, which should have been what happened given their difference in either seeing or not seeing an accomplice, there was almost 80% agreement on this issue after their conversation together—a remarkable example of "social contagion" from creating a shared reality.

There is also evidence that the social contagion effect on others is greater for more dominant members of a conversation. The participants in one study,[9] for example, read four short stories that each contained different details, such as one story about an extramarital affair that included a different detail about where the couple actually met (e.g., in a bar, in a steakhouse, in a café). Then they individually recalled the story. The next day the two group members, who were unrelated, met each other and had a chance to get to know each other. They then recalled together two of the stories. Afterwards they were given a recognition probe to test whether they would remember a detail that was not in the story they read but was in the story that the other group member read, such as where the couple met.

The major measure was such recognition errors—*false memories*—that could be traced back to the conversation that the participants had together. The study found that, indeed, participants remembered falsely a detail that was not in their story but was mentioned in the conversation by their partner when that partner told the story the day before. The study also found that the major contribution to this effect came from the group member who most dominated the conversation—the stronger the narrators, the more their partner had false memories that were in line with what these narrators said. Thus, the dominant conversationalists contributed most to the creation of a shared reality by the dyad—a shared reality, it should be noted, that was not contained in the information their partner actually received.

Socially Shared Meanings: The Case of Stereotypes

Thus far I have discussed how exposure to words that refer to shared concepts can bias our impressions, attitudes, and memory of particular people and events in our lives. The impact of our shared realities on our beliefs and what we know about the world is even greater than this, however. We create shared realities with others about what members of categories are like even *without* our having direct evidence for these beliefs. From these shared realities we *know* what category members are like, and then when we meet a new instance of that category, we believe that this instance has the typical characteristics of category members despite having no evidence for this belief. This effect from shared realities can be very beneficial—and it can be very costly as well.

Let's begin with the benefits. Imagine if everything that you perceived and interacted with in the present was experienced by you as being something new and *unique*. You could not connect your present experiences to your past experiences because all of these experiences are unique. *There would be no learning*. And for humans, like other animals, it is *essential* that we learn from our past experiences. To do so, we must connect current instances to some past instances and treat them as being related to one another, as being similar in some way. We need to develop categories of things in the world. And a major contributor to our doing this is our interactions with significant others who indicate in some way, most often with names, that some present instance is a member of a particular category whose instances you have encountered in the past.

This is highly beneficial because, by learning about the specific characteristics of each category, when you encounter a new instance of the category you can infer that it possesses the typical characteristics of that category without the need for direct evidence of those additional characteristics for this particular instance. You can go to the market, for example, and buy an instance of a "banana" and believe that, when you get home, it will taste like a banana and give you the energy-boosting benefits of a banana without having to eat the banana in the store to check. This is a blessing. Another blessing is assuming a "bartender" will take your order for a Stoli martini (extra dry, with a twist) and return with the drink you like (although I have found that the "extra dry" doesn't work in every country).

Speaking of bartenders, of major importance among our shared categories is our shared *social* categories like "bartender." A few of our social categories are universal like "baby," but many are not, like "bartender" (unfortunately). And having shared social categories where you know the characteristics of its members is again very beneficial. We know generally what to expect of a new instance of a social category without knowing anything other than his or her membership in that social category. And it is not only bartenders but also teachers, bus drivers, librarians, nurses, firemen, waitresses, and so on.

In sum, there is an essential benefit from acquiring our shared categories. But there is a downside as well. We can believe that all instances are similar enough that they can be treated the same way. We lose sight about what is *special* about each instance. "Oh, there's another sunset" rather than "Wow! Look at *that* sunset!" And when it comes to social categories, failing to recognize what is special about each instance of the category—what is special about each member of a social category—is especially problematic. Treating individuals as "just another waitress" or "just another librarian" can be insulting to a person and undermines our social fabric. Individuals deserve to be treated as more than just another member of their social category.

The worst case of treating individual members of a social category as being just like every other member of that category is *social stereotyping*. We all have a poor opinion of stereotyping others. But why exactly? Is it only bad for the reasons I just described? And that would be bad enough. But is there something else that we should be concerned about?

Years ago, Roger Brown, who made pioneering contributions to both psycholinguistics and sociolinguistics, addressed this issue brilliantly. My analysis is based on his analysis. In his landmark book, *Words and Things*,[10] he began with the standard criticism of social stereotypes, such as stereotypes in the 1930s about Jews and Germans, that they are generalizations that overlook individual differences within a social category. He pointed out, however, that all categories are generalizations that overlook differences among instances, like our previous "banana" example. If that's a problem, it is not unique to social stereotypes, although it *is* more problematic for how we treat members of a social category than how we treat members of the "banana" category. Yes, more problematic for a social category, but still not the real problem.

The next step in the argument was that the problem with stereotyping is not that there is a generalization but that the generalization is false. The problem here is what one means by being false. Is one instance that disconfirms what is claimed about category members in general sufficient to conclude that the generalization is false? We all know that dogs bark. Barking characterizes dogs. But hang on. What about the Basenji dog that does not bark? And what about the penguin bird that doesn't fly? Oh, *now* I get it. Saying dogs bark and birds fly is just stereotyping them, and it is in terribly bad taste. It is terribly unfair to Basenjis and penguins. *Really*, that is why stereotyping is a problem?

Well, we could always deal with a few exceptions, and Brown goes on to the next argument that stereotyping is not a problem because there is false generalizing to particular instances where it does not apply. Rather, it is a problem because we believe that some characteristic is much more preva-lent in a category than it actually is. This is the kind of argument that says, "Yes, there might be a kernel of truth, but you are claiming much more than a kernel. You make it sound like it is more often true than false, and this is not the case." But how big must the kernel be for there not to be a problem? And what evidence is there to justify that the kernel is big enough or not big enough?

Yes, making a characteristic sound much more prevalent in a social cat-egory than is justified by the evidence *is* a problem, and especially when it involves a *negative* characterization of category members. This is a serious shared reality problem that we have: overgeneralizing about negative char-acteristics of a social category when most members of the category do not possess that characteristic or do not possess it to any greater extent than the members of other social categories. But is this *the* fundamental problem of stereotyping? Brown argues that none of these issues is, fundamentally, what makes stereotyping a problem. I agree with him. There is, indeed, something else going on that is even more disturbing.[11]

The fundamental problem is that often there are characteristics in-cluded in the stereotype that do not describe category members to begin with. They are *not descriptions*. They are just opinions and feelings about members of a social category, but they are *treated as if* they represent actual knowledge or facts about them. Being both a Canadian and an American citizen, here is my example of this. There are reports that Americans, on average, shower six or more times a week, whereas Canadians, on average, shower five times a week. Americans and Canadians are *both* outraged to learn about this. American now know that they were right to believe that Canadians are "grimy." Canadians now know that they were right to believe that Americans are "wasteful."

Each group believes that what they now know about each other is simply descriptive: It's just the facts and only the facts. But it's not. The facts are only how often each group showers or bathes each week. Period. Each group is taking a fact and then evaluating it in relation to their own standards of how to behave. The evaluation itself cannot be proven or disproven because it goes beyond the facts themselves. The label applied to the other group represents an opinion, a feeling based on a standard of evaluation that is shared by Americans or is shared by Canadians. It is not knowledge, although it is treated as such. And each group considers its own shared standards to be the *right* standards. This is *ethnocentrism*. It is ethnocentrism that is the problem with stereotypes.

When judgments about out-group others derive from shared in-group standards, which are biased in favor of the in-group, they constitute stereotyping as ethnocentrism. That is why it is a serious problem. And such shared ethnocentric realities *are* definitely a problem. By the way, if I shower five times one week and seven times on another week, I will be "grimy" to Americans one week and "wasteful" to Canadians the other week. Ethnocentric shared realities can be annoying—and obviously worse than annoying.

If stereotypic beliefs about social categories include evaluations of category members in relation to specific shared standards, then individuals can have different beliefs about a social category at different times depending on which standard is salient or accessible at the time. When I am home in the United States, for example, I don't believe that showering or bathing five times a week is wasteful. But this could depend on my wanting to connect to other Americans because creating shared realities with others is motivated by social relational motives, by wanting to be connected to others. There is evidence for this kind of social relational effect for positive or negative beliefs about African Americans.

In one study, for example, with White undergraduate participants and experimenters,[12] the experimenter either wore an *antiracism* shirt that had the letters "Eracism" written on it or wore a shirt of the same color with no lettering on it. Liking for the experimenter was also manipulated by having the experimenter either thank the students for participating and telling them that out of appreciation she brought some candy for them (friendly) or move the candy away and tell the students that she thinks they are lucky just to get credit for participating (rude). The participants were then given a computer task measuring prejudice against African Americans where they were asked to press as quickly as possible one key when they recognized the word *good* and another key when they recognized the word *bad*. Unbeknownst to them, pictures of either White or Black faces appeared subliminally prior to their seeing the words.

Prejudice was indicated by responding more quickly to the word *good* than the word *bad* after subliminal exposure to a White face and responding more quickly to the word *bad* than the word *good* after subliminal exposure to a Black face. The study found that there was no difference in prejudice responses between exposure to the antiracism shirt versus the blank shirt when the experimenter had been rude to participants. But when the experimenter had been friendly to participants, there was significantly less prejudice—indeed, no prejudice—when the experimenter wore the antiracism shirt versus the blank shirt. Thus, when the experimenter was likable such that participants would feel connected to her and want to create a shared reality with her, the standard that she endorsed (i.e., antiracism) was adopted (unconsciously) by the participants as reflected in their no longer sharing the evaluative belief that Blacks are bad.

By the way, it was Roger Brown again who, over half a century ago, first brought attention to the fact that the same object can be categorized in multiple ways with each alternative being a *correct* alternative rather than a competing alternative. In his classic paper, "How Shall a Thing Be Called?" he highlighted that there are hierarchical options for every target object.[13] His example was the option of calling what is in your pocket "a 1952 dime," "a dime," "money," "a metal object," or even "a thing." There are clearly many possible names, and they are all correct. Which name should be used to create the right shared reality with others? Brown points out that despite there being multiple alternatives, many objects are given the same name by the entire community, such as a spoon typically being called a "spoon" rather than "silverware" or something else it could be called, such as "a metal object." Our shared reality is that this object should be called "spoon," and this is because when interacting together what matters is distinguishing a spoon from other silverware such as a fork or a knife. Our shared reality is to use the name that allows us to work together effectively by best distinguishing something from alternatives.

Using the name that is best for distinguishing an object from alternative objects typically creates a useful shared reality when interacting with others. But not always. Referring to someone simply by their ethnicity name is troubling because it sends the message that what matters about this person is their ethnic social category membership in contrast to all the other social categories to which they belong. When people refer to a Black psychology professor simply as "Black," it sends the message that the distinction that matters about this person is that he is Black instead of White, rather than, for example, that he is a professor instead of an airline pilot, or, at a lower level in the hierarchy, that he is a psychology professor rather than a physics professor. The shared reality that is created from choosing a particular ethic name when there are legitimate alternative names is clear: What is important about this person is that he is Black and not White. This is another example of the downside of what can happen when we create shared realities with others.[14]

Constructing Shared Beliefs from Interactions with Others

Thus far, I have discussed how our shared knowledge about the world, including our shared word meanings and shared social categories, can, when they are activated, influence what we believe and know about particular individuals and events that we observe. But where does such shared knowledge come from to begin with? In Chapters 2 and 3, I discussed developmental sources of such shared knowledge, and in Chapter 8, I will discuss more about how different kinds of caretaker–child interactions contribute to acquired shared goals and standards in particular.

When these adult–child interactions occur, children recognize that the older adults know more about how the world works than they do, and thus it makes sense for children to choose to follow the adults' lead regarding what to feel and what to believe.[15] But when an adult confronts a new situation with other adults for whom the situation is also new, who should they believe—themselves or others? Should they believe what they see, or should they try to create a shared reality with others? This was the fundamental question that Muzafer Sherif, a pioneer in the early history of social psychology, asked in his research on social norm construction.

Social Norm Construction

I described in Chapter 4 the studies by Sherif on how individuals' judgments of the movement of a light become more and more similar over time (i.e., converge) until they construct a group norm about the movement of the light. And this happens despite the fact that the light is actually stationary—does not move at all. It was the observers' saccadic eye movements in the completely dark room that made the stationary light appear to move.[16]

This research nicely illustrates how, when it comes to our beliefs, there is more than meets the eye—literally in this case, given that the light was stationary. What is going on here? It is surprising that each of these men gradually gave up their personal opinion about the light's movement, changing their judgment to be more like the judgments of the other group members, despite the fact that there was no evidence that their judgment was any less accurate than the others' judgments. Indeed, the others' judgments were *false* because each of them said that the light moved when it didn't. This choice to give up your personal opinion—one that you have previously held over many trials—to move closer to others' judgments, without any evidence that supports their judgments, is not just surprising. For many people, it is also troubling. In fact, such a choice is labeled with a derogatory term—both popularly and in most social psychology textbooks. It is called *conformity*. Conformity is seen as a sign of weakness, as giving up basic principles like "tell the truth" and "stick to your guns" just to curry favor with others or avoid rejection.

For many people, then, Sherif's research reveals a downside of human nature. Regarding shared reality, it suggests that people's desire to share reality with others—to have a common belief about something—is so strong that they will go along with others' beliefs even in the absence of any evidence to support those beliefs. And, yes, that *is* a potential downside of our human desire to share reality with others. The motivation to create a shared reality with others can lead us to accept something as true that is, in fact, *not* true. It can lead us to accept others' opinions less critically than we should, treat false "alternative facts" as the truth.

But this potential downside of what happened in this study is not the whole story. And, from my perspective, it does not justify calling people "conformists." Indeed, there is an upside of being human that is also part of this story that deserves attention—more attention than it gets in most social psychology textbooks. For Sherif, this research was not about "conformity." The word *conformity* does not even appear in his book. Instead, for him, the results illustrate how *group norms* are created from a convergence in judgments. And group norms are critical to the functioning of human societies. Effective cooperation and coordination among humans, especially in large societies, require the presence and use of social norms. And, yes, these social norms can be arbitrary like the agreement within a linguistic community about the word sound pattern to use to name a particular object, like using the word "dog" to name that four-legged furry animal that barks and fetches sticks as English speakers do. The choice of name is arbitrary, and it is not based on evidence. It is just a social norm. But this shared reality about the names of objects and events is extremely useful within a linguistic community for coordinating communicative interactions.

This analogy to the use of words in linguistic communities becomes even stronger when further results of the Sherif studies are considered. The research found that the group norm for how much the light moved was different for different groups, just like different linguistic communities have different social norms about the names of things. Also consistent with the notion that the common group judgment functioned like a norm, when the individuals subsequently made *private* judgments without the others being present, they tended to stick with the group's judgment rather than return to their original pregroup judgment. For an English speaker, the name of that animal remains "dog" even in private.

Subsequent research by others provided additional evidence that the common group judgment created in Sherif's studies functions the same way as do regular norms, like the names for things.[17] When the original members of a group were replaced, one at a time, by new participants until there were no longer any members of the original group (i.e., a totally new generation of group members), this new group maintained the original group's judgment of the light's movement. And, impressively, this persistence in group judgment continued over several generations of replacing all the members of a group. It is like new generations of English speakers, generation after generation, still using the word *dog* for that four-legged furry animal that barks and fetches sticks.[18]

Yes, there is a downside of our human motivation to create shared realities with others through constructing social norms. The creation of a group norm can result in our having false beliefs like the false beliefs in the Sherif study about the movement of the light and false beliefs about the nature of the physical world (flat earth anyone?) or the spiritual world (tree spirit anyone?). But the creation of group norms also has enormous benefits, like the benefits for interpersonal communication from agreeing about the meaning of those arbitrary word sound patterns. And, generally speaking, norms reflecting group consensus are generally adaptive. Most important, as Sherif said when discussing social rules and social products such as language, humans "cannot help producing rules, customs, values and other sorts of norms whenever they come together in a situation that lasts for any considerable time."[19] Creating shared realities in the form of group norms is neither simply bad nor simply good—it is simply what we do as humans.

What this research on social norm construction illustrates is the basic process by which people work together to create a shared belief about something in the world. This process of co-construction is a major way that we acquire shared knowledge of the world. And what is so important about this research is that it also illustrates how the same process can even occur when constructing a shared belief that is factually *false*, because the shared belief about the light's movement has to be false given that the light is actually stationary. Nonetheless, it is believed. Similarly, we can create false shared beliefs about the natural world, such as the world being flat, and shared false beliefs about the supernatural world, such as children's shared belief in Santa Claus or adults' belief that finding a four-leaf clover brings good luck.

By the way, my wife and I worked to maintain (helped create?) our daughter Kayla's belief in Santa Claus. She never saw the Santa presents until Christmas morning when they were all wrapped simply in thin red tissue paper and were all together in their own pile that was separate from the presents that we gave her as her parents. Our presents to her were wrapped in thicker multicolor wrapping paper with ribbons and bows. On occasion we would even refuse as parents to give her what she told us she most wanted for Christmas, such as the new pink Barbie car, but to her amazement and delight Santa, apparently, knew what she wanted and gave her the new Barbie car. When she opened it, screamed out in glee and then, finally, turned hesitantly to look at us, we shook our heads gently and gave her a weak, resigned look that said, "Ok, you can keep it given that it's from Santa." That kept her believing in Santa for a few more years.

Why all this trouble to create for our daughter the experience of a shared belief that Santa Claus is real? Because when you are a child it is a joy to believe that there is a very special and magical person who cares about you and wants to make you happy. And later when you learn that Santa is really Mommy and Daddy, you realize how much they love you and want to make you happy. They may not be as special and magical as Santa, but they are there for you all the time and not just at Christmas.

I should note that convergence of group members toward a group norm is not restricted to convergence in group members' judgment about something. There can also be convergence toward a group norm about the *strategy* that underlies group members' judgments. Rather than being about the judgment itself, the norm is about what strategy to use when making a judgment. In one study, for example, the participants performed a recognition memory task where they are shown a set of target stimuli and then later are shown one stimulus at a time that either was in the target set ("old") or was not in the target set ("new"). They can make a judgment error either by saying "old" to a "new" stimulus that was not in the target set, which is called a "false alarm," or by saying "new" to an "old" stimulus, which is called a "miss."

Prior research[20] had shown that promotion-focused individuals in this task are inclined to say "old," which is strategically risky (or lenient), because they prefer a "false alarm" error rather than miss an "old" stimulus. For them, to miss an "old" stimulus would be an error of omission, which is like a negative nongain. In contrast, prevention-focused individuals in this task are inclined to say "new," which is strategically conservative, because they prefer a "miss" rather than a "false alarm." For them, a "false alarm" would be an error of commission, which is like a negative loss.

The new study examined the decision strategies of different groups who were given a recognition memory task.[21] Either a promotion focus or a prevention focus was experimentally induced in *all* of the members in each group, thereby creating promotion groups and prevention groups. The study found that the members of the promotion group *converged* over time toward making risky choices whereas the members of the prevention group converged over time toward making conservative choices. Note that by the end of the task the members of each group shared a judgmental strategy, with the shared judgmental strategy being different for the promotion and prevention groups, *and* the shared judgment strategy was a judgmental *bias*. Once again, a shared reality need not be correct.

Establishing Truth with Unanimous Others

The *co*-construction of shared realities, like what happened in Sherif's studies, is one way that we create shared realities with others. Having parents tell us how the world works, and accepting what they say (think Santa Claus), is another. A third way is to hear the unanimous consensus of several other persons about something.

A study using the "sharing-is-believing" paradigm described in Chapter 1 provides an example of this third way. Participant communicators learned that their audience seemed to like or seemed to dislike a (male) target person before reading a passage that described his behaviors. All of the communicators prepared to communicate, but only half of them ended up doing so (there was a supposed technical glitch for the other half). As had been found in previous standard studies when the audience is a single person,[22] knowing about the audience's attitude toward the target person impacted communicators' memory for the target person when the communicators actually went on to produce a message for their audience but *not* when they did not go on to produce a message. Message production was necessary for the memory effect to occur.

However, something different happened when the audience was not a single person but, instead, was three people who were unanimous in either liking the target person (*all three* liked him) or disliking the target person (*all three* disliked him). [23] In this case, there was a direct effect on memory of the unanimous audience attitude even when no message was produced. Message production was no longer necessary for the memory effect to occur. The unanimous opinion of other people about the target was enough for participants to create a shared reality with them about whether he was likable or dislikable. This, in turn, impacted memory for the target's behaviors, with participants' memory being distorted to evaluatively match the attitude.

In this study, like previous "sharing-is-believing" studies, the behavioral descriptions of the target person were evaluatively ambiguous. In Sherif's studies, the information about the target light's "movement" was also unclear. Thus, this raises the question whether shared reality occurred in these cases because the individuals in these studies were confused or uncertain about what the truth is. There was no strong conflict between what an individual believed to begin with and what was being expressed by others because it was unclear what was, in fact, the correct answer. But what would happen if the correct answer *was* clear? Would people still move their belief in the direction of the group norm? Would they change their belief to create a shared reality with others?

I mentioned before in Chapter 1 that Leon Festinger argued that people only look to social reality for the truth when their belief in physical reality is weak.[24] From this perspective, people should not change their belief to create a shared reality with others when the correct answer is clear. This was what Solomon Asch, another great pioneer of experimental social psychology, also thought might be the case. So he investigated it.[25]

In the standard study, there is a group of seven to nine students who gather together in a classroom. They are told that they will be shown lines differing in length, and their task is to match a standard line with one of three other comparison lines that they are shown. What this task looks like is shown in the following figure. Which comparison line matches the standard line? Is it line 1, line 2, or line 3? That seems easy enough—except that Asch adds a twist to the study.

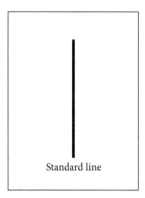
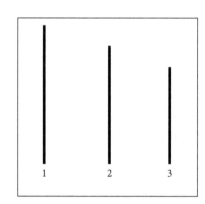

It turns out that there is only one actual participant among the group of seven to nine students. All the other students present in the room are confederates working with the experimenter. In addition, the students are seated in such a way that the real participant is always the last person to give his answer on each trial. The session begins in a straightforward manner with all of the confederates always giving the correct answer, which is also the participants' answer. Everything starts off fine. But then trouble begins. On some trials, beginning with the third trial, all of the confederates (unanimously) give the *same, incorrect* judgment about which of the comparison lines is the same length as the standard line. Referring to the figure, it would be as if they *all* said that line 3 is the correct answer.

On these conflict trials (i.e., conflict between the correct answer and the confederates' unanimous incorrect answer), sometimes the difference in length between the line unanimously chosen by the confederates and the line that was the correct answer was large (i.e., an easy discrimination) and sometimes it was small (i.e., a difficult discrimination). But, notably, control subjects who performed the task alone and did not hear anyone else's answer, almost always got the correct answer (92% of them got, on average, 94% correct), and they did well even on the more difficult trials. Thus, the discrimination in some cases was not easy but it was still easy enough to get the right answer. This means that when there were conflict trials in the group experiment, the real participants *felt conflict* between what they believed was the correct answer and what the others in the group were unanimously saying was the correct answer. It also means that the correct answer was clear enough from physical reality. With Festinger in mind, there was no need to turn to social reality for help because physical reality was clear enough.

So what did the experimental participants do on these conflict trials? On every conflict trial, including on the easier trials, there were some participants who gave the incorrect answer that was expressed unanimously by all the others in the group. Overall, the experimental participants gave incorrect answers on the critical trials one third of the time—more than *five times* as much as the control subjects who performed the task alone!

Asch's findings upset many people. Once again, they were taken as evidence that people are conformists, unable to stand by the truth when pressured by others. Once again, this became a story about weak and wishy-washy humans. But I believe there is something else going on here. So did Asch.

The issue is that most people, and social psychology textbooks, represent what happened as the participants in the group condition knowing the truth and being unwilling to stand up for it—caving in. But did they know *the* truth? They had no idea that the other students were confederates. You knew, but they didn't. From their perspective, they heard the independent judgments of several separate individuals, and these individuals *all* agreed that a particular answer was the correct answer. Given that other people are honest and trustworthy, which the participants would believe about these other students, then their stated beliefs deserve to be taken seriously. And the participants *did* take them seriously. As Asch says, "doubt sets in,"[26] and participants displayed a touching sense of humility, such as the following report by one of them: "I doubt that so many people could be wrong and I alone right."[27]

What this means is that they don't know that what they thought was the correct answer is, *in fact*, the truth. It is not that they are unwilling to stand up for the truth. Rather, they are no longer sure what the truth is, and they are willing to trust other honest people who, unanimously, know what the truth is. This is not conformity. It is part of the motivation to create a shared reality with others. It has the significant upside of humility and trust and respect for others. It is, indeed, how we learn correct beliefs about the world from others.[28]

I began this chapter with the story of Sue as an initial example of "there is more than meets the eye." Beyond what you see, there are our shared realities. The Asch findings also illustrate this. Beyond what *you* see, there are our shared realities with *others*. We learn from others what lies beyond what we can see. What we believe and know about the world is not re- stricted to what we perceive. Until recently thanks to space travel, we could not *see* the shape of the earth. Now we can see a beautiful blue marble. Notably, our most significant beliefs concern things that are not directly observable or could ever be observed. Learning about such things from others that otherwise we would never know is a major upside of shared reality.

As I discussed in Chapter 2, *learning from others* is essential for children's development, as well as adults' development. And children, as well as adults, not only are willing to learn from others. They *seek out* others to learn from. Moreover, children, as well as adults, seek out others *to teach* what they know that they believe is not known by these others, such as there is some- thing worth looking at that is sitting on the tree branch over there. Being teachers and learners is essential to what makes us human. It can also be a downside, however, as it was in Asch's study, when we create a shared be- lief about something as being true when it is actually *false*. There are many versions of this downside of false beliefs learned from trusted others, and some of them produce very serious problems indeed. They will be discussed further in Chapter 7 regarding false beliefs about ourselves.

Before leaving this section, I do want to say something more about Asch. I had lunch with him many years ago, and he told me that he was very upset about how others had interpreted his findings. He had conducted this research soon after the end of World War II. Because of Americans' perceptions of the Nazis being "mindless followers" of Hitler and because Americans believed in "rugged individualism," they were disgusted by any behavior that looked like "conformity" to pressures from others. "Stand up and be counted." Many people, including social psychologists, had nothing but contempt for those in Asch's experiment who gave the incorrect answer on the conflict trials. But Asch saw them very differently. He saw them struggling for the truth. And it was a struggle because they trusted the other students and believed that they were saying what they honestly believed. They tried their best to find the truth, with the motivation to create a shared reality being a powerful force on them.[29] Asch was so upset at how these student participants were insulted in academic publications and scientists' inability to see them humanely, that he quit social psychology and worked instead on learning in rats. Hearing this from Asch was painful for me— what a tragedy for social psychology to lose such a brilliant scientist in this way.

Communication Chains That Establish Relevance

I described in Chapter 1 how dyadic communication can influence what people end up believing and knowing—the "sharing-is-believing" effect. But the effects of communication on what is believed and what is known is not restricted to a single conversation between just two people. Whatever one person tells a second person, that second person will then tell a third person, and that third person will tell a fourth person, and so on and so on. We know this is how gossip works and how rumors are transmitted. We know that this is what humans love to do all the time. And we also know that whatever was the original information that was talked about, by the end of the communication chain, it is no longer the same.

The first person to study this phenomenon scientifically was Frederic Bartlett, a pioneer in studying social forces in reconstructing memories. In his classic book, *Remembering*,[30] he introduces his "method of serial reproduction." Person A reads an original story and then reproduces it, and then person B reads Person A's reproduction and reproduces it, and then Person

C reads Person B's reproduction and reproduces it, and so on over many different people.

As others found afterwards about rumor transmission generally,[31] Bartlett found that the story slowly changes as different people reproduce it. It becomes simpler over time, losing the title and some other details for example. But, most important, the story is changed to become more meaningful to the audience. This can include adding a moral message that would be significant within the participants' community, such as advocating about how family members should behave toward one another.

Consider the story with the title *The Son Who Tried to Outwit His Father*. The story begins with a son simply saying to his father one day: "I will hide, and you will not be able to find me." He changes himself into a kernel of a peanut, which then is swallowed by a fowl that is eaten by a cat that is eaten by a dog that is swallowed by a python that was caught in a fish trap. The father finds the python and opens up everything inside until he reaches the peanut, breaks the shell, and reveals his son. The story then ends: "The son was so dumbfounded that he never again tried to outwit his father."[32]

By the 20th reproduction,[33] the title is gone and now the story begins: "A small boy, having got into some kind of mischief, wished to hide himself from his father." The endless swallowing remains in the story, as does the father cutting up the python and everything within it to reveal his son. Now the story ends: "The son was overjoyed at seeing his father once more, and promised that he would never again conceal anything from him. He said that he would submit to the punishment he deserved, whatever his crime might be." Huh, where did that come from? We now have a morality tale to tell our children. It advocates a shared reality norm similar to the fifth commandment: *Honor thy father and thy mother*. Well, come to think of it, not a bad idea.

Thanks to the important work of Kashima and his colleagues that has extended and elaborated on Bartlett's work,[34] we now know much more about the dynamic process whereby social knowledge in general, and social stereotypes in particular, are strengthened and maintained through communication chains. One study,[35] for example, investigated whether the known tendency for stereotype-consistent information to be retained better than stereotype-inconsistent information over a communication chain was due to the "sharedness" of the stereotype-consistent knowledge across the communicators. The study also considered whether or not only the actual sharedness mattered but also the *perceived* sharedness.[36]

The participants first learned about a fictitious group, the Jamayans. They learned that the Jamayans live in a village on an island. They then learned what kind of people they were like as a group. This was used to create stereotype-like characterizations of the group, such as their being intelligent and honest and preferring to eat only fruits and vegetables. Following this information characterizing the group members as a whole, they read a story with a main character who was a specific member of the group and behaved in some ways that were consistent with the group-level category and in other ways that were inconsistent.

After reading the story, participants retold the story in writing for another participant to read. The subsequent communication chain consisted of four participants. No one knew which position they were in this chain. Actual sharedness was manipulated by either having all participants in each chain position read the same passage (actual shared knowledge) or read different passages from one to the next participant (actual unshared knowledge). Perceived sharedness was manipulated by telling participants that their audience would receive the same passage that they read (perceived shared knowledge) or would not receive the same passage (perceived unshared knowledge).

Not surprisingly, the effect of there being greater memory for the stereotype-consistent than inconsistent information was greater in the actual shared condition than the actual unshared condition because unshared information would disrupt the flow of information in the communication chain. However, and interestingly, the stereotype-consistency bias appeared in the *perceived unshared* knowledge condition but not in the perceived shared knowledge condition. What is going on here?

If communicators' message tuning is motivated by their wanting to create a shared reality with their audience, then they don't need to tune their message when they believe that they already have a shared reality with their audience (i.e., the perceived shared knowledge condition). But if they believe that they do not already have a shared reality with their audience (i.e., the perceived unshared knowledge condition), then they must tune their message to achieve this. And they do, by telling a story in their reproduction that *strengthens the stereotype knowledge* about the Jamayans that they are sharing. Once again, this illustrates a downside of our motivation to create shared realities with others.

This chapter has reviewed evidence for how people's beliefs and knowledge about objects, people, and events in the world are influenced by our shared realities with others. These studies clearly demonstrate that what we believe and what we know is more than meets the eye. Instead, it depends on constructed shared realities. There is another kind of knowledge that is very important to each of us that also involves constructed shared realities—our *self-knowledge*. Here too, it is not about physical and behavioral evidence. It is about socially constructed realities from interactions with others. This significant shared reality is considered next in Chapter 7.

Notes

1. See Higgins and Brendl (1995). A trait concept is considered to be chronically accessible for an individual if, when asked "What kind of people do you like?" "What kind of people do you dislike?" "What kind of people do you approach?" "What kind of people do you avoid?" and "What kind of people do you frequently encounter?" that individual spontaneously mentions that trait (e.g., conceited) frequently when answering these questions and the trait appears early among those traits that are mentioned (a frequency and recency measure of accessibility).
2. See Higgins (1998a).
3. See Higgins, Rholes, and Jones (1977).
4. To check on any possible demand effects, participants were asked to help us out by telling us whether there was *anything* about the first task that could have influenced what happened in the second task so we could change the procedure to avoid such problems. Only one participant noticed anything about the first task that related to the second task. The data from this participant were removed from the analysis.
5. See Kelley (1950).
6. See Loftus (2005).
7. See Loftus and Palmer (1974).
8. See Wright, Self, and Justice (2000).
9. See Cuc, Ozuru, Manier, and Hirst (2006).
10. See Brown (1958b).
11. I should note that there is some disagreement about how accurate or inaccurate stereotypes are—what is the size of the kernel of truth (for a review, see Jussim, Crawford, & Rubinstein, 2015). This is an important issue, but, as you will see, I do not believe that it is the fundamental problem about stereotypes because an accurate expression of your opinion about members of a social category is not the same as an accurate description of those people.
12. See Sinclair, Lowery, Hardin, and Colangelo (2005).
13. See Brown (1958a).
14. Notably, it would be different if the person was referred to as a "Black psychology professor" rather than just "Black" because this could highlight that psychology professors are not all White.

15. See Harris (2012).

16. See Sherif (1936). To do his research, Sherif took advantage of a visual perception phenomenon called the "autokinetic effect" where a stationary light, when it is looked at in a completely dark room, appears to move. In this dark room, both eyes will simultaneously move in the same direction involuntarily (saccadic eye movements), and this eye movement is experienced as object movement because the completely dark room provides no contextual cues or reference points regarding the eye movement. There are individual differences in judging the distance the light moved because different observers set different frames of reference for judging the amplitude of the movement. What Sherif found was that when individuals make their judgments in the presence of each other it influences their subsequent judgments so that they become more similar to each other with repeated judgment trials.

17. Jacobs and Campbell (1961).

18. As discussed earlier, the motivation to create a shared reality with others increases when individuals have a need for epistemic certainty (truth), as occurs when the "right" answer is unclear or there is no right answer. For further evidence of the role in group norm stability of the need for epistemic certainty, see Livi, Kruglanski, Pierro, Mannetti, and Kenny (2015).

19. See Sherif (1936, p. 3).

20. See Crowe and Higgins (1997).

21. See Levine, Higgins, and Choi (2000).

22. See, for example, Higgins and Rholes (1978).

23. See Higgins, Echterhoff, Crespillo, and Kopietz (2007).

24. See Festinger (1950, 1954).

25. See Asch (1952, 1956).

26. See Asch (1952, p.463).

27. See Asch (1952, p. 464).

28. For thoughtful reviews of group influence and the implications of Asch's findings for when people do and do not create shared realities with others, see Levine (1999) and Levine and Tindale (2015).

29. Ross, Bierbrauer, and Hoffman (1976) provide an additional shared reality perspective on why the Asch situation is so difficult for participants, and what motivates them to give the incorrect answer on conflict trials that agrees with the unanimous judgment of the other group members. Ross et al. suggest that participants want the other group members to understand, share with them, why they would give an answer different from them (i.e., give the correct answer on conflict trials rather than the others' incorrect answer), but the Asch situation does not contain information that participants can use to create a shared reality that would make sense of why the participant is giving a different answer than all the other group members. Because of this, the participants feel pressured to give the same (incorrect) answer as the other group members. Ross et al. reasoned that if information was available in the situation that would allow a shared reality for why different answers could be given, then participants would be less likely to give the incorrect answer on conflict trials. And this was what they found.

30. See Bartlett (1932).
31. See Allport and Postman (1945, 1947).
32. See Bartlett (1932, p. 129).
33. See Bartlett (1932, pp. 135–136).
34. See, for example, Kashima (2000), Kashima, Bratanova, and Peters (2018), Kashima et al. (2010), Kashima, Lyons, and Clark (2013), and Lyons and Kashima (2003).
35. See Lyons and Kashima (2003).
36. For a further discussion of this distinction, see Clark (1996).

7

Our Sense of Self

Who Am I? How Am I Doing?

Among all the objects in the world, the one that we experience most often is our self. Humans have a viewpoint on what kind of person they are—their "own" viewpoint on themselves. They also represent the viewpoint of significant others (e.g., mother, father, romantic partner, best friends, co-workers, managers, advisors) on what kind of person they are—the "other" viewpoint on themselves. Our own and others' beliefs and opinions about us matter a lot. Indeed, they are central to how we think, feel, and act.

Although the viewpoints of different others on what kind of person you are may not always agree, what they have in common is that they matter to you. If someone's viewpoint on you does not matter, then that person is not (or is no longer) a significant other to you. Of all the objects you know and have beliefs about, you are the object you pay most attention to and want to understand best. For this reason, when it comes to sharing beliefs and opinions about the world, you care most about whether significant others share your beliefs and opinions about who you are.

In fact, many of us don't have an "own" viewpoint on ourselves that is different from the "other" viewpoints on us. Instead, we have a viewpoint on ourselves that is shared with others. It may be that your viewpoint on some aspect of you is shared with one significant other and some other aspect is shared with another significant other, but typically there is at least one significant other who you believe shares your viewpoint on each aspect of yourself. Interestingly, this shared viewpoint is not always positive.

The Self-Digest

How do we learn to know who we are?[1] It all begins with how others respond to you.[2] And it starts in infancy. Children learn that they can achieve their goals by acting in particular ways. If they want to be picked up, they can raise their arms. If they want to share what they are finding interesting at the moment, they can grab the attention of caretaker and point to what is interesting them. As I discussed in Chapter 2, this is the beginning of shared reality, and infants can initiate that shared reality.

When caretakers respond to children's actions by picking them up or expressing interest in what they pointed to, the children experience control over making something happen, and, importantly, they feel that they matter. They develop a *social contingent* self—self-knowledge of the form, "Do X with A, and A will do Y," where X is the child's action, A is the significant other, and Y is the significant other's response to the child's action.[3] This is the start of children developing a belief about who they are by observing how others react to what they do. The renowned sociologist Charles Cooley referred to this process as the "looking glass self."[4]

Developing a social contingent self is part of children's development of their self-digest, which is a summary of *what the world is like in relation to you*. The self-digest serves self-regulatory functions by summarizing how children relate to the world and the personal consequences of these relations. I believe that what is most critical about self-knowledge is its contribution to effective self-regulation, to getting along in the world. Other perspectives on the self emphasize its cognitive properties, such as self traits being interconnected to form a cognitive structure, and this does matter.[5] But I believe that what matters most about the self is that we use our knowledge about ourselves as a distinct object that relates to the world in specific ways to make choices about what to do or not to do.[6]

The notion that self-knowledge is a self-digest that serves self-regulatory functions is compatible with the widespread assumption that human survival requires that children adapt to their surrounding environment and to their social environment in particular. To obtain the nurturance and security they need to survive, children must establish and maintain relationships with other people, especially adult caregivers who will fulfill their basic needs. This means that children must learn what is it about themselves and what they do that determine how others respond to them as an object in the world. They must learn these interpersonal contingencies and regulate what they do to increase the likelihood that others will provide them the nurturance and security they need.[7]

To regulate their behavior effectively, children also need to learn about their personal capabilities and competencies, about their own strengths and weaknesses. They must learn, for example, that although some older children can do certain tricks on the jungle gym, if they try to do the same tricks, they will fall and hurt themselves. They must learn their limits. And as their abilities change, their self-digest will change to reflect their new competencies. Knowing your strengths and weaknesses, what you can and cannot do, is adaptive. When choosing between alternative ways to attain a goal, it is adaptive to know which alternative best suits your capabilities. When deciding whether to pursue a goal, it is adaptive to know whether you can achieve it and, if you can, how much effort it will require to achieve it given your capabilities.

This kind of self-knowledge is also part of the self-digest. And, importantly, it is also influenced by other people and involves shared realities because children receive feedback from others about what they can and cannot do, and they typically accept what these experts have to say. On the upside, receiving positive feedback from others creates a positive shared reality entry in a child's self-digest, such as "I am good at numbers," which is likely to boost his or her confidence in math. On the downside, receiving negative feedback from others can create a negative shared reality entry, such as "I am tone deaf," which is likely to decrease the child's interest in becoming a musician. And both kinds of self-knowledge continue to be learned beyond childhood into adulthood.

I should emphasize that there are other kinds of knowledge that are relevant for self-regulation beyond the self-digest. Knowing that you are human—and only human—is very useful knowledge for self-regulation because it has implications for what you can and cannot do. For example, it is important for humans to breathe, and humans cannot breathe under water (without special equipment). This is useful knowledge about yourself, but it is not stored in the self-digest because the implications of being human are not specific to *you* as a *distinct* object in the world.

Our self-knowledge, our self-digest, has a unique status among all of our stored knowledge because the self is the one object that is always with us. Thus, it is highly significant that much, if not most, of this self-knowledge is a shared reality with others. Let us now discuss the three different functional selves that make up the self-digest—the social contingent self, the expectant self, and the monitored self—and consider the role of shared reality in their construction.

The Social Contingent Self

Even young infants learn that if they perform a particular action with a certain person, then that person will respond in a specific way. "When I eat my food, Mommy smiles at me." "When I throw my food, Mommy frowns at me." These are shared realities because the adult in the relationship knows that he or she treats Susie differently depending on what she does with her food. Indeed, and importantly, the adult often teaches the child the contingency: "Susie, eat your food; don't throw it." While the child eats her food, the mother looks at her and smiles. When the child throws her food, the mother looks at her and frowns. In this way, the social contingencies are shared realities.

The social contingent self begins early in development, but it also continues over the lifespan. Adults have social contingent selves. "When I forget my wife's birthday, she gets very sad." "When I beat my best time for the 100-meter dash, my coach slaps me on the back." And, again, these are shared realities because, for example, the wife knows that she is sad when her husband forgets her birthday. And it is not as if this is a universal contingency. Many people around the world do not even celebrate birthdays; for example, in some countries what is celebrated is not the day of the year when you were born but the day of the year that is associated with your name (in my case, born March 12; Edward, March 18). And some wives get angry rather than sad when their husband forgets their birthday.

What is remarkable is how much social contingent self-knowledge is stored by each of us. Most of us have many significant relationships—and some of us have a huge number of such relationships (check Facebook if you can believe it)—and for each relationship there can be multiple contingencies. You may not be fully aware of them all: Social contingent self-knowledge can be tacit. But it is very important interpersonal knowledge nonetheless because its use supports our relationships with others, and failure to use it can harm relationships. Moreover, as I mentioned earlier, it can be very specific to particular relationships. That is, you cannot assume that two (or more) of the people with whom you have relationships will respond similarly to the same behavior. "When I tell an off-color joke, my friend John laughs but my mother gets annoyed." Getting along with others takes a lot of social contingent knowledge, and it is not easy. I will talk more about this in Chapter 11.

The Expectant Self

The expectant self involves what I said earlier about knowing your competencies—your strengths and weaknesses. It also involves knowing your likes and dislikes. Together, it answers the question, "What am I *likely* to do or have happen to me? What can I *expect*?"

Expectant self-knowledge can be very specific. For young children, for example, a spoon is not just some object in the world. It is something that they use to eat. They may initially find it difficult not to spill food that they have on their spoon, leading to the perception that "When I pick up food with a spoon, I often spill it." This expectant self-knowledge is useful for the child because it allows him or her to try harder next time to make something better happen. In other cases, expectant self-knowledge can lead the child to avoid doing something, such as eating certain food (e.g., "When I eat peanuts, I get sick.").

Notably, a particular expectant self can change as a function of experience, as when a child gets better at doing something: "When I pick up food with a spoon, I *don't* spill it." Indeed, once the skill reaches the same level as that of other children doing the activity, then the particular expectant self is likely to disappear altogether. There is no point storing something about yourself that is true for everyone else. This is because, as I noted earlier, the purpose of the self-digest is to store knowledge about you that is distinct to you.

Importantly, children's knowledge about what makes them distinct often derives from what other people say about them. A classic example of a message that provides such information is a sentence like: "You are such a ___ __" If the child is fortunate, the parent or teacher or older sibling might insert the word "hard worker." If not, the word might be "slacker." And the recipient of such messages often takes it to heart. It becomes a shared reality.

Just as social contingent self-knowledge can vary across relationships (e.g., a close friend vs. your mother), expectant self-knowledge can also vary across relationships. For example, you can experience yourself as a more or less competent tennis player depending on the quality of your tennis partner. You can also receive different feedback from others, with your wife telling you how excellent you are while your father-in-law damns you with faint praise. The good news is that you can always choose to play with whomever makes you feel more competent. Later in this chapter I will talk more about self-enhancement.

As just mentioned, different others, like your wife versus your father-in-law, can have different standards for judging your performance and thereby your underlying competence. And this difference can affect your beliefs about your performance or competence, even without their giving you explicit feedback. These significant others can be an *inner audience* that becomes a standard for judging your performance/competence. In one study,[8] for example, participants first visualized two different inner audiences—either a good friend who would stick by them and support them through ups and downs or a new acquaintance who liked them contingent on their success. Importantly, participants in both conditions felt liked by the person who was the inner audience. Participants then performed a difficult memory task designed to make them believe they had performed badly. Because the task was difficult, the participants could have decided that their performance did not reflect their general competence. The study found that, compared to participants whose inner audience was a good friend, those whose inner audience liked them contingent on their success were more likely to attribute their poor performance on the memory task to their personal failings (low competence). And this self-criticism was especially strong for participants who performed the task with a mirror present (supposedly left over from another study) that made them self-conscious.

Self-evaluative judgments also vary depending on which shared belief about your self is salient. All of us are members of more than one social category. I am a senior citizen, Caucasian, male, New York City resident, and professor. I am a member of all five of these social categories—although if you asked me, I would say first that I am a New Yorker. In other words, my New Yorker identity is chronically accessible to me—it is the one that comes to mind most easily. Each of these categories has various stereotypes associated with it. Some of the stereotypes are even contradictory, such as seniors citizens walking slowly and New Yorkers walking quickly. So which it is? Am I a slow or quick walker? I think of myself more as a New Yorker than as a senior citizen, so my answer is "quickly."

But category membership salience is not immutable—there are situations in which one of my other memberships might become more salient that my New Yorker membership. For example, what if I were in a room filled with young people, as happens when I teach undergraduates? Here I might well think of myself more as a senior citizen than I usually do, in which case my answer to the walking speed question would be "slowly."

Research has demonstrated the relative ease of changing the salience of category memberships and the intriguing results of doing so. Let's take the case of ethnic and gender category memberships. Do Asian American women have higher math ability or higher verbal ability? As stereotypical women, they should have higher verbal than math ability. But as stereotypical Asian Americans, they should have higher math than verbal ability. In a study that investigated the impact of varying the salience of gender and ethnic category membership,[9] Asian American women were told that the study examined how students react to stressful academic situations. All participants first answered a "demographics" set of questions that included their age and their year in college. Then the salience of one or the other of their social category memberships was manipulated by having them answer a question about either their gender (women salient condition) or their ethnicity (Asian American salient condition). Next, the participants were asked to imagine, as vividly as possible, that they were the person in the story they were reading who was about to take a very difficult GRE-type exam with both math and verbal sections. The study found that the Asian American women evaluated themselves as better in math when their ethnicity was made salient, but better in verbal when their gender was made salient.

There is a further point that needs to be emphasized. What is stored in expectant self-knowledge is knowledge about yourself that is useful for self-regulation. It is information that matters for the choices that you make. It is not enough that something about you is distinctive, such as most other people are better at playing chess than you. For something distinctive about you to be part of your expectant self-knowledge, it must matter to you.[10] If playing chess doesn't matter to someone, then being worse at it than others, a "poor chess player," would not place that information into that person's expectant self-knowledge.

Importantly, the salience or perceived distinctiveness of a self-property will also vary depending on the shared realities that it creates. There is evidence, for example, that when schoolchildren are asked to describe themselves ("Tell me about yourself"), they are more likely to mention their gender as a self-property when they live in households where their gender is in the minority.[11] This would mean that their gender at home would be salient to both their family and to themselves—it would be a salient shared reality about them. But that is not all. They would be treated differently and have different demands placed on them at home because of their minority gender in the family. And what is expected of them at home because of their gender would be known by them and their family. Again, it would be a shared reality. Thus, for individuals with the same self-property, such as gender, the salience of that self-property will vary depending on the shared realities that it creates.

Information about self-competencies is an important part of expectant self-knowledge, but it is not the only expectant self-information that is stored in the self-digest. There is also information about your personal preferences, your likes and dislikes. A person might have the expectant self-knowledge that she loves powder skiing, tarte flambé, spy movies, and so on. You do not store information about everything you like or dislike, however. If you believe that you like to watch sunsets, for example, you would not store that information if you thought that everyone likes to watch sunsets because they are so beautiful. That is, enjoying sunsets says something about sunsets, how beautiful *they* are. It doesn't say anything about *you* as a distinct viewer of sunsets.[12] Under your knowledge of sunsets you would store that they are beautiful and that people love to watch them. Given that you are a person, you also love them. You do not need, then, to store your enjoyment of them as part of your self-knowledge.

There is an exception to this, however, depending on how strongly you like something. Take chocolate, for example. Almost everyone likes chocolate, but my wife doesn't like chocolate. She *loooves* chocolate. She is a chocoholic, although she would disagree with this term because she does not believe that her love of chocolate is excessive. She brings a bag of chocolate on all of our out-of-town trips (a box if it is a long trip). Her love of chocolate is part of her expectant self-knowledge.

Well, I *looove* sunsets. My love of sunsets is part of my expectant self-knowledge, with the additional information that I love in particular the sunsets I see from the front window of my apartment that looks West across the Hudson River to New Jersey. I try to be at home at the time of day that the sun sets, which varies throughout the year, because I expect to enjoy it very much. That is why my love of sunsets is in my expectant self-knowledge. Sunsets and sunshine are not the same. I like sunshine, but I do not love sunshine. I don't like sunshine more than anyone else. I don't store in my expectant self-knowledge that I like sunshine. Sunsets are different because my choices about when to get home in the evening are influenced by my love of sunsets. And, importantly, I especially enjoy watching sunsets with other people who love them. That shared reality makes them even more wonderful. And my wife is the same way with chocolate. For her, nothing is better than sharing chocolate with another chocolate lover.

The Monitored Self

The monitored self is the third functional component of the self-digest. At any point in time that you are doing something, performing some action, you can evaluate your self in relation to some standard. As discussed in classic cybernetic or control models of self-regulation, the process of goal pursuit involves monitoring the relation between the current state and the desired end-state (the goal).[13] If the monitoring process indicates a discrepancy between the two states, action is taken to reduce the discrepancy. The standards defining the desired end-state can be chronic, such as your *ideal* aspirations or your *ought* responsibilities. Discrepancies produce feedback that is experienced as negative emotion, such as feeling sad when your current self is discrepant from an ideal aspiration or feeling worried when your current self is discrepant from an ought responsibility.

The monitored self is the part of the self-digest that attends to and provides feedback about the success of your personal goal pursuits: "How am I doing?" The answer to this question is often a shared reality with a significant other. Because people typically have more than one significant other, they can have more than one answer to "How am I doing?" depending on which significant other they have in mind. If a mother has a young, 4-year-old daughter and an older, 13-year-old daughter, she might believe that she is a good mother in the eyes of her preschool daughter but a bad mother in the eyes of her teenage daughter (a rather common pattern, as many parents will attest). When she thinks about her preschool daughter she begins to smile, but when she thinks about her teenage daughter she begins to frown. As another example, employees often think and feel about themselves differently when they are pursuing their boss's goals for them versus their spouse's goals for them because these two "evaluators" are perceived as having different standards regarding how they should behave.

A major consequence of the monitored self is its impact on self-esteem, which is your respect for yourself, or your belief about your worth. Because people are often motivated to have high self-esteem, they use self-enhancement techniques to boost their self-esteem. Let's consider next how this works from the perspective of shared reality.

Self-Esteem and Self-Enhancement

Historically, global self-esteem has referred to individuals' overall evaluation or appraisal of themselves—whether they approve or disapprove of themselves, or like or dislike themselves.[14] The problem is that it is not always clear which "self" is being appraised or approved or liked. As suggested by the self-digest, there are different possibilities.

Mark Leary and his colleagues have suggested that individuals' self-esteem at any moment signals where they stand in their interpersonal relationships. In this formulation, self-esteem functions as a gauge, or "sociometer," of how effective you are in your social interactions with others, which has consequences for their acceptance or rejection of you.[15] And, notably, it is others' acceptance or rejection feedback, and your internalization of it—a shared reality—that produces high or low self-esteem. If you didn't believe or care about others' feedback, it would not impact your self-esteem. The sociometer perspective on self-esteem is a "social contingent self" perspective. You can have high self-esteem by remembering your wife's birthday and doing other things that she likes you to do. You can thus be "a good boy" or "a good girl," even though you are no longer a child.

A different perspective on self-esteem assumes that it reflects your evaluation of your competencies and abilities. Do you believe that your competencies and abilities will allow you to meet the demands of life and succeed in your endeavors? Can you accomplish the tasks on your plate? In many respects, this is the classic "self-description" perspective on self-esteem in which you describe who you think you are in more positive or more negative ways. And, as mentioned earlier, the "looking glass self," based on others' feedback about your competencies and abilities, creates a shared reality self that determines your self-esteem. This is an expectant self perspective on self-esteem.

A third perspective on self-esteem, which also has a long history, posits that self-esteem derives from individuals having congruencies (high self-esteem) or discrepancies (low self-esteem) between who people believe they actually are and who they ideally want to be or believe they ought to be.[16] This is a monitored self perspective on self-esteem. Shared reality plays a critical role here as well because it impacts both who you believe you actually are *and* who you ideally want to be and believe you ought to be.

There is some good news from the fact that our actual selves and our ideal and ought selves are shared realities with others. Because of this, individuals' low self-esteem, and the depression or anxiety often associated with it, can be improved by creating either a new shared reality about who you actually are or a new shared reality about what are your ideals or oughts. Thus, you can add a new significant other or subtract a current significant other depending on whether their shared reality about who you are and/ or their ideals and oughts for you increases or decreases your self-esteem. Indeed, therapists, as new significant others, can engage in both kinds of interventions when they challenge clients' "false" negative beliefs about who they are and/or their unrealistic or overly demanding ideals or oughts for themselves.[17] As a consequence, clients can create new shared realities with their therapists that help them think and feel better about themselves.

I need to emphasize something here. It is common to assume that everyone wants high emotional well-being and high self-esteem. But this is not the case. Although everyone wants high emotional well-being, not everyone wants high self-esteem. Indeed, it is not good for everyone to increase their self-esteem. Raising your self-esteem—*inflating* yourself—is an effective tool to increase your eagerness, which is what you want to do if you are pursuing promotion ideal goals. Self-enhancement is a fit with promotion. But raising your self-esteem can reduce vigilance (e.g., make you feel more content and relaxed), and reducing vigilance is *not* what you want to do if you are pursuing prevention ought goals. Instead, you want to increase vigilance, and this is achieved better by *deflating* yourself.

Indeed, there is strong cross-cultural evidence that individuals who are effective in promotion motivation have higher self-esteem, but there is no such positive correlation for individuals who are effective in prevention motivation.[18] If being effective simply raises your self-esteem, then individuals who are effective in promotion *and* those who are effective in prevention would have high self-esteem. But they do not. The positive relation is only there for promotion. Why? Because high self-esteem facilitates promotion motivation but not prevention motivation.

There is additional evidence that promotion and prevention motivations use self-inflation and self-deflation differently. In one study, for example, participants completed six anagrams.[19] Half of them thought that there were only six anagrams to work on and thus felt the task was over after they completed the six anagrams. The other half thought that there were 12 anagrams and thus expected to continue after doing 6 anagrams. At this point, all participants were given a standard measure of self-esteem, which provided an opportunity for participants who thought they had more anagrams to solve to "use" self-esteem as a motivational tool. The promotion-motivated participants expressed *higher* self-esteem in the continuing than in the completed condition (i.e., self-inflation), whereas the prevention-oriented participants expressed *lower* self-esteem in the continuing condition than in the completed condition (i.e., self-deflation).[20]

The promotion–prevention difference in motivation is of special interest because it is also associated with cultural differences in shared self-beliefs. People can have *independent* self-construals, whereby they represent themselves in terms of attributes that make them separate and unique from other individuals, or *interdependent* self-construals, whereby they represent themselves as being embedded within the larger society. Independent self-construals are more common in Western cultures, whereas interdependent self-construals are more common in Asian cultures.[21] There is also evidence that independent self-construals are more strongly associated with promotion motivation, whereas interdependent self-construals are more strongly associated with prevention motivation.[22] Finally, tying it altogether, members of Western cultures are likely to have predominant promotion motivation, whereas members of Asian cultures are likely to have predominant prevention motivation.[23]

What this all suggests is that important differences between cultures reflect differences in shared beliefs and motivational concerns. For example, there is a tendency for Americans to present themselves to others in a positive manner and to be self-enhancing. In contrast, Japanese tend to be more self-effacing and more realistic, even self-critical.[24] These differences are consistent with Americans sharing cultural beliefs and concerns related more to independence and promotion and Japanese sharing cultural beliefs and concerns related more to interdependence and prevention.

Before leaving this section on self-esteem and self-enhancement, I want to make an additional comment about the popular notion that there is a universal human need for people to view themselves positively. I believe that this notion is based on the broader assumption that the dominant human motivation is to maximize pleasure and minimize pain—*hedonism*. In my earlier book, *Beyond Pleasure and Pain: How Motivation Works*,[25] I discussed several reasons why this notion is false. Here, I want to emphasize the shared reality rebuttal to this.

People do not simply want to have desired outcomes in their lives. They want to establish what's real and what's right instead of what's fantasy (illusion) and what's wrong. And people establish the *truth* together with others—it is a *shared* reality. Moreover (and here's the point), this motivation is so strong that people will often choose a negative self-belief over a positive self-belief if they think that it portrays who they are more accurately. They want to know the truth about themselves. As they should, because they are using their self-knowledge to make choices that allow them to get along effectively in the world. We cannot afford to base those choices on illusions we created to make us feel more positive about ourselves. A major way that we learn what is *really* the truth about us is to have our self-beliefs verified by others, in the same way that scientists want other scientists to verify their findings. And we want such verification of our self from others even when our self-beliefs are *negative*. [26] The role of social verification—having others create a shared reality with us about who we are and how we are doing—is critical to our developing and maintaining our self-beliefs.

Self-Verification

According to Bill Swann's self-verification theory, for people to be successful in their social relationships, they need to learn how others' perceive and react to them and then use this knowledge to construct a self-concept to predict and prepare for how others will respond to them in the future.[27] Given this goal, it is useful to have stable perceptions of our self-attributes that others share. Any substantial change in these perceptions is a threat to effective functioning. Thus, people are motivated to have others verify their self-concept (i.e., create a shared reality with them) even when it concerns negative attributes. There is research with married couples that nicely illustrates this.[28]

Each partner separately rated himself or herself relative to others of the same age and gender on a list of attributes (e.g., social skills, intellectual capability). These self-ratings by each partner were combined to determine whether that person's self-concept was relatively positive or negative. Similarly, each participant's ratings of his or her partner were combined to determine the positivity or negativity of those ratings. Finally, both participants indicated their commitment to their marriage on dimensions such as desire to remain in the relationship, satisfaction with the relationship, and amount of time spent with the partner.

The study found that participants who had more positive self-concepts were more committed to their marriage when their partner appraised them positively rather than negatively. This is not surprising. However, what is surprising, but is predicted by self-verification theory, is that the study also found that participants who had more negative self-concepts were more committed to their marriage when their partner appraised them *negatively* rather than positively. Thus, for people with negative self-concepts, having their partner verify their beliefs about their negative attributes was more important than having the partner provide a glowing assessment of them. Other results indicated that, regardless of whether participants had a positive or negative self-concept, what produced commitment to the marriage was believing that their partner had an accurate view of them—with perceived accuracy requiring a shared reality.

Swann and his colleagues have found that individuals' motivation for social verification of their self-beliefs is especially strong when they already have high certainty about those self-beliefs. Notably, such certainty could itself derive from a prior history of significant others sharing those self-beliefs.[29] For example, it might matter to a husband that his wife believes he is a caring but forgetful person because his mother and father hold those beliefs about him. Given his long history with his parents, he has high certainty that he is that kind of person. If his wife says that he is caring and *not* forgetful, then he is caught between conflicting shared realities about whether he is forgetful or not. He needs his wife to verify his (and his parents') belief that he is forgetful because, if she did not, there would be both social relational and epistemic problems in his overall social network. There is, in fact, evidence that individuals whose self-views are high (vs. low) in certainty have stronger relationships with others whose appraisals of them agree with their self-views.[30] Thus, a nonverifying wife would not only create an epistemic conflict for her husband but also a social conflict with his parents.

There is evidence that self-verification matters so much to people that they evaluate the extent to which another person is *generally* a good a judge of others in terms of that person's agreement with them about their *self* characteristics—"If she verifies my self-beliefs, then she is generally a good judge of others."[31] Not surprisingly, the research found that people consider another person to be a good judge of others when that person agrees with them about the characteristics of target others that they both judged. But what was found to matter most in their evaluation of another person's judgment-of-others ability was that this person agrees with their judgment of themselves.

There is substantial evidence, then, that individuals want others to verify their self-views. They want a shared reality with others about their self-views. Notably, individuals in close relationships want even more than that. They also want their partner to perceive himself or herself in a way that establishes a shared reality with their *ideal* view of him or her. And they don't leave this to chance. They affirm and support the actual self of their partner so that it will match their ideal view of him or her. For example, if their ideal for their partner is that he or she be "affectionate," each time their partner acts affectionate they might say things like, "Thank you, that was so sweet of you" or "I'm so lucky to have such an affectionate partner," while not saying anything when their partner fails to act in an affectionate manner.

The good news is that this shaping of the partner's actual image often works, with their behavior toward their partner producing movement toward their ideal view of him or her.[32] It is a benevolent version of a "self-fulfilling prophecy," such that a partner's original idealized view of his or her partner that looked like a case of "love is blind" now looks prescient as the result of successful shaping.[33] Over time, the partner ends up sharing this idealized reality about what kind of person he or she *really* is—a very happy ending indeed.

One final point. Recognizing the different functions of the self-digest allows a better understanding of how self-enhancement and self-verification can *both* occur. The social contingent self can learn which "public selves," including "false fronts," are effective in self-presentation or impression management to get acquaintances to react positively by making them believe you have capabilities or preferences that you don't have (a form of self-enhancement). Moreover, at the same time, your expectant self can retain the truth about your capabilities and preferences that you want your close significant others to verify (self-verification), even when they are less positive than what you are presenting to others—wanting your intimates to know "the real you."

Self-Beliefs and Self-Knowledge from Identifying with a Social Category

A person's self-digest is "social" in that it contains information about how others respond to what you do, what kind of person they perceive you to be, and how well you are meeting their goal and standards for you. The self-digest, which is about *you* as an individual, impacts your beliefs and feelings about yourself and your choices in self-regulation. However, there is another important kind of "social" information that is not just about you as an individual, and it also impacts your beliefs and feelings about yourself and your choices in self-regulation. It is information about your *social identities,* and it too involves shared realities.[34]

As John Donne said, "no man is an island, entire of itself." That is, we belong to different groups, and we embrace them as reflecting who we are and want to be. We have social identities and not just personal identities. Henri Tajfel and John Turner, pioneers in understanding the significance of our social memberships, studied how the groups to which we belong and embrace can be a critical source of pride to us.[35] For example, when our personal failures bring us down, pride in the accomplishments of our social identity groups, such as our favorite sports team winning the championship, can bring us up.

To understand what makes us human, it is critical to appreciate that we do not simply belong to groups and cooperate with other members of those groups. We also define ourselves in terms of the social categories to which we belong. We have seen that the self-digest *I* is itself a shared reality with others. But there is also a *we* and *us* shared reality, and most individuals have multiple social identities that matter to them and impact what they do.

Social Identities

From the perspective of Tajfel and Turner and their colleagues, social identification occurs when individuals include themselves and others in a social category with shared attributes that differ from those possessed by members of a different social category.[36] This leads to different perceptions of and behaviors toward in-group and out-group members, which has been the main focus of social identity theorists and will be discussed more fully in Chapter 11 when we consider how humans get along with each other. Here I am more concerned with the fact that when individuals embrace a social identity, they have a collective bond that is based on their common attributes (i.e., the prototypic qualities of in-group members).

According to social identity theory, when individuals identify with a group, they do not relate to other members on the basis of their unique personal qualities but, instead, relate to them on the basis of the qualities they share in common. It a *we* group identity rather than a close-knit family of *I*s.

This has important implications for how group members see themselves as well as others. As social identification increases, the personal self becomes increasingly less salient and accessible, and individuals more and more see themselves as exemplifying the prototypical qualities of the group.[37] " I am a Mets fan." They are also motivated to behave in ways that are prototypical of the group and different from how other groups behave, like wearing a Mets cap. In addition, when a specific social identity is made salient, such as women's identity as female, they see themselves as having attributes that are stereotypic of that social category, such as women representing themselves as being "dependent" or "nurturant"—*self*-stereotyping.[38]

Social Fusion

Bill Swann and his colleagues have recently described a related but different way in which individuals' group memberships become part of who they believe they are—*social fusion*.[39] Social fusion is similar to social identity in that individuals perceive themselves as being members of a group, and they embrace that membership as a major part of who they are. However, social fusion differs from social identities in that individuals maintain their personal identities and do establish unique personal relationships with other members of the group based on each of their distinctive qualities. Thus, members experiencing social fusion function more like members of a family where each member is loyal to the "family" as a whole but still has distinctive relationships with individual family members (e.g., father vs. sister). The "fusion" derives from their experiencing an intimate connection between their personal identity and their social identity—"I am one with my family." Significantly, the unique social relationship ties that individuals form with other members of the group strengthen the fusion with the group.

A good example of social fusion outside one's biological family are fighting units formed in wars, like the famous "Band of Brothers," Easy Company of the 101st Airborne Division of the United State Army in World War II.[40] Swann and his colleagues have found that social fusion in such fighting units is associated with group members being willing to make extreme sacrifices for their group, including sacrificing their lives for one another.[41] Swann and his colleagues also found that Americans expressed more willingness to carry out extreme behaviors in support of their country (e.g., willingness to die for their country) when they felt a strong fusion with America, and this effect was even stronger when the participants were reminded of the core values that Americans share (e.g., democracy, freedom).[42] Finally, another study with Spanish students found that for participants who felt strong (vs. weak) fusion with Spain, priming shared core values (e.g., honesty) increased their perception of other Spaniards being like family to them (e.g., "I see other members of my country as brothers and sisters"). And this perception of other Spaniards as family was the factor underlying (i.e., mediating) the influence of fusion on the participants' willingness to make extreme sacrifices for their country.[43]

For humans, then, there are many different answers to the (apparently) simple questions, "Who am I?" and "How am I doing?" There are answers from our social contingent self, from our expectant self, and from our monitored self. Our sense of self also derives from our social identities and our social fusions. And all of these are shared realities that have a major impact on how we feel about ourselves and the choices we make in our lives, including choosing to make the ultimate sacrifice for others.

What makes us human? In the previous chapters, I have discussed how the human motivation to create shared realities with others impacts our feelings and our knowledge, including our feelings and knowledge about our self. But it also does more: It impacts our attitudes and opinions, which I consider next.

Notes

1. For excellent discussions of self development, see Harter (2015) and Nelson (2007).
2. For excellent reviews of this symbolic interactionist perspective, see Stryker (1980) and Stryker and Statham (1985).
3. For a discussion of the social contingency self, which I previously called the *instrumental* self, as well as other functions within the self-digest, see Higgins (1996a).
4. For the original work of this pioneer in sociology generally, and symbolic interactionism in particular, see Cooley (1902/1964, 1909/1962). See also Mead's (1934) discussion of symbolic gestures. For an even earlier discussion of the "looking glass self," see Smith (1759).
5. See, for example, Markus and Smith (1981), Rogers (1981), and Sarbin (1952).
6. See Higgins (1996a).
7. See, for example, Bowlby (1969, 1973), Cooley (1902/1964), Mead (1934), and Sullivan (1953).
8. See Baldwin and Holmes (1987).
9. See Sinclair, Hardin, and Lowery (2006).
10. See Markus (1977).

11. See McGuire, McGuire, and Winton (1979).
12. See Kelley (1973).
13. See, for example, Carver and Scheier (1981, 1998), Miller, Galanter, and Pribram (1960), and Wiener (1948).
14. See, for example, Greenwald and Pratkanis (1984), Rosenberg (1965, 1979), and Wylie (1979).
15. See, for example, Leary, Tambor, Terdal, and Downs (1995).
16. See, for example, Cooley (1902/1964), Duval and Wicklund (1972), James (1890/1948), Mead (1934), Piers and Singer (1971), and Rogers (1961). For an integrative review of this perspective, see Higgins (1987).
17. See, for example, Beck, Rush, Shaw, and Emery (1979), Ellis (1973), and Rogers (1959). For a related perspective on treatment, see Moretti, Higgins, and Feldman (1990).
18. See Higgins (2008).
19. See Scholer, Ozaki, and Higgins. (2014).
20. This self-deflation effect in prevention motivation was even stronger in another study by Scholer et al. (2014) where participants were predominant in prevention motivation.
21. See Markus and Kitayama (1991). For a related distinction between *individualism* and *collectivism*, see Triandis (1989).
22. See Lee, Aaker, and Gardner (2000).
23. See Higgins (2008).
24. See, for example, Akimoto and Sanbonmatsu (1999), Heine, Lehman, Markus, and Kitayma (1999), and Yamagishi, Hashimoto, Cook, and Li (2012).
25. See Higgins (2012).
26. For a discussion of the role of social verification in shared reality, see Hardin and Higgins (1996). I should also note here that the socially verified self beliefs, although experienced as objective and thus fulfilling our motivation for truth, are not necessarily the truth, just as verified scientific results are not necessarily the truth. As discussed in Chapter 7, there can be "false objectivity." The point here is that we want such verification even for negative self-beliefs.
27. Although there were early proposals about the importance of self-consistency (e.g., Lecky, 1945), I focus on Bill Swann's analysis because it is the most theoretically developed and most heavily researched.
28. See Swann (1984, 1990).
29. See Hardin and Higgins, (1996).
30. See Pelham and Swann (1994).
31. See Chun, Ames, Uribe, and Higgins (2017) and Kwang and Swann (2010).
32. See Murray, Holmes, and Griffin (1996), Rusbult, Finkel, and Kumashiro (2009), and Rusbult and Van Lang (2003).
33. For this point, and the evidence supporting it, see Murray, Holmes, and Griffin (1996). See also Rusbult, Finkel, and Kumashiro (2009).
34. See Hogg and Rinella (2018).

35. See Tajfel (1974), Tajfel and Turner (1979), and Turner, Hogg, Oakes, Reicher, and Wetherell (1987).
36. See Tajfel and Turner (1979) and Turner et al. (1987).
37. See Turner et al. (1987).
38. See, for example, Brewer (2007) and Hogg and Turner (1993).
39. See, for example, Swann and Buhrmester (2015) and Swann, Jetten, Gómez, Whitehouse, and Bastian (2012).
40. For the historial account of this company, see Ambrose (1992).
41. See Whitehouse, McQuinn, Buhrmester, and Swann (2014).
42. See Swann et al. (2014).
43. See Swann et al. (2014).

8

Our Attitudes and Opinions

Experiencing the Subjective as Objective

What does it mean when we experience our judgments or beliefs as being "objective"? Consider again the classic Asch study where participants chose which comparison line matches the standard line after hearing the unanimous choice of several other individuals (confederates). When a participant goes along with the others in the group even when they are incorrect, is that choice *experienced* as subjective or objective? One might assume that for participants to experience their judgment as objective, they would have to base their judgments solely on the physical evidence about the standard line and the comparison lines. Given that their judgments were instead shared realities that they created with the other group members, we would expect that the participants would not experience their judgments as objective. But is this the case?

What matters is a person's *experience* of objectivity, and people have an experience of objectivity when they believe that they and others agree on a judgment.[1] Creating shared realities with others can generate an experience of objectivity that goes beyond the available information. This is surprising because what is supposed to be objective (i.e., based on the available information) is actually *not*; it is a shared reality that creates an *experience of objectivity*.

And there is something else that is surprising about how humans comprehend their world. Having an objective response to something is supposed to be different from having a subjective response. In contrast to an objective response, a subjective response to something does not need to be based on an unbiased reaction to the available information about that thing. Instead, it can be a person's private, and potentially biased, reaction to that thing. There need be no social consensus in the latter case because the reaction is attributed to the individual person, to something about him or her personally, rather than to the properties of that thing per se.[2] Thus, it is not necessary that there be a shared reality with others to support a subjective reaction to something. After all, it is just personal, like loving pistachio ice cream. But, surprisingly, this is not enough for humans. *We want our subjective reactions to be verified by others.*[3] We want to have shared realities about our subjective reactions just like our objective reactions. We want others to agree that pistachio ice cream *is* wonderful. Thus, in contrast to the classic subjective versus objective distinction, we do not have purely subjective personal reactions to things versus objective information-based reactions to things. For humans, we have shared realities about things—and we experience them as objective.

What are the implications of all this for the distinction between facts and opinions? In contrast to facts, opinions are responses to something that do not require conclusive supporting information, such as a person's particular food preferences. Unlike for a fact, a person supposedly does not need other people to agree with his or her opinion about something for it to be considered legitimate: "Well OK, you don't agree, but that's my opinion." Nonetheless, we humans want our opinions to be shared realities with others, and we prefer to interact with others who share them. By so doing, we *experience* our opinions as being objective rather than subjective. This has significant consequences for what makes us human: (a) We are motivated to learn from others, *motivated to be influenced by others*, in order that our opinions be a shared reality that makes our opinions objective and not just subjective, and (b) we treat our subjective opinions as if they were objective facts—the *false objectivity* effect of shared reality.

Creating Attitudes and Opinions as Shared Realities with Others

The human motivation to share our attitudes and opinions with others means that others *can* and *will* influence our evaluations of things in the world, *over and above* our own response to those things. Others also influence our moral evaluations of our own and others' actions.

Others' Influence on What We Like and Dislike

The human motivation to learn from others what to feel about things in the world is evident early in child development. As discussed in Chapter 2, it is evident in the emergence of shared feelings during infancy. Infants try to get the person they are with to share their interest in something they are looking at—their opinion that this is worth looking at. But they also are responsive to feedback from that person about whether it *is* something worth looking at, as shown in the study in which infants pointed more often at a moving object when their partner looked at both the infant's face and the object while expressing excitement about what was happening.[4] This back-and-forth between infants and their interaction partners is the starting point for children's creation of a shared opinion about something.

The development of shared opinions about things is also evident in children learning from others how to evaluate something. As mentioned earlier, 12-month-old infants can even learn how to evaluate a novel object in a televised scenario from observing an adult's emotional reaction to that object. And they are selective about whose evaluation they should share, such as learning from an experimenter rather than from their mother how to evaluate a novel toy that is approaching them in the experimenter's room.

Another case of children learning from others how to evaluate things is their learning what foods to like or dislike. I discussed earlier the case of learning to like spicy food. As I said, it is not natural to eat spicy food. It is also not natural to eat sour food, and the term *sour* is even used metaphorically to denote something bad, like a relationship that has "soured." Nonetheless, children learn to eat food that is spicy *and* sour. This does not happen spontaneously. Children observe their parents and older children react positively to eating such food. Other people send the clear message that they like to eat this kind of food. Motivated to share that reality, children eat it and learn to like it too. Notably, they are not simply imitating the behavior of eating the food. They are not just sharing the practice of eating the food. They learn to share the positive attitude toward the food, *to share liking it*.

By the way, it is evident that many parents have at least a tacit understanding that their young child's affective reaction to something can be influenced by how they affectively respond to that thing. An especially compelling example is what many parents do when their wobbly young toddler falls while trying to walk. Falling is inherently a negative event for children. For young infants, falling produces a reflex startle response that usually includes crying (the Moro reflex). Thus, we would expect that toddlers, and their parents, would feel negative about it, end of story. But often toddlers who fall check to see how their parents feel about what just happened, and often their parents *act* as if nothing significant, nothing negative, just happened—all is well. Some parents even display a gentle, benign smile when it happens (despite what they are feeling inside). And the toddlers often accept this message from their parents and learn to treat most falls as no big deal. They want to share the opinion, which their parents have communicated, that falling is fine. By creating a shared reality, a naturally negative event is transformed to something more benign. This is an upside of humans wanting to create shared realities.

It is not just children, of course, whose opinions are influenced by messages from others about what to like and dislike. Teenagers and adults are influenced by messages from their friends, romantic partners, teachers or managers, and, pervasively, from the media. Historically, the largest research question in the field of social psychology, as well as in the field of marketing and consumer behavior, has been concerned with how messages from others influence people's attitudes and opinions. It is not possible to cover this huge literature on attitude formation and change,[5] but I do want to discuss some of its findings from the perspective of shared reality motivation in effective persuasion from others.

The traditional literature on attitudes did not relate them to shared reality motivation per se. However, two proposed functions of attitudes are related to shared reality motivation. One was the *knowledge* function, whereby attitudes help people to make sense of their life experiences.[6] This function relates to the epistemic motive of creating shared realities with others. The other function of attitudes was the *formation and maintenance of social relationships*,[7] which relates to the social relational or connectedness motive of creating shared realities with others.

The distinction between epistemic and social relational motives is also relevant to the literature on types of social influence. John French and Bertram Raven, pioneers in analyzing social power, distinguished between referent power and expert power.[8] An agent of influence has *referent power* to the extent that the recipient of influence has or wants to have a feeling of "oneness" with that agent. An agent of influence has *expert power* to the extent that the recipient perceives the agent as having knowledge or expertise that the recipient does not have. Thus, referent power relates to the social relational or connectedness motive of creating a shared reality with others, whereas expert power relates to the epistemic motive.

Similar to French and Raven's distinction, Herbert Kelman distinguished between social influence based on *identification*, whereby the influence recipient adopts the agent's viewpoint to establish a relationship with that agent, versus influence based on *internalization*, whereby the recipient adopts the agent's viewpoint because it seems sensible and valid.[9] A classic study by Kelman nicely illustrates how the former social relational motive and the latter epistemic motive underlying shared reality creation can play out differently over time.

The study was conducted in 1954, just before the US Supreme Court was to make a decision on desegregating public schools. The participants were Black students who attended an all-Black college. They received a persuasive message advocating that some all-Black private colleges should remain all-Black to preserve Black culture, history, and tradition—an opinion contrary to that held by a large majority of the participants. In the "attractive influence agent" condition, the ostensible source of the message was a college senior who was president of the student council at a top all-Black university. In the "credible influence agent" condition, the ostensible source was a highly respected professor and expert on the history and problems of minority groups. The salience of the influence agent study was also manipulated to be "high" (the dependent measures were collected soon after the persuasive message) or "low" (the measures were collected one to two weeks later).

The study found that participants in the "attractive influence agent" condition were more receptive to the persuasive message when the agent had high versus low salience. In contrast, participants in the "credible influence agent" condition were highly and equally receptive to the persuasive message in both the high *and* low salience conditions. Thus, consistent with Kelman's distinction, the influence of an attractive agent, but not a credible agent, depended on the relationship being salient. This shows how shared realities with others can play out differently over time when they are based on the epistemic motive versus the social relational motive. In the former epistemic case, social influence does not depend on there being a strong relationship with the influence agent, and thus the influence can continue even when that agent is no longer salient.

As another example of this phenomenon, consider an additional finding from the original "saying-is-believing" study discussed in Chapter 1. The participants in this study were assigned to the role of communicator, and their topic was the evaluatively ambiguous behaviors of a person called Donald. The participants labeled Donald's behaviors with more positive trait names when the audience liked him (e.g., "confident," "persistent") and with more negative trait names when the audience disliked him (e.g., "conceited," "stubborn"). Note that the participants have epistemic uncertainty about how to characterize Donald because his behaviors were evaluatively ambiguous. In addition, the audience is a stranger to them, as is the target person Donald. They believe they are unlikely to meet either the audience or Donald in the future.

Given all this, it is likely that the epistemic motive for creating a shared reality with the audience—*to make sense* of Donald's ambiguous behaviors—is stronger than the social relational motive. If so, then there should be a shared reality effect on participants' attitude toward Donald both immediately after they have tuned their message toward their audience and weeks later. In fact, this was the case.

As these examples illustrate, there are times when it is the epistemic motive for creating a shared reality that underlies social influence. But there are other times when it the social relational motive for creating a shared reality that rules the day. I discussed in Chapter 3 how preschoolers deal with a conflict between two adult models when one model is more accurate and the other has a stronger relationship to them. One model talks with a native accent but gives incorrect names for familiar objects, whereas the other model talks with a foreign accent but gives correct names. When these models give different novel names for a novel object, whose lead did the children follow? The four- and five-year-olds chose the name suggested by the foreign-accented speaker, choosing epistemic accuracy over in-group relationship. *But,* for the younger children, the in-group relationship beat out epistemic accuracy.[10]

Notably, relationships can beat out epistemic accuracy for adults as well. There is evidence, for example, that the quality of the arguments in a message (i.e., epistemic support) carries less weight when the influence agent is high in attractiveness to the message recipients.[11] Indeed, wanting to share others' attitudes or opinions, independent of these others' expertise or arguments, can be so important to people that they will change their attitude on the topic toward what they know is another person's position even before they have received a message from that person—the phenomenon of anticipatory attitude change.[12]

Also relevant to shared reality motivation is the social influence distinction between *membership* groups and *reference* groups. A membership group is a group to which you belong. A reference group is a group whose attitudes and opinions (and values) you use as a guide for your own attitudes and opinions. In the case of a positive reference group, you are motivated to share, or accept, the group's attitudes and opinions. In the case of a negative reference group, you are motivated not to share, or to reject, group members' attitudes and opinions. Your own membership group can be either a positive or a negative reference group.[13] For example, some members of minority groups disparage their groups in an effort to distance themselves from these groups, with the goal of avoiding the societal costs of membership. In such cases, they treat their membership group as a negative reference group. It is also the case that someone can have a positive reference group of which they are not a member. For some working-class individuals, "billionaires" is such a positive reference group. The remarkable thing about reference groups is that they can shape the attitudes and opinions of people who do not belong, are unlikely to ever belong, and, in many cases, have never interacted with a single member of that group.

Theodore Newcomb, a pioneer in social psychology, conducted a longitudinal study on reference groups in the late 1930s during the period of President Roosevelt's New Deal. [14] The entire student body at Bennington College, an all-female college, participated in the study over several years. All of the participants, then, were members of the Bennington College community as well as members of their own home family. Significantly, most of the participants' parents were conservative on political and economic public issues, whereas most members of the Bennington College community (e.g., older students and teachers) were liberal. What varied among the students was whether their family or the Bennington College community was the more positive reference group regarding political and economic opinions.

One would expect that, generally speaking, as students spent more time participating in the Bennington College community, that community would become a more positive reference group, which would be revealed in juniors and seniors being less conservative than first-year students. This was indeed the case. In the 1936 presidential election, 62% of the first-year students voted for the Republican candidate versus 29% for the liberal Roosevelt and 9% for socialist candidates. In stark contrast, among the juniors and seniors, only 14% voted for the Republican candidate versus 54% for Roosevelt and 30% for socialist candidates.

That is a remarkable difference. And the development of the Bennington College community into a positive reference group with a less conservative viewpoint had another consequence. As a measure of students' prestige, or status, within the community, the students were asked to choose (as one of five students) a student who was "most worthy to represent the college" at an intercollegiate gathering. Overall, the students who were chosen for this prestigious position were less conservative than those who were not chosen, and this was especially true for the junior and senior classes.

Sharing opinions with the local community on political and economic issues increased students' prestige within the community. This was a social benefit of shared reality for these students. However, for those students who continued to treat their home family as the more positive reference group, there was a definite downside from shared reality in terms of lower prestige within the Bennington community. And I wonder whether there was also a cost of shared reality back home for those who treated the Bennington College community as the more positive reference group. Did these students perhaps lose status within their family? As always, there is likely to be a trade-off from choosing one reference group over another. I wonder what this trade-off looks like when someone chooses a group as a positive reference group despite not being a member of that group (now or ever), as when working class individuals choose "billionaires" as their positive reference group?

Social Influence on Our Moral Opinions

Other people influence not only our likes and dislikes but also our moral opinions, and moral opinions are different than just preferences. For example, children can learn from their family to eat nonspicy food, and if they observe other children eat spicy food, they might consider this to be odd or even unwise, but not immoral. On the other hand, children from some communities, as in Britain, would consider it immoral to eat horse meat, as happens in France. Such moral opinions are not biological imperatives. After all, is it really morally worse to eat horse meat than cow meat? But if a community shares the opinion that horses or dogs or some other animal are really members of the *family*, then killing them and eating them becomes a moral issue—a shared opinion that it is morally wrong to do so.

I discussed in Chapter 2 how toddlers learn to share their community's social practices. They learn how to dress, how to use eating utensils (including their hands), how to name objects, and so on. Most of these social practices are not considered moral issues. Dressing with one black sock and one brown sock is a mistake, even an embarrassing mistake, but it is not immoral. Calling something by the wrong name, or mispronouncing the name, can also be an embarrassing mistake, but again it is not immoral. (Whenever I mispronounce a name, which happens too often, I say that this is how it is pronounced in Canada, or at least the part of Canada in which I grew up. That usually works, although my wife and daughter roll their eyes.) Even young children can understand the difference between a social practice that is a shared social convention in their community and a social practice that is a shared moral opinion.[15]

There are some shared moral opinions that are found in many cultures, including both Western and Eastern cultures. Richard Shweder, a renowned cultural anthropologist and psychologist, and his colleagues report that respondents from both the United States and India judge the following types of behavior to be morally wrong: harming another person, breaking promises, and incest.[16] There were also differences between Americans and Indians regarding what is morally wrong.

One example Shweder gives is a husband in India punishing his wife after she disobeys him, for example, by going to a movie alone without his permission. Shweder argues that the family unit in India is treated analogously to a military unit, and a low-ranking member who leaves a military base without permission in the US army would be punished. From this broader perspective, if the wife's behavior is viewed through the lens of the Indian shared viewpoint (i.e., that the family unit is analogous to a military unit), then one would share the Indian moral opinion that leaving home (the base) without permission should be punished. However, if the wife's behavior is not viewed through this lens, then one would not share the Indian moral opinion.

What this highlights is that what is or is not shared is a set of viewpoints and opinions that work together in a coherent manner. There is not just *a* moral opinion. There are other shared viewpoints that justify the moral opinion. Without sharing those background viewpoints, the moral opinion seems unjustified. This can create misunderstandings and conflict between individuals from different cultures.

The importance of background factors is not limited to background shared viewpoints. It is also true for background shared concerns. For example, moral judgments about others' actions can vary depending on whether the person making the judgment has shared promotion concerns with others (i.e., shared concerns with growth and advancement) or shared prevention concerns with others (i.e., shared concerns with safety and security). Consider the following scenario:

> A brother and sister are alone in the house and decide to make love just once. The sister is already taking birth control pills and the brother uses a condom. They both enjoy the act but decide not to do it again. They promise each other to keep it a secret.

What is your opinion of what these siblings did? Most people's opinion is negative. And, more than just negative, their opinion is that what they the siblings did was morally wrong. They cannot always justify their moral opinion, however, and often give reasons that are not supported by the scenario, such as saying that the sister will get pregnant even though her birth control pills and his condom make that highly unlikely, or saying that their parents will be upset by what happened even though the brother and sister promise to keep it a secret and not do it again.[17]

Would you change your opinion if your reasons for judging the siblings' behavior as being morally wrong were shown to be weak? Many people would not because they go with their gut, their feelings, which continue to tell them that what happened was wrong even if they can't give good reasons why. But there are individuals who do care about whether their reasons do or do not justify their opinion. Recent research has found that moral opinions regarding this scenario are based more on *feelings* for people with shared *promotion* concerns but are based more on *reasons* for people with shared *prevention* concerns.[18] Given that the reasons for condemnation are weak in this scenario, prevention participants judged the siblings' action to be significantly *less wrong* than did promotion participants.[19] Thus, different background shared concerns can influence whether some action is perceived to be morally wrong.

As mentioned earlier, incest, as in the previous example, is one of those actions that most people judge to be morally wrong. Another is breaking a promise, or not keeping commitments. In his book, *Trusting What You're Told*,[20] Paul Harris describes the moral judgments about eating meat that are made by children, 6 to 10 years of age, who decided to be vegetarians within a family that eats meat. Harris calls these children "independent" vegetarians because their decision was independent of their meat-eating family. However, this does not mean that they did not share opinions about eating meat with other people outside their family (other vegetarians).

Thus, like Harris, I will put "independent" in quotations. In addition to the "independent" vegetarians, the research included two other groups of children of the same age and background—*family vegetarian* children whose family also did not eat meat and *family meat-eater* children who were nonvegetarian like their family and ate meat regularly.

These three different kinds of children were asked how bad it would be for someone to eat meat if, in one case, that person were a morally committed vegetarian who had promised not to eat meat because animals were friends and this would hurt them or, in another case, that person was uncommitted to vegetarianism and had never made a promise not to eat meat. There was no difference between the moral judgments of the "independent" vegetarians, the family vegetarians, and the family meat-eaters. They all condemned the person who was a committed vegetarian and broke the promise not to eat meat, and they all did not condemn the person who was uncommitted and had never made a promise not to eat meat.

What's happening here? An earlier study had found that, when asked to think of a kind of meat that they did not ordinarily eat and give reasons why they didn't, "independent" vegetarians overwhelmingly gave an animal welfare reason such as "I don't like the idea of killing animals." In contrast, meat-eaters most often gave a reason about the bad taste, such as "It tastes kind of . . . like, weird." Given this, one might think that there would be a difference between the "independent" vegetarian children and the meat-eater children in their moral condemnation of eating meat. I believe that what this research shows is that shared attitudes should be distinguished from shared moral opinions.[21] The "independent" vegetarians do not share the same attitude toward eating meat with the meat-eating children. The latter like eating meat (when it tastes good), but the former do not (even when it tastes good). But these different children can share, and this research suggests that they do share, the same moral opinion about *keeping commitments*: It is wrong to do something that you promised not to do, but it is okay if you did not promise not to do it.

Distinguishing between shared attitudes and shared moral opinions provides a nice solution to a potential problem for the "independent" vegetarian children. They share with some nonfamily members the commitment not to eat meat because of a shared dislike for hurting or killing animals. But this attitude about disliking to eat meat is not shared with their own family. If these vegetarian children make a moral issue out of their dislike of people eating meat, such as telling their mother or father "You are a bad person to eat meat," then there could be a serious conflict. Instead, these children can decide not to make a moral issue out of it. They can create a shared moral opinion on the commitment issue instead, by all agreeing that what matters is following commitments: "If you are committed to not eating meat, then you should not eat meat, and it would be bad if you did so. But if you are not committed to not eating meat, then you can eat meat, and you are not bad for doing so." The vegetarian children and their meat-eating family can all share this moral opinion about commitment. Problem solved—and they lived happily ever after.

When a moral opinion has been previously established with others as a shared reality, can it be influenced in a current situation by the judgments of others who are present and express their unanimous contrary opinion? This is like the conflict in the Asch situation except that it is not between a perceptual judgment and the consensus of the other group members. Now, the conflict is between two shared realities—a prior norm about the right moral judgment and a current contrary norm expressed unanimously by other members in the group. This conflict was examined in a recent study.[22]

Consistent with Asch's findings, there was a significant tendency for the undergraduate participants to match the moral judgment of the other group members on the conflict trials (compared to the nonconflict, control condition), and this tendency was greater when there was some ambiguity about what the correct moral judgment was. Moreover, the participants continued to support their new moral judgments when they later made private judgments. Thus, there was an actual change in shared reality regarding the moral judgments. It was not the case that participants were simply "going along to get along."[23]

The study also found that the participants supported (i.e., justified) their new moral judgment by modifying their position on the issue. For example, one scenario was the following: *To avoid upsetting her friend, Kimberly lies by saying, "No! You don't look fat in those jeans."* The standard response from most participants was that this behavior was morally acceptable because kindness matters more than honesty—a little white lie. But those participants who changed their judgment when faced with other group members declaring this behavior to be morally unacceptable modified their original position on this moral issue. They changed their priority by arguing that honesty was more important than kindness, saying something like "Friends should be honest with each other." This change from a shared opinion previously established with others to a new opinion shared with a current group is similar to what happened in Newcomb's Bennington College study when students changed their political and economic opinions from those they grew up with at home to those that were dominant in their current college community.

If It's Just about Wanting Shared Reality, Why Is There Resistance to Persuasion?

There is substantial evidence—much more than I have been able to review—that people's attitudes and opinions are influenced by others. I have suggested that a major reason for this is that people are motivated to create shared realities with others. But if people are open to influence by others to create a shared reality with them, then why is there also clear evidence that people often resist being persuaded by others? Where does this resistance come from?

Before beginning this discussion, it is important to be clear what "resistance to persuasion" means. A failure of a persuasion attempt does not mean that it failed because of resistance to it. A persuasion attempt can fail because it had little persuasive force on the recipient to begin with—there was no need to resist it. It is like walking forward against a light breeze rather than a strong wind. There is little need to resist the light breeze because its force is so weak. If a persuasive attempt is not relevant to a recipient's epistemic motive or social relational motive, then there is little motivation to create a shared reality with the agent of influence. The persuasion attempt would fail but not because there was resistance to creating a shared reality; there was simply no motivation to create a shared reality to begin with.

What we are discussing here is the case where a persuasive attempt is relevant to a recipient's epistemic motive and/or social relational motive, and, therefore, there should be some motivation to create a shared reality with the agent of influence. Given this, why would there be resistance? That is the question.

A classic case of resistance to persuasion derives from work testing the theory of psychological reactance that proposes that people resist another person pressuring them to do something, such as telling them that they *must* believe something.[24] People resist to maintain their independence or show the person pressuring them (or others observing what happens) that they are autonomous.[25] This work demonstrates that when people have an initial attitude about something and then receive a message that not only challenges their attitude but does so in a coercive way, they are likely to maintain their initial attitude (i.e., resist the persuasive message). Moreover, pressure tactics can produce change opposite to what a message is advocating (a "boomerang" effect) even when the message is consistent with the recipient's original attitude. In addition, this resistance is more likely if recipients must publicly express their attitude after receiving the pressure tactics.[26]

What does this literature on resistance tell us? This literature is showing that people are not motivated to create a shared reality with someone if that person is pressuring them to agree in a way that makes them feel or look as though they are being controlled by that person. If they were to go along with what that person wants, it would be compliance (superficial agreement) and not internalization (genuine agreement). Thus, it would *not* be a shared reality. Given this, there is no shared reality motivation to do it.

There is another finding about resistance to changing attitudes that should be noted. There is evidence that individuals are more susceptible to changing their political attitudes when they are young adults than when they are older—a so-called impressionable period.[27] This is the same age period studied by Newcomb in his Bennington College study. It is interesting that two follow-up studies using many of the students who participated in Newcomb's original study, one 25 years later and another 40 years later, found that these students had *remained* quite liberal.[28] The earlier change persisted. What is happening here? Let's now consider this impressionable period phenomenon as well as the other resistance phenomena that we have discussed in terms of the motivation to create shared reality with others.

Where does resistance come from if people want to create shared reality with others? One answer that I previously mentioned is that people resist when they feel that to go along with someone pressuring them would be mere compliance and thus would not create a shared reality with that person. Another more general reason is that people have prior beliefs that they share with significant others, and they are *defending those* shared realities against current pressure to change. Take the Bennington College students for example. When they were students, they had the Bennington College community as a positive reference group with which they shared new liberal political attitudes. And this Bennington College community continued to be a positive reference group. It was the shared reality associated with this community that was internalized and remained stable over time and even decades later was defended against attack.

When individuals have prior attitudes that are threatened by a current message arguing against them, the social relationships associated with those prior attitudes will be defended. And this includes public displays to others in the current situation about what kind of person you are, such as being autonomous, to support that view of yourself that you also *share* with significant others. I agree with experts on attitudes when they say that strong attitudes are more likely to persist and are more resistant to change than are weak attitudes because strong attitudes are more motivationally significant and are linked to many other attitudes and beliefs.[29] But I would add that strong attitudes are motivationally significant and linked to many other attitudes and beliefs precisely because they are part of a coherent system of shared realities with significant others.

Treating Subjective Attitudes and Opinions as if They Were Objective Facts

Let's return to the subjective/objective distinction with which I began this chapter. As I mentioned then, people want their subjective attitudes and opinions to be verified by others. In so doing, they create shared realities such that their attitudes and opinions are now experienced as objective rather than subjective. One of the clearest, and most troubling, examples of how people treat subjective attitudes and opinions as if they were objective facts is people's use of *stereotypes* to characterize members of different groups.

I discussed several problems with stereotypes in Chapter 6 and concluded (following Roger Brown) that the fundamental problem is that characteristics included in stereotypes often do not describe category members because they are actually not descriptions. Instead, they are opinions and attitudes about category members. That is, when using stereotypes, people treat subjective opinions and attitudes about social category members as if they were objective facts. And not only that, the social category members are evaluated using the perceivers' own standards, which the perceivers assume are universally valid and correct—the *right* standards.

This last aspect of stereotypes needs to be emphasized. Stereotypes are not facts about social category members. They are instead *value judgments* based on standards that people share with members of their in-group. Even when stereotypes are considered to be positive, like saying that Canadians are "polite" or Germans are "hard-working," the perceivers who are making this evaluation based on their own standards rather than offering a simple description of the target group. In fact, the target group often evaluates itself differently based on its own standards, such as Germans characterizing themselves as "skillful" rather than "hard-working." "Hard-working" and "skillful" both sound positive, but if you ask why Germans workers are so productive, it is quite different to say that their productivity is due to effort versus ability. What evidence would justify making an effort versus an ability attribution in this case? It is not about facts; it is an opinion that suits a preferred conclusion for those using the stereotype.

And, of course, in many cases the stereotypes about social category members are not positive. They are negative. They represent failures to meet the standards of the stereotype users. For example, to be "dependent," "emotional," and "sensitive" is not inherently bad, but if perceivers value people who are "independent," "unemotional," and "tough," then the former characteristics are, by definition, bad.[30] Thus, it matters that Americans in the land of "rugged individualism" traditionally stereotyped females as dependent, emotional, and sensitive in contrast to men who were independent, unemotional, and tough. And when stereotypes are negative in this way, they function as negative attitudes (i.e., prejudices) and not just negative opinions. And these prejudices can, in turn, lead to discrimination. Women in the workplace, for example, have been discriminated against by men who held these stereotypes about them. And, importantly, when such discrimination occurs, the perpetrators think their stereotypes about females are *simply facts* about females. Indeed, for some sexist males today, anyone who says otherwise is just being "politically correct."

There are other consequences of people's subjective attitudes and opinions being experienced as objective when shared realities are created. One consequence is that the attitudes and opinions can become more extreme. Early studies of group polarization had small groups (five or so members) discuss what advice to give another person who was facing a choice dilemma. The dilemma was between a more attractive option that was relatively risky and a less attractive option that was less risky. One choice dilemma, for example, concerned an engineer who was choosing between staying in his current job that was adequate but afforded little opportunity for significant salary improvement (less attractive but less risky) versus a job with a new company, which, if all went well, offered the opportunity for significant salary improvement (more attractive but riskier). The group's task was to recommend how much risk the target person should be willing to take if he were to choose the new job. For this engineer case, the group indicated the lowest likelihood that the new company would prove to be financially sound (e.g., not lower than 90%, as low as 30%) to make it acceptable for the target person to change to the new job.

The study began with the participants first making their recommendation as individuals, and then they met together as a group to reach consensus on what to recommend. The early research found that the recommendation by a group was riskier than the average of the prior individual recommendations of its group members. Given this, the phenomenon was called the "risky shift." However, subsequent research found that decisions made by a group sometimes were more cautious than the average of the individual decisions of the group members.[31] The more general phenomenon, then, is that the group decisions are more extreme, or more polarized, than the decisions made by individual members in whatever direction the members were initially leaning.

This group polarization phenomenon can be understood in terms of the group discussion creating a shared reality among its members. When the individuals, prior to meeting as a group, make their decision, that individual decision is experienced as being subjective, *not* objective, and thus not necessarily valid, or conclusive. It is not clear that recommending that the target person move in a risky direction, or in a cautious direction, is the best advice. However, the decision that is reached after the group arrives at a consensus is a shared reality, and, as such, it is treated as being objective and thus valid and conclusive. Now it is clear that recommending that the target person move in a risky direction, or move in a cautious direction, *is* the best advice. There is no need to waffle, to moderate the advice. It is the best advice and thus should be sent unambiguously. This results in the group recommendation being more extreme than the average of the members' individual recommendations.

There is evidence that one shared reality mechanism underlying group polarization is social validation. Earlier studies had found that attitudes become polarized when group members repeatedly express the same attitude. But there is also evidence that this effect is especially large when the arguments given by one group member in support of an attitude are picked up by another group member and repeated back to him or her in subsequent interactions.[32] Such repeating back serves as social validation—an important mechanism in shared reality creation.

There is another consequence of people's subjective attitudes and opinions being experienced as objective when shared realities are created. If an opinion is objective, is now a fact about the world, then it can be the basis for understanding what happens in the world. And if something happens that *appears* to contradict this shared opinion, then arguments need to be constructed to explain what happened in a way that maintains the opinion. This is similar to what I discussed earlier regarding resistance to persuasion, but this time it occurs not in response to an agent of influence trying to change your opinion but in response to something happening in the world that appears to contradict your opinion—the opinion that to you is not just an opinion but rather a fact about the world.

Perhaps the most compelling example of this phenomenon is the research conducted by John Jost, a major figure in political psychology, and his colleagues on how people justify the sociopolitical status quo, even when their status in the existing social arrangement is *disadvantageous* to them.[33] The opinion in this case, which is treated like a fact, is that the current, existing social arrangements are fair and legitimate.

But how can certain conditions, such as millions of people living in poverty in the United States, be fair and legitimate? The answer is that such conditions are fair and legitimate because America is a meritocracy in which those who are poor *deserve* to be poor because they lack the motivation and/or ability to earn more money. This belief is quite common in the United States. For example, poor African Americans in the South are *more* likely to subscribe to meritocratic ideologies than more affluent African Americans in the North. Moreover, there is evidence that low-income Americans are more likely than higher-income Americans to believe that large differences in pay are *necessary* to encourage effort and that economic inequality is legitimate and necessary.[34] There is also evidence that the social relational motive associated with creating shared realities with others supports such *system-justifying world views*.[35]

In sum, there are some major downsides of what might be called the "false objectivity" effect of shared reality. This effect can cause us to create stereotypic beliefs about members of out-groups—beliefs that are treated as factual descriptions but are really evaluations based on our own in-group values. It can also lead to more extreme opinions than would have occurred from just combining our individual judgments. Finally, it can also cause us to justify and defend opinions that are not supported by evidence, even when these opinions are not in our self-interest. Thus, we need to be careful to recognize many of our opinions for what they truly are—evaluative judgments with limited evidence to support them. We should stop treating them as facts. This means that when there are political conflicts, often there is not really a competition between "alternative facts." If it were, then we could determine which side has the correct facts. But it is not a competition between alternative facts. Rather, it is a competition between *alternative evaluations*.

In concluding this chapter, it is important to mention a pervasive bias that can exacerbate the downsides of the false objectivity effect. This is the tendency to see more consensus with our attitudes and opinions than actually exists—the so-called false consensus effect.[36] People have a tendency to think that their attitudes and opinions are shared by others and are relatively common. When young children do this, we call it "egocentrism." When adults do it we often call it "projection," which, given that this was considered to be a defense mechanism in the psychodynamic literature, makes it sound aberrant. But it is not limited to young children or aberrant adults. It is actually quite common and pervasive. Normal adults do it all the time. And, because of shared reality, false consensus contributes to the false objectivity effect.

One of my favorite examples of false consensus (sometimes called "assumed similarity") is an early study that was ostensibly studying communication techniques. In this study, students were asked to walk around their college campus for 30 minutes wearing a sandwich board that said "Repent." Half of the students agreed to do so, and half did not agree. They were all then asked to estimate what percentage of their fellow students would agree or disagree to do this activity. Those students who had agreed to wear the sign estimated that 63.5% of their fellow students would, like them, agree to wear the sign. Those students who did *not* agree to wear the sign estimated that 76.6% would, like them, *not* agree to wear the sign.

Note that both groups of the students estimated that a clear majority had the same opinion as they did about walking around wearing the sign. In actual fact, there was no consensus on this issue (it was split evenly), but the students generated a consensual shared reality for their opinion. This is important because it would support a shift from their seeing their opinion as subjective to seeing it as objective—this *is* what most people would choose to do. In this way, the false consensus effect can make the false objectivity effect even more prevalent and problematic.

Thus far, I have discussed how our shared realities fundamentally shape our feelings, our beliefs and knowledge including our self-knowledge, and our attitudes and opinions. But that is not the end of the shared reality story because our shared realities not only impact how we experience our world. Our motivation to create shared realities also determines what goals we pursue—what we strive for and value in life. This central part of what makes us human is considered next.

Notes

1. See Hardin and Higgins (1996).
2. See Kelley (1973).
3. See Hardin and Higgins (1996).
4. See Liszkowski, Carpenter, Henning, Striano, and Tomasello (2004).
5. For a thoughtful and extensive review of this literature, see Eagly and Chaiken (1993). They define attitude as "*a psychological tendency that is expressed by evaluating a particular entity with some degree of favor or disfavor*" (p. 1; emphasis in original).
6. Daniel Katz and his colleagues (e.g., Katz, 1960) introduced and named this function of attitudes.
7. Classic discussions of this attitude function were provided by Kelman (1958) and Smith, Bruner, and White (1956).
8. See, for example, French (1956) and French and Raven (1959).
9. See Kelman (1958).
10. See Corriveau, Kinzler, and Harris (2013).
11. See, for example, Norman (1976).
12. See, for example, Cialdini, Levy, Herman, and Evenbeck (1973), Cialdini, Levy, Herman, Kozlowski, and Petty (1976), and Cialdini and Petty (1981).
13. See, for example, Kelley (1952), Merton (1957), and Newcomb (1958).
14. See Newcomb (1958).
15. See Turiel (2006).
16. See Shweder, Mahapatra, and Miller (1987).
17. For a thoughtful discussion of the psychology of people's reactions to this scenario, see Haidt (2001).
18. Why this difference between promotion and prevention? People with prevention concerns want to maintain the current satisfactory status quo. The current "nonloss" status quo is fine with them. Taking unnecessary risks could land them in a worse "–1" state. They need clear reasons to choose to do that. Reasons are in the service of effective prevention. In contrast, people with promotion concerns want to advance from the current status quo to a better state. The current "nongain" status quo is not

fine with them. They are willing to take a chance to move to a better "+1" rather than stay in an unsatisfactory nongain state. Waiting for clear reasons frustrates this movement. There will always be some uncertainty about moving to a better future, but sticking with the current status quo is a certain negative condition (a certain nongain). Going with your feelings, then, even if they cannot be justified with reasons, is in the service of effective promotion.

19. See Cornwell and Higgins (2016).
20. See Harris (2012).
21. For other arguments why this distinction should be made, see Heiphetz, Spelke, Harris, and Banaji (2013).
22. This study was conducted as part of Carl Jago's Columbia University Honors Thesis under the supervision of James Cornwell and me.
23. Another finding from this study also makes clear that the participants were concerned about making the *right* judgment rather than just trying to get along. The study included a manipulation that made some participants feel high power and others feel low power. High power is a fit with participants who are dominant promotion, and low power is a fit with participants who are dominant prevention. Those participants with regulatory fit should "feel right" about their initial opinion on each moral scenario—an opinion that reflects the normative standard they shared prior to the conflict situation. Moreover, this "feel right" feeling should make them believe that this normative moral judgment *is* right (Camacho, Higgins, and Luger 2003). If this is the case, then they should be less open to changing this judgment and agreeing with the current group's contrary judgment. And, indeed, this is what happened—regulatory fit reduced the current group's influence.
24. See Brehm (1966).
25. See Baer, Hinkle, Smith, and Fenton (1980) and Heilman and Toffler (1976).
26. See Baer et al. (1980).
27. See Krosnick and Alwin (1989).
28. See Alwin, Cohen, and Newcomb (1991) and Newcomb, Koenig, Flacks, and Warwick (1967).
29. See, for example, Eagly and Chaiken (1993, p. 680).
30. For an extensive and thoughtful review of gender stereotypes, and stereotyping more generally, see Schneider (2004).
31. See Stoner (1961, 1968).
32. See Brauer and Judd (1996).
33. See, for example, Jost, Banaji, and Nosek (2004), Jost, Ledgerwood, and Hardin (2008), Jost and Hunyady (2005), and Jost, Pelham, Sheldon, and Sullivan (2003).
34. See Jost et al. (2003).
35. See Jost et al. (2008).
36. See Marks and Miller (1987) and Ross, Greene, and House (1977).

9

What We Strive For and Value

What do we strive for? What is it that we want? Historically, classic psychology, as well as classic economics and other disciplines, have had a simple answer to this question. *We want what other animals want: need satisfaction and the pleasure that accompanies it.* That was the basic answer. Unlike intelligence where our extraspecial gifts were extolled, when it came to motivation we were just like any other animal. The only difference in opinion was which motivation that we had in common with other animals should be emphasized most. Was it biological needs that must be satisfied, such as the need for food, water, and sex? Was it the hedonic motivation to maximize pleasure and minimize pain?[1] Whichever one it was, it was a motive that humans had in common with other animals. We were not considered to be special from other animals when it came to motivation. We were basically the same.

Well, humans are *not* the same as other animals motivationally.[2] We are different in significant ways—the most important being how we are motivated to create shared realities with others. How humans are motivated to create shared realities with others is special—"special" in the sense of being remarkable. The ways in which humans create shared realities with others reveals who we are, why we deal with the world and get along in the world, or don't, in the particular ways that *we* do that is different from other animals.

This chapter highlights a critical and central aspect of the shared reality motivation that makes humans special motivationally—our *self-regulation* in relation to internalized goals and standards that we share with significant others. This phase of shared reality development was discussed in Chapter 3—*shared self-guides*. It is remarkable to me that children as young as three years old, and in some cases even younger, can infer that other people have particular goals for them about what they want them to attain and particular standards for them that they want them to follow. Yes, this does require an impressive kind of *social* intelligence. But what is even more remarkable to me is that children *want* to share these goals and standards that others have for them. They accept them as their *own* personal goals and standards for their *own* self-regulation (internalization).[3]

Because young children do this all the time, it can seem unremarkable, even ordinary. But consider for a moment what is happening. A parent can show a child how to use a spoon or engage in some other social practice. But a parent's goals and standards for a child are not directly observable. They have to be inferred by the child. And among the parent's goals and standards are some that are just for this particular child. They are not a general social practice. In addition, and importantly, the goals and standards are often not just about who the child needs to be right now, but who the child needs to *become* in the *future*. On top of all this, children do not just comply with these goals and standards when they are being observed but also accept them as personal goals and standards to be attained and followed without surveillance, even when they are alone. The fact that very young children can do all this *is* remarkable. And for parents of young children, quite wonderful.

How Children Acquire Shared Ideal and Ought Self-Guides for Self-Regulation

How do we know that young children have accepted others' goals and standards for them in their own self-regulation? As I discussed in Chapter 3, they follow rules set for them by others even when they are not being observed. Even more striking, they feel shame or guilt when they behave in a way that is discrepant from others' standards for them, even when they are alone and others don't know what they did. And there is more to this child development story of self-regulation. Children learn to distinguish between two kinds of self-guides (goals and standards)—what kind of person they would ideally like to be, or aspire to be (*ideal* self-guides), and what kind of person they believe they should be, or have a responsibility to be (*ought* self-guides).[4] And they learn from others how much to emphasize each of these different types of self-guides in their self-regulation. How does this happen?

Caretaker–Child Interactions That Create Shared Ideal versus Ought Self-Guides

Everyone knows that caretaker–child interactions are very important in the development of children. And we also know that caretakers, such as a child's parents, can have very different styles of interacting with a child, with some being more supporting and managing (positive interactions) and others being more disciplining (negative interactions). But *within* positive interactions and *within* negative interactions, there can still be other important distinctions in how parents (which I will now use to represent caretakers in general) interact with their children. And these distinctions are important for how much and in what way children share reality with their parents.

Parents' interactions with their child create different psychological situations for the child. Consider the following interaction: A girl toddler smiles at her mother, the mother responds by picking her up and hugging her, and the girl feels happy. The child's psychological situation from this interaction is to experience the *presence of a positive outcome*. In contrast, consider the following different interaction between this girl and her mother: While walking outside with her mother, the girl is scared by a dog off its leash and cries out in distress, the mother responds by shooing the dog away and reassuring the child, and the girl feels relieved. The child's psychological situation from this interaction is to experience the *absence of a negative outcome*.

These are *both positive* interactions for the child, but they are two different kinds of positive interactions. In the first case, the parent's reaction to the child moves the child from a satisfactory status quo (zero) to something better (+1). Another example of such positivity from the presence of a positive outcome is when parents help their child to make progress on some activity or to advance from how they are currently doing to a better state. This kind of parental help has been called "scaffolding." It relates to Vygotsky's conception of the zone of proximal development in which children receive assistance that allows them to move from their current state to a higher skill set, as what happens when parents help their child learn a social practice like what are the names of different things.[5]

In the second case, the parent's reaction to the child moves the child from an unsatisfactory state (−1) back to a satisfactory state (zero). Safety and security is restored. Another example of positivity from the absence of a negative outcome is when parents intervene to prevent something bad from happening, such as stopping their child from touching a hot stove or walking into traffic. Here the current satisfactory state (zero) is retained by preventing −1 from happening—positivity from the absence of a negative outcome.

Parents, then, can create two different kinds of positivity for their child that send very different messages to the child about what kind of world the child is living in.[6] In the first case (presence of positive), the message is that the world is a place where nurturance, mastery, and growth occurs: *Your life can get better and better.* This message between parent and child creates a shared *promotion* viewpoint on the world. The parents' goals and standards for the child are experienced by the child as hopes and aspirations for the child's future—shared *ideal* self-guides.

In the second case (absence of negative), the message is that the world is a place where you have to be on your guard because bad things can happen. You have to work to maintain or restore safety and security: *Your life will remain fine only if you are careful.* This message between parent and child creates a shared *prevention* viewpoint on the world. The parents' goals and standards for the child are experienced by the child as the child's duties, obligations and responsibilities—shared *ought* self-guides.

These different shared self-guides and viewpoints on the world are also created by different negative interactions that children can have with their parents. Let's begin with a promotion failure. Consider the following interaction: A boy toddler spills some food while eating, the father responds by no longer smiling at him, and the boys feels sad. The child's psychological situation from this interaction is the *absence of a positive outcome*. It represents a failure to be nurtured. Another example of negativity from the absence of a positive outcome is when parents express disappointment at their child's failure to make progress on some activity, such as failing to make a new toy work. Combining the presence of positives with such absence of positives, promotion success and failure messages from parent to child create a shared viewpoint that the world is a world of potential *gains* and possible *nongains*, respectively. Children learn from these messages that to deal with this world and work effectively in it, they need to be eager and anticipate how things can go right.

Let's now discuss prevention failure. Consider a different interaction between the father and son: While the son is getting dressed, he is not focused and puts the wrong shoe on the wrong foot, the father angrily yells at the child to pay attention, and the child feels nervous. The child's psychological situation from this interaction is the *presence of a negative outcome*. It represents a failure of security. Another example of negativity from the presence of a negative outcome is when a child falls on the jungle gym at the playground and the father, clearly upset, rushes over and says, "You have to be more careful!" Combining the absence of negatives with such presence of negatives, prevention success and failure messages from parent to child create a shared viewpoint that the world is a world of potential *nonlosses* and possible *losses*, respectively. Children learn from these messages that to deal with this world and work effectively in it, they need to be vigilant and anticipate how things could go wrong.

What the promotion–prevention distinction suggests is that different types of parent–child interactions will lead to children acquiring different types of self-guides. And there is evidence that this is the case.[7] The research on self-guides began by examining the parenting styles of mothers with their five-year-old preschoolers. Three different types of parenting styles were identified: *nurturance* (maternal warmth and affection), *control* (the child must follow specific rules for obedience), and *punishment* (punitive maternal behaviors and derogation). The research then investigated how these three types of parenting received by preschoolers led to their acquiring by first grade either strong ideal self-guides or strong ought self-guides.

To measure the first graders' strength of *ideal* self-guides, they were asked the following questions: "What kind of kid would you like to be if you were the best you could possibly be?" and "Tell me about the kind of kid you would be if you could be perfect?" To measure the first graders' strength of *ought* self-guides, they were asked the following questions: "What kind of kid are you supposed to be to stay out of trouble?" and "Tell me about the kind of kid you have to be so you don't break any rules?" Following the procedure of previous studies with adults,[8] response latencies in answering these questions were used to measure strong ideal and ought self-guides, with faster responses indicating stronger self-guides.

The study found that a nurturance style of parenting five-year-olds predicted their acquiring strong ideal self-guides by first grade. In contrast, a control style of parenting five-year-olds, combined with a moderate amount of punishment (not too little or too much punishment), predicted their acquiring strong ought self-guides by first grade. Consistent with the earlier discussion, these findings show that different types of parent–child interactions result in children acquiring different types of self-guides.[9] Whether they are ideals or oughts, these self-guides are the goals that children believe *they need to attain* and the standards that they believe *they need to follow*. They are internalized as their own goals and standards to guide them even without surveillance. Once again, *sharing is believing*.

Before ending this section, I need to emphasize that it is not the goal content or topic of the parent–child interaction that is critical for children acquiring ideal or ought self-guides. Rather, it is the psychological situation produced in the child by that interaction, and that psychological situation depends on how the message about the goal or standard was delivered to the child.[10] Imagine, for example, that two different parents both want their child to work hard in school and be polite to others. Consider the differences below in how the parents deliver their message:

Parental goal: It's Important to work hard in school
  Promotion delivery:
  If you work hard in school, you'll be able to have any career you want!
  (positive end-state; eager optimistic message)
  Prevention delivery:
  If you work hard in school, you'll avoid getting into trouble.
  (positive end-state; vigilant careful message)

Parental goal: It's important to be polite

  Promotion delivery:
  If you are polite, you will always be welcome everywhere!
  (positive end-state; eager optimistic message)
  Prevention delivery:
  If you are polite, you will not lose your friends.
  (positive end-state; vigilant careful message)

There is something else I need to add. Children do not necessarily receive only one kind of parenting. If a child has two parents, they can interact with the child differently. And even the same parent can emphasize either prevention security or promotion nurturance at different times. And this can be a good thing because when the children are effective in their self-regulation, they can experience *both* peace (prevention success) and joy (promotion success). There are children, in fact, who receive both prevention- and promotion-style parenting, and they develop into individuals with strong ideal and strong ought self-guides. It is not necessarily one or the other, although often one or the other predominates.

Caretaker–Child Interactions That Impact the Strength of Shared Self-Guides

It is clear from the previous examples that the promotion and prevention messages that children receive from their parents, and which they accept as a shared reality about the world, can be very different. Consider now the following examples of parental messages from American history:

> *I have placed my happiness on seeing you good and accomplished, and no distress which this world can now bring on me could equal that of your disappointing my hopes. If you love me, then strive to be good under every situation.* (Thomas Jefferson to his 11-year-old daughter)
>
> *I would rather see you find a grave in this ocean you have crossed than see you an immoral profligate or graceless child.* (Abigail Adams to her 11-year-old son, John Quincy, 1780)

Both messages are about what negative outcome will happen or should happen if the child fails and what the child needs to do to avoid it (an if–then contingency message). However, the first message from Thomas Jefferson to his daughter is a strong promotion message about avoiding disappointing his hopes for her, and the second message from Abigail Adams to her son is a strong prevention message about avoiding being an immoral profligate or graceless child. Although the former message is promotion and the latter is prevention, both are very strong messages. Indeed, it is difficult to imagine a message much stronger than these two. And, along with the promotion versus prevention distinction, the *strength of the message*, and how that translates into children acquiring strong self-guides, is another parenting variable that goes beyond the simple distinction between positive versus negative parent–child interactions.

Thomas Jefferson and Abigail Adams are each sending clear if–then contingency messages to their child: "If you do X, then Y will happen." *Message clarity* is one major contributor to the strength of the message that results in children acquiring strong shared self-guides.[11] For children to create a shared self-guide with a parent, they need the epistemic motive of shared reality to be satisfied. If parents don't communicate clearly what goal or standard they want the child to attain or follow, then the epistemic motive will be disrupted. Children will be confused about what goal or standard their parent wants them to accept and share. Thomas Jefferson and Abigail Adams got this right.

They also got something else right. Another major contributor to the strength of the message that results in children acquiring strong shared self-guides is that attaining the goal or following the standard must be experienced by them as something that is important to do. They must experience their choices in relation to the self-guides as having significant consequences. That is, the parental message must convey that the self-guide contingency is consequential—*message significance*. In the "If you do X, then Y will happen" contingency message, the Y must matter to them. For Thomas Jefferson's message to his daughter Martha, the Y is disappointing and distressing him, her father, and Martha revered her father. That is a very strong consequence. Not to be outdone, for Abigail Adams's message to her son John Quincy, the Y is wanting him to drown in the ocean.

In addition to having consequential significance, both messages also contribute to shared reality motivation by highlighting the social relationship motive of shared reality. If the children do *not* attain their parent's self-guide for them, their relationship with their parent would be disrupted. In the case of the Jeffersons, Thomas would be disappointed in his daughter Martha. In the case of the Quincys, Abigail would want Quincy to drown. Well, Quincy drowning would certainly disrupt the relationship.

By the way, I do need to note something else about these two parental messages. They are not just strong. They are harsh. One is promotion harsh (Jefferson), and one is prevention harsh (Adams). This makes the point again that promotion and prevention messages can be distinguished *within negative* parenting, even when the negative is harsh. It is not that promotion is positive and prevention is negative. But beyond that point, one has to wonder why Thomas Jefferson and Abigail Adams both chose a negative path to create a shared reality with their child rather than a positive path. It reminds me of old black-and-white photographs where the adult family members look so grim. How about a smile? And, yes, we *can* also parent with a smile. This might seem more natural to promotion parenting than prevention parenting, but prevention success produces serenity and peacefulness, like a smiling Buddha. Thus, there is no reason that a prevention parent cannot send his or her child a smiling prevention message.

Having a clear and consequential parental message is critical for motivating children to create a shared reality with their parents. There are also two other contributors to children acquiring strong self-guides from parental messaging that should also be mentioned. The parental messages also need to be consistent and frequent. If a parent sends contradictory contingency messages to a child—sometimes the message is "If you do X, then Y will happen" while other times the message is "If you do X, nothing will happen"—then the child will be confused about the parent's goal or standard for him or her. The child will also be confused if the two parents send opposite, contradictory messages. This is why *message consistency* matters. Note that if a Mom and Dad were to send the same contingency message, "If you do X, then Y will happen" in both a promotion manner (Mom) and in a prevention manner (Dad), this would constitute message consistency.

Finally, children must receive the parental message often—*message frequency*. Like learning in general, frequent exposure to a learning situation matters. And frequency has both epistemic and social relational advantages. If information about a self-guide is repeated frequently by parents, then children are more likely to experience it as *the truth* about what to do— what goal they should *really* try to attain or what standard they should *really* try to follow. In addition, if parents frequently remind children of what goals they should attain and what standards they should follow, then the children are likely to infer that these goals and standards matter a lot to their parents. This contributes to the shared reality experience: "If it matters so much to them, then it matters to me too." Frequent messages also constitute frequent interactions between a parent and child, which contributes to the parent–child connectedness.

I will conclude this section by providing examples of socialization differences between the members of different demographic categories that produce a difference in the strength of self-guides that matters for self-regulation. I begin by describing a study that both provided an initial test of socialization conditions that would create stronger self-guides and examined the motivational and emotional consequences of people acquiring stronger self-guides.[12] Two separate groups of adolescents were identified who, according to the logic of the previously described factors that contribute to acquiring strong self-guides, should differ in self-guide strength: *first-borns* (including those first-borns who ended up as the only child in their family) versus *later-borns*. First-borns should acquire stronger self-guides than later-borns because message frequency, consistency, clarity, and significance would all tend to be greater for them than later-borns.[13]

If first-borns have stronger self-guides than later-borns, as predicted, what would this mean motivationally and emotionally? To answer this question, it is important to remember that self-guides function as *both* goals to attain and standards to follow. Children with stronger self-guides, then, should be more motivated to attain their goals, but they should also be more upset by any failure to do so. Self-guides functioning as goals predicts that first-borns, compared to later-borns, should generally have smaller discrepancies between their actual self (who they are now) and their self-guides because they are more motivated to attain their self-guide goals. On the other hand, self-guides functioning as standards predicts that first-borns, compared to later-borns, should suffer more from any discrepancy that remains because their strong self-guide standards should make any failure more emotionally painful. The study found precisely this combination of benefits and costs for both the ideal self-guides and the ought self-guides of first-borns compared to later-borns. Once again, the trade-offs from shared reality were evident.

The difference between first-borns versus later-borns provides one example of how a demographic variable can be associated with a difference in the strength of self-guides, while also illustrating the trade-offs from strong self-guides. Is there another example? When I give lectures on parenting, I talk about the fact that most parents want their young children to be happy and at ease, be nice and polite to others, be liked by others, not get into trouble, and work hard and do well at school. What if we could study children in early elementary school and find one category of children who had these qualities more than children not in that category? Then we could rear all children to be like that successful category.

How great would that be? Guess what, if you look at the literature, you will find that these two different categories *do* exist. They are called *girls* and *boys*. Compared to boys in early elementary school, girls are happier and less anxious, nicer and politer to others, less aggressive, have fewer conduct disorders, work harder in school, and get better grades. Well that was simple. All we need to do now is rear boys more like we rear girls.

How do we rear girls differently than boys? Generally speaking, the answer is that girls are treated more like first-borns than boys are. That is, girls receive more of the kind of parent–child interactions, especially mother–daughter interactions, that produce strong ideal and ought self-guides. They receive more clear, consistent, and frequent parental messages about what is expected of them.[14] Girls' stronger self-guides motivate them to attain and follow the ideal and ought goals and standards that they share with their parents. Given that their parents want them to be nice and polite to others, be liked by others, not get into trouble, and work hard and do well at school, girls accept these goals and standards for themselves and are motivated to meet them. And, generally speaking, they succeed. And this makes them feel happy (promotion ideal success) and at ease (prevention ought success).[15]

So all is good—except that it's not. Everything works out fine as long as the motivation to meet the shared self-guides is enough to succeed. But once boys and girls become high schoolers and teenagers, it becomes much more difficult to succeed at everything. Not only are the demands themselves greater, but social comparisons and curved grading make it impossible for everyone to be popular, talented, sexually attractive, a top student, and so on. It is not possible for every girl, or every boy, to be "better than average." Inevitably, both boys *and* girls will fail or will be "less than average" at something.

Because girls have not only stronger goals but also stronger standards of self-evaluation, failure will be more painful for the girls. Failing ideal self-guides will make them sad or even depressed. Failing ought self-guides will make them nervous or even clinically anxious. Indeed, in adolescence and adulthood, females are more likely than males to become clinically depressed or anxious. They still have fewer conduct problems than males (e.g., less substance abuse, fewer antisocial behaviors) because that is something their higher motivation to meet self-guides can still control. But even their higher self-control has drawbacks because females are more likely to have *over*control problems (e.g., anorexia, bulimia). Once again, the trade-offs of having strong shared self-beliefs is evident. So rearing all our children like we rear girls is not the answer.

Kinds of Shared Reality from Different Types of Parenting

Table 9.1 shows the kinds of shared reality that children experience as a function of whether their parental interactions are positive (desired end-state for child) or negative (undesired end-state for child), are oriented toward promotion ideals or prevention oughts, and create stronger or weaker self-guides (from stronger or weaker contingency messages).[16] Table 9.1 highlights the fact that *within* positive and *within* negative parent–child interactions, there are four different kinds of shared realities that children experience. Some of these parent–child interactions lead children to acquire

Table 9.1 Kinds of Shared Reality from Different Types of Parent–Child Interactions

Positive Interaction for Child		Negative Interaction for Child	
Strong	Managing	Disciplining	
Promotion Ideal	Prevention Ought	Promotion Ideal	Prevention Ought
Bolstering	*Prudent-Controlling*	*Love Withdrawal*	*Punitive/Critical*
Weak	Doting	Rejecting	
Promotion Ideal	Prevention Ought	Promotion Ideal	Prevention Ought
Spoiling	*Overprotective*	*Neglectful*	*Abusive*

strong shared self-guides—managing and disciplining. Other parent–child interactions produce weak shared self-guides—doting and rejecting. Children acquire strong promotion ideals when their parenting combines the bolstering version of managing (presence of positive) and the love withdrawal version of disciplining (absence of positive).[17] They acquire strong prevention oughts when their parenting combines the prudent-controlling version of managing (absence of negative) and the punitive/critical version of disciplining (presence of negative).

Note that the difference between promotion parenting and prevention parenting is not that promotion parenting is more positive than prevention parenting. It is *not* a positive versus negative difference. As shown in Table 9.1, both strong promotion parenting and strong prevention parenting involve positive parent–child interactions (managing) and negative parent–child interactions (disciplining).

The difference between promotion parenting and prevention parenting is also *not* an approach versus avoidance difference. Although promotion-bolstering involves strategic behaviors to approach an improved state for the child whereas prevention prudent-controlling involves strategic behaviors to avoid a worse state for the child, promotion love *withdrawal* involves suppressing (avoiding) positive actions after the child fails, and prevention punitive/critical involves taking (approaching) negative actions after the child fails. An example of love withdrawal discipline would be parents stopping a story when their child is not paying attention. An example of punitive/critical discipline would be parents yelling at their child when the child doesn't listen.

By the way, when I talk to a general audience about the different kinds of parental disciplining, often someone in the audience says that the punitive/critical type of discipline seems more harsh and painful for the child than the love withdrawal type of discipline. It is as if "presence of negative" seems more painful than "absence of positive." This is not the case. They can both be painful for the child. I was once told by a graduate student in my lab that he and other lab members he had talked to had the common experience that when they told me about something that had gone awry with our research plan, such as being delayed or not working out, I never got annoyed or critical but just looked disappointed. And he went on to say that sometimes he wished that I had instead got annoyed or critical because seeing me disappointed was more painful to him. That was a good lesson for me—not that I should now become angry and critical but to be more careful about expressing my disappointment. I am reminded of Thomas Jefferson telling Martha that his happiness depended on her being accomplished, that nothing would distress him more than her disappointing him: "If you love me, then strive to be good under every situation." Ouch! That must be painful for Martha—and my students.

Given that both types of disciplining can be painful for children, it is not surprising that parents also often ask me whether disciplining is really necessary for children to acquire strong self-guides. Why not use only the positive managing types of parenting? Wouldn't this be enough? I know of no scientific evidence that directly answers this question. I have friends that took this approach, and it seems to have worked out fine. I also know that it is difficult for many parents to eschew discipline completely. And by "discipline," I do not mean physical punishment. As illustrated by the discipline examples I have given previously, parents do not need to use physical punishment. Indeed, physical punishment can produce weak self-guides, as in the case of abuse.

Why is it difficult to eschew discipline completely? Because discipline can send a clear contingency message about the negative outcomes that will occur from behaving in a way that a parent finds unacceptable. When a child behaves in an unacceptable way, it is difficult for a parent not to send a disciplinary message about it, even if only nonverbally. And disciplinary messages about how *not* to behave can complement management messages about how to behave. It is not about inflicting pain, it is about providing clear *feedback* about how not to behave. This can complement a positive managing message to send a clear overall message to a child about what to do and what not to do.

This is not to say that managing and disciplining are equally effective for children's creating a shared reality. They may be equally effective for the epistemic motive of learning correct contingency rules regarding what to do and what not to do, but positive managing could better support children's social relational motive than negative disciplining. What is clear is that parents feel better when their child has positive feelings than negative feelings, and children don't enjoy being disciplined.

Thus far, my discussion has emphasized the different types of parenting that create strong self-guides in children. What about the types of parenting that do not have this effect? There is a natural tendency when thinking about this issue to focus on the clearly bad parenting like the two rejecting types of parenting in Table 9.1—*neglectful* and *abusive*. These types of parenting are, indeed, very bad for children because, in addition to the direct harm that they can do to a child, they destroy children's creation of shared reality with respect to both their social relational motive and their epistemic motive. Neglect and abuse both send the message that the parent does not care about or want to be close to the child. In addition, children cannot learn the contingency rules about what they need to do if they are being neglected or abused. These rejecting types of parenting make it very difficult for children to create shared realities with their parents.

Compared to neglect and abuse, the two doting types of parenting—spoiling and overprotective—seem pretty good. And they are pretty good with respect to the social relational motive because they both send the message that the parent cares about the child. The doting types of parenting also create a shared reality with the child about what kind of world they live in. For spoiling, it is a shared reality that the world has opportunities for gains. For overprotective, it is a shared reality that, by being careful, the world can be safe and secure. However, the doting types of parenting do not support children acquiring strong self-guides because the parents' responses to the child are *noncontingent*. The parental message is either that everything the child does is great (spoiling) or that everything the child does is potentially dangerous (overprotective). There are no contingencies. Contingencies would look more like the following: "If you do X, then that is great, but if you do Y, then not so great" (how to succeed in promotion) or "If you do X, then danger, but if you do Y, then not so dangerous" (how to succeed in prevention). But very spoiled or overprotected children don't even have those messages; instead, it's all gains or nonlosses, respectively.

By the way, for centuries, classic advice for parents has been "Spare the rod, spoil the child." Take a look at Table 9.1. *Sparing* the rod (where "the rod" is a metaphor for punitive discipline) entails *not* using punitive/critical discipline, which means *not* using a negative prevention type of parenting that *does* support a child acquiring strong self-guides. "Spoiling the child" would entail using the spoiling version of doting, which entails using a positive promotion type of parenting that does *not* support a child acquiring strong self-guides. These types of parenting are extreme opposites in Table 9.1: *Not* using a negative prevention type of parenting that supports a child acquiring strong self-guides (*not* using or sparing the rod) could lead to its extreme opposite happening—using a positive promotion type of parenting that does not support a child acquiring strong self-guides (spoiling). Not using the rod option could lead to the spoiling option.

Given all this, the advice "Spare the rod, spoil the child" has an impressive psycho-logic underlying it. It makes sense if you restrict the options to these two options. But Table 9.1 also makes it clear that there are many more parenting options than is suggested by this advice. It is *not* the case that the only alternative to using the rod is to spoil the child. Rather than using the rod as discipline, for example, a parent could try love withdrawal as discipline. But it is not necessary to use discipline at all. Rather than using the rod, a parent could use a managing type of parenting, like bolstering. Bolstering, like spoiling, is also quite different than the punitive/critical discipline of using the rod, but it is different than spoiling because it *does* support children acquiring strong self-guides. I should note that Proverbs 13:24 is even more prorod when it says: "Whoever spares the rod hates their children." But that's not the case. Bolstering spares the rod, and it is a loving and effective parenting method.

How Strong Promotion versus Prevention Self-Guides Impact What We Strive For

I mentioned earlier that we can have both strong promotion and strong prevention self-guides (or both weak promotion and weak prevention self-guides). But many of us have stronger self-guides of one sort or the other, which makes our goal pursuits predominant promotion-oriented or predominant prevention-oriented. It turns out that this matters, even for the same goal such as having straight As in college, being physically healthy, or being a good friend. What this means is that for the same goal, which shared reality you have regarding that goal, whether it is a promotion or prevention shared reality, matters significantly for how your goal pursuit plays out.

Consider, for example, students who want straight As in college. This goal can be experienced predominantly as a promotion ideal aspiration or a prevention ought obligation. But does this matter for *how* the goal is pursued? It's the same goal, so shouldn't the means of goal pursuit be only an issue of which means are more instrumental, more likely to lead to reaching the goal of getting straight As? That makes sense, but it is *not* how it works motivationally.

It matters whether shared promotion ideals or prevention oughts predominate. That will determine which manner of pursuing the goal "feels right" to the students.

When we have a predominant promotion ideal orientation, we prefer to pursue goals in an eager manner, selecting means of advancement to a better state. In contrast, when we have a predominant prevention ought orientation, we prefer to pursue goals in a vigilant manner, selecting careful means that will avoid mistakes. For example, those students who pursue straight As in college as a promotion goal are more likely to do extra assignments to gain extra points, whereas those who pursue straight As a prevention goal are more likely to doublecheck the assignments they hand in to make sure there are no spelling errors or, heaven forbid, a dangling participle. When we pursue a goal in a manner that fits our predominant orientation, we engage in the goal pursuit more strongly and "feel right" about it; when the manner of goal pursuit is a nonfit, engagement is weakened and we "feel wrong" about it.[18]

As we have seen, our predominant goal orientation—whether it is a predominant promotion ideal orientation or a predominant prevention ought orientation—can have its history in a shared reality we created with a parent about how goal pursuit works in the world. Are your goal pursuits about your aspiring to get better and better (promotion ideals), or are they about your responsibility to maintain a satisfactory state (prevention oughts)? This difference in shared reality regarding what we strive for can impact whether we experience *the manner of our goal pursuits* as being a fit that makes us "feel right" or a nonfit that makes us "feel wrong."

Unfortunately, and notably, our strategic preferences are not the end of the fit versus nonfit story. If it were, then we would mostly experience fit because we would just choose the manner of our goal pursuit (eager or vigilant) that was a fit for our predominant orientation (ideal or ought). But we are not always in control of how we pursue a goal. Other people can tell us how to pursue our goal. If you are predominant promotion ideal-oriented, for example, you would prefer to pursue a goal in an eager manner, but someone else with power over you, such as your boss at work, might make you pursue the goal in a vigilant manner. This would be a nonfit for you. Different tasks or social roles can also create nonfit, such as predominant promotion individuals having to be vigilant when they balance their checkbook or when they are assigned the role of treasurer in their club or organization.

The fact that fit or nonfit means of goal pursuit can be induced by external forces independent of what we would prefer given our predominant motivational orientation has broad significance in our lives. It can impact whether we feel right or wrong about what we are doing and how strongly or weakly we engage in what we are doing. Thus, fit and nonfit affects the quality of our life experiences. But that's not all. These effects, in turn, influence how much we value things in the world and how well we perform the tasks we are doing. Such fit and nonfit effects are considered next.

Fit and Nonfit Effects on Value and Performance

Let's begin with an early study on fit that my colleagues and I conducted at Columbia.[19] The undergraduate participants were shown a Columbia coffee mug and an inexpensive pen and were asked to decide which of these two objects they would prefer to own. The experimenter suggested *how* they should make their decision by varying the instructions she gave them prior to their making their choice. Half of them were told to think about what they would *gain by choosing* the mug and what they would gain by choosing the pen, which is an *eager* way to make the decision. The other half were told to think about what they would *lose by not choosing* the mug or what they would lose by not choosing the pen, which is a *vigilant* way to make the decision.

Note that in both cases the decision requires thinking about the positive qualities of each choice—the positive qualities that would be gained by choosing the mug or the pen or the positive qualities that would be lost by not choosing the mug or the pen. It is simply that the former process is experienced as an eager way to make the choice whereas the latter process is experienced as a vigilant way to make the choice. Importantly, this difference in the manner of goal pursuit did not influence their actual choice because we purposely selected two options where one of them—the Columbia coffee mug—would be clearly preferred by these Columbia students. Indeed, the Columbia mug was chosen by almost everyone, and only the results of those who chose the mug were considered for the results.

The participants in this study varied in whether they were predominant promotion or predominant prevention based on the relative strength of their ideal and ought self-guides. The measure of the relative strength of their ideal and ought self-guides used a response latency measure like the longitudinal developmental study described earlier.[20] Stronger self-guides come to mind more easily, and thus the strength of promotion ideals and prevention oughts can be measured by how quickly individuals can express their ideal and ought self-guides: the more quickly, the stronger the self-guide.

Participants are first given a definition of their ideal self (the type of person they ideally would like to be, the type of person they hoped, wished, or aspired to be) and their ought self (the type of person they believed they ought to be, the type of person they believed it was their duty, obligation, or responsibility to be). They are told to provide examples of their ideal self when asked about it and examples of their ought self when asked about it and to provide each example as quickly as possible. We averaged the response times for their ideal self examples, and we averaged the response times for their ought self examples. In this way, we measured the relative strength of their ideal self and the relative strength of their ought self, where faster was stronger.

In the mug study, after participants chose the mug as their preferred option, they were then given the opportunity to buy it *with their own money*. Following standard procedure in experimental economics for measuring the value of something, as mentioned earlier, the participants where shown an envelope and told that there was a fair price inside for buying the mug. They were then told that if they offered to buy the mug for that price or any higher price, they would get the mug for *whatever amount they offered* to buy the mug, but if their offer was less than that price, they would not get the mug.

The study found that neither the manner of choosing the mug (eager vs. vigilant), by itself nor whether participants' predominant orientation was promotion or prevention by itself affected how much participants were willing to pay to own the mug.[21] Instead, there was a fit effect. Promotion predominant participants who chose the mug in an eager manner (fit) and prevention predominant participants who chose the mug in a vigilant manner (fit) offered almost 70% more money to own the mug than promotion predominant participants who chose the mug in a vigilant manner (nonfit) and prevention predominant participants who chose the mug in an eager manner (nonfit).

In another study, the participants performed a task that involved solving anagrams with the goal of ending up with enough tokens to win a coffee mug as the prize. In one condition, the participants began with zero tokens and needed to solve enough of the anagrams to gain 100 tokens by the end to win the prize. In the other condition, the participants began with 100 tokens and needed to solve enough anagrams not to lose the tokens and lose the prize. The former condition is an eager attainment way to win the prize, and the latter condition is a vigilant maintenance way to win the prize. After winning the prize (which they all did), they were asked how much money they would be willing to pay for it if they saw it in a store for sale. The study found that promotion predominant participants who won the prize in an eager attainment manner (fit) and prevention predominant participants who won the prize in a vigilant maintenance manner (fit) said they would pay 90% more money to buy it in a store than did promotion predominant participants who won it in a vigilant maintenance manner (nonfit) and prevention predominant participants who won it in an eager attainment manner (nonfit).

What the results of these and other studies like them demonstrate is that regulatory fit can intensify the value of a chosen object or activity.[22] Fit occurs when the manner of goal pursuit (e.g., eager manner or vigilant manner) matches the motivational orientation toward the goal pursuit (e.g., promotion orientation or prevention orientation). And, as described earlier, the relative strength of our promotion versus prevention motivation can derive from our shared realities with significant others. In this way, our shared realities can influence how much we value what we strive for and choose to do in our lives.

Fit from shared realities can also influence how well we perform. In one study examining the regulatory fit effect on goal completion, undergraduates were asked to write a report on how they planned to spend their upcoming Saturday and to turn it in by a certain deadline to receive a cash payment.[23] Previous research had found that the likelihood that individuals would achieve their goal was increased when they mentally simulated the steps needed to implement goal completion, as by thinking about *when*, *where*, and *how* they would complete the goal.[24] The implementation steps that they planned to use to complete their goal were manipulated so that the when, where, and how were either eager means to pursue their goal or vigilant means to pursue their goal. The study found that promotion predominant participants who planned eager implementation means (fit) and prevention predominant participants who planned vigilant implementation means (fit) were almost 50% more likely to turn in their reports than promotion predominant participants who planned vigilant means (nonfit) and prevention predominant participants who planned eager means (nonfit).

Another study examined motivational *persistence* by measuring how long participants spent working on anagrams where each anagram had multiple solutions.[25] The anagrams appeared in either a green color or a red color. For the green anagrams, the participants were told that if they found all of the possible words, they would gain a point, but if they did not find all of the possible words they would not gain a point (eager gain that fits promotion). For the red anagrams, they were told that if they found all of the possible words, they would not lose a point, but if they did not find all of the possible words they would lose a point (vigilant nonloss that fits prevention).

The participants knew that there were five green anagrams and five red anagrams for them to solve. Thus, as they went along working on the anagrams, they knew how close they were to finishing the task. This created a "goal looms larger" situation. "Goal looms larger" refers to the fact that motivational strength while pursuing a goal increases as distance from the goal decreases.[26] A well-known example of this is horses running faster as they get closer to the barn. My favorite illustration of this phenomenon is a study where hungry rats were trained to run down a short alley to obtain food, and each rat wore a little harness that was connected to an electronic device that measured (in grams) how strongly a rat pulled when the harness stopped it before getting to the food.[27] The study found that the rats pulled harder when they were stopped closer to the food than when they were stopped further away from the food.

A "goal looms larger" effect was also expected in this anagram study. It was predicted that participants would spend more time (persist) trying to solve anagrams that were closer to the goal, but this would be more evident for predominant promotion participants on the green anagrams (fit) than on the red anagrams (nonfit) and for predominant prevention participants on the red anagrams (fit) than the green anagrams (nonfit). This is exactly what the study found.

These studies on value creation and performance demonstrate that the relative strengths of shared promotion ideal and prevention ought self-guides, which develop as shared realities with others, have significant effects on what we strive for, how much we value what we strive for, and how hard we work to make what we strive for happen. These are major consequences of our shared realities with others. The central point is that even for *the same goal*, such as having a successful career, having a good marriage, being a good friend to those you care about, or the nature of your goal pursuit and how it plays out, will be *different* when the goal is a promotion ideal than a prevention ought. Whether you play to win or play not to lose in goal pursuit will depend on whether your goals are more promotion ideals or prevention oughts. And whether your goals are promotion ideals or prevention oughts will depend on your shared realities with significant others.

As I mentioned earlier, you do not always have control over selecting how to pursue your goals. Other people and situations can determine how you pursue your goals, just as the experimenters did in the previously discussed studies and as a boss does in the workplace. For this reason, you can end up in regulatory nonfit. As one general example of this, you could live in a culture with situational pressures to pursue goals in either an eager manner (e.g., United States, Italy, Spain) or in a vigilant manner (e.g., Japan, South Korea, China). These cultural pressures create a nonfit, respectively, if you personally have strong prevention oughts or strong promotion ideals.[28] Indeed, there is cross-cultural evidence that such person–culture *nonfit* can reduce individuals' well-being.[29]

I should also note that whether we have stronger promotion ideals or stronger prevention oughts has a major impact on how we pursue our goals and make decisions beyond just fit and nonfit effects. And how we pursue our goals and make decisions, including whether and when we are willing to choose a riskier option over a less risky option, fundamentally defines who we are motivationally. Thus, it matters whether shared promotion self-guides or shared prevention self-guides are emphasized in our lives because it influences our goal pursuit choices and experiences. This *how* of goal pursuit is an important part of what makes us human. This chapter has told some of that story (e.g., eager for promotion vs. vigilant for prevention). The next chapter tells this story more fully.

Notes

1. For an extensive review of these different perspectives on what motivates humans and other animals, see Higgins (2012).
2. For a broader discussion of this point and a review of the research literature to support it, see Higgins and Pittman (2008).
3. This is not to say that children during Phase 3 can distinguish their own standpoint from the standpoint of a significant other. That comes later. But they can accept the standpoint of a significant other and make it their own.
4. See Manian, Papadakis, Strauman, and Essex (2006).
5. See Vygotsky (1978, p. 86). The term *scaffolding* was used by Bruner (1983).
6. See Higgins (1989a) and Higgins (1991).
7. See Manian et al. (2006).
8. See Higgins, Shah, and Friedman (1997).
9. There is evidence that different kinds of parent–child interactions contribute to children acquiring strong promotion ideal self-guides and/or prevention ought self-guides. This is not an argument against biological inheritance also contributing to children having strong ideal and ought self-guides. In this regard, there is evidence that children's temperament can contribute to the development of strong ideal and ought self-guides, but, interestingly, the contribution is through impacting parent–child interactions rather than being a direct effect on strength of ideal and ought self-guides (see Manian et al., 2006).
10. See Grant Halverson and Higgins (2013)
11. For a discussion of the factors that contribute to children developing strong self-guides, see Higgins (1989a, 1991).
12. See Neuman, Higgins, and Vookles (1992)
13. For a review of the socialization literature that supports this conclusion, see Neuman et al. (1992).
14. For a discussion of how girls and boys are reared differently, see Higgins (1991).
15. As noted in an earlier footnote, the difference in parenting received by boys and girls that produces a difference in self-guide strength is not an argument against biological inheritance also contributing to self-regulatory differences between boys and girls. However, as also mentioned earlier, the biological inheritance difference might contribute to self-regulatory differences through influencing how parents interact with their boy and girls rather than having a direct effect on self-regulatory differences.
16. For earlier discussions of these modes, see Higgins (1991) and Higgins and Silberman (1998).
17. I need to make clear that when I say "love withdrawal": I am not saying that the parent no longer loves the child. I am not saying that the parent's love is contingent on the

child's behavior. That would be very hurtful and damaging to the child. Instead, I am referring to a current interaction that a child is experiencing as the presence of a positive, and then the child does something that disrupts that interaction. The child's experience of the positive interaction ends, and there is the absence of a positive. By "love withdrawal," I am referring to the child's experience in a particular interaction of doing something that ends a positive interaction with his or her parent. An example of a love withdrawal interaction would be parents stopping a story when their child is not paying attention. What was a positive interaction has now ended. The child experiences the absence of a positive. The child is not experiencing the loss of his or her parent's love.

18. See Higgins (2000, 2006).
19. See Higgins, Idson, Freitas, Spiegel, and Molden (2003).
20. For a comparable measure of attitude strength, see Bassili (1995) and Fazio (1995).
21. Readers who are familiar with Kahneman and Tversky's (1979) prospect theory might find it surprising that there was no effect on value from the gain of eager framing versus the loss of vigilant framing. But both framing conditions referred to the positive qualities of the mug and the pen, to be gained or not lost, and thus it was not the case that some participants were in an area of gains whereas others were in an area of losses.
22. For a review of other studies, see Higgins (2006).
23. See Spiegel, Grant-Pillow, and Higgins (2004).
24. See Gollwitzer (1996).
25. See Förster, Higgins, and Idson (1998).
26. See Lewin (1935) and Miller (1944).
27. See Brown (1948).
28. For a discussion of such cross-cultural differences in promotion and prevention, see Higgins (2008).
29. See Fulmer et al. (2010).

10

How We Strive

The good life is a process, not a state of being. It is a direction not a destination.

Carl Rogers

Life is a journey, not a destination.

Ralph Waldo Emerson

We spend much of our lives on a journey to desired destinations, experiencing the striving process itself. Given this, *how* we strive is as important as *what* we strive for. Indeed, it can be argued that how we strive *is* our life. And, just as what we strive for involves shared realities with others, how we strive also involves shared realities with others. We learn from others what are the appropriate ways to pursue particular goals. These include the shared practices that toddlers learn that were discussed in Chapter 1. Children in all cultures, for example, strive to consume food, but how they do so—the local shared practice for consuming food—can vary from using a spoon, chopsticks, or your own hand.

Shared practices for how to strive range from everday activities like eating and dressing, to games and leisure activities, to long-term goals such as finding a life partner and vocation. Although different cultures vary in what they strive for and value, many of the cross-cultural differences that we notice are differences in *how* we strive rather than *what* we strive for—differences in shared practices. For example, wanting a life partner is quite common across human cultures, but how this is done can be quite different—from arranged marriages (marrying the boy or girl chosen for you by your family) to personally looking for "the one" who is "right for me."

It was Robert Merton, a towering figure in sociology, who noted: "Every social group invariably couples its cultural objectives with regulations, rooted in the mores or institutions, of allowable procedures for moving toward these objectives."[1] The cultural objectives are the shared realities about what is worth striving for, what has value. The "allowable procedures" are the shared practices concerning *how* to strive for what has value. They can be conventions or customs, and they can be laws and moral demands. The Ten Commandments constitute shared practices at the highest level of moral force—God-given. Some regulate how we should treat God: "Thou shalt not have strange gods before me" and "Thou shalt not take the name of the Lord thy God in vain." Others regulate how we should behave toward other people, and often are included within the legal system as well: "Thou shalt not kill" and "Thou shalt not steal." And some regulate how we should feel: "Thou shall not covet thy neighbor's house: neither shalt thou desire his wife" and "Honor thy father and thy mother."

Generally speaking, for Christian and Jewish communities historically, and other communities as well, the shared practices associated with the Ten Commandments were taken very seriously (and still are today in many cases). They were considered practices that everyone ought to do, had an obligation to do. As prevention shared practices, everyone must maintain them, obey them, all the time. It is *not* about making progress. It is not acceptable to claim, "I really had a great week last week. I obeyed eight of the Ten Commandments, compared to obeying only six the previous week." All ten must be obeyed. Failing to obey any one of them, and you experience guilt and shame.

There are other shared practices that are taken more seriously by some members of a community than others, and not everyone is expected to carry out the practices with the same zeal that they do. Not everyone is expected to be "devout." Being devout means being totally committed, and this means carrying out all of the shared practices with full diligence. For devoted sports fans, this can mean wearing the colors of your team—on your hat, your jacket, your shirt, your scarf, even on your face and cheering and screaming constantly during the game and joining in "the wave." For deeply pious Christians or Jews, this can mean carrying out each day all of the religious rituals, including those that are voluntary. It is not necessary, for example, that a Catholic say a prayer each night for each bead on the rosary, with the right prayer for a bead being different on different days. But devout Catholics will do so.

Carrying out shared practices and rituals connects people to others who have done so in the past, are doing so in the present, and will do so in the future. Renowned scholars of sociology and religion, such as Emile Durkheim and Mordecai Kaplan, have proposed that people achieve self-transcendence by sharing a community of faith. By carrying out shared ritual practices, the community creates a "collective effervescence" that *is* God.[2]

The importance of shared reality in how we go about our daily lives is evident not only in our customs or rituals but also in the strategies we choose when pursuing goals or making decisions. I discussed in the previous chapter how pursuing goals and making decisions in an eager manner is a fit for individuals with shared ideal self-guides (goals and standards) whereas pursuing goals and making decisions in a vigilant manner is a fit for individuals with shared ought self-guides. *How* these individuals strive is different. A life of eager goal pursuit is different than a life of vigilant goal pursuit. And the promotion–prevention difference in how we strive is not only about eager versus vigilant striving. There is cross-cultural evidence, for example, that individuals with a shared prevention orientation, which is relatively common in Japan, are more likely to pursue goals in a conscientious manner, whereas individuals with a shared promotion orientation, which is relatively common in the United States, are more likely to pursue goals in an extroverted manner.[3] The entire process of our goal pursuits is shaped by whether we strive for shared promotion ideals or shared prevention oughts: what counts as success and failure, the significance of success and failure, and what we choose to emphasize, including when to be more or less risky in our choices. Our shared realities with others impact how we carry out our goal pursuits and *who we are motivationally*.

The shared realities that were discussed in Chapter 9 were chronic shared realities that derive mostly from our long-term relationships with others, including not only our parents and other caretakers but also our teachers, supervisors, close friends and partners, co-workers, and so on. In these long-term relationships, we develop shared promotion ideal self-guides and shared prevention ought self-guides that vary in strength. It should be emphasized, however, that shared realities involving promotion ideals and prevention oughts can also be created momentarily in a particular interaction with another person who is especially relevant in that situation, such as a team leader who tells team members how to pursue their task. This includes laboratory studies where an experimenter, who is especially relevant in that situation, gives participants instructions about a task that create either a promotion or a prevention orientation toward the task. Such momentary shared realities are common in everyday life and have significant consequences for how we pursue our goals. In what follows, both chronic and momentary shared realities will be discussed.[4]

What Counts as Success and Failure

What we strive for in our goal pursuits are the outcomes that we want at the end—to end up satisfying our desired promotion ideals and prevention oughts. Thus, what could be more fundamental to the goal pursuit process than whether it succeeds or fails? Surely, it is quite straightforward whether a goal pursuit succeeds or fails. Yes, we might be motivated to believe we succeeded when we really didn't or believe we didn't fail when we really did. And, yes, we are biased in favor of perceiving success-related outcomes more than perceiving failure-related outcomes (self-enhancement). Nonetheless, generally speaking, we basically know what outcomes count as success and what outcomes count as failure, and once we see a given outcome, then that's the end of the story. Or is it? It turns out that, thanks to the difference between shared promotion ideals versus prevention oughts, it is *not* the end of the story. What *counts* as success or failure is different when we have promotion ideals than when we have prevention oughts.

To understand what counts as success or failure for promotion and prevention, we need to consider again what we want when we pursue promotion ideals versus prevention oughts. For promotion ideals, we want advancement or improvement from our current state—progress toward our hopes and aspirations. Our current status quo (zero) might be satisfactory, and maintaining it is better than changing to a worse state. Nonetheless, it is not enough for us when we have a promotion goal. To stay at the current status quo (zero) is a *failure* because it is a *nongain* (i.e., not a +1). For something to count as a success, there needs to have been a change to a better state (+1). Only a *gain* counts as a *success*.

What counts as success or failure is very different for prevention. For prevention ought goals, we want to meet our duties and obligations. We don't need to exceed or excel beyond our duties and obligations. We just need to meet them. And our most central duty and obligation is to maintain peace and order, safety and security, and ensure against an unsatisfactory (−1) alternative. Thus, if the current status quo (zero) is satisfactory, if it constitutes being safe and secure, it counts as a *success* by being a *nonloss*.

What counts as a failure would be to move to an unsatisfactory state (−1). It is a *loss* that counts as a *failure*.

This difference in what counts as success or failure creates very different worlds when we pursue shared promotion ideals versus shared prevention oughts. When we pursue strong promotion ideals, we must continue to do better and better to feel successful. Just maintaining a satisfactory life is not enough. In competition, a tie is not enough. We play to win; we must win. As the legendary Green Bay Packers coach Vince Lombardi put it, "winning isn't everything, it's the *only* thing." In contrast, when we pursue strong prevention oughts, we focus on doing what's necessary to ensure that we do not lose our safety and security. In competition, we play to *not lose* rather than to win. As the famous tennis player Jimmy Connors put it, "I hate to lose more than I love to win."

This difference in what counts as success or failure also influences how we strategically pursue our goals. Imagine that on New Year's Eve we (or some of us) resolve to weigh 10% less by next New Year's Eve. That is our new goal. By making that resolution, there is now a discrepancy between our current weight and the weight that is our new goal. What strategies can we use to move from our current weight to that goal? There are actions that we can take that would support the move, such as eating low-calorie healthy food and exercising each day. Such actions are matches to moving toward the goal. As a strategy to end up at the desired weight, we can *approach these matches*. There are also actions that we have taken in the past—bad habits— that if we were to continue doing them would be obstacles to our moving toward our goal, such as our eating high-calorie junk food and lounging around home each day. Such actions are mismatches to our moving toward our goal. As a strategy to end up at the desired weight, we can *avoid these mismatches*.

Imagine now that our goal to weigh 10% less by next New Year's Eve was shared with our life partner who was also concerned about our current weight. It was a shared reality. This kind of shared reality concern is quite common. Also imagine that for some of us the shared goal to weigh 10% less by next New Year's Eve is experienced as a promotion ideal whereas for others of us it is experienced as a prevention ought. We have the same goal to weigh 10% less by next New Year's Eve, and, because it is shared with our partner, we are strongly committed to this goal. Why would it matter whether it is a shared promotion ideal or a shared prevention ought? It would matter because different strategies of goal pursuit are relevant for promotion ideals versus prevention oughts given the difference between promotion and prevention in what counts as success or failure.

When the shared goal to weigh 10% less by next New Year's Eve is a promotion ideal, then success would entail approaching matches to the desired end-state to make steady advances, steady progress, toward the desired end-state (gains). Failure would be not to approach matches to the desired end-state (nongains). Strategically, those of us for whom the resolution is a shared promotion goal are more likely to seek out low-calorie healthy food and find ways to exercise each day.

In contrast, when the shared goal to weigh 10% less by next New Year's Eve is a prevention ought, then success would entail avoiding mismatches to the desired end-state to ensure against mistakes, stop disruptions, while moving toward the desired end-state (nonlosses). Failure would be not avoiding mismatches to the desired end-state (losses). Strategically, those of us for whom the resolution is a shared prevention goal are more likely to avoid situations where they might be tempted by high-calorie junk food and resist engaging in long-lasting lounging activities (e.g., lying on the couch to read the entire Sunday New York Times).

What this illustrates is that even for the same shared goal to which we are strongly committed, how the goal pursuit process plays out can depend on whether we experience the goal as a shared promotion ideal or a shared prevention ought. Although there is not a study precisely like the just described scenario, there is one that is quite similar.[5]

In this study, participants were asked to imagine being on a diet and wanting to keep their diet but being tempted by a slice of pizza when they are hungry. They were then presented with possible actions that they could do to keep their diet. Some actions, such as thinking about the health benefits of the diet, would be effective for keeping the diet (matches to the desired end-state) and thus should be approached. Other actions, such as thinking about how yummy the pizza is, would be ineffective for keeping the diet (mismatches to the desired end-state) and thus should be avoided. The study found that participants with stronger promotion chose to engage in the effective match actions (think about the diet's health benefits), whereas participants with stronger prevention chose not to engage in the ineffective mismatch actions (not think about how the pizza's yumminess).

The promotion–prevention difference in what counts as success or failure even affects our social relationships. There is evidence, for example, that what counts as "not belonging" is different for promotion and prevention.[6]

When people with strong prevention are asked to describe a time when they "did not belong," they are likely to describe a time when they were actively *rejected*, which would be a –1 loss for them. In contrast, when people with strong promotion are asked the same question, they are more likely to describe a time when they had been *ignored*, which would represent a missed opportunity to advance from zero (i.e., a nongain). Consistent with these findings, another study found that when there is social discrimination involving –1 unsatisfactory states, distress increases for people with strong prevention but not for people with strong promotion.[7]

The Motivational Significance of Success and Failure

The difference between what counts as success or failure for individuals with shared promotion versus prevention goals also produces differences in the intensity of the success experience and the intensity of the failure experience. For shared promotion goals, what really matters is the eager success of moving from a current state (zero) to a better state (+1)—success as a gain. In contrast, what really matters for shared prevention goals is the vigilance failure to maintain the current state (zero) and moving to a worse state (–1)—failure as a loss.

This difference predicts that success should be experienced more intensely for people with shared promotion ideals than shared prevention oughts because for promotion it is eagerly attaining a gain success that really matters. On the other hand, failure should be experienced more intensely for people with shared prevention oughts than shared promotion ideals because for prevention it is vigilantly preventing a loss failure that really matters. Indeed, this is what has been found.

In one study that used the measure of promotion ideal strength and prevention ought strength described in Chapter 9, participants were given 10 anagrams to solve and were told that they would be paid $9 if they scored above the 70th percentile (relative to other students who had already participated) and would be paid $8 if they scored below the 70th percentile.[8] After working on the anagrams, they were given the bogus feedback that they had scored either in the 61st percentile (failure feedback) or in the 79th percentile (success feedback).[9] After this feedback, they rated how intensely they felt different positive and negative emotions. Not surprisingly, the participants overall felt better after success feedback than failure feedback. But in addition to this, the study found that after being given the *same* success feedback, the positive emotions felt by the promotion participants were more intense than the positive emotions felt by the prevention participants, and after being given the *same* failure feedback, the negative emotions felt by the prevention participants were more intense than the negative emotions felt by the promotion participants.

By the way, one should not conclude from these kinds of findings that it is better to have shared promotion ideals than shared prevention oughts. At first glance, these findings seem to say that people with shared promotion ideals, compared to those with shared prevention oughts, experience more pleasure from success and less pain from failure. If that were the case, then it would be better to have shared promotion ideals than shared prevention oughts. But, in fact, it confuses motivational intensity with pleasure and pain intensity. What is happening is that promotion and prevention participants are feeling different emotions after success and feeling different emotions after failure.

Promotion ideal success makes people feel happy or joyful, which is more intense than prevention ought success that makes people feel at ease or at peace. Promotion success is more intense because it increases motivational eagerness whereas prevention success *decreases* motivational vigilance. But this does not mean that the former is more pleasant than the latter. A life of peace and a life of joy both sound very good to me. Heaven, after all, is described as an afterlife of "peace and joy."

Prevention ought failure makes people feel tense or nervous, which is motivationally more intense than promotion ideal failure that makes people feel sad or discouraged. Prevention failure is more intense because it increases motivational vigilance whereas promotion failure *decreases* motivational eagerness.[10] But, again, this does not mean that the former is more painful than the latter. Indeed, the depression that is associated with extreme promotion failure can be more painful than the anxiety that is associated with extreme prevention failure. In fact, there is evidence that the promotion–prevention difference in the intensity of feelings after success versus failure relates to a difference in *motivational* intensity rather than a difference in pleasure or pain.[11]

One should also not conclude that people pursuing promotion ideals simply give up after failure. While it is true that certain kinds of failure, like being fired or divorced, can cause promotion-oriented people to become depressed and give up, that is not what failure typically does to people who have a strong promotion orientation. Instead, they respond to failure in ways to remain eager. One study, for example, found that when prevention-oriented participants received failure feedback on a task, their expectancies for how well they would perform next on that task dropped about 20%.[12] This considerable drop is what you might expect to happen after receiving failure feedback. After all, if you just performed relatively poorly on a task, it is realistic to lower your expectations for how well you will perform next on the task. But this is not what happened with the promotion-oriented participants. After receiving failure feedback, their expectancies dropped much less (about 6%). By maintaining positive expectancies, they can remain eager.

What should happen to individuals' expectancies for future performance on a task after they receive feedback that so far their performance on the task has been *successful*? Their expectancies should *increase*. And this is exactly what happened for the promotion-oriented participants. Their expectancies for how well they would perform next went up (about 11%), which kept them eager. But this is not what happened with prevention-oriented participants. Their expectancies for how well they would perform next actually *dropped* (about 8% down)! How could this happen? Normally, prevention-oriented people are realistic. But they are not motivated in this case to be realistic and raise their expectations because this would reduce their vigilance. That is, *feeling at ease* from higher expectations following success would have reduced their vigilance, and they did not want this to happen. Instead, they wanted to maintain or even increase their vigilance. They did so by dropping their expectations after success.

Raising or lowering our expectancies for future performance is one strategy we use to control our motivation. Another strategy is to generate counterfactuals, or thoughts about what might have happened differently. People generate counterfactuals especially after they have failed at something. They reflect upon either how things could have turned out better (upward counterfactual reflection) or how things could have turned out worse (downward counterfactual reflection). Which kind of reflection would be more motivating for people with a promotion versus a prevention orientation?

Let's look at a study that was designed to answer this question.[13] The participants were instructed to find as many words as possible for the anagrams they were given and were told that each anagram might have no solution, one solution, or multiple solutions. After completing the first set of anagrams, they received feedback that they had found half of the solutions. They then received either upward or downward counterfactual reflection instructions. In the upward counterfactual reflection condition, participants were told: "Think about how your performance on the anagrams might have turned out BETTER than it actually did. Close your eyes and VIVIDLY imagine what might have been. Spend about a minute VIVIDLY IMAGINING how your performance on the anagrams might have been BETTER." In the downward counterfactual reflection condition, participants were told: "Think about how your performance on the anagrams might have turned out WORSE than it actually did. Close your eyes and VIVIDLY imagine what might have been. Spend about a minute VIVIDLY IMAGINING how your performance on the anagrams might have been WORSE."

The measure of performance motivation in this study was the change in persistence (time spent working to find solutions) from the first set to the second set of anagrams. What the study found was that for the promotion-oriented participants, persistence increased on the second set of anagrams more when they engaged in upward counterfactual reflection (how their performance might have been better) than downward counterfactual reflection (how their performance might have been worse). By imagining how their performance could have been better on the first set, they could imagine how it could be better on the next set, which restored their eagerness after hearing that they performed rather poorly on the first set.

What about the prevention-oriented participants? Their persistence increased more when they engaged in *downward* counterfactual reflection than upward counterfactual reflection. By imaging how their performance could have been worse on the first set, they reminded themselves that they could do really poorly on the second set. The way to stop this from happening was to be highly vigilant on the second set.

By the way, in this study participants' promotion versus prevention orientation did not derive from chronic differences in relative strength of promotion ideal self-guides versus prevention ought self-guides. Instead, promotion and prevention orientations were created by instructions from the experimenter. Specifically, participants in the promotion condition were told to find 90% or more of all the possible words, and if they did they would earn an extra dollar (gain). Participants in the prevention condition were told not to miss more than 10% of all the possible words, and if they did they would not lose a dollar (nonloss). With whom did participants share reality in this situation? The answer is, the experimenter who is the local expert in this situation. This kind of shared reality creation is actually quite common in our everyday lives when we receive instructions from others on how to do some activity. It is also similar to the shared reality that we create when we communicate to others, even when the audience is a stranger (see Chapter 1). And, of course, participants creating a shared reality with the experimenter is common in research studies where participants treat the experimenter as the local expert, as even toddlers did when they looked to the experimenter rather than their mother to learn how they should feel about the object moving toward them (see Chapter 2).

How We See the World

Promotion–prevention differences in what counts as success or failure and in the motivational significance of success and failure are examples of how sharing promotion versus prevention goals and standards with others has a major impact on our lives. In addition to these effects, there are other important effects of the promotion–prevention difference. Let's begin with how we see the world.

We all know the expression, "Can't see the forest for the trees." Less common is the opposite expression, "Can't see the trees for the forest." Seeing the forest is seeing the world in a more global manner, whereas seeing the trees is seeing the world in a more local manner. There is a clever way of testing whether someone processes things in the world more globally or more locally. It is called the Navon task.[14] There are different versions of this task, but, generally, participants are asked to respond as quickly as possible when they see a target letter, such as an H or an S. Among the stimulus figures they are shown, there is a large shape that forms that letter, and this large shape is composed of multiple copies of small shapes that either also form that same letter (the first and fourth shapes in the following figures) or form a different letter (the second and third shapes in the following figure).

```
H   H   S     S    H H H      S S S
                    H   H              S
H   H   S     S    H                  S
                                       S
H H H H S S S S    H H H      S S S
                        H              S
H   H   S     S        H              S
                                       S
H   H   S     S    H H  H H    S S S S
```

Not surprisingly, people are typically fastest to respond that they see the letter when it is *both* the global letter and the local letter (the first and fourth shapes in the figure). In addition, they are also generally faster when the target letter, such as H, is the global letter but not the local letter (the second shape in the figure) than when it is the local letter and not the global letter (the third shape in the figure).

Would you expect there to be promotion–prevention differences in this effect? When we have shared prevention ought self-guides, we feel responsible for peace and order and use strategic vigilance to maintain safety and security. Given this, perhaps we would pay more attention to our concrete surroundings because we need to be prepared for potential threats and are careful to screen the local environment for them. Over time, this vigilant strategy could become an automatic habit of looking for even very subtle cues of something threatening. We need to pay attention to details because the devil is in the details. This means that when we have shared prevention ought self-guides, we might be more likely to process input locally.

It is quite different when we have shared promotion ideal self-guides. Then we are concerned with growth and expansion and use strategic eagerness to move ahead. We need to go beyond the given details, the concrete status quo, and discover the whole meaning. Given this, perhaps we would then look for the big picture. Again, over time, such eagerness to see the big picture beyond the details could become an automatic habit, making us more likely to process input globally.

Is there, in fact, evidence to support this proposed promotion–prevention difference in global versus local processing of input? Yes, there is. One study measured participants' strength of promotion ideal self-guides and strength of prevention ought self-guides using the method described in Chapter 9.[15] They were then given a version of the Navon task.[16] They were instructed to press a blue response key if the stimulus contained the letter L and to press a red response key if the stimulus contained the letter H, and they were asked to respond as quickly as possible. Four of the figures included global targets (an H made of Fs, an H made of Ts, an L made of Ts, and an L made of Fs). Four other figures included local targets (a large F made of small Hs, a large F made of small Ls, a large T made of small Hs, and a large T made of small Ls). The performance of individuals with stronger promotion ideal self-guides was like the standard finding: They were quicker to respond to the large global letters than the small local letters. And the *more* promotion they were, the *more* this was true. However, individuals with stronger prevention ought self-guides were quicker to respond to the small local letters than to the large global letters.

The results of this study provide clear evidence that we see the world differently depending on whether we have stronger prevention ought self-guides or stronger promotion ideal self-guides. Other studies provide additional, complementary evidence for this conclusion. One research program examined whether people with a promotion orientation (vs. a prevention orientation) use more abstract than concrete language when talking about their goal pursuits.[17] When we have shared promotion ideal goals, we have broad aspirations and hopes that we eagerly pursue. We do not want to miss any gains; we want to cover all possible ways for growth and advancement. Thus, we would benefit from representing our goal pursuit broadly and abstractly rather than concretely, such as the abstract "having a wonderful dinner party" rather than the concrete "arranging the guests at the table." In contrast, when we have shared prevention ought goals, we have clear responsibilities that we vigilantly pursue. We do not want to make any mistakes; we want to make sure that nothing goes wrong. This means that we need to think about the concrete rather than the abstract details of the goal pursuit (i.e., the concrete "arranging the guests at the table").

It was predicted that this difference would translate into how people talk about their goal pursuits, with promotion-oriented people talking relatively more abstractly and prevention-oriented people talking relatively more concretely. To measure participants' language use along a concrete–abstract dimension, the researchers used a model that distinguishes among different categories of language terms.[18] Along the concrete–abstract dimension, it goes from the most concrete, which are descriptive action verbs that describe a single observable event and its perceptual features (e.g., "Tom punches Sam"), to the most abstract, which are adjectives that generalize across events and are relatively context independent (e.g., "Tom is aggressive").

In one study, the experimenter created different shared realities with the participants about the same basic goal of having a positive friendship by framing this goal as either a promotion goal pursuit or a prevention goal pursuit. In the promotion goal pursuit condition, the participants were instructed: "Imagine that you are the kind of person who likes to be a good friend in your close relationships. What would your strategy be to meet this goal?"

In the prevention goal pursuit condition, the participants were instructed: "Imagine that you are the kind of person who believes you should try not to be a poor friend in your close relationships. What would your strategy be to meet this goal?"[19]

The participants provided a written answer to the question, and their answer was coded in terms of the concrete–abstract nature of the terms that were used. As predicted, the descriptions of friendship strategies in the promotion goal condition were more abstract than those in the prevention goal condition. Specifically, participants with a promotion goal orientation were more likely to use abstract adjectives, such as "To be a good friend, I would be supportive" and "I would be caring and helpful." In contrast, participants with a prevention goal orientation were more likely to use concrete action verbs, such as "Not to be a poor friend, I would ring [phone] him often" and "I would visit her."

The results from this research program on concrete–abstract language use nicely complements the promotion global–prevention local distinction by finding a promotion abstract–prevention concrete distinction. There is additional complementary evidence from another research program on thinking about future goals.[20] In one study, the participants were asked to generate and record three goals. Instructions in the promotion future goal condition were: "What are some positive things that you expect to be successful at achieving? Please take a moment to think about your future, focusing on desirable things that you expect to attain." Instructions in the prevention future goal condition were: "What are some negative things that you expect to be successful at avoiding? Please take a moment to think about your future, focusing on undesirable things that you expect to prevent."

The participants were also asked to try to estimate when they might start working actively toward achieving each goal and when each might be achieved. The study found that, compared to participants thinking about prevention future goals, participants thinking about promotion future goals gave estimates of when they would initiate and complete their goal that were more distant in the future (over twice as long).[21] What these results show is that psychological *distance*—in this case, temporal distance—is greater for promotion goals than prevention goals. A prevention goal places us more in the here and now. And consistent with the previous discussion, there is evidence that greater psychological distance, including temporal distance in particular, is associated with more *abstract* conceptions of goal pursuit activities.[22]

How We Deal with the World

The previously discussed studies show that individuals with shared promotion goals (chronically or momentarily) see the world differently than individuals with shared prevention goals. They also deal with the world differently. To demonstrate this difference, I begin with a classic trade-off in goal pursuit—speed versus accuracy.

The speed versus accuracy (or quantity vs. quality) trade-off is common in everyday life. It is a major issue in many companies that are creating products that they need to get to market soon (speed) but don't want recalls after they do get to market (accuracy). Some managers are more concerned about getting to market whereas others are more concerned with recalls. Which shared goal orientation—promotion or prevention—should the managers create with their employees so that the employees emphasize either speed or accuracy?

In one study designed to address this issue,[23] participants were asked to complete a series of four connect-the-dot pictures. When correctly completed, each picture was a cartoon of an animal, such as an hippopotamus. [A partially completed connect-the-dot picture is shown in the following graphic. Can you guess what it shows? Have fun completing it.] Similar to what different managers might do when trying to motivate their employees, the experimenter's instructions for the participants varied in whether they created a shared promotion goal or a shared prevention goal.

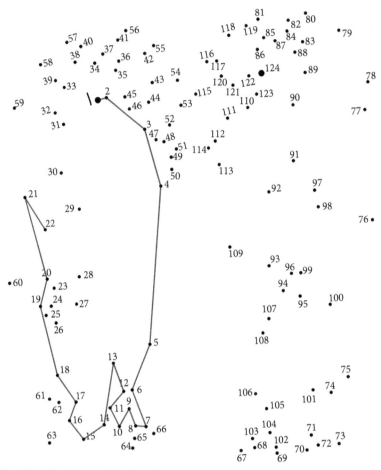

A Partially Solved Connect-Dots Puzzle

In the promotion goal condition, participants were told that they would gain extra money if they performed above a certain score based on a fast and accurate criterion (gain), but they would not gain this extra money if they did not perform above this criterion (nongain). In the prevention goal condition, participants were told that they would lose money if they did not perform above the fast and accurate criterion (loss), but they would not lose the money if they did perform above this criterion (nonloss). The criterion for success was the same for both conditions, and what participants would earn by being successful was also the same. What differed was the motivational message about how to view task performance—to share the experimenter's promotion orientation toward success and failure in one condition (gain/nongain) or the experimenter's prevention orientation toward success and failure in the other condition (nonloss/loss).

This study also examined the "goal looms larger" effect discussed in Chapter 9 whereby people are more motivated as they get closer to completing a task. To examine this, half of the participants in both the promotion and prevention goal conditions were told that they would work on four pictures, whereas the other half were told that they would work on eight pictures. Although all participants actually worked on the same four pictures, the participants who thought they would work on four pictures (vs. eight pictures) experienced the third and fourth pictures as being closer to completing the task. This allowed a test of the "goal looms larger" effect.

The first performance measure was the number of dots participants connected for each picture within the allotted time frame. The *greater number of dots connected*, the greater the *speed*. The second performance measure was the number of dots participants *missed* up to the last dot they reached for each picture within the allotted time frame. The *lower the number of dots missed*, the greater the *accuracy*.

Because people with a promotion orientation want to make progress and advance toward their goal, they should want to connect the dots as fast as possible to find the animal in each picture. In contrast, people with a prevention orientation should emphasize accuracy because they want to be careful and not make mistakes. This is precisely what was found. The shared promotion goal participants connected more dots in the allotted time, but the shared prevention goal participants made fewer errors in connecting the dots (i.e., fewer dots missed). And there was a "goal looms larger" effect as well. For those participants who thought there were four pictures but not those who thought there were eight pictures, performance was significantly better on the fourth and final picture compared to the earlier pictures, with the promotion goal participants being significantly faster (i.e., connected more dots) and the prevention goal participants being significantly more accurate (i.e., missed fewer dots for the portions of the pictures they had completed).

These and other findings[24] demonstrate that having a shared promotion versus prevention goal orientation changes the strategic emphasis on speed versus accuracy. We emphasize speed more when we have a shared promotion orientation, and we emphasize accuracy more when we have a shared prevention orientation. Notably, these shared promotion or prevention orientations can be chronic (e.g., the relative strength of participants' ideal vs. ought self-guides) or, as in the just described study, they can be induced by sharing the orientation of a significant other, who in this case was the experimenter. This promotion–prevention difference provides a clear example of a trade-off from sharing others' promotion orientation or prevention orientation.

Generally speaking, there are benefits from completing a task quickly and costs from being slow to complete a task, as in the earlier example of getting a product to market in a timely fashion. Another example would be meeting the deadline for turning in a research grant. And, obviously, there are benefits from doing accurate work and costs from making mistakes. The earlier example was the costs from mistakes leading to a product having to be recalled. But it can be worse than that. Product mistakes, as with cars and airplanes, can cause injuries or even death. Which benefits are better? Which costs are worse? For many products, it is not always clear. What is clear is that emphasizing one more and the other less has *both* benefits and costs. Thus, it matters whether you are sharing with others a promotion orientation or a prevention orientation.

Another promotion–prevention difference in emphasis is between being open to new options and new possibilities versus sticking with the status quo, with what is given. The former is emphasized more when we have a strong promotion orientation, whereas the latter is emphasized more when we have a strong prevention orientation. This difference in emphasis shows up in several ways. One way is how we respond to being interrupted when doing an activity. Later, after the interruption, do we prefer to resume that interrupted activity, or, instead, do we want to switch to another activity?[25]

In one study, participants, in the role of the communicator, were asked to describe each of three different abstract figures to another person who was in the role of the audience. For each description, the job of the audience was to select which figure was being described from among a set of 10 different abstract figures (a referential communication task).[26] Either a shared promotion goal orientation to the task or a shared prevention goal orientation was induced by the experimenter telling the participants that they would, respectively, either gain or not gain points (gain) or lose or not lose points (nonloss) depending on how well they described each figure. The points that participants earned if they were successful was the same for both conditions because in the promotion condition they started with no points and then attained points, whereas in the prevention condition they started with points and needed to maintain them.

While they were describing the third figure, all participants were interrupted by the computer screen (asking questions) and could not complete the description. After the interruption, the participants were asked if they wanted to return to describe the figure on which they had been interrupted or, instead, describe a new figure they had not seen before. Participants with a promotion goal orientation were twice as likely as those with a prevention goal orientation to choose a new figure to describe rather than return to the original figure. A follow-up study measured participants' strength of ideal and ought self-guides. Participants' preference to describe a new figure (rather than return to the old figure) increased as ideal self-guide strength increased and decreased as ought self-guide strength increased. A clear majority of predominant ideal self-guide participants (60%) chose to describe a new figure, whereas only one third of predominant ought self-guide participants did so.

Where does this promotion–prevention difference come from? Compared to returning to the original figure, describing a new figure represents a change. It allows someone to proceed ahead rather than go back. It is more like making progress, and this should appeal more to participants who have a promotion goal orientation. In addition, the new figure is "new" rather than "old," and to find something better, which is what strong promotion individuals want, they need to be open to new alternatives. From a prevention perspective, on the other hand, there was nothing wrong with the old figure. And, by having already started describing it, it is a "known" object. In this sense, it is safe. "Better safe than sorry." "Better the devil you know than the devil you don't." This line of reasoning predicts that the prevention goal participants will choose to stick with the old figure, which is exactly what happened.

This promotion–prevention difference in emphasis on being open to new possibilities versus sticking to the known and the status quo should also produce a difference in the famous "endowment" effect, which refers to people's reluctance to exchange an object that they already possess for something else, including money, that has comparable dollar value.[27] A well-known demonstration of this effect uses three groups.[28] One group is given an object, such as a coffee mug, and a second group is given another object of comparable dollar value, such as a candy bar. To demonstrate that the value of the mug and the candy bar are approximately equal, a third group is given a choice between the two objects. About half of those in this third group choose the mug, and the other half choose the candy bar.

Despite this demonstration that the value of the mug and the candy bar is approximately equal, few individuals in the first two groups are willing to exchange the object that they happened to be given (the endowed object) for the other object.

The choice of the endowed participants can be considered as a choice between an old object that is the participants' status quo (the endowed object) and the other object, which is a new alternative. Given what I just said about the promotion–prevention difference in goal orientation, do you think the endowment effect would differ between people with a promotion orientation versus those with a prevention goal orientation? If so, what would the difference be?

In a study that addressed these questions,[29] participants who varied in the strength of ideal self-guides and ought self-guides performed an incidental task that allowed the experimenter to thank them and tell them that, in appreciation for their taking part in this study, they would receive a pen, over and above the payment they had been promised for participating in a study. The pen was randomly selected from two pens with different styles that both cost $2.50. After the participants received the pen, the experimenter casually mentioned that there were actually two kinds of pens that were being used as gifts for participation, and they were welcome to look at the other pen and try out both pens to decide if they wanted to keep the pen they had been given or exchange it for the other pen.

Only one third of the participants wanted to exchange the pen they were given for the alternative pen—a strong demonstration of the endowment effect. This happened despite the fact that the pens cost the same *and* the fact that which of the two pens participants received as the endowed pen was random. However, this is not all that happened. The endowment effect depended on participants' strength of ideal and ought self-guides. As participants' prevention ought self-guides increased in strength, their willingness to exchange the old pen for the new pen *decreased*; that is, the endowment effect was *stronger* as participants' prevention orientation was stronger. In contrast, as participants' promotion ideal self-guides increased in strength, their willingness to exchange the old pen for the new pen *increased*; that is, the endowment effect was *weaker* as participants' promotion orientation was stronger. Indeed, the endowment effect was found for the predominant prevention-oriented participants but was *not* found for the predominant promotion-oriented participants.

There is clear evidence, then, that when we have a prevention orientation, we emphasize sticking with the status quo—with what is old and known, with what is given—whereas when we have a promotion orientation we are open to new alternatives, to changing the status quo. This difference in emphasis, like those discussed earlier, also has its trade-offs. And the trade-offs are significant because they impact creativity and analytical reasoning.

Our openness to new alternatives when we have a promotion orientation supports the creative process, whereas our emphasis on sticking with what is given when we have a prevention orientation does *not* support the creative process. There is a nice and simple study that illustrates this.[30] Like other studies that I have described earlier, either a shared promotion goal orientation or a shared prevention goal orientation was induced by the experimenter giving different goal instructions. In the promotion goal orientation condition, the participants were told that if they did well on the exercises to follow they would be given as their final task an activity that they liked. In the prevention goal orientation condition, the participants were told that as long as they did not do poorly on the exercises to follow they would not be given a disliked task to do as their final task.

One of the exercises was a sorting task. They were shown a set of 12 fruits and a set of 12 vegetables (with the order counterbalanced across participants) and were told that they could use any criterion to sort each set, including the same criterion for both sets (e.g., by color for both sets). The study found that, although most participants generally switched the sorting criterion from the first to the second set, participants given a prevention goal orientation were twice as likely as participants given a promotion goal orientation to stick to the same criterion for the second set that they used in the first set.

In another study where the participants varied in the strength of their ideal self-guides and the strength of their ought self-guides, participants performed an object-naming task.[31] They were given a booklet that contained four pictures, each picture on a separate page. Although the objects depicted were familiar objects, they were taken from unusual angles and thus were difficult to recognize. The participants were instructed to try to guess what the object was in each picture, and they could list as many or as few answers as they wanted. The study found that as the strength of participants' ideal self-guides increased, the more alternative possibilities were generated, but as the strength of participants' ought self-guides increased, the fewer alternative possibilities were generated.

What these and other studies have found is that individuals with a promotion orientation, compared to those with a prevention orientation, are more open to new possibilities and generating new alternatives, which supports creativity.[32] In contrast, individuals with a prevention orientation, compared to those with a promotion orientation, emphasize more sticking with the status quo, with what is given. This does not support creativity. But it *does* support analytical reasoning.[33] This benefit on analytical tasks from having a prevention orientation could derive in part from the fact that, as discussed earlier, those with a prevention orientation are more likely to use local (vs. global) processing, and local processing facilitates analytical thinking.[34] In addition, the emphasis of a prevention orientation on sticking with the status quo, on sticking with what is given, benefits analytical reasoning because such reasoning requires sticking with the given premises. You need to follow the facts you are given and follow the stated rules. In analytical reasoning tasks, generating alternative possibilities is *not* what you want to do. Yet another example of the trade-off from shared promotion versus shared prevention.

Promotion–Prevention Differences in Risky Decision-Making

I end this chapter with an especially significant promotion–prevention difference in strategic motivation—a difference in what motivates our willingness to choose a more risky option over a less risky option when we make a decision. When we are willing to take risks, and when we are not, is critical to the choices that we make. If motivation is fundamentally about people's preferences that direct their choices, as I have argued in an earlier book[35], and there is a promotion–prevention difference in when risky choices are preferred, then the presence of different shared realities with others that create either a promotion or prevention goal orientation is highly significant.

Prior research has generally shown that when the current condition is a satisfactory status quo, those people who have promotion concerns are more willing to take risks than those who have prevention concerns.[36] After all, when we have prevention concerns, we want to maintain a satisfactory status quo, remain safe and secure, and avoid taking any unnecessary risks that could move us to −1. In contrast, when we have promotion concerns, we are not content with the status quo and are willing to take a risk if that is necessary to move us to +1.

This is the story when we are currently at a satisfactory status quo (zero). However, we are not always at the status quo. We can find ourselves below the status quo in the −1 domain of losses or above the status quo in the +1 domain of gains. What happens then? What do we do if we have shared promotion versus shared prevention concerns?

When We Find Ourselves in the Domain of Losses

The domain of losses is more relevant to prevention concerns than promotion concerns. For promotion, −1 losses is pretty much the same as the status quo (zero) because both represent a failure to move to a +1 gain; it is a nongain in both cases. Staying at a −1 loss and returning to the status quo (zero) are both failures to advance to +1. Why take a risk just to return to the status quo? In contrast, the domain of −1 losses is highly relevant to prevention because it is precisely the end-state that vigilance is meant to ensure against. It represents unacceptable danger, and anything and everything must be done to restore safety and security. When we have prevention concerns and find ourselves at a −1 loss, we should become risky, even highly risky, if that is what is necessary to get back to our satisfactory status quo, to restore our safety and security.

This difference between prevention and promotion concerns in willingness to take a risk in the domain of losses was investigated in several studies.[37] The participants began by completing the measure of ideal self-guide strength and ought self-guide strength. For completing this task, they were given $5. They were then told that they had the option to participate in a second part of the study session, in which they could invest the $5 they had just earned to play a stock market game. They were told that they could potentially increase their original $5, lose it completely, or potentially end up owing money if they lost more than the $5.

Those who elected to play the stock market game were given a choice of stocks in which to invest their $5. After their investment, participants watched the progress of their selected stock. They learned that their initial stock pick was down a total of $9. This was clearly below the status quo—a definite −1 loss. The participants were then given the option to invest in a second stock, choosing between a less risky option (75% chance of winning $7; 25% chance of losing $10) and a more risky option (25% chance of winning $20; 75% chance of losing $4).

It should be noted that the more risky option was, indeed, perceived by participants as being more risky, in addition to being actually riskier in the sense that there was greater uncertainty in what would happen (i.e., higher variance in possible outcomes). It is also important to note that the more risky choice in this case was the *only* option that had the potential to return the participants back to their original status quo. The less risky option would not return the participants back to their original status quo. As expected, under these circumstances, the prevention-oriented participants were significantly more likely to choose the more risky option compared to the less risky option. In contrast, the promotion-oriented participants showed no reliable preference between the more and less risky choice.

Subsequent studies showed that prevention-oriented participants' preference for the more risky option was not due to their suddenly becoming "risky" people when they were in the domain of –1 losses.[38] It was due to the specific nature of the more risky option in comparison to the less risky option. It was due to the more risky option having the potential for restoring the status quo and the less risky option *not* having that potential. When *neither* option had the potential to restore the status quo, prevention-oriented participants' preference for the more risky option disappeared. They were now indifferent between the more risky option and the less risky option. And when *both* the more risky option and the less risky option had the potential to restore the status quo, now prevention-oriented participants' had a preference for the *less risky* option (with its higher certainty). They are *not* risky people. They prefer the less risky option if it also has the potential to restore the status quo and with more certainty.

Other findings showed that when prevention-oriented participants do choose the more risky option, it is not because they are risk-seeking. It is *not* because they *like* that option.[39] The participants were asked, in random order, how much they liked the more risky option, how much they liked the less risky option, how much they disliked the more risky option, and how much they disliked the less risky option. The results showed that when prevention-oriented participants chose the more risky option because it was the only option that could restore the status quo, they did not like the more risky option more. Instead, they *disliked it less*.

What this tells us is that people with prevention concerns don't like the more risky option. They actually dislike the more risky option and prefer the less risky option when it can also restore the status quo. But when the less risky option cannot restore the status quo, then they dislike the more risky choice less because it is the only way to get back to the status quo. It is not about people with prevention concerns seeking risk in the domain of –1 losses. It is about them doing what is necessary to restore the status quo and get out of danger.

When We Find Ourselves in the Domain of Gains

Another set of studies examined what happens to the risk preferences of people with promotion versus prevention concerns when they find themselves in the domain of +1 gains.[40] In contrast to the domain of –1 losses that has greater motivational relevance for people with prevention concerns than promotion concerns, the domain of +1 gains has greater motivational relevance for people with promotion concerns than prevention concerns. For prevention concerns, there is little difference between the status quo (zero) and a +1 state because they are both successes in relation to a –1 loss state. They are both nonlosses. For promotion concerns, however, there is a fundamental difference between the status quo (zero) and a +1 state because only the +1 state represents an advancement, a move to a better state. Thus, in the domain of +1 gains, it is people with promotion concerns rather than those with prevention concerns whose preference for a more risky option versus a less risky option will vary under different conditions. What would dictate their preference?

What matters for people with promotion concerns is experiencing success in advancing to a better state, in making progress. If progress has not been made and the more risky option is needed to make progress, then it will be preferred by those with promotion concerns. But if progress has been made, +1 has been attained, then choosing the more risky option is not worth it, and they will shift to a less risky option. This issue of *progress* will not affect the choices of people with prevention concerns. Once they are in the domain of +1 gains, and neither option will put them in danger of a −1 loss, they should be relatively indifferent to the choice between a more risky option and a less risky option.

These predictions were tested using the same basic stock market paradigm just described. This time, after their initial stock investment, participants were told that they either had no change, a small gain (£4), or a large gain (£20). Following this report, participants were given the opportunity to make either a less risky choice (100% chance of staying in the same place) or a more risky choice (50% chance of gaining £5; 50% chance of losing £5).

As expected, stronger prevention concerns did not predict preference between the more risky and less risky options. But stronger promotion concerns did. What mattered to the participants with stronger promotion concerns was their perception of whether or not they had made real progress: Was their gain large enough to count as real progress? When perceived progress was high, they were more likely to choose the less risky option than the more risky option. But when perceived progress was low, those with promotion concerns were more likely to choose the more risky option than the less risky option. Thus, the participants with promotion concerns were *not* risk averse in the domain of gains. They preferred the more risky option if they believed that they had not yet gained enough to count as real progress, had not yet clearly reached a better +1 state, and needed to choose the more risky option to do so.[41]

People acquire shared goals and standards for self-regulation in their long-term relationships with significant others, including not only their parents but also their teachers, managers, and so on. The shared ideals and oughts are chronic guides for self-regulation. More temporary shared guides can also be created in short-term interactions with others who are perceived as relevant to the current task or activity (e.g., a supervisor giving instructions). The promotion–prevention differences that I have described in this chapter and Chapter 9 derive from both of these kinds of shared realities. And the results of the studies that I have discussed demonstrate the deep and broad significance of the difference between shared promotion ideals versus prevention oughts for *what* humans strive for and *how* we strive for it. But there is still more to this shared reality story because what we strive for and how we strive for it takes place not only in our individual goal pursuits but also when we function as partners in close relationships and as members of social groups. That major story is next.

Notes

1. See Merton (1957, p. 133).
2. See Rosati (2009).
3. See Higgins (2008). It should also be noted that individuals in Japan who are more promotion oriented will pursue goals in a more extroverted manner, and individuals in the United States who are more prevention oriented will puruse goals in a more conscientious manner.
4. A reader might ask whether what matters is simply the difference between the promotion and prevention orientations. Does the fact that a promotion orientation or prevention orientation is "shared" with a relevant other make a difference? Does the shared reality matter? As discussed earlier, shared reality transforms a subjective experience into an objective experience. It increases the relevance of the motivational orientation, which, in turn, makes that orientation more salient and accessible (see Eitam & Higgins, 2010).
5. See Higgins et al. (2001, Study 3).
6. See Molden, Lucas, Gardner, Dean, and Knowles (2009).
7. See Sassenberg and Hansen (2007).
8. See Idson, Liberman, and Higgins (2000). For other evidence of this promotion–prevention asymmetry in success versus failure intensity, see Idson, Liberman, and Higgins (2004).
9. These percentiles for success and failure feedback were selected after extensive piloting. For most of the undergraduates in this study, anything less than being in the top quartile (better than 75% of the other students) is experienced as a failure.
10. What does it mean for performance that after success motivational intensity increases for promotion goals (more eager) but decreases for prevention goals (less vigilant), whereas after failure it increases for prevention goals (more vigilant) but decreases for promotion goals (less eager)? This promotion–prevention difference in motivational intensity after success versus failure suggests that performance would be better for promotion-oriented than prevention-oriented individuals after success feedback, whereas performance would be better for prevention-oriented than promotion-oriented individuals after failure feedback. This is, indeed, what has been found (e.g., Idson & Higgins, 2000; Van-Dijk & Kluger, 2004).
11. See Idson, Liberman, and Higgins (2004). I should note that in this study the positive and negative feelings were from anticipated success and anticipated failure.
12. See Förster, Grant, Idson, and Higgins (2001).
13. See Markman, McMullen, Elizaga, and Mizoguchi (2006).
14. See Navon (1977).
15. See Förster and Higgins (2005).
16. See Derryberry and Reed (1998).
17. See Semin, Higgins, Gil de Montes, Estourget, and Valencia (2005).
18. See Semin (2000) and Semin and Fiedler (1988, 1991).
19. It should be noted that, as an additional check, the participants were asked to evaluate their friendship goal from positive to negative. There was no difference between

the promotion and prevention conditions in the positivity of the goal. What mattered was whether this positive friendship goal was a promotion goal or a prevention goal.

20. See Pennington and Roese (2003).

21. This latter finding replicates the results of research by Freitas, Liberman, Salovey, and Higgins (2002), who found that individuals with a prevention orientation initiate their goal pursuit activities sooner than do individuls with a promotion orientation.

22. See Liberman and Trope (2008), Liberman, Trope, and Stephan (2007), and Trope and Liberman (2003, 2010).

23. See Förster, Higgins, and Bianco (2003).

24. For other studies, see Förster et al. (2003).

25. For classic discussions and research on this choice, see Atkinson (1953), Lewin (1935, 1951), and Zeigarnik (1938).

26. See Liberman, Idson, Camacho, and Higgins (1999).

27. See Kahneman, Knetsch, and Thaler (1990; 1991) and Thaler (1980).

28. See Knetsch (1989).

29. See Liberman et al. (1999).

30. See Crowe and Higgins (1997).

31. See Liberman, Molden, Idson, and Higgins (2001).

32. For additional evidence that participants with a promotion goal orientation perform better on a creativity task, see Friedman and Förster (2001). It should be noted, however, that there is also a relation between creativity and willingness to take a risk, and when individuals with a prevention orientation experience themselves as being in danger (−1), they become more willing to take a risk (see Scholer, Zou, Fujita, Stroessner, and Higgins 2010). This can translate into being more creative (see Baas, De Dreu, & Nijstad, 2011).

33. See Friedman & Förster (2001) and Seibt & Förster (2004).

34. See Friedman, Fishbach, Förster, & Werth (2003)

35. See Higgins (2012), *Beyond Pleasure and Pain: What Makes Us Human*

36. See, for example, Crowe & Higgins (1997) and Levine, Higgins, & Choi (2000). For other research related to promotion-prevention differences in risk perception, see Lee & Aaker (2004).

37. See Scholer, Zou, Fujita, Stroessner, and Higgins (2010).

38. See Scholer et al. (2010).

39. See Scholer et al. (2010).

40. See Zou, Scholer, and Higgins (2014)

41. For readers familiar with Kahneman and Tversky's (1979) highly influential prospect theory, I should note that the different psychological factors associated with prevention and promotion concerns contribute to understanding individuals' preferences for risky versus conservative options *independent* of the factors described in their theory.

11

How We Get Along

Bringing Us Together and Tearing Us Apart

Consider the following study. The participants were male students, 14- to 15-years-old, and they were all from the same school. They were shown slides of reproductions of various abstract paintings by two different modern painters, Klee and Kandinsky. They were shown one pair of paintings at a time, with one Klee painting and one Kandinsky painting in each pair. They were told that the paintings were by Klee and Kandinsky, whose names were written on the blackboard, but they were *not* told who painted each painting in a pair. For each pair of paintings, they were asked to state which painting they preferred. In this way, the students could be divided into one group of students who supposedly preferred Kandinsky and another group who supposedly preferred Klee.

After expressing their preferences, their answers were scored by one experimenter while another experimenter introduced them to a second (ostensibly unrelated) part of the experiment where they would be allotting money as rewards or penalties to the other participants. They would not know who the individual was, but they would know whether each person was part of the group who preferred Kandinsky or part of the group who preferred Klee. Importantly, it was emphasized that they would never be rewarding or penalizing themselves. Before starting this second part of the study, they were told (based on random assignment and not on their actual expressed preferences) either that they were part of the group who preferred Kandinsky or that they were part of the group who preferred Klee.

The study found that in the second part of the experiment, the percentage of students who most of the time favored their own group (either their Kandinsky group or their Klee group) when rewarding and penalizing others was 72%, compared to less than 20% who favored the other group (8% favored neither group). In addition, the students had the opportunity to make choices that would either benefit everyone, maximize the absolute outcomes of the members of their own group, or maximize the winning advantage of their group versus the other group. The study found that the students chose to maximize the winning advantage of their group versus the other group, that is, to maximize the advantage *difference* between their group and the other group. All this from simply experiencing shared reality with those other students who supposedly shared their painter preference and not experiencing shared reality with those who had a different painter preference—a painter preference that they did not even know about or care about before the study.

What is surprising is that these students knew each other well and could have acted to benefit everyone. Instead, an ad hoc distinction between Kandinsky fans versus Klee fans was enough for them not only to favor their own group but also to try to maximize the financial advantage of the students in their own painter-preference group *over* those in the other group.[1] Notably, they could also have chosen to maximize the *absolute* outcomes of their own group, but they chose instead to maximize the *advantage*, the winning difference between their own group and the other group—a clear in-group versus out-group effect.

Social Identities

The study just described is a classic social psychology study by Henri Tajfel who, with his collaborators, pioneered the study of intergroup discrimination and its relation to social identity. Let us now consider social identities and intergroup discrimination in more detail.

Social Identities and In-Group–Out-Group Discrimination

The innovative methodology that Tajfel and his colleagues used in the described study is called the "minimal group paradigm" because it reveals the minimal conditions necessary to observe intergroup discrimination. What this study demonstrates, and many others like it, is that it doesn't take much of a difference between groups to make discrimination occur. Let me give one more example of this—a more popularly known example often called the "blue eyes–brown eyes" experiment. This study took place, not in a lab study, but as a class exercise in an Iowa third-grade classroom with eight-year-old students.[2] Jane Elliott was the teacher of the class, and she was moved by the recent murder of Martin Luther King Jr. She wanted the children to experience what it felt like to be discriminated against because she believed that her all-White students, who had very little exposure to African Americans, would not understand what racism was like from just talking about it in class. The students agreed to do an exercise that might help them to feel what it was like to be treated the way that African Americans are treated in America.[3]

On the first day of the exercise, the teacher said that blue-eyed children are superior in many ways to brown-eyed children. The blue-eyed children were told to wrap brown fabric collars around the necks of the brown-eyed children in the class so that these children could be easily identified. The blue-eyed children were given extra privileges, including extra food helpings at lunch and extra minutes at recess. While the blue-eyed children sat in the front of the classroom, the brown-eyed children had to sit in the back. The blue-eyed children were encouraged to ignore the brown-eyed children and play only with other blue-eyed children. The differences between the two groups were emphasized by highlighting the mistakes and the negative characteristics of the brown-eyed children. Although there was some initial resistance from the students, it was not long before some of the blue-eyed children acted as superior to the brown-eyed children and behaved in bossy and unpleasant ways to them. In contrast, the brown-eyed children became more timid, even isolating themselves during recess, and performed more poorly in class than usual.

The teacher in this study did much more to create group differences than Tajfel's minimal group paradigm. Nonetheless, the group difference was only eye color, and now there were blue-eyed children who felt superior and acted superior because of their eye color. And it was very fast, considering that these children had known each other for a long time. This is both surprising and disturbing.

The discrimination that occurred in the Tajfel study is perhaps even more surprising considering that not only did the students also know each other well, the difference between the groups was simply preference for Kandinsky versus Klee as abstract painters, which had little if any relevance to the students prior to the study. In addition, there was no mention that this difference in preference had anything to do with group superiority. Nonetheless, it was enough to produce discrimination in rewarding and penalizing others.

The minimal conditions for producing competition between groups is also illustrated in a classic field study by Sherif and his colleagues. There were two separate groups of boys who had just come to a holiday camp. As soon as they became aware of each other's existence, they developed competitive in-group–out-group attitudes despite there being no prior competition between them.[4] The results of Tajfel, Sherif, and other studies like them highlight a striking and very disturbing intergroup downside of people creating shared realities—how our motivation for shared reality with others can function to tear us apart.

Motives Underlying Intergroup Discrimination

How was the shared reality created in the Tajfel study, and why did such minimal group conditions produce in-group–out-group discrimination? There are two different social identification mechanisms that each contribute to in-group–out-group discrimination. And these mechanisms relate to the epistemic and the social relational motives underlying shared reality creation.

The Epistemic Motive Involved in Social Identification

When explaining the results of their research, Tajfel and his colleagues highlight the *beneficial* process of social categorization.[5] They argue that a social world where different social categories are not differentiated is not meaningful, nor does it provide guidelines for how to conduct oneself or take action when interacting with different people in different social situations. It is unclear and confusing. By differentiating among social categories, people can make sense of their social world; they can give it order and coherence. Thus, social categorization processes support the beneficial epistemic motive of creating shared realities with others about others.

Donald Campbell and Gordon Allport, two other giants and pioneers of social psychology, had earlier noted this epistemic function of social categorization.[6] They emphasized that *differences* between social categories are *accentuated* to distinguish them more clearly, and they pointed out that social categorization, as is found in stereotyping, is just a special case of how categorization generally functions.[7] To know the difference between apples and oranges, we need to know not only what makes apples similar to each other and what makes oranges similar to each other but also what makes apples and oranges different from each other. The distinct categories we form then guide our actions toward category members.

In the case of our social world, we distinguish among many different kinds of social categories, among different kinds of religions, nations, ethnic groups, professions, family roles, sports teams and their fans, and so on. And these distinctions guide our actions in our social world. It contributes in a major way to how we interact with others in our everyday lives. By accentuating similarities within social categories and differences between them, we can order, simplify, and make sense of our complex social world.[8] This is an upside, an epistemic benefit, of creating shared realities about the differences among social categories.

The Social Relational Motive Involved in Social Identification

The epistemic function of creating shared realities that I have just described can account for Tajfel's finding that the students created a difference between their group and the other group by assigning different rewards and penalties to the two groups. They created in-group–out-group social category differences by their own discriminating actions toward the two social categories (Kandinsky fans and Klee fans), and they even *accentuated* this difference by maximizing the advantage *difference* between the two groups. But this epistemic function is not enough to account for the discrimination of *favoring* your own group over the other group. I could distinguish between apples and oranges and accentuate this difference by liking apples more than oranges *or* by liking oranges more than apples. Likewise, people could distinguish between their in-group and an out-group by either favoring their in-group *or* by favoring the out-group. But this is not what happened in Tajfel's study (or in other studies). They favored the in-group. Where does this in-group favoritism come from? It cannot be explained just in terms of the epistemic function of distinguishing between social categories.

The answer is that it comes from the second, social relational motive of creating a shared reality with others, with wanting a positive connection to those with whom you have a shared reality. Let's reconsider the term *identification*. This term can be used as a synonym of *categorization*: to judge that something is a member of a particular category. For example, you can *identify* an object as being an apple rather than an orange, or a dog rather than a cat. In social categorization, you *identify* someone as being a member of a social category, such as being a Kandinsky fan rather than a Klee fan.

This sense of the term *identification* concerns the epistemic function of identification. But, as was discussed in Chapter 7, this is not the only meaning of *identification*. Identification with others is also a form of social influence that impacts attitudes and opinions. The classic case, which is discussed in the psychodynamic literature, is identifying with significant others, having a feeling of attachment to them, and making them positive role models. In the attitude literature, identification occurs when the recipient of an influence attempt is attracted to the agent of influence and wants to be connected to that person, to experience a "*we*-ness" with that person. It is as if influence recipients want to experience themselves as being in the same category as the influence agent, belonging together in the same category, hence, the use of the term *identification*.

This social relational function of identification is not neutral. It is not just epistemic. If we identify an object as an apple rather than an orange, we do not want to *be* like that apple. But when we identify with a person, we do want to *be* like that person. Similarly, when we identify with a social category or a group, we want to be connected to that group, extend our self into the group.[9] That group is a *positive* reference group, and we will take actions that are consistent with it being a positive group to us, such as showing in-group favoritism. This is the social relational motive of creating a shared reality with others and it accounts for the in-group favoritism that Tajfel found and that is pervasive in our social world. It is what Tajfel and his colleagues later called "positive group distinctiveness."[10]

Regulatory Focus Differences
in Intergroup Discrimination

It should also be noted that intergroup discrimination can be accomplished in two different ways—by responding more positively to the in-group or by responding more negatively to the out-group. It is interesting in this regard that promotion shared concerns and prevention shared concerns produce different ways of creating positive group distinctiveness. Promotion shared concerns produce more positive responses to the in-group whereas prevention shared concerns produce more negative responses to the out-group—*promoting us* versus *preventing them*.

As one example of this, participants in one study were told to sit in a room while they waited for a study to begin in which they and their teammate would compete against another team.[11] In the waiting room was a backpack on a chair that was owned supposedly by either their future partner or a future opponent in the upcoming task. There were also other chairs in the room that were different distances away from the chair with the backpack. The participants freely chose where to sit. The study found that the participants with a stronger promotion focus chose to sit *closer* to their *teammate*, whereas a stronger prevention focus had no such relation to the teammate. In contrast, participants with a stronger prevention focus chose to sit *further away* from their *opponent*, whereas a stronger promotion focus had no such relation to the opponent.

This difference between prevention and promotion in how discrimination plays out is interesting in the context of racist rhetoric. There is evidence, for example, that White supremacists engage in more hate speech against out-groups than love speech about their in-group, despite their claims that their purpose is to support the White race.[12] The concerns of these groups as reflected in their messages are prevention concerns with safety and security—the threats posed by the out-group.

Different Levels of Social Identities

The importance of social identification or social identities in our social lives is not restricted to its effects on in-group–out-group discrimination, as significant as that is. The students in the Tajfel study did not experience who they were fundamentally or define their basic selves in terms of being a Kandinsky fan or a Klee fan. But people can and will define themselves in terms of their social identities, such as their ethnic identity (e.g., Serbian, French Canadian) or religious identity (e.g., Sunni Muslim, evangelical Christian) or political identity (e.g., progressive Democrat, conservative Republican). And these identities can and do instill intense emotional commitment that includes a willingness to die for one's group.

Marilynn Brewer, who has made landmark contributions to understanding the nature and consequences of social identity, emphasized the importance of social identities to humans and points out that our social identities exist at different levels in the social network; that is, they are *hierarchical*.[13] Going up my academic social identity hierarchy, for example, I have shared realities with the other social psychologists who are faculty in the two departments at Columbia to which I belong (the psychology department and the management department), shared realities with all of the faculty in my two departments, shared realities with all of the faculty at Columbia University, and shared realities with other academics at other universities in the world.

These social identities at different levels of my hierarchy are all significant to me and can influence what I feel, what I believe, and what I choose to do. Like others, I will choose to take on effortful tasks that serve the interests of these social identities (i.e., service). But at any particular time, whose interests I favor will vary as a function of which social identity level is salient. When what is salient is my social identity with the faculty in my departments, then it is their interests that I favor in contrast to the interests of faculty in other departments. But when my social identity with Columbia University is salient, then it is all of the faculty at Columbia that I favor in contrast to the faculty at other universities.

What is notable about these comparisons is the specificity of the "in contrast to." The contrast is in relation to another social category at the same level and along the same dimension. When my social identity as a Columbia faculty member is salient, it is the interests of Columbia faculty that I favor in contrast to the interests of faculty at other universities rather than in contrast to the interests of faculty in the botany department at Princeton University or in contrast to the interests of the members of the Conservative Party in Canada.

By the way, this specificity is something that political and media commentators should pay more attention to when they discuss social conflicts. When they refer to someone as a Muslim terrorist, they are specifying a level of comparison where the contrast is a non-Muslim religion, which makes salient comparisons of, and conflict between, religious groups. This is precisely what terrorist groups want—to make the conflict a religious war between different shared beliefs and shared values. It would be better to simply refer to them as terrorists.

Note that the existence of different levels of social identities means that a contrast social category (e.g., Columbia faculty who are not psychologists) to a currently salient social identity (Columbia faculty who are psychologists) can be people with whom you have a common membership and social identity (Columbia faculty). But, by being in contrast to the identity that is currently salient, that contrast category is treated like an out-group with respect to favorability. At other times that same membership group (Columbia faculty) can be an in-group in contrast to some other group (faculty not at Columbia). This reveals the psychological subtlety of human social identities. It is not simply about membership versus non-membership groups mapping directly onto in-groups versus out-groups.

That said, membership in-groups are important to humans. Indeed, it has been argued that in-group identification is primary.[14] This makes sense because we are most likely to create our major shared realities, our shared feelings, shared beliefs, and shared concerns with the members of the in-groups to which we belong. As noted earlier, this does not mean that we respond to this primary identification only by rewarding our in-group members. We could respond by punishing out-group members, especially when the out-group is perceived as a threat to the safety and security of our in-group (i.e., prevention concerns). But, importantly, we do not need to punish out-group members to experience in-group positivity. Our positive feelings toward in-group members and our inclination to benefit them does *not* mean that we must also experience negativity toward out-groups.[15] There is evidence, for example, that children show a positivity bias toward members of their in-group while not displaying any negativity toward out-groups.[16]

Competition versus Cooperation as Characterizing Humans

There is a common misunderstanding about in-group–out-group discrimination that I need to address. It begins with the common idea that people are aggressive and competitive. People point to the Freudian notion of an instinct of aggression, and the supposed Darwinian notion of "survival of the fittest," as referring to the winner of interindividual or intergroup competition. We end up characterizing human motivation in terms of aggressive competition—the "dog-eat-dog" notion of what motivates us.

This leads to the mistaken belief that in-group–out-group discrimination involves our behaving aggressively and competitively toward the out-group, and that is why in-group–out-group discrimination is bad. Well, this can happen, but what usually happens is that we behave cooperatively with our in-group members to improve our group's status relative to the out-group. We cooperative with our in-group members to give our in-group an advantage. Even when we build defenses, like trenches (or moats) and walls, we do so by working together with others to build them. Even when we fight, we work together in units to defeat the enemy. In terms of what we are actually doing, even when preventing the out-group, *we are cooperating with in-group members*. Players on sports teams, like basketball, volleyball, and soccer (football in the rest of the world) cooperate with one another on the court or on the field—whether they win or lose. Yes, they can be characterized as trying to beat the other team, but to do so they need to cooperate with their teammates. If they refuse to cooperate with their teammates, they won't last long on the team.

What we are doing is cooperating with our in-group members to yield a positive advantage for "us" over "them." However, the fact that what we are doing is cooperating does not make what we are doing a good thing. Cooperation involves creating a shared reality with others, and this can have consequences that often are beneficial, but it can have harmful consequences as well. In the case of in-group–out-group discrimination, it can benefit the in-group while also hurting the out-group. Indeed, we can cooperate with in-group members to hurt out-group members. But, to repeat, hurting the out-group is not a necessary part of cooperation with our in-group members. For example, you can want to give some of your personal funds to help out a family member in need without wanting to hurt any out-group members.

By the way, if humans are really "dog-eat-dog" extreme competitors, why don't we refer to what we do when we compete as our "man-eat-man" behavior? It doesn't seem very fair to dogs, who after all evolved from highly social wolves whose signature characteristic is their cooperation in hunting other animals. They don't kill and eat each other. There is more evidence of that kind of behavior among humans (think human cannibalism), but it is rare for us as well and is mostly taboo. I think it is time to retire the "dog-eat-dog" expression.

In addition to wanting a positive advantage for "us" over "them," cooperation from shared social identities can have another negative consequence that is unintended and goes unrecognized. When people work together in groups, they often perceive each other as in-group members, as having a common social identity. This makes their interactions relatively smooth, effortless, and pleasant. But it does *not* necessarily make them more *productive*. Indeed, making their shared identity salient also makes their shared feelings, shared beliefs, and shared interests more accessible than whatever it is that they do *not* share. This can be a problem for groups because the group members will often discuss what they share with one another rather than what they don't share. This means that the information that is uniquely possessed by each group member will not be exchanged with other group members, which can make the group decision-making process *less* effective than it would be otherwise.[17]

As an illustration of the group process trade-offs from group members having (vs. not having) shared realities from a common social identity, one study examined the effects of a newcomer joining a group of old-timers where the newcomer was either an in-group member that kept the group of old-timers homogeneous or was an out-group member that made the group more diverse. [18] Three individuals began a discussion of the problem assigned to them (the old-timers) before the fourth member arrived (the newcomer). The old-timers were members of the same fraternity (or same sorority), and the newcomer was also a member of that fraternity (in-group) or was a member of a different fraternity (out-group). Fraternity membership had been made salient as a social identity at the beginning of the study by having large banners with the names of the fraternities posted on the walls.

Importantly, the groups with *out-group* newcomers performed significantly *better* on the task, especially when they paid more attention to the newcomer. But, interestingly, this superior performance went *unrecognized*. Indeed, when the newcomer was an in-group member rather than an out-group member, the group members were more confident in their performance and reported that their group interactions were more effective. Having shared realities with others creates an *experience* of connectedness and of epistemic authority, but these experiences do *not* necessarily reflect actual performance.

Group homogeneity can be a problem because the group members assume shared realities with other group members and thus do not make the effort to learn from one another about what, in fact, they don't share.[19] Having, instead, an out-group member in a group can increase effort to learn about all the different information on an issue because you cannot take for granted that you all share the same feelings, beliefs, opinions, or knowledge. This can be an advantage for group processes. Indeed, there is evidence that even a minimal source of social category diversity, such as wearing different colored shirts that match different colored sections of a room (blue vs. red), can lead to greater consideration of all the information available for a group discussion, which, in turn, improves the group's performance (e.g., deciding who committed the murder in a murder mystery).[20]

Social Roles and Social Positions

Working together in coordinated social roles is pervasive in human society. Indeed, whenever we communicate with each other we are coordinating the roles of speaker and listener. And not only are we coordinating roles, we are also switching roles. Taking turns being the speaker or the listener is fundamental to interpersonal communication, and, as was discussed in Chapter 3, it is something that takes children time to learn to do effectively. It is a fundamental part of human development in creating shared realities with others.

Performing and Coordinating Social Roles

The shared realities that are associated with different social roles impact what we do. This was demonstrated in a classic study on the role of speaker versus listener by Bob Zajonc, another major figure in the history of social psychology. All of the participants read a letter written by a job applicant to a potential employer that included information about his qualifications and background. They were all told to imagine what kind of person he is. After reading the letter, they were assigned either the role of speaker (transmitter) or the role of listener (recipient) where they would, respectively, either transmit a message about the letter writer so that the message recipient can know him, or they would receive more information about the letter writer from a message sent to them. Before the communication took place, both the speakers and listeners were asked to write down the things they learned about the job applicant from his letter. The study found that, even before the communication took place, the information that was written down about the letter writer by those in the speaker role was more organized and more specific than what was written down by those in the listener role.[21] This difference is consistent with the role expectations for speakers to be clear about a message topic, and the role expectations for listeners to be open about a message topic (as discussed in Chapter 1).

The shared realities that are associated with different social roles not only impact what we do. They also impact how we see the world. Read the following story as if you were a burglar gathering information:

The two boys ran until they came to the driveway. "See, I told you today was good for skipping school," said Mark. "Mom is never home on Thursday," he added. Tall hedges hid the house from the road so the pair strolled across the finely landscaped yard. "I never knew your place was so big," said Pete. "Yeah, but it's nicer now than it used to be since Dad had the new stone siding put on and added the fireplace."

There were front and back doors and a side door that led to the garage, which was empty except for three parked 10-speed bikes. They went in the side door, Mark explaining that it was always open in case his younger sisters got home earlier than their mother.

Pete wanted to see the house so Mark started with the living room. It, like the rest of the downstairs, was newly painted. Mark turned on the stereo, the noise of which worried Pete. "Don't worry, the nearest house is a quarter of a mile away," Mark shouted. Pete felt more comfortable observing that no houses could be seen in any direction beyond the huge yard.

The dining room, with all the china, silver, and cut glass, was no place to play so the boys moved into the kitchen where they made sandwiches. Mark said they wouldn't go to the basement because it had been damp and musty ever since the new plumbing had been installed.

"This is where my dad keeps his famous paintings and his coin collection," Mark said as they peered into the den. Mark bragged that he could get spending money whenever he needed it since he'd discovered that his dad kept a lot in the desk drawer.

There were three upstairs bedrooms. Mark showed Pete his mother's closet, which was filled with furs, and the locked box, which held her jewels. His sisters' room was uninteresting except for the color TV, which Mark carried to his room. Mark bragged that the bathroom in the hall was his since one had been added to his sisters' room for their use. The big highlight in his room, though, was a leak in the ceiling where the old roof had finally rotted.

Now look away from the book, get a piece of paper or go to your computer, and write down what you can remember about this house. *Don't look back at the story.*

Now that you have written down what you can remember, take a look at what you have written. Is it relevant to the role of burglar? Is there other information that you did not write down? Now let's switch your role. Imagine that instead of being a burglar, you are now a homebuyer. Now as a homebuyer, is there any additional information in the story that you can think of?

I conduct this study in my introductory social psychology course, and I find the same basic result that was found in the original study.[22] By switching roles, people usually remember additional information—about a 20% increase in remembering items relevant to homebuyer that were not previously remembered in the burglar role. This recall of additional items relevant to homebuyer means that the items were attended to originally and even stored. But when taking the role of burglar, they were not recollected because they were not relevant to that role, and the accessibility of information depends on its relevance.[23] It should also be noted that in the role of burglar some of the homebuyer-relevant items did not receive much attention to begin with and were not stored to begin with—about another 20% in the original study. For example, did you remember in your first recall that the yard of the house was "finely landscaped" or that the house had "new stone siding"? These items are more likely to be recalled when participants begin in the role of homebuyer rather than beginning in the role of burglar.

Our shared realities about what is expected for those who perform a social role effectively, even being an effective burglar, create a viewpoint on the world that influences our perception and memory of the world by determining what is relevant and significant. As we switch from role to role, what matters about the world changes. Although you are unlikely to switch between the role of homebuyer and the role of burglar, you will frequently switch between a career role and a family role, and this switch in shared relevance will impact what you attend to and what you remember in your life. And it needs to be emphasized that these roles—even those we have not personally enacted (think burglar)—are shared realties that we have learned by being a member of a given group. Moreover, what is expected for a particular role, such as the role of wife or the role of husband, can vary among groups.

An especially interesting case of switching between different roles in close relationships was described by the pioneer of transactional analysis, Eric

Berne, in his book, *Games People Play*.[24] Berne was inspired by the work of Freud, as well as the work of Harry Stack Sullivan who was another pioneer in psychoanalysis. Using Freud's ego states as an analogy, Berne described what happens in close relationships when individuals play the roles of child, parent, and adult, analogous to Freud's ego states of id, superego, and ego, respectively. According to Berne, carrying out these roles produces the following psychological characteristics:

CHILD *role*: Intuitive, creative, spontaneous, have fun.
PARENT *role*: Conventional, authoritative, responsible, nurturant.
ADULT *role*: Mature, practical, executive, problem-solver.

When two people interact, they can each perform any one of these three roles. But the stability of the different role combinations vary. For example, a parent-to-parent combination will not be stable. It will produce conflict because you cannot have two people who both take the authoritative, supervisor position in an interaction. The different role combinations can also vary in effectiveness, but this also depends on the situation, on what the dyad is doing together. For example, the adult-to-adult combination can be very effective, but, according to Berne, when having sexual relationships the child-to-child combination is more effective because that activity is more about being spontaneous and having fun than it is about being practical or solving problems (e.g., "Alright now, let's think about how we can get this done in a practical way.")

An interesting feature of these role combinations is that supposedly the same utterance could be made in different ways that creates different role combinations. For example, the question "Where is the butter?" could be expressed with a neutral, purely information-seeking manner that creates an adult-to-adult combination, which could produce an adult answer like, "I think it is on the top shelf of the refrigerator door." Alternatively, the same utterance could be expressed in a whining manner that creates a child-to-parent combination, which could produce a parent answer like, "Keep looking. I know you can find it yourself." Or it could be expressed in an angry demanding manner that creates a parent-to-child combination, which could produce a child answer like, "I didn't move it. Why are you blaming me?"

What is notable about these roles is that you can have role switching. In a husband and wife relationship, for example, there can be adult-to-adult when problem-solving together, child-to-child when having fun together, and parent-to-child where the husband and wife take turns at each role depending on who needs comforting at the moment. Such role-switching is healthy for the relationship and illustrates an upside of our creating shared realities with others by coordinating our social roles.

But, unfortunately, role-switching can also be unhealthy. An especially pernicious example of this is what some male bosses do with their female employees. This relationship is supposed to be professional, which means being in an adult-to-adult relationship. But male bosses can take on a playful child role, so-called flirting, to pressure the female employee into a child-to-child combination for sexual activities. This could lead to sexual harassment. Moreover, faced with a boss taking on a playful child role, the female employee cannot just respond instead as the parent to her child because she typically would not have the authority to be the parent in a parent-to-child relationship with her boss as the child. Indeed, it is much more likely for male bosses to act like an authoritative figure to create a parent-to-child combination that forces the female employee into the role of the child being dependent on the boss. These are very unhealthy role combinations for a professional female to be forced into. Once again, it illustrates a downside of our human motivation to create shared realities with others.

What I find fascinating about Berne's analysis is the conclusion that people can be pressured or constrained by their interaction partner to play certain roles. This can occur in something as simple as the manner in which the partner asks, "Where's the butter?"—with the tone of an adult, a child, or a parent. There is another, relatively common example of a downside from shared realities in role relationship dynamics. This can occur when college students go home during a semester break and want their parents to treat them in their new "grown-up college student" adult identity. They want adult-to-adult interactions. The problem is that their parents quite naturally initiate interaction with them in terms of the previously established parent-to-child role combination. When they do so, the college student adult feels pressure to adopt the role of child. This is not the adult role that they prefer to perform. My advice to my students is to talk to their parents about their preference for more adult-to-adult interactions but to remember as well that a little parent-to-child can also be a wonderful thing. And who better to do this with than your actual parents? Oh, and one more thing. Sometimes the parent can need comforting, and the student can take the role of a nurturant parent.

People not only perform roles, but they also are perceived by others as performing roles. There are two roles that others perceive us as performing that are especially significant in human society—the male role and the female role. For many people, the shared realities about these roles are traditional viewpoints on what is expected of males and females. For example, males are expected traditionally to be assertive while females are not. Females are expected traditionally to be nurturant while males are not. These different role expectations create pressure on individuals to act in ways that are consistent with these expectations.

Because of these different role expectations and demands, males and females can be perceived differently even when their actual behavior is the *same*.[25] For example, a male's assertive behavior can be perceived as being strong and decisive like men are supposed to be, whereas the same behavior by a female can be perceived as surprising and inappropriate, as being aggressive or even rude. As another example, a female's caring and supportive behavior can be perceived as just what females are supposed to do, whereas the same behavior by a male can be perceived as surprising, as being exceptionally kind and helpful. Put these two cases together, and the potential disadvantage to females from these differences in male and female roles is clear.

Social Positions

A social position is any socially recognized category (i.e., shared reality) that has associated with it expectations about the attributes of its members.[26] Social roles constitute social positions that have *injunctive* expectations associated with them about how someone enacting that role *should* behave (i.e., their responsibilities and obligations). There are other social positions in a society that are also shared realities about the members of a social category, but rather than involving injunctive expectations about how category members should behave, they involve *descriptive* expectations about how social category members *will* behave. These descriptive social expectations can also influence behavior.[27]

One significant way that this can play out is through what Robert Merton called the "self-fulfilling prophecy." Simply because of their membership in a social category, individuals can be perceived by others as possessing certain attributes (even when they don't). Then, others will respond to them as if they had these attributes. And these responses to them will, in turn, cause them to react in a manner that ends up fulfilling the expectation about them.

A well-established example of such a process is teachers' having expectancies about a particular category of students that results in the teachers behaving toward the students in a way that ends up causing the students to fulfill those expectancies. This was found in the research by Robert Rosenthal and Lenore Jacobson that was described in their classic book, *Pygmalion in the Classroom*.[28] A random set of students was selected, and their teachers, who were not aware of this random selection, were told that these students were potential "late bloomers." This social category assignment produced expectations that these students would excel if given the appropriate support and guidance. This resulted in the teachers behaving differently to them than they did before. Assigning these students to the social position category of late bloomer mattered because their school performance improved over time more than that of the other students—they ended up, in fact, blooming.

This research illustrates the potential upside of the self-fulfilling prophecy. But there is often a downside. An elegant set of studies clearly demonstrated how the dynamic of the self-fulfilling prophecy process can play out negatively.[29] The first study examined how White male college student interviewers behaved while interviewing young male high school students who were applicants for a position. The high school applicants were either White or Black. One of the measures was the physical distance that the interviewer chose to place himself while interviewing the applicant. To obtain this measure, the experimenter pretended to discover that there was no chair in the room for the interviewer and told the interviewer to bring in a chair from the adjoining room. This study found that the White interviewers placed their chair further away from the Black applicant than the White applicant. The interviewers also chose to end the interview sooner for the Black applicant than the White applicant, and spoke less fluently and coherently when interviewing the Black applicant than the White applicant.

In the second study, White interviewers were trained to conduct their interview of applicants either in the way that White interviewers had with the Black applicant in the first study (Black-applicant interview style) or in the way that White interviewers had with the White applicant in the first study (White-applicant interview style). After training in these two different interview styles, all of the White interviewers interviewed only actual White applicants, either using the White-applicant interview style or the Black-applicant interview style. The White applicants who received the Black-applicant interview style performed more poorly in the interview than the White applicants who received the White-applicant interview style. Of course, in the normal course of things, it would be young Black male applicants who would receive the Black-applicant interview style and thus end up victims of a self-fulfilling prophecy.

By the way, another situation where the self-fulfilling prophecy can play out in damaging ways is during therapist–client social interactions. In my experience while being trained as a therapist, the client categories that had a high risk of creating a damaging self-fulfilling prophecy were clients being diagnosed as "dependent" and "passive-aggressive." But the worst social category assignment that I dealt with in my training was when I was told that my next client had been consistently diagnosed by his previous therapists as having "Munchausen syndrome." These are patients believed to be *faking their illness*. Imagine how they will be responded to and how these responses will affect them. Avoiding a self-fulfilling prophecy for this category is a big challenge.

I discussed Susan Andersen's important work on emotional transference in Chapter 5. Her work can be conceptualized as people assigning a new person they meet to a person category comprised of one of their significant others, such as their mother. In transference, the category is defined in terms of the attributes of the significant other, such as their mother, to whom the new person has some resemblance, even if the resemblance is quite minimal. Despite this new person not possessing many of the attributes of their significant other, people will often respond as if the new person *did* possess the missing attributes as well. It is as if a significant other in an individual's life has developed into a specific social position in the social world of that individual—a social category with descriptively expected attributes—and it is now possible for a new person to be perceived as a member of that social category. What Andersen and her colleagues have found is that the transference to the new person can involve not only feelings that are shared with the significant other but also a world view that is shared with the significant other.

The new person's resemblance to the participants' significant other activates the world view they share with their significant other, including shared values, shared political and religious beliefs, and shared meaning systems.[30] This leads the participants to believe that they are likely to develop a mutual understanding about life while interacting with this new person. Moreover, when asked to select a topic of conversation for their upcoming interaction with this person, they are more likely to choose a topic associated with a value they share with their significant other but do not necessarily share with this new person. This means that shared realities with a significant other provide a scaffold for creating shared realities with a new person who resembles the significant other in some way. This is certainly efficient, but given that the resemblance can be rather superficial (e.g., personal habits) and have little actual relation to the new person's world views, such transference can also be a problem with respect to knowing the truth about that person. And the conversation itself might not go very well if this new person's values are actually quite different from the significant other.

Creating a *We* from Shared Realities

Fritz Heider is one of social psychology's most important historical figures. He is famous for his contributions to the areas of causal attribution and cognitive consistency. Indeed, I had always thought that the title of his classic book, *The Psychology of Interpersonal Relations*,[31] was a little odd given that he was talking about person perception and cognitive consistency. To me, he was a pioneer in social cognition and motivated cognition. I now appreciate better that he was, indeed, concerned with interpersonal relations and had important insights about the dynamics of social relationships.[32]

One of Heider's insights was to distinguish between *sentiment* relations and *unit* relations and then consider how they can impact one another. Sentiment relations can be positive or negative—*like* or *dislike*, respectively. Unit relations can also be positive or negative—*associated* or *disassociated*, respectively. Sometimes the sentiment and unit relations in social relationships go together. For example, the relation between *me* and *my friend* is positive with respect to both sentiment and unit (i.e., I like my friend, and we have a close relationship together), and the relation between *me* and *my enemy* is negative with respect to both sentiment and unit (i.e., I dislike my enemy, and we avoid each other). But sentiments and units can be independent or even opposite. People can like members of a positive reference group but have no unit membership with them, like blue-collar workers admiring billionaires. People can also have a unit relationship with a sibling who they dislike or even a marital partner who they now detest (positive unit, negative sentiment).

Close relationships are complex precisely because of the different combinations of sentiment and units that are possible within the relationship and its contrast relationships. For example, there is really a problem in a marriage if a wife not only detests her husband (positive unit with negative sentiment) but loves her married yoga instructor who has never even talked to her (negative unit with positive sentiment). What is fascinating about Heider's discussion of the dynamics of social relationships is his analysis of how people try to make sense of and deal with experienced problems by changing the units and sentiments to create *balance* among them. In the previous example, the wife could divorce her husband and get the yoga instructor to divorce his wife and marry her. Short of that, which is, after all, a tall order, she can decide that, all things considered, her husband really is a better partner for her than the yoga instructor. This change in perception may also take some major cognitive effort.

Heider's ideas are broadly applicable to the shared realities that create satisfying close relationships. Take, for example, the phenomenon of couples creating shared realities, that is, perceiving that they and their partner have the same feelings and beliefs about things in the world, despite them actually not having the same feelings and beliefs about things in the world. For instance, there is evidence that a marital relationship is more satisfying when the husband and wife perceive that they share opinions about what an ideal marriage is like (even when the ideal is stereotypic) or believe that they and their partner resolve marital conflicts in the same constructive way, regardless of whether those perceived shared opinions are *actually* shared.[33] Indeed, the perceived or experienced shared realities matter *more* to the success of the relationship than the actual reality, which says a lot about the critical importance to humans of experiencing shared realities.

There is also evidence that actually being similar to someone, such as a student having the same gender as another student and being from the same hometown, is *not* what's critical for liking that person. Experiencing a shared reality with them is more important, especially in the form of believing that you share with that person the same subjective experience about something, such as both of you reacting in the same way to a third student—what has been called *I* sharing (seeing "I to I").[34] As discussed in Chapter 2, this is what happens when a child and a parent show interest and excitement about the same object they are looking at. Because this shared reality involves the social relational motive, we would expect that *I* sharing would be an even more important factor in creating a positive feeling about another person when the motive to be close to others is stronger. This is, in fact, the case.[35] Moreover, there is also evidence that just like the first phase of shared reality development in children is shared feelings with their significant others, the first phase of adults' creating a close relationship with one another is shared feelings.[36]

What Heider highlighted is that *perceptions* of sharing units and sentiments really matter for relationship satisfaction. In particular, as I just mentioned, perceived similarity matters more than actual similarity. Although it has been suggested in the literature that perceived similarity occurs because partners project their own perceptions of the relationship onto their partner, I believe that it occurs because the partners in a positive unit relationship want to experience shared realities with one another—for both epistemic and social relational motives.

A significant extension of Heider's idea of a *unit* has been made in the work of Art Aron and his colleagues on the implications for close relationships of including another person in the self (i.e., expanding the self from a *me* element to a *we* unit). Aron and his colleagues developed an interpersonal closeness measure of experiencing others in the self using Venn diagrams like the one displayed in the following figure.[37]

Please circle the picture below which best describes your relationship

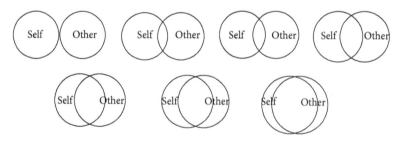

Research using this Inclusion of Other in the Self scale has found that it predicts whether romantic relationships will still be intact three months later, as well as marital satisfaction more generally. It also positively relates to other measures of closeness or "*we*-ness" that have very different characteristics than the pictorial Venn diagrams. For example, participants who were in romantic relationships were asked to share some thoughts, either positive or negative, about their current relationship. Their sentences were coded in terms of whether they included plural nouns (we, us, our) or singular pronouns (I, me, mine). The research found that there was a significant positive relation between participants' Inclusion of Other in the Self and the frequency of their using plural *we*-related words.[38]

The literature on close relationships has identified different kinds of interpersonal exchanges that enhance feelings of intimacy and closeness between partners. Some researchers have highlighted the importance of each person in the relationship telling his or her partner about his or her feelings, beliefs, concerns, fears, and dreams (i.e., *self-disclosure*).[39] This kind of intimacy was discussed in Chapter 3 as something that begins when shared coordinated roles emerge. In addition to such back and forth self-disclosure, what is also important is that partners who receive the self-disclosure validate and verify the feelings, beliefs, and concerns that their partner has disclosed to them (i.e., actually *be responsive*) and that the self-disclosing partner *perceive* that he or she has been responsive.[40]

There is yet another kind of interpersonal exchange that has been found to be a strong predictor of relationship satisfaction—having your partner be responsive to your good news. Indeed, *sharing your good news* with your partner and having your partner express positive feelings about it that match your positive feelings (social verification of your feelings) can contribute more to a close relationship than having him or her respond appropriately to your bad news (i.e., providing appropriate support).[41] Responding positively to your partner's good news intensifies the positivity of the good news—the shared reality makes the positive news more *real*.

What is notable about these kinds of interpersonal exchanges that contribute to relationship satisfaction is that they all involve creating shared realities between partners—disclosing to each other, being responsive to each other, sharing good news with each other. More specifically, what is often happening is that shared feelings, attitudes, and opinions are being created. And this, in turn, creates connectedness. What does this mean? Not only do the partners share sentiments, but a positive unit is also created between them from the connectedness—a "*we*-ness." As Heider would say, a *well-balanced* relationship is created from this combination of sentiments and units.

There is also some recent evidence that directly supports the idea that when people create shared realities with each other, it increases their sense of closeness or "*we*-ness."[42] One study used the "say-is-believing" paradigm discussed in Chapter 1 and manipulated whether communicators received feedback that their audience had succeeded (shared reality) or failed (no shared reality) to identify whom they were talking about. Using the Inclusion of Other in the Self measure of closeness or "*we*-ness," the study found that the communicators who received the success feedback (shared reality) felt closer to their audience than the communicators who received the failure feedback (no shared reality). This study also found that the effect of the success (vs. failure) feedback on closeness was driven by the participant communicators having both greater epistemic trust and greater social relational trust in their audience partner.

Another study found that participants who were asked to write about a discussion they had with their partner in which they experienced high (vs. low) shared reality felt closer to their partner as measured by greater use of plural nouns (we, us, our) in their writing. Finally, for partners in romantic relationships, higher scores on a questionnaire measuring perceived shared reality in their relationship (e.g., "We typically share the same thoughts and feelings about things." "Through our discussions, we often develop a joint perspective") predicted feeling closer on both the Inclusion of Other in the Self measure and the measure of use of plural nouns (we, us, our) when describing their relationship.[43]

What we have learned from past research on human relationships is that creating shared realities with others is a mixed blessing. It can bring us together by making us feel connected to other people—a *we* feeling—or it can tear us apart by making us feel that our in-group is *special* and out-group members are to be avoided and even punished. And interacting with out-group members can itself be a trade-off because it can reduce feelings of interpersonal connectedness and even create conflict, but it can also increase attention to all the available information on an issue, which, in turn, improves performance.

What is fascinating—or disturbing, or hopeful—about humans is that the same group can be experienced as an in-group or an out-group at different times (depending on the current level of social categorization and contrast). Moreover, a group can impact us without our needing to be a member of that group or even having met a member of that group. And these effects of shared reality on our social interactions derive from both epistemic and relational motives. Yes, humans are complex, but what is clear is that shared reality is fundamental to how we get along with others.

Notes

1. For more details about the methodology and results of this study, see Tajfel, Flament, Billig, and Bundy (1971).
2. A gripping movie about the original study that you can see on YouTube is called, "The Eye of the Storm" (also called the "Brown Eyes and Blue Eyes Racism Experiment").
3. Jane Elliott received strong negative feedback from her community at the time for carrying out this study. One criticism was that the children were too young to participate in this study, and it could have negative consequences for them. I believe that this is a reasonable criticism. At the very least, the parents of these children should have given their permission for their child to participate. In addition, it is possible that these children would have negative experiences that they would not have had otherwise in their lives and that they would continue to do so after the study was completed. All of this, according to the ethical code for conducting psychological research, would have meant that this study should not be conducted. In fairness to Jane Elliott, these ethical rules were not as clear when the study was done, and what was done was a class exercise and not as research for publication. She also intended that the children learn something important and beneficial, and she did not criticize the children for what they did. Thus, this exercise is *not* like Milgram's (1974) infamous research program (which I discuss in detail, from a shared reality perspective, in my *Beyond Pleasure and Pain* book; see Higgins, 2012). Still, such a study should not be done the way that it was done.
4. See Sherif, Harvey, White, Hood, and Sherif (1961).
5. See Tajfel et al. (1971).
6. See Allport (1954) and Campbell (1956).
7. For further discussion of social categorization, see also Brewer (2007).
8. See Tajfel (1982). See also Hogg and Abrams (1993) and Hogg and Rinella (2018).
9. See, for example, Turner, Hogg, Oakes, Reicher, and Wetherell (1987).
10. See Tajfel (1974, 1981) and Tajfel and Turner (1979). See also Commins and Lockwood (1979).
11. See Shah, Brazy, and Higgins (2004).
12. See Gonsalkorale and von Hippel (2012).
13. See, for example, Brewer (1991).
14. For a comprehensive and thoughtful review, see Brewer (2007).
15. See, for example, Brewer (2007).
16. See Cameron, Alvarez, Ruble, and Fuligni (2001).
17. See, for example, Stasser (1992, 1999). For a review of the potential productivity downsides of shared reality in groups, see Levine, Resnick, and Higgins (1993).
18. See Phillips, Liljenquist, and Neale (2009).
19. For a related perspective, see Apfelbaum, Phillips, and Richeson (2014).
20. See Loyd, Wang, Phillips, and Lount (2013).
21. See Zajonc (1960).
22. See Anderson and Pichert (1978).
23. See Eitam and Higgins (2010).

24. See Berne (1964).

25. For classic discussions and evidence about how role demands impact perceptions, see Jones and Davis (1965) and Jones, Davis, and Gergen (1961).

26. See Stryker and Statham (1985).

27. For further discussion of the difference between injunctive norms and descriptive norms, and how they can independently influence behavior, see Cialdini (2003) and Cialdini, Reno, and Kallgren (1990).

28. See Rosenthal and Jacobson (1968).

29. See Word, Zanna, and Cooper (1974).

30. See Andersen and Przybylinski (2018) and Przybylinski and Andersen (2015).

31. See Heider (1958).

32. For a fuller discussion of the shared reality and interpersonal relationship implications of Heider's work, as well as the work of other "cognitive consistency" theorists, see Rossignac-Millon and Higgins (2018a).

33. See, for example, Acitelli, Douvan, and Veroff (1993) and Acitelli, Kenny, and Weiner (2001). For a sociological, symbolic interactionist perspective on this, see also Berger and Kellner (1964) and Stephen (1984).

34. See Pinel, Long, Landau, Alexander, and Pyszczynski (2006).

35. See Pinel et al. (2006).

36. For a review of such evidence, see Rossignac-Millon and Higgins (2018b).

37. See Aron, Aron, and Smollan (1992). This Venn diagram idea for representing closeness in self–other relationships relates to the earlier work of Levinger and Snoek (1972) and especially to Lewin (1948), who represented relationships within the life space in terms of degrees of overlap between life space regions, such as overlap between the life space region representing the self and the life space region representing a partner. An extension of *we* experiences in close relationships has recently been proposed by Fitzsimons, Finkel, and vanDellen (2015) in their model of transactive goal dynamics, which proposes that repeated instances of working together on shared goals and shared pursuit of those goals, such as couples having children and/or buying a home together, leads partners to become a single regulatory system.

38. See Agnew, Van Lange, Rusbult, and Langston (1998).

39. See, for example, Derlega, Metts, Petronia, and Margulis (1993).

40. See, for example, Laurenceau, Barrett, and Pietromonaco (1998), Reis and Patrick (1996), and Reis and Shaver (1988).

41. See, for example, Gable, Gonzaga, and Strachman (2006), Gable, Gosnel, Maisel, and Strachman (2012), Gable and Reis (2010), Gable, Reis, Impett, and Asher (2004), and Reis et al. (2010).

42. See Rossignac-Milon, Bolger, and Higgins (2016).

43. See Rossignac-Milon et al. (2016).

Epilogue

It Begins with Shared Relevance

"May you live in interesting times." I used to think that I wanted to live in interesting times, despite this English expression purportedly being a translation of a Chinese curse. Now I am not so sure—maybe it is a curse. The conflicts that are currently happening between people with different political views have reached an intensity that is very disturbing, despite their creating interesting (i.e., attention-grabbing) times. These political conflicts clearly illustrate the trade-offs from shared reality that are described in this book. Each political group is *stronger* from its shared feelings, beliefs, and opinions. But the differences between these shared realities are *tearing us apart*.

The new media technologies available to people in today's world are not helping. The supporters of each political group can choose to be exposed only to information in the social media that supports their shared realities—ushering in the now famous phrase, "political bubble." When we enter a bubble, we bathe in pure social verification. How wonderful to have others agree with all our feelings, beliefs, and opinions about the world! For some, it is Fox News; for others, it is MSNBC. Importantly, for the supporters of each political group, what *they* are learning about is not "fake news" or "alternative facts." It is *the* truth, the whole truth, and nothing but the truth. It is the *other* group who are sadly, maddeningly, hearing "fake news" and "alternative facts." Our new political bubble world contributes significantly to differing shared realities tearing us apart. "So, OK," you say, "what can we do about it?" I believe that we must find a way to create a shared reality between supporters of different political groups. Only in this way can these two groups begin to feel connected and trust one another. Where do we begin? We begin with shared relevance.

To understand what we need to do and how to do it, let's go back to the beginning—to the development of shared reality between children and their caretakers. Even infants can experience that they have a shared reality with their caretaker. I discussed in Chapter 2 how infants learn to like the same things or dislike the same things as their caretakers—shared evaluative reactions. But I also emphasized that before shared evaluative reactions there is shared relevance.

When a child and a caretaker pay attention to the same object or event, treat that object or event as being worthy of receiving attention, it is often the case that not only do they both find it interesting (i.e., of interest), but they also have the same evaluative reaction to it. They both find it appealing, or they both find it disturbing. However, although it is common for children and their caretakers to have a shared evaluative reaction to something they both find interesting, it is not necessary that this be the case for them to experience a shared reality. Children and their caretakers do not need to have a shared evaluative reaction to something to signal to one another that they both find it worthy of attention; both find it relevant. Indeed, beginning with shared relevance, parents often try to change how their child is reacting to something when they believe that their child's reaction is too positive or too negative.

If a toddler excitedly walks toward a mean-looking dog to pet it, the parent will signal that this particular dog should not be approached. There is shared relevance that this dog, and perhaps this type of dog, is worthy of attention, but there is not shared reality regarding how to react to it evaluatively. The caretaker believes that the child's reaction to this dog is too positive. The opposite case is also common—when parents try to reduce their child's too negative reaction to something. Children can overreact with fear to some strange object or event. Taking dogs again as an example, a child could feel threatened by a dog that the parent knows is friendly to children, and the parent could bring the dog over to the child and have the child pet it to reduce the child's negative reaction to it. The fact that the parent brought the dog over signals that the parent shares with the child that the dog is relevant. The child and parent share that this dog is worthy of attention. It is the child's initial evaluative reaction to the dog that the parent does not share.

What happens when a toddler falls down and is upset? Parents don't ignore the event. They might go over and lift the child up and gently brush the grass or dirt off the child. They signal to the child that his or her falling is worthy of attention. They share its relevance. But they often want the child to feel less upset about the fall and thus don't signal to the child that this event is something to feel upset about (even when they actually are upset).

Having shared relevance sets the stage for creating other shared realities. Experiencing that another person agrees about which objects and events in the world are worthy of attention creates a connection with that person and some initial trust: This person and I agree on what matters in the world. Right now we don't have the same evaluative reactions or beliefs about these things, but we agree that they matter. This is critical for building child–caretaker relationships. It is also important in building therapist–client relationships.

Consider this example. A male client begins the session by saying, "My wife doesn't love me, and I feel lonely." His therapist says, "You believe that your wife doesn't love you. And you feel lonely." The therapist is paying close attention to what the client says and simply repeats it. This is called "mirroring" because the therapist simply reflects back what the client is saying. Note that the therapist is *not* agreeing with the client's belief or the client's emotional reaction to this belief. There is no shared belief or shared emotional reaction. In that sense, it is not empathy per se, not "I feel your pain." Instead, there is shared relevance. The therapist is communicating that the client's belief about his wife's feelings about him and the client's emotional reaction to this is highly relevant to the therapist—so relevant it is worth the therapist's close attention and worth repeating. Like the previously discussed caretaker–child examples, therapists often begin with this shared relevance and acknowledge it, but then work to *change* the client's beliefs and emotional reactions. After all, this is a therapy session.

The therapist might begin with the client's belief about his wife. "Your belief that your wife doesn't love you is important. Let's talk about it." That said, the therapist will not simply accept or verify that belief: "You are absolutely right. Your wife does not love you." Instead, the therapist will question how valid the belief is, trying to determine or discover what the source of the belief is. The therapy need not, and typically does not, begin with the client and therapist having shared beliefs and emotional reactions to the people and events in the client's life. And typically by the end of the therapy, the client's beliefs and emotional reactions will have changed.

What does the shared relevance of therapeutic mirroring do? It is known to build a connection between the client and the therapist. It is a starting point, a foundation for future interactions where changes in emotional reactions and beliefs can happen, where new shared evaluations and beliefs can be created. This is also true for caretaker–child relationships. I believe this can be true as well for in-group–out-group relationships, for different political groups.

Let me be clear. I am not saying different political groups are like children or caretakers or clients or therapists. Nor am I saying that they should be treated as such. Indeed, they should *not* be because the relationship between these groups is very different, and no one group should take on any particular role in relation to the other group. No political group should be treated as children or as clients in need of therapy. What I am saying is that what happens in the early stages of developing a relationship between child and caretaker and between client and therapist should also happen in the early stages of developing a relationship between an in-group political group and its out-group—using shared relevance to build a connection and initiate trust.

How might this be done? Taking a leaf out of the child–caretaker book, one can begin by recognizing that there are many political and policy issues that both sides in a political contest consider important and believe are highly deserving of close attention. There is already substantial shared relevance that is often overlooked. Imagine for a moment the following scene:

> Two guys who support different political parties are engaged in a heated argument over what the government should or should not do on various issues. They argue about what should be done about immigrants who want to come into their country. They argue about what should be done about citizens being killed by guns. They turn to taxes and argue about tax cuts. Next, it's about improving the healthcare system, and that goes on for quite a while. While they are still arguing, a third guy comes up to them and asks them what they are arguing about. They answer that they have been arguing about immigrants, guns, tax cuts, and the healthcare system. The newcomer is bewildered, surprised. He says: "Why waste your time talking about those issues? They don't matter. Hakuna matata. Worry-free is my philosophy."

How do you think the original two guys who were arguing with each other would react to this? I know how I would react. I would find the newcomer annoying and would have no interest in talking with *him*.[1] And I would suddenly feel more connected with my debating partner: "At least he knows what is important in the world. He cares about what matters. We don't agree right now about what to do about these issues, but we agree that they deserve close attention. We should talk more to see if we might find some more common ground and can identify some policies that we both agree would make sense to institute."

We should look for the shared relevance that exists between different groups that are expressing different opinions and beliefs on political issues. We could have more shared relevance between us and them than we have with other people, such as people who only care about what happens to them personally as individuals or who cynically believe that everybody is a crook and nothing can be done to make things better or who have given up worrying about how to solve the problems in the world (Hakuna matata). It is not uncommon for members of different political groups to be dissatisfied with the current situation and want change and to be willing to take action to make things happen. This means that in addition to shared relevance (what issues deserve attention), they also have some shared feelings (they are both dissatisfied with the current situation) and shared beliefs (they both believe that action is needed for change to happen). That's a beginning.[2]

Now let's take a leaf out of the client–therapist book. When engaged in an argument with someone with different political views, listen carefully to your conversational partner and then indicate that you have listened to him or her by repeating it in some form: "What I'm hearing you say is . . ." or "If I'm hearing you right, you are saying . . ." Identify what is the general issue that is important to your conversational partner and separate this from his or her specific opinions and beliefs about that issue. In the previous client–therapist example, the issue that matters to the client is how his wife feels about him, and that is separate from the client's belief that his wife does not love him. The therapist can signal sharing the relevance of the client's issue without needing to share the client's beliefs about the issue and emotional reactions to the issue. Similarly, you can signal that you agree that the issue raised by your conversational partner is important, that it deserves close attention. Then, try to understand what the source is of his or her evaluative reactions and beliefs on that issue. Then, because this is not therapy, try to help your conversational partner understand the source of your feelings and evaluative reactions on the issue that you both agree is important. Try to build from the experience of shared relevance to co-constructing together some shared beliefs and opinions.

By the way, I am not saying that it is easy for members of different political groups to establish shared relevance with each other. After all, it is still politics, and there are different ways that politics can work against establishing shared relevance. One obvious problem for establishing shared relevance is that two political groups, given their distinct ideologies, can have competing ideas about what really matters even for the same issue that they both consider important. For example, both groups can consider that lowering taxes is important, but one group believes that what deserves attention is lowering taxes on small businesses whereas the other group believes that lowering taxes on workers is what deserves attention.

Another problem for establishing shared relevance is more subtle and strategically political. This is when members of different political parties choose what to emphasize as important not because it fits their ideology but because it gives them a political advantage. For example, a political group can decide that their group has a political advantage over their competition on a particular issue, such as their group having a position on a health-care issue that voters prefer to their competition's position on that issue.

They will then try to set the political agenda with that issue having priority. A classic case occurred during the 1992 presidential campaign between Bill Clinton and George H. W. Bush when James Carville coined the expression: "The economy, stupid!" This emphasis on the economy as *the* issue was originally intended to strengthen the Clinton in-group but it became the de facto slogan for the Clinton campaign and was considered an advantage for them in the election.

This attempt to control what is worthy of attention for political advantage can even be used to select the personality dimension of the candidates running for election that is ostensibly most relevant for the office. Two major dimensions that people use to evaluate others is *warmth* and *competence*.[3] If you had to choose between them, which is more relevant for being an effective president of the United States? Does the answer depend on your political party? The following maxim seems to suggest that it does: "If you're not a Democrat when you're 20, you're heartless. If you're not a Republican when you're 40, you're brainless."[4]

If you are a Democrat, what kind of person should a president be? Of course, a warm and caring person (and preferably young). If you are a Republican? Of course, a competent and wise person (and preferably older). It turns out, however, that the dimension that Democrats and Republicans actually emphasize depends on which dimension gives their candidate an advantage in a particular election. If it is the 2012 presidential election between Barach Obama (perceived advantage on warm) and Mitt Romney (perceived advantage on competence), then, yes, Democrats emphasize warmth and Republicans emphasize competence. But if it is the 2004 presidential election between George W. Bush (perceived advantage on warm) and John Kerry (perceived advantage on competence), Democrats emphasize competence and Republicans emphasize warmth. Which personality dimension is treated as more relevant depends on which gives your candidate the advantage.[5]

Thus, it is not always easy to establish shared relevance, especially between political groups. But there are areas of broad consensus, high shared relevance, such as children's health, safety, and education being important and worthy of attention. And after a back-and-forth discussion, an initial disagreement on what deserves attention could lead to an agreement. For example, there could be agreement that attention should be paid to decreasing the taxes on *both* small businesses and the working class. Cuts in the taxes of small businesses and workers both deserve our attention because with lower taxes small businesses can hire more workers, and with lower taxes workers would have more money to spend on the goods and services provided by small businesses. And what would be wrong with our insisting that our political leaders be high on both warmth and competence?

Yes, we need to establish shared relevance. And, to do so, we need to do a better job of connecting to others, learning from others, identifying commonalties and co-constructing shared realities. This is true for our relationships with other humans and, as discussed in Chapter 4, our relationships with other animals as well. The survival of humans and other animals depends on our connecting with each other and learning from one another. We don't need to travel to exotic places, or other planets, to discover new worlds. We just need to pay close attention to what matters to other humans and other animals around us that we have overlooked or ignored—other worlds right in front of us that we have missed.

It begins with shared relevance. Whether it is caretaker–child relationships, client–therapist relationships, close peer relationships, human–other animal relationships, or in-group–out-group relationships, to build a sense of connectedness and initiate trust, creating an experience of shared relevance is where we need to begin. Yes, we want to build beyond that to shared evaluative reactions and shared beliefs, but creating shared relevance provides the foundation that we can build upon. My hope is that we will look for opportunities to build this foundation.[6]

Notes

1. It is interesting in this regard that Levine and Ruback (1980) found that someone who was *indifferent* on an issue that others cared about were more negatively evaluated than someone who actually disagreed a little with them on the issue and significantly decreased any desire to have a further discussion with this person.

2. I recognize that my suggestion to look for shared relevance when there is a conflict between you and another person might be surprising to some readers who have been taught to avoid negotiating on issues that are important to both parties. Instead, we are taught, look for issues where the parties differ in the importance they assign to them. In this way, the parties can trade-off on those issues ("logrolling"), with the parties giving away more to their partner on the issue that is less important to them and receiving more from their partner on the issue that is more important to them— a loss on the less important issue is traded for a gain on the more important issue. Having taught negotiation for several years, I agree with this "integrative" negotiation strategy. But for a negotiation on a topic to occur, both parties must feel that the

topic is worthy of attention, worthy of talking about to begin with. Without shared relevance regarding a topic, there will be no conversation on that topic—there won't be a negotiation. Once shared relevance is established, then the conversation can begin, with the parties feeling some connection to each other through knowing that they both consider this to be an issue worth talking about.

3. See Fiske, Cuddy, and Glick (2007).
4. This is a modern version of a well-known statement that purportedly originated with Francois Guizot, a mid-19th-century historian and statesman. It stereotypes Republicans as lacking feelings for others (heartless) and Democrats as lacking realism (brainless). See Cornwell, Bajger, and Higgins (2015).
5. See Cornwell et al. (2015).
6. The title of this epilogue is, "It begins with shared relevance." From what I have discussed, the "it" has been "relationships." So why not just say that: Relationships begin with shared relevance. The reason is that "it" is not restricted to relationships. As one example, the shared practice within a language community of using a particular name to refer to a particular thing, such as a particular name for a particular kind of snow, only happens because members of that language community, such as the Inuit, consider that particular thing to be worthy of attention to begin with—there is the experience of shared relevance with respect to that thing. As another example, the shared coordinated roles involved in playing a particular game, such as baseball, only occur if there are people who consider that game to be worthy of their attention to begin with—there is the experience of shared relevance with respect to that activity. Again, the connectedness that is produced by recognition of the shared relevance would be strengthened if those with the shared relevance were to meet others who did not share that relevance: "Snow is just snow. It's all alike. Why are you making up additional names for the same thing? One name is enough." or "Why would anyone want to throw around some small ball or try to hit it with a stick?" *It* begins with shared relevance.

References

Acitelli, L. K., Douvan, E., & Veroff, J. (1993). Perceptions of conflict in the first year of marriage: How important are similarity and understanding? *Journal of Social and Personal Relationships, 10,* 5–19.

Acitelli, L. K., Kenny, D. A., & Weiner, D. (2001). The importance of similarity and understanding of partners' marital ideals to relationship satisfaction. *Personal Relationships, 8,* 167–185.

Agnew, C. R., Van Lange, P. A. M., Rusbult, C. E., & Langston, C. A. (1998). Cognitive interdependence: Commitment and the mental representation of close relationships. *Journal of Personality and Social Psychology, 74,* 939–954.

Akimoto, S. A., & Sanbonmatsu, D. M. (1999). Differences in self-effacing behavior between European Americans and Japanese Americans: Effect on competence evaluations. *Journal of Cross-Cultural Psychology, 30,* 159–177.

Allport, G. W. (1954). *The nature of prejudice.* Cambridge, MA: Addison-Wesley.

Allport, G. W. (1955). *Becoming: Basic considerations for a psychology of personality.* New Haven, CT: Yale University Press.

Allport, G. W., & Postman, L. J. (1945). Psychology of rumor. *Transactions of the New York Academy of Sciences, 8,* 61–81.

Allport, G. W., & Postman, L. J. (1947). *The psychology of rumor.* New York, NY: Holt, Rinehart, & Winston.

Alwin, D. F., Cohen, R. L., & Newcomb, T. M. (1991). *The women of Bennington: A study of political orientations over the life span.* Madison: University of Wisconsin Press.

Ambrose, S. E. (1992). *Band of brothers: E Company, 506th Regiment, 101st Airborne from Normandy to Hitler's Eagle's Nest.* New York, NY: Simon & Schuster.

Andersen, S. M., & Baum, A. (1994). Transference in interpersonal relations: Inferences and affect based on significant-other representations. *Journal of Personality, 62,* 459–497.

Andersen, S. M., & Berk, M. S. (1998). Transference in everyday experience: Implications of experimental research for relevant clinical phenomena. *Review of General Psychology, 2,* 81–120.

Andersen, S. M., & Chen, S. (2002). The relational self: An interpersonal social-cognitive theory. *Psychological Review, 109,* 619–645.

Andersen, S. M., & Cole, S. W. (1990). "Do I know you?" The role of significant others in general social perception. *Journal of Personality and Social Psychology, 59,* 384–399.

Andersen, S. M., Glassman, N. S., Chen, S., & Cole, S. W. (1995). Transference in social perception: The role of chronic accessibility in significant-other representations. *Journal of Personality and Social Psychology, 69,* 41–57.

Andersen, S. M., & Przybylinski, E. (2018). Shared reality in interpersonal relationships. *Current Opinion in Psychology, 23,* 42–46.

Andersen, S. M., Reznik, I., & Glassman, N. S. (2005). The unconscious relational self. In R. R. Hassin, J. S. Uleman, & J. A. Bargh (Eds.), *The new unconscious* (pp. 421–481). New York, NY: Oxford University Press.

Anderson, R. C., & Pichert, J. W. (1978). Recall of previously unrecallable information following a shift in perspective. *Journal of Verbal Learning and Verbal Behavior, 17,* 1–12.

Apfelbaum, E. P., Phillips, K. W., & Richeson, J. A. (2014). Rethinking the baseline in diversity research: Should we be explaining the effects of homogeneity? *Perspectives on Psychological Science, 9,* 235–244.

Aron, A., Aron, E. N., & Smollan, D. (1992). Inclusion of Other in the Self Scale and the structure of interpersonal closeness. *Journal of Personality and Social Psychology, 63,* 596–612.

Asch, S. E. (1952). *Social psychology.* Englewood Cliffs, NJ: Prentice-Hall.

Asch, S. E. (1956). Studies of independence and conformity: A minority of one against a unanimous majority. *Psychology Monographs, 70*(9), 1–70.

Atkinson, J. W. (1953). The achievement motivation and recall of interrupted and completed tasks. *Journal of Experimental Psychology, 46,* 381–390.

Austin, J. L. (1962). *How to do things with words.* Oxford, England: Oxford University Press.

Baas, M., De Dreu, C. K. W., & Nijstad, B. A. (2011). When prevention promotes creativity: The role of mood, regulatory focus, and regulatory closure. *Journal of Personality and Social Psychology, 100,* 794–809.

Baer, R., Hinkle, S., Smith, K., & Fenton, M. (1980). Reactance as a function of actual versus projected autonomy. *Journal of Personality and Social Psychology, 38,* 416–422.

Baillargeon, R., Scott, R. M., & He, Z. (2010). False-belief understanding in infants. *Trends in Cognitive Sciences, 14,* 110–118.

Baldwin, J. M. (1897). *Social and ethical interpretations in mental development.* New York, NY: Macmillan.

Baldwin, M. W., & Holmes, J. G. (1987). Salient private audiences and awareness of the self. *Journal of Personality and Social Psychology, 52,* 1087–1098.

Bandura, A. (1986). *Social foundations of thought and action: A social cognitive theory.* Englewood Cliffs, NJ: Prentice-Hall.

Baron-Cohen, S. (1995). *Mindblindness: An essay on autism and theory of mind.* Cambridge, MA: MIT Press.

Bartlett, F. C. (1932). *Remembering.* Cambridge, England: Cambridge University Press.

Bar-Yosef, O. (2002). The Upper Paleolithic revolution. *Annual Review of Anthropology, 31,* 363–93.

Bassili, J. N. (1995). Response latency and the accessibility of voting intentions: What contributes to accessibility and how it affects vote choice. *Personality and Social Psychology Bulletin, 21,* 686–695.

Bates, E., Camaioni, L., & Volterra, V. (1975). The acquistion of performatives prior to speech. *Merrill-Palmer Quarterly, 21,* 205–226.

Beck, A. T., Rush, A. J., Shaw, B. F., & Emery, G. (1979). *Cognitive therapy of depression.* New York, NY: Guilford.

Berger, P., & Kellner, H. (1964). Marriage and the construction of reality. *Diogenes, 46,* 1–24.

Berk, M. S., & Andersen, S. M. (2000). The impact of past relationships on interpersonal behavior: Behavioral confirmation in the social-cognitive process of transference. *Journal of Personality and Social Psychology, 79,* 546–562.

Berndt, T. J. (1983). Social cognition, social behavior, and children's friendships. In E. T. Higgins, D. N. Ruble, & W. W. Hartup (Eds.), *Social cognition and social development: A socio-cultural perspective* (pp. 158–1189). New York, NY: Cambridge University Press.

Berne, E. (1964). *Games people play.* New York, NY: Ballantine Books.

Blos, P. (1961). *On adolescence.* New York, NY: Free Press.

Bowlby, J. (1969). *Attachment and loss: Vol. 1. Attachment.* New York, NY: Basic Books.

Bowlby, J. (1973). *Attachment and loss: Vol. 2. Separation: Anxiety and anger.* New York: Basic Books.

Boyd, R., Richerson, P. J., & Henrich, J. (2011). The culural niche: Why social learning is essential for human adaptation. *Proceedings of the National Academy of Sciences of the United States of America, 108,* 10918–10925.

Bratman, M. E. (1992). Shared cooperative activity. *Philosophical Review, 101,* 327–341.

Brauer, M., & Judd, C. M. (1996). Group polarization and repeated attitude expressions: A new take on an old issue. *European Review of Social Psychology, 7,* 173–207.

Brehm, J. W. (1966). *A theory of psychological reactance.* New York, NY: Academic Press.

Bretherton, I. (1991). Pouring new wine into old bottles: The social self as internal working model. In M. R. Gunnar & L. A. Sroufe (Eds.), *Self processes and development: The Minnesota Symposia on Child Psychology* (Vol. 23, pp. 1–41). Hillsdale, NJ: Erlbaum.

Brewer, M. B. (1991). The social self: On being the same and different at the same time. *Personality and Social Psychology Bulletin, 17,* 475–482.

Brewer, M. B. (2007). The social psychology of intergroup relations: Social categorization, ingroup bias, and outgroup prejudice. In A. W. Kruglanski & E. T. Higgins (Eds.), *Social psychology: Handbook of basic principles* (2nd ed., pp. 695–715). New York, NY: Guilford.

Brown, J. S. (1948). Gradients of approach and avoidance responses and their relation to motivation. *Journal of Comparative and Physiological Psychology, 41,* 450–465.

Brown, R. W. (1958a). How shall a thing be called? *Psychological Review, 65,* 14–21.

Brown, R. W. (1958b). *Words and things.* New York, NY: Free Press.

Brownell, C. A., Nichols, S., & Svetlova, M. (2005). Early development of shared intentionality with peers. *Behavioral and Brain Sciences, 28,* 693–694.

Bruner, J. S. (1983). *Child's talk: Learning to use language.* New York, NY: Norton.

Butterworth, G., & Jarrett, N. (1991). What minds have in common is space: Spatial mechanisms serving joint visual attention in infancy. *British Journal of Developmental Psychology, 9,* 55–72.

Camacho, C. J., Higgins, E. T., & Luger, L. (2003). Moral value transfer from regulatory fit: "What feels right *is* right" and "what feels wrong *is* wrong." *Journal of Personality and Social Psychology, 84,* 498–510.

Cameron, J. A., Alvarez, J. M., Ruble, D. N., & Fuligni, A. J. (2001). Children's lay theories about ingroups and outgroups: Reconceptualizing research on prejudice. *Personality and Social Psychology Review, 5,* 118–128.

Campbell, D. T. (1956). Enhancement of contrast as composite habit. *Journal of Abnormal and Social Psychology, 3,* 350–355.

Carmichael, L., Hogan, H. P., & Walter, A. A. (1932). An experimental study of the effect of language on the reproduction of visually perceived form. *Journal of Experimental Psychology, 15,* 72–86.

Carpenter, M., Nagel, K., & Tomasello, M. (1998). Social cognition, joint attention, and communicative competence from 9 to 15 months of age. *Monographs of the Society for Research in Child Development, 63*(4), 1–143.

Carver, C. S., & Scheier, M. F. (1981). *Attention and self-regulation: A control-theory approach to human behavior.* New York, NY: Springer-Verlag.

Carver, C. S., & Scheier, M. F. (1998). *On the self-regulation of behavior.* New York, NY: Cambridge University Press.

Carver, C. S., & Scheier, M. F. (2008). Feedback processes in the simultaneous regulation of action and affect. In J. Y. Shah and W. L. Gardner (Eds.), *Handbook of motivation science* (pp. 308–324). New York: Guilford Press.

Case, R. (1985). *Intellectual development: Birth to adulthood.* New York, NY: Academic Press.

Case, R. (1992). *The mind's staircase: Exploring the conceptual underpinnings of children's thought and knowledge.* New York, NY: Psychology Press.

Chouinard, M. (2007). Children's questions: A mechanism for cognitive development. *Monographs of the Society for Research in Child Development, 72*(1), 1–112.

Chun, J. S., Ames, D. R., Uribe, J. N., & Higgins, E. T. (2017). Who do we think of as good judges? Those who agree with us *about us. Journal of Experimental Social Psychology, 69,* 121–129.

Cialdini, R. B. (2003). Crafting normative messages to protect the environment. *Current Directions in Psychological Science, 12,* 105–109.

Cialdini, R. B., Levy, A., Herman, C. P., & Evenbeck, S. (1973). Attitudinal politics: The strategy of moderation. *Journal of Personality and Social Psychology, 25,* 100–108.

Cialdini, R. B., Levy, A., Herman, C. P., Kozlowski, L., & Petty, R. E. (1976). Elastic shifts of opinion: Determinants of direction and durability. *Journal of Personality and Social Psychology, 34,* 663–672.

Cialdini, R. B., & Petty, R. E. (1981). Anticipatory opinion effects. In R. E. Petty, T. M. Ostrom, & T. C. Brock (Eds.), *Cognitive responses in persuasion* (pp. 217–235). Hillsdale, NJ: Erlbaum.

Cialdini, R. B., Reno, R. R., & Kallgren, C. A. (1990). A focus theory of normative conduct: Recycling the concept of norms to reduce littering in public places. *Journal of Personality and SocialPsychology, 58,* 1015–1026.

Clark, H. H. (1996). Communities, commonalities, and communication. In J. J. Gumperz & S. C. Levinson (Eds.), *Rethinking linguistic relativity* (pp. 324–355). Cambridge, England: Cambridge University Press.

Commins, B., & Lockwood, J. (1979). The effects of status differences, favored treatment, and equity on intergroup comparisons. *European Journal of Social Psychology, 9*, 281–289.

Cooley, C. H. (1964). *Human nature and the social order.* New York, NY: Schocken Books. (Original work published 1902)

Cooley, C. H. (1962). *Social organization: A study of the larger mind.* New York, NY: Schocken Books. (Original work published 1909)

Cornwell, J. F. M., Bajger, A. T., & Higgins, E. T. (2015). Judging political hearts and minds: How political dynamics drive social judgments. *Personality and Social Psychology Bulletin, 41*, 1053–1068.

Cornwell, J. F. M., & Higgins, E. T. (2015). The "ought" premise of moral psychology and the importance of the ethical ideal. *Review of General Psychology, 19*, 311–328.

Cornwell, J. F. M., & Higgins, E. T. (2016). Eager feelings and vigilant reasons: Regulatory focus differences in judging moral wrongs. *Journal of Experimental Psychology: General, 145*, 338–355.

Corriveau, K. H., Kinzler, K. D., & Harris, P. L. (2013). Accuracy trumps accent in children's endorsement of object labels. *Developmental Psychology, 49*, 470–479.

Crowe, E., & Higgins, E. T. (1997). Regulatory focus and strategic inclinations: Promotion and prevention in decision-making. *Organizational Behavior and Human Decision Processes, 69*, 117–132.

Cuc, A., Ozuru, Y., Manier, D., & Hirst, W. (2006). The transformation of collective memories: Studies of family recounting. *Memory and Cognition, 34*, 752–762.

Damon, W. (1977). *The social world of the child.* Washington, DC: Jossey-Bass.

Darwin, C. (1859). *Origin of species.* London, England: John Murray.

Darwin, C. (1868). *The variation of animals and plants under domestication.* London, England: John Murray.

Deaux, K. (1996). Social identification. In E. T. Higgins & A. W. Kruglanski (Eds.), *Social psychology: Handbook of basic principles* (pp. 777–798). New York, NY: Guilford.

De Beaune, S. A., & White, R. (1993). Ice Age lamps. *Scientific American, 268*(3), 108–113.

Deci, E. L., & Ryan, R. M. (1985). *Intrinsic motivation and self-determination in human behavior*. New York, NY: Plenum.

Deci, E. L., & Ryan, R. M. (2000). The "what" and the "why" of goal pursuits: Human needs and the self-determination of behavior. *Psychological Inquiry, 11*, 227–268.

Derlega, V. J., Metts, S., Petronia, S., & Margulis, S. T. (1993). *Self-disclosure*. Newbury Park, CA: SAGE.

Derryberry, D., & Reed, M. A. (1998). Anxiety and attentional focusing: Trait, state and hemispheric influences. *Personality and Individual Differences, 25*, 745–761.

Dix, T., Cheng, N., Day, W. (2009). Connecting with parents: Mothers' depressive symptoms and responsive behaviors in the regulation of social contact by one- and young two-year-olds. *Social Development, 18*, 24–50.

Dodge, K. A., Coie, J. D., & Lynam, D. (2006). Aggression and antisocial behavior in youth. In N. Eisenberg (Ed.), *Handbook of child psychology: Vol. 3. Social, emotional, and personality development* (6th ed., pp. 719–788). Hoboken, NJ: Wiley.

Dorval, B., & Eckerman, C. O. (1984). Developmental trends in the quality of conversation achieved by small groups of acquainted peers. *Monographs of the Society for Research in Child Development, 49*(2), 1–91.

Duval, S., & Wicklund, R. A. (1972). *A theory of objective self-awareness*. New York, NY: Academic Press.

Dweck, C. S., & Elliot, E. S. (1983). Achievement motivation. In P. H. Mussen (Ed.), *Handbook of child psychology, Volume IV: Socialization, personality, and social development* (pp. 643–691). New York: John Wiley & Sons.

Eagly, A. H., & Chaiken, S. (1993). *The psychology of attitudes*. New York, NY: Harcourt Brace Jovanovich.

Echterhoff, G., Higgins, E. T., & Groll, S. (2005). Audience-tuning effects on memory: The role of shared reality. *Journal of Personality and Social Psychology, 89*, 257–276.

Echterhoff, G., Higgins, E. T., Kopietz, R., & Groll, S. (2008). How communication goals determine when audience tuning biases memory. *Journal of Experimental Psychology: General, 137*, 3–21.

Echterhoff, G., Higgins, E. T., & Levine, J. M. (2009). Shared reality: Experiencing commonality with others' inner states about the world. *Perspectives on Psychological Science, 4*, 496–521.

Echterhoff, G., Kopietz, R., & Higgins, E. T. (2013). Adjusting shared reality: Communicators' memory changes as their connection with their audience changes. *Social Cognition, 31*, 162–186.

Echterhoff, G., Kopietz, R., & Higgins, E. T. (2017). Shared reality in intergroup communication: Increasing the epistemic authority of an out-group audience. *Journal of Experimental Psychology: General, 146,* 806–825.

Echterhoff, G., & Schmalbac, B. (2018). How shared reality is created in interpersonal communication. *Current Opinion in Psychology, 23,* 57–61.

Eckerman, C., Davis, C., & Didow, S. (1989). Toddlers' emerging ways to achieve social coordination with a peer. *Child Development, 60,* 440–453.

Eckerman, C., & Whitehead, H. (1999). How toddler peers generate coordinated action: A cross cultural exploration. *Early Education and Development, 10,* 241–266.

Eimas, P. D., Siqueland, E. R., Jusczyk, P., & Vigorito, J. (1971). Speech perception in infants. *Science, 171,* 303–306.

Eisenberg, N., & Fabes, R. A. (1998). Prosocial development. In W. Damon & N. Eisenberg (Eds.), *Handbook of child psychology: Social, emotional, and personality development* (5th ed., Vol. 3, pp. 701–778). New York, NY: Wiley.

Eisenberg, N., & Fabes, R. A. (1999). Emotion, emotion-related regulation, and quality of socioemotional function. In L. Balter and C. S. Tamis-LeMonda (Eds.), *Child psychology: A handbook of contemporary issues* (pp. 318–336). Philadelphia: Psychology Press.

Eisenberg, N., Fabes, R. A., & Spinrad, T. L. (2006). Prosocial development. In N. Eisenberg (Ed.), *Handbook of child psychology: Vol. 3. Social, emotional, and personality development* (6th ed., pp. 646–718). Hoboken, NJ: Wiley.

Eitam, B., & Higgins, E. T. (2010). Motivation in mental accessibility: Relevance of a Representation (ROAR) as a new framework. *Social and Personality Psychology Compass, 4,* 951–967.

Ellis, A. (1973). *Humanistic psychotherapy: The rational-emotive approach.* New York, NY: McGraw-Hill.

Erikson, E. H. (1963). *Childhood and society* (Rev. ed.). New York: Norton.

Fabes, R. A., Carlo, G., Kupanoff, K., & Laible, D. (1999). Early adolescence and prosocial/moral behavior I: The role of individual processes. *Journal of Early Adolescence, 19,* 5–16.

Fazio, R. H. (1995). Attitudes as object-evaluation associations: Determinants, consequences, and correlates of attitude accessibility. In R. E. Petty & J. A. Krosnick (Eds.), *Attitude strength: Antecedents and consequences* (pp. 247–282). Mahwah, NJ: Erlbaum.

Festinger, L. (1950). Informal social communication. *Psychological Review, 57,* 271–282.

Festinger, L. (1954). A theory of social comparison processes. *Human Relations, 1,* 117–140.

Festinger, L. (1957). *A theory of cognitive dissonance.* Evanston, IL: Row, Peterson.

Fischer, K. W. (1980). A theory of cognitive development: The control and construction of hierarchies of skills. *Psychological Review, 87,* 477–531.

Fischer, K. W., & Lamborn, S. D. (1989). Sources of variation in developmental levels: Cognitive and emotional transitions during adolescence. In A. de Ribaupierre, K. Scherer, & P. Mounod (Eds.), *Transition mechanisms in child development: The longitudinal perspective* (pp. 33–67). Paris: European Science Foundation.

Fischer, K. W., & Watson, M. W. (1981). Explaining the Oedipus conflict. In K. W. Fischer (Ed.), *Cognitive development* (pp. 79–92). San Francisco, CA: Jossey-Bass.

Fiske, S. T., Cuddy, A. J. C., & Glick, P. (2007). Universal dimensions of social cognition: Warmth and competence. *Trends in Cognitive Science, 11,* 77–83.

Fitzsimons, G. M., Finkel, E. J., & Vandellen, M. R. (2015). Transactive goal dynamics. *Psychological Review, 122,* 648–673.

Flavell, J. H. (1999). Cognitive development: Children's knowledge about the mind. *Annual Review of Psychology, 50,* 21–45.

Flavell, J. H. (2004). Theory-of-Mind development: Retrospect and prospect. *Merrill-Palmer Quarterly, 50,* 274–290.

Förster, J., Grant, H., Idson, L. C., & Higgins, E. T. (2001). Success/failure feedback, expectancies, and approach/avoidance motivation: How regulatory focus moderates classic relations. *Journal of Experimental Social Psychology, 37,* 253–260.

Förster, J., & Higgins, E. T. (2005). How global vs. local perception fits regulatory focus. *Psychological Science, 16,* 631–636.

Förster, J., Higgins, E. T., & Bianco, A. T. (2003). Speed/accuracy decisions in task performance: Built-in trade-off or separate strategic concerns? *Organizational Behavior and Human Decision Processes, 90,* 148–164.

Förster, J., Higgins, E. T., & Idson, C. L. (1998). Approach and avoidance strength as a function of regulatory focus: Revisiting the "goal looms larger" effect. *Journal of Personality and Social Psychology, 75,* 1115–1131.

Fusaro, M., & Harris, P. L. (2013). Dax gets the nod: Toddlers detect and use social cues to evaluate testimony. *Developmental Psychology, 49,* 514–522.

Freitas, A. L., Liberman, N., Salovey, P., & Higgins, E. T. (2002). When to begin? Regulatory focus and initiating goal pursuit. *Personality and Social Psychology Bulletin, 28,* 121–130.

French, J. R. P. (1956). A formal theory of social power. *Psychological Review, 63,* 181–194.

French, J. R. P., & Raven, B. (1959). The bases of social power. In D. Cartwright (Ed.), *Studies in Social power* (pp. 150–167). Ann Arbor, MI: Institute of Social Relations.

Freud, A. (1937). *The ego and the mechanisms of defense.* New York: International Universities.

Freud, S. (1958). The dynamics of transference. In J. Strachey (Ed. & Trans.), *The standard edition of the complete psychological works of Sigmund Freud* (Vol. 20, pp. 99–108). London, England: Hogarth. (Original work published 1912)

Freud, S. (1961). The ego and the id. In J. Strachey (Ed. & Trans.), *Standard edition of the complete psychological works of Sigmund Freud* (Vol. 19, pp. 3–66). London, England: Hogarth. (Original work published 1923)

Friedman, R. S., Fishbach, A., Förster, J., & Werth, L. (2003). Attentional priming effects on creativity. *Creativity Research Journal, 15,* 277–286.

Friedman, R. S., & Förster, J. (2001). The effects of promotion and prevention cues on creativity. *Journal of Personality and Social Psychology, 81,* 1001–1013.

Fulmer, C. A., Gelfand, M. J., Kruglanski, A. W., Kim-Prieto, C., Diener, E., Pierro, A., & Higgins, E. T. (2010). On "feeling right" in cultural contexts: How person–culture match affects self-esteem and subjective well-being. *Psychological Science, 21,* 1563–1569.

Gabard-Durnam, L. J., Flannery, J., Goff, B., Gee, D. G., Humphreys, K. L., Telzer, E., . . . Tottenham, N. (2014). The development of human amygdala functional connectivity at rest from 4 to 23 years: A cross-sectional study. *Neuroimage, 95,* 193–207.

Gable, S. L., Gonzaga, G. C., & Strachman, A. (2006). Will you be there for me when things go right? Supportive responses to positive event disclosures. *Journal of Personality and Social Psychology, 91,* 904–917.

Gable, S. L., Gosnell, C. L., Maisel, N. C., & Strachman, A. (2012). Safely testing the alarm: Close others' responses to personal positive events. *Journal of Personality and Social Psychology, 103,* 963–981.

Gable, S. L., & Reis, H. T. (2010). Good news! capitalizing on positive events in an interpersonal context. *Advances in Experimental Social Psychology, 42,* 195–257.

Gable, S. L., Reis, H. T., Impett, E. A., & Asher, E. R. (2004). What do you do when things go right? The intrapersonal and interpersonal benefits of sharing positive events. *Journal of Personality and Social Psychology; Journal of Personality and Social Psychology, 87,* 228–245.

Garfinkel, H. (1967). *Studies in ethnomethodology.* Englewood Cliffs, NJ: Prentice-Hall.

Gergely, G., Bekkering, H., & Király, I. (2002). Rational imitation in preverbal infants. *Nature, 415,* 755.

Gibbons, A. (2007). Food for thought: Did the first cooked meals help fuel the dramatic evolutionary expansion of the human brain? *Science, 316,* 1558–1560.

Glassman, N. S., & Andersen, S. M. (1999). Activating transference without consciousness: Using significant-other representations to go beyond what is subliminally given. *Journal of Personality and Social Psychology, 77,* 1146–1162.

Glucksberg, S., & Krauss, R. M. (1967). What do people say after they have learned how to talk? Studies of the development of referential communication. *Merrill-Palmer Quarterly, 13,* 309–316.

Glucksberg, S., Krauss, R. M., & Higgins, E. T. (1975). The development of referential communication skills. In F. Horowitz, E. Hetherington, S. Scarr-Salapatek, & G. Siegel (Eds.), *Review of child development research* (Vol. 4. pp. 305–345). Chicago, IL: University of Chicago Press.

Goffman, E. (1959). *The presentation of self in everyday life.* Garden City, NY: Doubleday.

Goffman, E. (1961). *Encounters.* Indianapolis, IN: Bobbs-Merrill.

Gollwitzer, P. M. (1996). The volitional benefits of planning. In P. M. Gollwitzer and J. A. Bargh (Eds.), *The psychology of action: Linking cognition and motivation to behavior* (pp. 287–312). New York: Guilford.

Gonsalkorale, K., & von Hippel, W. (2012). Intergroup relations in the 21st century: Ingroup positivity and outgroup negativity among members of an internet hate group. In R. Kramer, G. Leonardelli, & R. Livingston (Eds.), *Social cognition, social identity, and intergroup relations: Festschrift in honor of Marilynn Brewer* (pp. 163–188). Boston, MA: Taylor & Francis.

Gopnik, A., & Graf, P. (1988). Knowing how you know: Young children's ability to identify and remember the sources of their beliefs. *Child Development, 59,* 98–110.

Grant Halvorson, H., & Higgins, E. T. (2013). *Focus: Use different ways of seeing the world for success and influence.* New York, NY: Penguin.

Greenwald, A. G., & Pratkanis, A. R. (1984). The self. In R. S. Wyer & T. K. Srull (Eds.), *Handbook of social cognition* (Vol. 3, pp. 129–178). Hillsdale, NJ: Erlbaum.

Grice, H. P. (1971). Meaning. In D. D. Steinberg & L. A. Jakobovits (Eds.), *Semantics: An interdisciplinary reader in philosophy, linguistics, and psychology* (pp. 436–444). London, England: Cambridge University Press.

Grice, H. P. (1975). Logic and conversation. In P. Cole & J. L. Morgan (Eds.), *Syntax and semantics: Vol. 3. Speech acts* (pp. 365–372). New York, NY: Seminar.

Guide. (1989). *Webster's Ninth New Collegiate Dictionary.* Springfield, MA: Merriam-Webster.

Gumperz, J. J., & Hymes, D. (Eds.). (1972). *Directions in sociolinguistics: The ethnography of communication.* New York, NY: Holt, Rinehart & Winston.

Hackman, J. R., & Katz, N. (2010). Group behavior and performance. In S. T. Fiske, D. T. Gilbert, and G. Lindzey (Eds.), *Handbook of social psychology, 5th Edition, Volume 2* (pp. 1208–1251). Hoboken, NJ:John Wiley & Sons.

Haidt, J. (2001). The emotional dog and its rational tail: A social intuitionist approach to moral judgment. *Psychological Review, 108,* 814–834.

Hamlin, J. K., Mahajan, N., Liberman, Z., & Wynn, K. (2013). Not like me = bad: Infants prefer those who harm dissimilar others. *Psychological Science, 24,* 589–594.

Harari, Y. N. (2015). *Sapiens: A brief history of humankind.* New York, NY: HarperCollins.

Hardin, C., D., & Higgins, E. T. (1996). Shared reality: How social verification makes the subjective objective. In R. M. Sorrentino & E. T. Higgins (Eds.), *Handbook of motivation and cognition: Vol. 3. The interpersonal context* (pp. 28–84). New York, NY: Guilford.

Harris, P. L. (2000). *The work of the imagination.* Oxford, England: Blackwell.

Harris, P. L. (2012). *Trusting what you're told: How children learn from others.* Cambridge, MA: Harvard University Press.

Harris, P. L., & Kavanaugh, R. D. (1993). Young children's understanding of pretense. *Monographs of the Society for Research in Child Development, 58*(1), 1–107.

Hart, D., & Matsuba, M. K. (2007). The development of pride and moral life. In J. L. Tracy, R. W. Robins, and J. P. Tangney (Eds.), *The self-conscious emotions: Theory and research* (pp. 114–113). New York: Guilford.

Harter, S. (1983). Developmental perspectives on the self-system. In P. H. Mussen (Ed.), *Handbook of child psychology: Vol. 4. Socialization, personality, and social development* (pp. 275–385). New York, NY: Wiley.

Harter, S. (1986). Cognitive-developmental processes in the integration of concepts about emotions and the self. *Social Cognition, 4,* 119–151.

Harter, S. (1999). *The construction of the self: A developmental perspective.* New York, NY: Guilford.

Harter, S. (2006). The self. In N. Eisenberg (Ed.), *Handbook of child psychology: Vol. 3. Social, emotional, and personality development* (6th ed., pp. 505–570). Hoboken, NJ: Wiley.

Harter, S. (2015). *The construction of the self: Developmental and sociocultural foundations* (2nd ed.). New York, NY: Guilford.

Hawkes, K. (2003). Grandmothers and the evolution of human longevity. *American Journal of Human Biology, 15,* 380–400.

Hay, D. F., & Rheingold, H. L. (1983). The early appearance of some valued behaviors. In D. L. Bridgeman (Ed.), *The nature of prosocial development: Interdisciplinary theories and strategies* (pp. 73–94). New York, NY: Academic Press.

Heider, F. (1958). *The psychology of interpersonal relations.* New York, NY: Wiley.

Heilman, M. D., & Toffler, B. L. (1976). Reacting to reactance: An interpersonal interpretation of the need for freedom. *Journal of Experimental Social Psychology, 12,* 519–529.

Heine, S. J., Lehman, D. R., Markus, H. R., & Kitayma, S. (1999). Is there a universal need for positive self-regard? *Psychological Review, 106,* 766–794.

Heiphetz, L., Spelke, E. S., Harris, P. L., & Banaji, M. R. (2014). The development of reasoning about beliefs: Fact, preference, and ideology. *Journal of Experimental Social Psychology, 49,* 559–565.

Henrich, J. (2016). *The secret of our success: How culture is driving human evolution, domesticating our species, and making us smarter.* Princeton, NJ: Princeton University Press.

Higgins, E. T. (1977). Communication development as related to channel, incentive, and social oclass. *Genetic Psychology Monographs, 96,* 75–141.

Higgins, E. T. (1981a). The "communication game": Implications for social cognition and persuasion. In E. T. Higgins, C. P. Herman, & M. P. Zanna (Eds.), *Social cognition: The Ontario Symposium* (pp. 343–392). Hillsdale, NJ: Erlbaum.

Higgins, E. T. (1981b). Role-taking and social judgment: Alternative developmental perspectives and processes. In J. H. Flavell & L. Ross (Eds.), *Social cognitive development: Frontiers and possible futures* (pp.119–153). New York, NY: Cambridge University Press.

Higgins, E. T. (1987). Self-discrepancy: A theory relating self and affect. *Psychological Review, 94,* 319–340.

Higgins, E. T. (1989a). Continuities and discontinuities in self-regulatory and self-evaluative processes: A developmental theory relating self and affect. *Journal of Personality, 57,* 407–444.

Higgins, E. T. (1989b). Self-discrepancy theory: What patterns of self-beliefs cause people to suffer? In L. Berkowitz (Ed.), *Advances in experimental social psychology* (Vol. 22, pp. 93–136). New York, NY: Academic Press.

Higgins, E. T. (1991). Development of self-regulatory and self-evaluative processes: Costs, benefits, and tradeoffs. In M. R. Gunnar & L. A. Sroufe (Eds.), *Self processes and development: The Minnesota Symposia on Child Psychology,* (Vol. 23, pp. 125–165). Hillsdale, NJ: Erlbaum.

Higgins, E. T. (1992). Achieving "shared reality" in the communication game: A social action that creates meaning. *Journal of Language and Social Psychology, 11,* 107–131.

Higgins, E. T. (1996a). Knowledge activation: Accessibility, applicability, and salience. In E. T. Higgins & A. W. Kruglanski (Eds.), *Social psychology: Handbook of basic principles* (pp. 133–168). New York, NY: Guilford.

Higgins, E. T. (1996b). The "self digest": Self-knowledge serving self-regulatory functions. *Journal of Personality and Social Psychology, 71,* 1062–1083.

Higgins, E. T. (1997). Beyond pleasure and pain. *American Psychologist, 52,* 1280–1300.

Higgins, E. T. (1998a). The "aboutness principle": A pervasive influence on social inference. *Social Cognition, 16,* 173–198.

Higgins, E. T. (1998b). Promotion and prevention: Regulatory focus as a motivational principle. In M. P. Zanna (Ed.), *Advances in experimental social psychology* (Vol. 30, pp. 1–46). New York, NY: Academic Press.

Higgins, E. T. (2000). Making a good decision: Value from fit. *American Psychologist, 55,* 1217–1230.

Higgins, E. T. (2001). Promotion and prevention experiences: Relating emotions to nonemotional motivational states. In J. P. Forgas (Ed.), *Handbook of affect and social cognition* (pp. 186–211). Mahwah, NJ: Erlbaum.

Higgins, E. T. (2005). Humans as applied motivation scientists: Self-consciousness from "shared reality" and "becoming." In H. S. Terrace & J. Metcalfe (Eds.), *The missing link in cognition: Origins of self-reflective consciousness* (pp. 157–173). Oxford, England: Oxford University Press.

Higgins, E. T. (2006). Value from hedonic experience *and* engagement. *Psychological Review, 113,* 439–460.

Higgins, E. T. (2008). Culture and personality: Variability across universal motives as the missing link. *Social and Personality Psychology Compass, 2,* 608–634.

Higgins, E. T. (2012). *Beyond pleasure and pain: How motivation works.* New York, NY: Oxford University Press.

Higgins, E. T., & Brendl, M. (1995). Accessibility and applicability: Some "activation rules" influencing judgment. *Journal of Experimental Social Psychology, 31,* 218–243.

Higgins, E. T., Camacho, C. J., Idson, L. C., Spiegel, S., & Scholer, A. A. (2008). How making the same decision in a "proper way" creates value. *Social Cognition, 26,* 496–514.

Higgins, E. T., & Cornwell, J. F. M. (2016). Securing foundations and advancing frontiers: Prevention and promotion effects on judgment & decision making. *Organizational Behavior and Human Decision Processes, 136,* 56–67.

Higgins, E. T., & Eccles-Parsons, J. (1983). Social cognition and the social life of the child: Stages as subcultures. In E. T. Higgins, D. N. Ruble, and W. W. Hartup (Eds.), *Social cognition and social development: A socio-cultural perspective* (pp. 15–62). New York, NY: Cambridge University Press.

Higgins, E. T., Echterhoff, G., Crespillo, R., & Kopietz, R. (2007). Effects of communication on social knowledge: Sharing reality with individual versus group audiences. *Japanese Psychological Research, 49,* 89–99.

Higgins, E. T., Friedman, R. S., Harlow, R. E., Idson, L. C., Ayduk, O. N., & Taylor, A. (2001). Achievement orientations from subjective histories of success: Promotion pride versus prevention pride. *European Journal of Social Psychology, 31,* 3–23.

Higgins, E. T., Idson, L. C., Freitas, A. L., Spiegel, S., & Molden, D. C. (2003). Transfer of value from fit. *Journal of Personality and Social Psychology, 84,* 1140–1153.

Higgins, E. T., & Pittman, T. (2008). Motives of the *human* animal: Comprehending, managing, and sharing inner states. *Annual Review of Psychology, 59,* 361–385.

Higgins, E. T., & Rholes, W. S. (1978). "Saying is believing": Effects of message modification on memory and liking for the person described. *Journal of Experimental Social Psychology, 14,* 363–378.

Higgins, E. T., Rholes, W. S., & Jones, C. R. (1977). Category accessibility and impression formation. *Journal of Experimental Social Psychology, 13,* 141–154.

Higgins, E. T., Shah, J., & Friedman, R. (1997). Emotional responses to goal attainment: Strength of regulatory focus as moderator. *Journal of Personality and Social Psychology, 72,* 515–525.

Higgins, E. T., & Silberman, I. (1998). Development of regulatory focus: Promotion and prevention as ways of living. In J. Heckhausen & C. S. Dweck (Eds.), *Motivation and self-regulation across the life span* (pp. 78–113). New York, NY: Cambridge University Press.

Hill, J. P., & Lynch, M. E. (1983). The intensification of gender-related expectancies during early adolescence. In J. Brooks-Gunn & A. C. Peterson (Eds.), *Girls at puberty* (pp. 201–228). New York, NY: Plenum.

Hoffman, M. L., & Saltzstein, H. D. (1967). Parental Discipline and the child's moral development. *Journal of Personality and Social Psychology, 5*, 45–57.

Hogg, M. A., & Abrams, D. (1993). Towards a single-process uncertainty reduction model of social motivation in groups. In M. A. Hogg & D. Abrams (Eds.), *Group motivation: Social psychological perspectives* (pp. 173–190). London, England: Harvester Wheatsheaf.

Hogg, M. A., & Rinella, M. J. (2018). Social identities and shared realities. *Current Opinion in Psychology, 23*, 6–10.

Holden, C. (1998). No last word on language origins. *Science, 282*, 1455–1458.

Houston, D. A. (1990). Empathy and the self: Cognitive and emotional influences on the evaluation of negative affect in others. *Journal of Personality and Social Psychology, 59*, 859–868.

Howells, W. W. (1997). *Getting here: The story of human evolution*. Washington, DC: Compass.

Howes, C. (1988). Peer interaction of young children. *Monographs of the Society for Research in Child Development, 53*(1), 217.

Horner, V. K., & Whiten, A. (2005). Causal knowledge and imitation/emulation switching in chimpanzees (Pan troglodytes) and children. *Animal Cognition, 8*, 164–181.

Idson, L. C., & Higgins, E. T. (2000). How current feedback and chronic effectiveness influence motivation: Everything to gain versus everything to lose. *European Journal of Social Psychology, 30*, 583–592.

Idson, L. C., Liberman, N., & Higgins, E. T. (2000). Distinguishing gains from nonlosses and losses from nongains: A regulatory focus perspective on hedonic intensity. *Journal of Experimental Social Psychology, 36*, 252–274.

Idson, L. C., Liberman, N., & Higgins, E. T. (2004). Imagining how you'd feel: The role of motivational experiences from regulatory fit. *Personality and Social Psychology Bulletin, 30*, 926–937.

Jablonka, E., & Lamb, M. J. (2005). *Evolution in four dimensions: Genetic, epigenetic, behavioral, and symbolic variation in the history of life*. Cambridge, MA: MIT Press.

Jacobs, R. C., & Campbell, D. T. (1961). The perpetuation of an arbitrary tradition through several generations of a laboratory microculture. *Journal of Abnormal and Social Psychology, 62*, 649–658.

James, W. (1948). *The principles of psychology*. New York, NY: World Publishing. (Original work published 1890).

Jaswal, V. K., & Markman, E. (2007). Looks aren't everything: 24-month-olds' willingness to accept unexpected labels. *Journal of Cognition and Development, 8,* 93–111.

Johnston, A. M., Byrne, M., Santos, L. R. (2018). What is unique about shared reality? Insights from a new comparison species. *Current Opinion in Psychology, 23,* 30–33.

Jones, E. E., & Davis, K. E. (1965). From acts to dispositions: The attribution process in person perception. In L. Berkowitz (Ed.), *Advances in experimental social psychology* (Vol. 2, pp. 219–266). New York, NY: Academic Press.

Jones, E. E., Davis, K. E., & Gergen, K. J. (1961). Role playing variations and their informational value for person perception. *Journal of Abnormal and Social Psychology, 63,* 302–310.

Jost, J. T., Banaji, M. R., & Nosek, B. A. (2004). A decade of system justification theory: Accumulated evidence of conscious and unconscious bolstering of the status quo. *Political Psychology, 25,* 881–919.

Jost, J. T., & Hunyady, O. (2005). Antecedents and consequences of system-justifying ideologies. *Current Directions in Psychological Science, 14,* 260–265.

Jost, J. T., Ledgerwood, A., & Hardin, C. D. (2008). Shared reality, system justification, and the relational basis of ideological beliefs. *Social and Personality Psychology Compass, 2,* 171–186.

Jost, J. T., Pelham, B. W., Sheldon, O., & Sullivan, B. N. (2003). Social inequality and the reduction of ideological dissonance on behalf of the sysem: Evidence of enhanced system justification among the disadvantaged. *European Journal of Social Psychology, 33,* 13–36.

Jussim, L., Crawford, J. T., & Rubinstein, R. S. (2015). Stereotype (in)accuracy in perceptions of groups and individuals. *Current Directions in Psychological Science, 24,* 490–497.

Kahneman, D., Knetsch, J. K., & Thaler, R. H. (1990). Experimental tests of the endowment effect and the Coase theorem. *Journal of Political Economy, 98,* 1325–1348.

Kahneman, D., Knetsch, J. K., & Thaler, R. H. (1991). The endowment effect, loss aversion, and status quo bias. *Journal of Economic Perspectives, 5,* 193–206.

Kahneman, D., & Tversky, A. (1979). Prospect theory: An analysis of decision under risk. *Econometrica, 47,* 263–291.

Kashima, Y. (2000). Maintaining cultural stereotypes in the serial reproduction of narratives. *Personality and Social Psychology Bulletin, 26,* 594–604.

Kashima, Y., Bratanova, B., & Peters, K. (2018). Social transmission and shared reality in cultural dynamics. *Current Opinion in Psychology, 23,* 15–19.

Kashima, Y., Kashima, E. S., Bain, P., Lyons, A., Tindale, R. S., Robins, G., . . . Whelan, J. (2010). Communication and essentialism: Grounding the shared reality of a social category. *Social Cognition, 28,* 306–328.

Kashima, Y., Lyons, A., & Clark, A. (2013). The maintenance of cultural stereotypes in the conversational retelling of narratives. *Asian Journal of Social Psychology, 16,* 60–70.

Katz, D. (1960). The functional approach to the study of attitudes. *Public Opinion Quarterly, 24,* 163–204.

Keller, H. (1902). *The story of my life.* New York, NY: Grosset & Dunlap.

Kelley, H. H. (1950). The warm-cold variable in first impressions of persons. *Journal of Personality, 18,* 431–439.

Kelley, H. H. (1952). Two functions of reference groups. In G. E. Swanson, T. M. Newcomb, & E. L. Hartley (Eds.), *Readings in social psychology* (2nd ed., pp. 410–420). New York, NY: Holt, Rinehart & Winston.

Kelley, H. H. (1973). The process of causal attribution. *American Psychologist, 28,* 107–128.

Kelman, H. C. (1958). Compliance, identification, and internalization: Three processes of attitude change. *Journal of Conflict Resolution, 2,* 51–60.

Kim, G., & Kwak, K. (2011). Uncertainty matters: impact of stimulus ambiguity on infant social referencing. *Infant Child Development, 20,* 449–463.

Kinzler, K. D., Dupoux, E., & Spelke, E. S. (2007). The native language of social cognition. *Proceedings of the National Academy of Sciences of the United States of America, 104,* 12577–12580.

Kitcher, P. (2011). *The ethical project.* Boston, MA: Harvard University Press.

Knetsch, J. L. (1989). The endowment effect and evidence of nonreversible indifference curves. *American Economic Review, 79,* 1277–1284.

Kochanska, G., Aksan, N., Knaack, A., & Rhines, H. M. (2004). Maternal parenting and children's conscience: Early security as a moderator. *Child Development, 75,* 1229–1242.

Kochanska, G., Casey, R. J., & Fukumoto, A. (1995). Toddlers' sensitivity to standard violations. *Child Development, 66,* 643–656.

Kochanska, G., & Knaack, A. (2003). Effortful control as a personalitycharacteristic of young children: Antecedents, correlates, and consequences. *Journal of Personality, 71,* 1088–1112.

Kochanska, G., Murray, K. T., Jacques, T. Y., Koenig, A. L., & Vandegeest, K. A. (1996). Inhibitory control in young children and its role in emerging internalization. *Child Development, 67,* 490–507.

Krosnick, J. A., & Alwin, D. F. (1989). Aging and susceptibility to attitude change. *Journal of Personality and Social Psychology, 57*, 416–425.

Kruglanski, A. W., Bélanger, J. J., Gelfand, M., Gunaratna, R., Hettiarachchi, M., Reinares, F., . . . Sharvit, K. (2013). Terrorism—a (self) love story: Redirecting the significance quest can end violence. *American Psychologist, 68*, 559–575.

Kruglanski, A. W., Gelfand, M. J., Bélanger, J. J., Sheveland, A., Hetiarachchi, M., & Gunaratna, R. (2014). The psychology of radicalization and deradicalization: How significance quest impacts violent extremism. *Political Psychology, 35*, 69–93.

Kruglanski, A. W., Raviv, A., Bar-Tal, D., Raviv, A., Sharvit, K., Ellis, S., . . . Mannetti, L. (2005). Says who? Epistemic authority effects in social judgment. In M. P. Zanna (Ed.), *Advances in Experimental Social Psychology* (Vol. 37, pp. 345–392). New York, NY: Academic Press.

Kuhl, P. K. (1983). Perception of auditory equivalence classes for speech in early infancy. *Infant Behavior and Development, 6*, 263–285.

Kwang, T., & Swann, W. B., Jr. (2010). Do people embrace praise even when they feel unworthy? A review of critical tests of self-enhancement versus self-verification. *Personality and Social Psychology Review, 14*, 263–280.

Lagattuta, K. H., & Thompson, R. A. (2007). The development of self-conscious emotions. In J. L. Tracy, R. W. Robins, & J. P. Tangney (Eds.), *The self-conscious emotions: Theory and research* (pp. 91–113). New York, NY: Guilford.

Laurenceau, J., Barrett, L. F., & Pietromonaco, P. R. (1998). Intimacy as an interpersonal process: The importance of self-disclosure, partner disclosure, and perceived partner responsiveness in interpersonal exchanges. *Journal of Personality and Social Psychology, 74*, 1238–1251.

Leary, M. R., Tambor, E. S., Terdal, S. K., & Downs, D. L. (1995). Self-esteem as an interpersonal monitor: The sociometer hypothesis. *Journal of Personality and Social Psychology, 68*, 518–530.

Lecky, P. (1945). *Self-consistency: A theory of personality.* New York, NY: Island Press.

Lee, A. Y., & Aaker, J. L. (2004). Bringing the frame into focus: The influence of regulatory fit on processing fluency and persuasion. *Journal of Personality and Social Psychology, 86*, 205–218.

Lee, A. Y., Aaker, J. L., & Gardner, W. L. (2000). The pleasures and pains of distinct self-construals: The role of interdependence in regulatory focus. *Journal of Personality and Social Psychology, 78*, 1122–1134.

Legerstee, M. (1991). The role of person and object in eliciting early imitation. *Journal of Experimental Child Psychology, 51*, 423–433.

Leikin, M. (2012). The effect of bilingualism on creativity: Developmental and educational perspectives. *International Journal of Bilingualism, 17,* 431–447.

Levine, J. M. (1999). Solomon Asch's legacy for group research. *Personality and Social Psychology Review, 3,* 358–364.

Levine, J. M., Alexander, K., & Hansen, T. (2010). Self-control in groups. In R. R. Hassin, K. N. Ochsner, and Y. Trope (Eds.), *Self control in society, mind, and brain* (pp. 449–472). New York: Oxford University Press.

Levine, J. M., Higgins, E. T., & Choi, H-S. (2000). Development of strategic norms in groups. *Organizational Behavior and Human Decision Processes, 82,* 88–101.

Levine, J. M., & Moreland, R. L. (1986). Outcome comparisons in group contexts: Consequences for the self and others. In R. Schwarzer (Ed.), *Self-related cognitions in anxiety and motivation* (pp. 285–303). Hillsdale, NJ: Erlbaum.

Levine, J. M., Resnick, L. B., & Higgins, E. T. (1993). Social foundations of cognition. *Annual Review of Psychology, 44,* 585–612.

Levine, J. M., & Ruback, R. B. (1980). Reaction to opinion deviance: Impact of a fence straddler's rationale on majority evaluation. *Social Psychology Quarterly, 43,* 73–81.

Levine, J. M., & Tindale, R. S. (2015). Social influence in groups. In M. Mikulincer & P. R. Shaver (Eds.), *Handbook of personality and social psychology: Vol. 2. Group processes* (pp. 3–34). Washington, DC: American Psychological Association.

Levinger, G., & Snoek, J. D. (1972). *Attraction in relationship: A new look at interpersonal attraction.* Morristown, NJ: General Learning.

Lewin, K. (1935). *A dynamic theory of personality.* New York, NY: McGraw-Hill.

Lewin, K. (1948). The background of conflict in marriage. In G. Lewin (Ed.), *Resolving social conflicts: Selected papers on group dynamics* (pp. 84–102). New York, NY: Harper.

Lewin, K. (1951). *Field theory in social science.* New York, NY: Harper.

Lewis, M. (1995). Embarassment: The emotion of self-exposure and evaluation. In J. Tangney and K. Fischer (Eds.), *Self-conscious emotions: The psychology of shame, guilt, embarassment and pride* (pp. 198–218). New York: Guilford Press.

Lewis, M. (2003). The role of the self in shame. *Social Research, 70,* 1181–1204.

Lewis, M. (2007). Self-conscious emotional development. In J. L. Tracy, R. W. Robins, & J. P. Tangney (Eds.), *The self-conscious emotions: Theory and research* (pp. 134–149). New York, NY: Guilford.

Lewis, M., Alessandri, S. M., & Sullivan, M. W. (1992). Differences in shame and pride as a function of children's gender and task difficulty. *Child Development, 63,* 630–638.

Liberman, N., Idson, L. C., Camacho, C. J., & Higgins, E. T. (1999). Promotion and prevention choices between stability and change. *Journal of Personality and Social Psychology, 77,* 1135–1145.

Liberman, N., Molden, D. C., Idson, L. C., & Higgins, E. T. (2001). Promotion and prevention focus on alternative hypotheses: Implications for attributional functions. *Journal of Personality and Social Psychology, 80,* 5–18.

Liberman, N., & Trope, Y. (2008). The psychology of transcending the here and now. *Science, 322,* 1201–1205.

Liberman, N., Trope, Y., Stephan, E. (2007). Psychological distance. In A. W. Kruglanski & E. T. Higgins (Eds.), *Social psychology: Handbook of basic principles* (2nd ed., pp. 353–381). New York, NY: Guilford.

Liszkowski, U. (2005). Human twelve-month-olds point co-operatively to share interest with and provide information for a communicative partner. *Gesture, 5,* 135–154.

Liszkowski, U. (2018). Emergence of shared reference and shared minds in infancy. *Current Opinion in Psychology, 23,* 26–29.

Liszkowski, U., Carpenter, M., Henning, A., Striano, T., & Tomasello, M. (2004). Twelve-month-olds point to share attention and interest. *Developmental Science, 7,* 297–307.

Livi, S., Kruglanski, A. W., Pierro, A., Mannetti, L., & Kenny, D. A. (2015). Epistemic motivation and perpetuation of group culture: Effects of need for cognitive closure on trans-generational norm transmission. *Organizational Behavior and Human Decision Processes, 129,* 105–112.

Loevinger, J. (1976). *Ego development: Conceptions and theories.* San Francisco, CA: Jossey-Bass.

Loftus, E. F. (2005). Planting misinformation in the human mind: A 30-year investigation of the malleability of memory. *Learning and Memory, 12,* 361–366.

Loftus, E. F., & Palmer, J. C. (1974). Reconstruction of automobile destruction: An example of the interaction between language and memory. *Journal of Verbal Learning and Verbal Behavior, 13,* 585–589.

Loyd, D. L., Wang, C. S., Phillips, K. W., & Lount, R. B., Jr. (2013). Social category diversity promotes premeeting elaboration: The role of relationship focus. *Organization Science, 24,* 757–772.

Luby, J. L. (2010). Preschool depression: The importance of identification of depression early in development. *Current Directions in Psychological Science, 19,* 91–95.

Lyons, A., & Kashima, Y. (2003). How are stereotypes maintained through communication? The influence of stereotype sharedness. *Journal of Personality and Social Psychology, 85,* 989–1005.

Lyons, D. E., Young, A. G., & Keil, F. C. (2007). The hidden structure of overimitation. *Proceedings of the National Academy of Sciences, 104,* 19751–19756.

Mandler, G. (1975). *Mind and emotion.* New York, NY: Wiley.

Manian, N., Papadakis, A. A., Strauman, T. J., & Essex, M. J. (2006). The development of children's ideal and ought Self-Guides: Parenting, temperament, and individual differences in guide strength. *Journal of Personality, 74,* 1619–1645.

March, J. G. (1994). *A primer on decision making: How decisions happen.* New York, NY: Free Press.

Markman, K. D., McMullen, M. N., Elizaga, R. A., & Mizoguchi, N. (2006). Counterfactual thinking and regulatory fit. *Judgment and Decision Making, 1,* 98–107.

Marks, G., & Miller, N. (1987). Ten years of research on the false consensus effect: An empirical and theoretical review. *Psychological Bulletin, 102,* 72–90.

Markus, H. (1977). Self-schemata and processing information about the self. *Journal of Personality and Social Psychology, 35,* 63–78.

Markus, H., & Kitayama, S. (1991). Culture and the self: Implications for cognition, emotion, and motivation. *Psychological Review, 98,* 224–253.

Markus, H., & Smith, J. (1981). The influence of self-schema on the perception of others. In N. Cantor & J. F. Kihlstrom (Eds.), *Personality, cognition, and social interaction* (pp. 233–262). Hillsdale, NJ: Erlbaum.

Marques, J. M., & Yzerbyt, V. Y. (1988). The black sheep effect: Judgmental extremity towards ingroup members in inter- and intra-group situations. *European Journal of Social Psychology, 18,* 287–292.

Mascolo, M., & Fischer, K. (1995). Developmental transformations in appraisals for pride, shame, and guilt. In J. Tangney & K. Fischer (Eds.), *Self-conscious emotions: The psychology of shame, guilt, embarassment and pride* (pp. 64–113). New York, NY: Guilford.

McGuire, W. J., McGuire, C. V., & Winton, W. (1979). Effects of household sex composition on the salience of one's gender in the spontaneous self-concept. *Journal of Experimental Social Psychology, 15,* 77–90.

Mead, G. H. (1934). *Mind, self, and society*. Chicago, IL: University of Chicago Press.

Merton, R. K. (1957). *Social theory and social structure*. Glencoe, IL: The Free Press.

Milgram, S. (1974). *Obedience to authority*. New York, NY: Harper & Row.

Miller, G. A., Galanter, E., & Pribram, K. H. (1960). *Plans and the structure of behavior*. New York, NY: Holt, Rinehart, & Winston.

Miller, N. E. (1944). Experimental studies of conflict. In J. McV. Hunt (Ed.), *Personality and the behavior disorders* (Vol. 1, pp. 431–465). New York, NY: Ronald Press.

Molden, D. C. (Ed.). (2014). *Understanding priming effects in social psychology* [Special issue], *32*(Suppl).

Molden, D. C., Lucas, G. M., Gardner, W. L., Dean, K., & Knowles, M. L. (2009). Motivations for prevention or promotion following social exclusion: Being rejected versus being ignored. *Journal of Personality and Social Psychology, 96*, 415–431.

Moretti, M. M., & Higgins, E. T. (1999). Internal representations of others in self-regulation: A new look at a classic issue. *Social Cognition, 17*, 186–208.

Moretti, M. M., Higgins, E. T., & Feldman, L. (1990). The self-system in depression: Conceptualization and treatment. In C. D. McCann & N. S. Endler (Eds.), *Depression: New directions in research, theory, and practice* (pp. 127–156). Toronto, ON: Wall & Thompson.

Moses, L. J., Baldwin, D. A., Rosicky, J. G., & Tidball, G. (2001). Evidence for referential understanding in the emotions domain at twelve and eighteen months. *Child Development, 72*, 718–735.

Mumme, D. L., & Fernald, A. (2003). The infant as onlooker: Learning from emotional reactions observed in a television scenario. *Child Development, 74*, 221–237.

Mumme, D. L., Fernald, A., & Herrera, C. (1996). Infants' responses to facial and vocal emotional signals in a social referencing paradigm. *Child Development, 67*, 3219–3237.

Murray, S. L., Holmes, J. G., & Griffin, D. W. (1996). The self-fulfilling nature of positive illusions in romantic relationships: Love is not blind, but prescient. *Journal of Personality and Social Psychology, 71*, 1155–1180.

Navon, D. (1977). Forest before trees: The precedence of global features in visual perception. *Cognitive Psychology, 9*, 353–383.

Nelson, K. (1992). Emergence of autobiographical memory at age 4. *Human Development, 35*, 172–177.

Nelson, K. (2003). Narrative and self, myth, and memory: Emergence of a cultural self. In R. Fivush and C. A. Haden (Eds.), *Autobiographical memory and the construction of a narrative self: Developmental and cultural perspectives* (pp. 72–90). Mahwah, NJ: Erlbaum.

Nelson, K. (2005). Emerging levels of consciousness in early human development. In H. S. Terrace & J. Metcalfe (Eds.), *The missing link in cognition: Origins of self-reflective consciousness* (pp. 116–141). Oxford, England: Oxford University Press.

Nelson, K. (2007). *Young minds in social worlds: Experience, meaning, and memory.* Boston, MA: Harvard University Press.

Newcomb, T. M. (1958). Attitude development as a function of reference groups: The Bennington study. In E. E. Maccoby, T. M. Newcomb, & E. L. Hartley (Eds.), *Readings in social psychology* (2nd ed., pp. 265–275). New York, NY: Holt, Rinehart & Winston.

Newcomb, T. M., Koenig, K. E., Flacks, R., & Warwick, D. P. (1967). *Persistence and change: Bennington College and its students after years.* New York, NY: Wiley.

Neuman, L. S., Higgins, E. T., & Vookles, J. (1992). Self-guide strength and emotional vulnerability: Birth order as a moderator of self-affect relations. *Personality and Social Psychology Bulletin, 18,* 402–411.

Nielsen, M. (2006). Copying actions and copying outcomes: Social learning through the second year. *Developmental Psychology, 42,* 555–565.

Norman, R. (1976). When what is said is important: A comparison of expert and attractive sources. *Journal of Experimental Social Psychology, 12,* 294–300.

Parten, M. B. (1932). Social participation among pre-school children. *Journal of Abnormal and Social Psychology, 27,* 243–269.

Pelham, B. W., & Swann, W. B. (1994). The juncture of intrapersonal and interpersonal knowledge: Self-certainty and interpersonal congruence. *Personality and Social Psychology Bulletin, 20,* 349–357.

Pennington, G. I., & Roese, N. J. (2003). Regulatory focus and temporal distance. *Journal of Experimental Social Psychology, 39,* 563–576.

Perreault, C., Brantingham, P. J., Kuhn, S. L., Wurz, S., & Gao, X (2013). Measuring the complexity of lithic technology. *Current Anthropology, 54* (Suppl 8), S397–S406.

Phillips, K. W., Liljenquist, K., & Neale, M. A. (2009). Is the pain worth the gain? The advantages and liabilities of agreeing with socially distinct newcomers. *Personality and Social Psychology Bulletin, 35,* 336–350.

Pinel, E. C., Long, A. E., Landau, M. J., Alexander, K., & Pyszczynski, T. (2006). Seeing I to I: A pathway to interpersonal connectedness. *Journal of Personality and Social Psychology, 90,* 243–257.

Piaget, J. (1926). *The language and thought of the child.* New York: Harcourt Brace.

Piaget, J. (1962/1951). *Play, dreams and imitation in childhood.* New York: Norton.

Piaget, J. (1965). *The moral judgment of the child.* New York, NY: Free Press (Original translation published 1932)

Piaget, J. (1970). Piaget's theory. In P. H. Mussen (Ed.), *Carmichael's manual of child psychology* (3rd ed., Vol. 1, pp. 703–732). New York, NY: Wiley.

Pianta, R. C., Rimm-Kaufman, S. E., & Cox, M. J. (1999). Introduction: An ecological approach to kindergarten transition. In R. C. Pianta & M. J. Cox (Eds.), *The transition to kindergarten* (pp.3–12). Baltimore, MD: Brookes.

Piers, G., & Singer, M. B. (1971). *Shame and guilt.* New York, NY: Norton.

Przybylinski, E., & Andersen, S. M. (2015). Systems of meaning and transference: Implicit significant-other activation evokes shared reality. *Journal of Personality and Social Psychology, 109,* 636–661.

Reis, H. T., & Patrick, B. C. (1996). Attachment and intimacy: Component processes. In E. T. Higgins & A. W. Kruglanski (Eds.), *Handbook of personal relationships* (pp. 523–563). New York, NY: Guilford.

Reis, H. T., & Shaver, P. (1988). Intimacy as an interpersonal process. In S. Duck (Ed.), *Handbook of personal relationships* (pp. 367–389). Chichester, England: Wiley.

Reis, H. T., Smith, S. M., Carmichael, C. L., Caprariello, P. A., Tsai, F., Rodrigues, A., & Maniaci, M. R. (2010). Are you happy for me? how sharing positive events with others provides personal and interpersonal benefits. *Journal of Personality and Social Psychology, 99,* 311–329.

Reznik, I., & Andersen, S. M. (2007). Agitation and despair in relation to parents: Activating emotional suffering in transference. *European Journal of Personality, 21,* 281–301.

Rholes, W. S., Blackwell, J., Jordan, C., & Walters, C. (1980). A developmental study of learned helplessness. *Developmental Psychology, 16,* 616–624.

Rholes, W. S., & Ruble, D. N. (1984). Children's understanding of dispositional characteristics of others. *Child Development, 4,* 550–560.

Robson, D. (2013, January 14). There really are 50 Eskimo words for "snow." *Washington Post.* Retrieved from http://www.washingtonpost.com

Rokeach, M. (1973). *The nature of human values.* New York, NY: Free Press.

Rogers, C. R. (1959). A theory of therapy, personality, and interpersonal relationships, as developed in the client-centered framework. In S. Koch (Ed.), *Psychology: A study of a science: Vol. 3. Formulations of the person and the social context* (pp. 184–256). New York, NY: McGraw-Hill.

Rogers, C. R. (1961). *On becoming a person.* Boston, MA: Houghton Mifflin.

Rogers, T. B. (1981). A model of the self as an aspect of the human information processing system. In N. Cantor & J. F. Kihlstrom (Eds.), *Personality, cognition and social interaction* (pp. 193–214). Hillsdale, NJ: Erlbaum.

Rogoff, B. (1990). *Apprenticeship in thinking: Cognitive development in social context.* New York, NY: Oxford University Press.

Rogoff, B. (2003). *The cultural nature of human development.* New York, NY: Oxford University Press.

Rogoff, B., Paradise, R., Mejia Arauz, R., Correa-Chavez, M., & Angelillo, C. (2003). Firsthand learning through intent participation. *Annual Review of Psychology, 54,* 175–203.

Rommetveit, R. (1974). *On message structure: A framework for the study of language and communication.* New York, NY: Wiley.

Rosati, M. (2009). *Ritual and the sacred: A Neo-Durkheimian analysis of politics, religion and the self.* New York, NY: Routledge.

Rosenberg, M. (1965). *Society and the adolescent self-image.* Princeton, NJ: Princeton University Press.

Rosenberg, M. (1979). *Conceiving the self.* Malabar, FL: Krieger.

Rosenthal, R., & Jacobson, L. (1968). *Pygmalion in the classroom: Teacher expectancies and pupils' intellectual development.* New York, NY: Holt, Rinehart & Winston.

Ross, L., Bierbrauer, G., & Hoffman, S. (1976). The role of attribution processes in conformity and dissent: Revisiting the Asch situation. *American Psychologist, 31,* 148–157.

Ross, L., Greene, D., & House, P. (1977). The "false consensus effect": An egocentric bias in social perception and attribution precesses. *Journal of Experimental Social Psychology, 13,* 279–301.

Rossano, M. J. (2012). The essential role of ritual in the transmission and reinforcement of social norms. *Psychological Bulletin, 138,* 529–549.

Rossignac-Milon, M., Bolger, N., & Higgins, E. T. (2016, July). *Shared reality increases closeness in romantic and unacquainted dyads.* Paper presented at the International Association for Relationship Research Conference, Toronto, ON.

Rossignac-Milon, M., & Higgins, E. T. (2018a). Beyond intrapersonal cognitive consistency: Shared reality and the interpersonal motivation for truth. *Psychological Inquiry, 29,* 86–93.

Rossignac-Milon, M., & Higgins, E. T. (2018b). Epistemic companions: Shared reality development in close relationships. *Current Opinion in Psychology, 23,* 66–71.

Roth, M. T. (1997). *Law collections from Mesopotamia and Asia Minor* (2nd ed.). Atlanta, GA: Society of Biblical Literature.

Ruble, D. N. (1983). The development of social comparison processes and their role in achievement-related self-socialization. In E. T. Higgins, D. N. Ruble, & W. W. Hartup (Eds.), *Social cognition and social development: A socio-cultural perspective.* (pp. 134–157). New York, NY: Cambridge University Press.

Ruble, D. N., & Rholes, W. S. (1981). The development of children's perceptions and attributions about their social world. In J. D. Harvey, W. Ickes, & R. F. Kidd (Eds.), *New directions in attribution research* (Vol. 3, pp. 3–36). Hillsdale, NJ: Erlbaum.

Rusbult, C. E., Finkel, E. J., & Kumashiro, M. (2009). The Michelangelo phenomenon. *Current Directions in Psychological Science, 18,* 305–309.

Rusbult, C. E., & Van Lange, P. A. M. (2003). Interdependence, interaction, and relationships. *Annual Review of Psychology, 54,* 351–375.

Rutter, D. R., & Durkin, K. (1987). Turn-taking in mother–infant interaction: An examination of vocalizations and gaze. *Developmental Psychology, 23,* 54–61.

Saarni, C. (2000). Emotional competence: A developmental perspective. In R. Bar-On & J. D. A. Parker (Eds.), *The handbook of emotional intelligence: Theory, development, assessment, and application at home, school, and in the workplace* (pp. 68–91). San Francisco, CA: Wiley.

Saarni, C., Campos, J. J., Camras, A., & Witherington, D. (2006). Emotional development: Action, communication, and understanding. In N. Eisenberg (Ed.), *Handbook of child psychology: Vol. 3. Social, emotional, and personality development* (6th ed., pp. 226–299). Hoboken, NJ: Wiley.

Sapir, E. (1928). The unconscious patterning of behavior in society. In *The unconscious: A symposium* (pp. 114–142). New York, NY: Knopf.

Sarbin, T. R. (1952). A preface to a psychological analysis of the self. *Psychological Review, 59,* 11–22.

Sarbin, T. R., & Allen, V. L. (1968). Role theory. In G. Lindzey & E. Aronson (Eds.), *Handbook of social psychology* (2nd ed., Vol. 1, pp. 488–567). Reading, MA: Addison-Wesley.

Sassenberg, K., & Hansen, N. (2007). The impact of regulatory focus on affective responses to social discrimination. *European Journal of Social Psychology, 37,* 421–444.

Schachter, S. (1959). *The psychology of affiliation.* Stanford, CA: Stanford University Press.

Schachter, S. (1964). The interaction of cognitive and physiological determinants of emotional state. In L. Berkowitz (Ed.), *Advances in experimental social psychology* (Vol. 1, pp. 49–80). New York, NY: Academic Press.

Schachter, S., & Singer, J. E. (1962). Cognitive, social and physiological determinants of emotional state. *Psychological Review, 69,* 379–399.

Schmidt, M. F. H., Rakoczy, H., & Tomasello, M. (2012). Young children enforce social norms selectively depending on the violator's group affiliation. *Cognition, 124,* 325–333.

Scholer, A. A., Ozaki, Y., & Higgins, E. T. (2014). Inflating and deflating the self: Sustaining motivational concerns through self-evaluation. *Journal of Experimental Social Psychology, 51,* 60–73.

Scholer, A. A., Zou, X., Fujita, K., Stroessner, S. J., & Higgins, E. T. (2010). When risk-seeking becomes a motivational necessity. *Journal of Personality and Social Psychology, 99,* 215–231.

Schneider, D. J. (2004). *The psychology of stereotyping.* New York, NY: Guilford.

Schwartz, S. H. (1992). Universals in the content and structure of values: Theoretical advances and empirical tests in 20 countries. In M. P. Zanna (Ed.), *Advances in experimental social psychology* (Vol. 25, pp. 1–65). New York, NY: Academic Press.

Schwebel, D. C., Rosen, C. S., & Singer, J. L. (1999). Preschoolers' pretend play and theory of mind: The role of jointly constructed pretence. *British Journal of Developmental Psychology, 17,* 333–348.

Seibt, B., & Förster, J. (2004). Stereotype threat and performance: How self-stereotypes influence processing by inducing regulatory foci. *Journal of Personality and Social Psychology, 87,* 38–56.

Selman, R. L. (1980). *The growth of interpersonal understanding: Developmental and clinical analyses.* New York, NY: Academic Press.

Selman, R. L., & Byrne, D. F. (1974). A structural-developmental analysis of levels of role-taking in middle childhood. *Child Development, 45,* 803–806.

Semin, G. R. (2000). Agenda 2000: Communication: Language as an implementational device for cognition. *European Journal of Social Psychology, 30,* 595–612.

Semin, G. R., & Fiedler, K. (1988). The cognitive functions of linguistic categories in describing persons: Social cognition and language. *Journal of Personality and Social Psychology, 54,* 558–568.

Semin, G. R., & Fiedler, K. (1991). The linguistic category model, its bases, applications and range. In W. Stroebe & M. Hewstone (Eds.), *European review of social psychology* (Vol. 2, pp. 1–50). Chichester, England: Wiley.

Semin, G. R., Higgins, E. T., Gil de Montes, L., Estourget, Y., & Valencia, J. F. (2005). Linguistic signatures of regulatory focus: How abstraction fits promotion more than prevention. *Journal of Personality and Social Psychology, 89,* 36–45.

Shah, J. (2003). The motivational looking glass: How significant others implicitly affect goal appraisals. *Journal of Personality and Social Psychology, 85,* 424–439.

Shah, J. Y., Brazy, P. C., & Higgins, E. T. (2004). Promoting us or preventing them: Regulatory focus and manifestations of intergroup bias. *Personality and Social Psychology Bulletin, 30,* 433–446.

Shantz, C. U. (1983). Social cognition. In J. H. Flavell & E. M. Markman (Eds.), *Carmichael's manual of child psychology: Vol. 3. Cognitive development* (P. H. Mussen, Gen. ed., 4th ed., pp. 495–555.). New York, NY: Wiley.

Sherif, M. (1936). *The psychology of social norms.* New York, NY: Harper & Brothers.

Sherif, M., Harvey, O., White, B., Hood, W., & Sherif, C. (1961). *Intergroup conflict and cooperation: The robber's cave experiment.* Norman, OK: Institute of Group Relations, University of Oklahoma.

Shteynberg, G. (2015). Shared attention. *Perspectives on Psychological Science, 10,* 579–590.

Shteynberg, G. (2018). A collective perspective: Shared attention and the mind. *Current Opinion in Psychology, 23,* 93–97.

Shteynberg, G., & Apfelbaum, E. (2013). The power of shared experience: Simultaneous observation with similar others facilitates social learning. *Social Psychological & Personality Science, 4,* 738–744.

Shteynberg, G., Hirsh, J. B., Apfelbaum, E. P., Larsen, J. T., Galinsky, A. D., & Roese, N. J. (2014). Feeling more together: Group attention intensifies emotion. *Emotion, 14,* 1102–1114.

Shweder, R. A., Mahapatra, M., & Miller, J. G. (1987). Culture and moral development. In J. Kagan & S. Lamb (Eds.), *The emergence of morality in young children* (pp. 1–83). Chicago, IL: University of Chicago Press.

Sinclair, S., Hardin, C. D., & Lowery, B. S. (2006). Self-stereotyping in the context of multiple social identities. *Journal of Personality and Social Psychology, 90*, 529–542.

Sinclair, S., Lowery, B. S., Hardin, C. D., & Colangelo, A. (2005). Social tuning of automatic racial attitudes: The role of affiliative motivation. *Journal of Personality and Social Psychology, 89*, 583–592.

Smith, M. B., Bruner, J. S., & White, R. W. (1956). *Opinions and personality.* New York, NY: Wiley.

Smith, T. M., Tafforeau, P., Reid, D. J., Pouech, J., Lazzari, V., Zermeno, J. P., . . . Hublin, J-J. (2010). Dental evidence for ontogenetic differences between modern humans and Neanderthals. *Proceedings of the National Academy of Sciences of the United States of America, 107*, 20923–20928.

Sorce, J. F., Emde, R. N., Campos, J., & Klinnert, M. D. (1985). Maternal emotional signaling: its effect on the visual cliff behavior of 1-year-olds. *Developmental Psychology, 21*, 195–200.

Spelke, E. S. (2013). Developmental sources of social divisions. In A. M. Battro, S. Dehaene, and W. J. Singer (Eds.), *The proceedings of the Working Group on neurosciences and the human person: New perspectives on human activities. Pontifical Academy of Sciences, Scripta Varia, 121.* Vatican City.

Spiegel, S., Grant-Pillow, H., & Higgins, E. T. (2004). How regulatory fit enhances motivational strength during goal pursuit. *European Journal of Social Psychology, 34*, 39–54.

Stasser, G. (1992). Pooling of unshared information during group discussion. In S. Worchel, W. Wood, & J. A. Simpson (Eds.), *Group process and productivity* (pp. 48–67). Newbury Park, CA: SAGE.

Stasser, G. (1999). The uncertain role of unshared information in collective choice. In L. L. Thompson, J. M. Levine, & D. M. Messick (Eds.), *Shared cognition in organizations: The management of knowledge* (pp. 49–69). Hillsdale, NJ: Erlbaum.

Stenberg, G. (2009). Selectivity in infant social referencing. *Infancy, 14*, 457–473.

Stephen, T. D. (1984). A symbolic exchange framework for the development of intimate relationships. *Human Relations, 37*, 393–408.

Stern, D. N. (1985). *The interpersonal world of the infant.* New York, NY: Basic Books.

Stern, W. (1914). *Psychologie der fruehen Kindheit.* Leipzig, Germany: Quelle & Meyer.

Stipek, D. (1995). The development of pride and shame in toddlers. In J. Tangney & K. Fischer (Eds.), *Self-conscious emotions: The psychology of shame, guilt, embarassment and pride* (pp. 237–252). New York, NY: Guilford.

Stipek, D., Recchia, S., & McClintic, S. (1992). Self-evaluation in young children. *Monographs of the Society for Research in Child Development, 57,* 1–84.

Stoner, J. A. F. (1961). *A comparison of individual and group decisions involving risk.* Unpublished MA thesis, MIT.

Stoner, J. A. F. (1968). Risky and cautious shifts in group decisions: The influence of widely held values. *Journal of Experimental Social Psychology, 4,* 442–459.

Stout, D. (2011). Stone toolmaking and the evolution of human culture and cognition. *Philosophical Transactions of the Royal Society B: Biological Sciences, 366,* 1050–1059.

Striano, T., Reid, V. M., & Hoehl, S. (2006). Neural mechanisms of joint attention in infancy. *European Journal of Neuroscience, 23,* 2819–2823.

Stryker, S. (1980). *Symbolic interactionism.* Mendo Park, CA: Benjamin/Cummings.

Stryker, S., & Statham, A. (1985). Symbolic interaction and role theory. In G. Lindzey & E. Aronson (Eds.), *Handbook of social psychology* (Vol. 1, pp. 311–378). New York, NY: Random House.

Suddendorf, T. (2013). *The gap: The science of what separates us from other animals.* New York, NY: Basic Books.

Sullivan, H. S. (1953). *The collected works of Harry Stack Sullivan: Vol. 1. The interpersonal theory of psychiatry.* Edited by H. S. Perry & M. L. Gawel. New York, NY: Norton.

Svetlova, M., Nichols, S. R., & Brownell, C. A. (2010). Toddlers' prosocial behavior: From instrumental to empathic to altruistic helping. *Child Development, 81,* 1814–1827.

Swann, W. B., Jr. (1984). Quest for accuracy in person perception: A matter of pragmatics. *Psychological Review, 91,* 457–477.

Swann, W. B., Jr. (1990). To be adored or to be known? The interplay of self-enhancement and self-verification. In E. T. Higgins & R. M. Sorrentino (Eds.), *Handbook of motivation and cognition: Foundations of social behavior* (Vol. 2, pp. 408–448). New York, NY: Guilford.

Swann, W. B., Jr., & Buhrmester, M. D. (2015). Identity fusion. *Current Directions in Psychological Science, 25,* 52–57.

Swann, W. B., Jr., Buhrmester, M. D., Gómez, Á., Jetten, J., Bastian, B., Vázquez, A., . . . Zhang, A. (2014). What makes a group worth dying for? Identity fusion fosters perception of familial ties, promoting self-sacrifice. *Journal of Personalilty and Social Psychology, 106,* 912–926.

Swann, W. B., Jr., Hixon, J. G., Stein-Seroussi, A., & Gilbert, D. T. (1990). The fleeting gleam of praise: Cognitive processes underlying behavioral reactions to self-relevant feedback. *Journal of Personalilty and Social Psychology, 59,* 17–26.

Swann, W. B., Jr., Jetten, J., Gómez, Á., Whitehouse, H., & Bastian, B. (2012). When group membership gets personal: A theory of identity fusion. *Psychological Review, 119,* 441–456.

Tajfel, H. (1974). Social identity and intergroup behavior. *Social Science Information, 13,* 65–93.

Tajfel, H. (1981). *Human groups and social categories: Studies in social psychology.* Cambridge: Cambridge University Press.

Tajfel, H. (1982). Social psychology of intergroup relations. *Annual Review of Psychology, 33,* 1–39.

Tajfel, H., Flament, C., Billig, M., & Bundy, R. P. (1971). Social categorization and intergroup behavior. *European Journal of Social Psychology, 1,* 149–178.

Tajfel, H., & Turner, J. C. (1979). An integrative theory of intergroup conflict. In W. G. Austin & S. Worchel (Eds.), *The social psychology of intergroup relations* (pp. 33–47). Monterey, CA: Brooks/Cole.

Tamis-LeMonda, C. S., Bornstein, M. H., & Baumwell, L. (2001). Maternal responsiveness and children's achievement. *Child Development, 72,* 748–767.

Terrace, H. S. (2005). Metacognition and the evolution of language. In H. S. Terrace & J. Metcalfe (Eds.), *The missing link in cognition: Origins of self-reflective consciousness* (pp. 84–115). Oxford, England: Oxford University Press.

Thaler, R. H. (1980). Toward a positive theory of consumer choice. *Journal of Economic Behavior and Organization, 1,* 39–60.

Thompson, R. A. (2006). The development of the person: Social understanding, relationships, conscience, self. In N. Eisenberg (Ed.), *Handbook of child psychology: Vol. 3. Social, emotional, and personality development* (6th ed., pp. 24–98). Hoboken, NJ: Wiley.

Tomasello, M. (2014). *A natural history of human thinking.* Cambridge, MA: Harvard University Press.

Tomasello, M., Carpenter, M., Call, J., Behne, T., & Moll, H. (2005). Understanding and sharing intentions: The origins of cultural cognition. *Behavioral and Brain Sciences, 28,* 675–735.

Tomasello, M., Carpenter, M., & Liszkowski, U. (2007). A new look at infant pointing. *Child Development, 78,* 705–722.

Trevarthen, C. (1979). Commuication and cooperation in early infancy: A description of primary intersubjectivity. In M. Bullowa (Ed.), *Before speech. The beginning of interpersonal communication.* New York, NY: Caambridge University Press.

Triandis, H. C. (1989). The self and social behavior in differing cultural contexts. *Psychological Review, 93*, 506–520.

Trope, Y., & Liberman, N. (2003). Temporal construal. *Psychological Review, 110*, 403–421.

Trope, Y., & Liberman, N. (2010). Construal-level theory of psychological distance. *Psychological Review, 117*, 440–463.

Turiel, E. (2006). The development of morality. In N. Eisenberg (Ed.), *Handbook of child psychology: Vol. 3. Social, emotional, and personality development* (6th ed., pp. 646–718). Hoboken, NJ: Wiley.

Turner, J. C., Hogg, M. A., Oakes, P. J., Reicher, S. D., & Wetherell, M. S. (1987). *Rediscovering the social group: A self-categorization theory*. Oxford, England: Blackwell.

Van Dijk, D., & Kluger, A. N. (2004). Feedback sign effect on motivation: Is it moderated by regulatory focus? *Applied Psychology: An International Review, 53*, 113–135.

Van Dijk, T. A. (1977). Context and cognition: Knowledge frames and speech act comprehension. *Journal of Pragmatics, 1*, 211–232.

Van Hook, E., & Higgins, E. T. (1988). Self-related problems beyond the self-concept: The motivational consequences of discrepant self-guides. *Journal of Personality and Social Psychology, 55*, 625–633.

Vygotsky, L. S. (1962). *Thought and language*. Translated by E. Hanfmann & G. Vakar. Cambridge, MA: MIT Press.

Vygotsky, L. S. (1978). *Mind in society: Development of higher psychological processes*. Edited by M. Cole. Cambridge, MA: Harvard University Press.

Wameken, F., Chen, F., & Tomasello, M. (2006). Cooperative activities in young children and chimpanzees. *Child Development, 77*, 640–663.

Warneken, F., & Tomasello, M. (2007). Helping and cooperation at 14 months of age. *Infancy, 11*, 271–294.

Watson, A. J., & Valtin, R. (1997). Secrecy in middle childhood. *International Journal of Behavioral Development, 21*, 431–452.

Wellman, H. M. (2014). *Making minds: How theory of mind develops*. New York, NY: Oxford University Press.

Wellman, H. M., Cross, D., & Watson, J. (2001). Meta-analysis of theory-of-mind development: The truth about false belief. *Child Development, 72*, 655–684.

Werker, J. F., & Tees, R. C. (1984). Cross-language speech perception: Evidence for perceptual reorganization during the first year of life. *Infant Behavior and Development, 7*, 49–63.

Whitehouse, H., McQuinn, B., Buhrmester, M., & Swann, W. B., Jr. (2014). Brothers in arms: Libyan revolutionaries bond like family. *Proceedings of the National Academy of Sciences, 111*, 17783–17785.

Whiten, A., McGuigan, N., Marshall-Pescini, S., & Hopper, L. M. (2009). Emulation, imitation, over-imitation and the scope of culture for child and chimpanzee. *Philosophical Transactions of the Royal Society B, 364*, 2417–2428.

Whiting, B. B., & Whiting, J. W. M. (1975). *Children of six cultures: A psycho-cultural analysis.* Cambridge, MA: Harvard University Press.

Whorf, B. L. (1956). *Language, thought and reality.* Boston, MA: MIT Press.

Wiener, N. (1948). *Cybernetics: Control and communication in the animal and the machine.* Cambridge, MA: MIT Press.

Wiessner, P. W. (2014). Embers of society: Firelight talk among the Ju/'hoansi Bushmen. *PNAS, 111*, 14027–14035.

Wimmer, H., & Perner, J. (1983). Beliefs about beliefs: Representation and constraining function of wrong beliefs in young children's understanding of deception. *Cognition, 13*, 103–128.

Winnicott, D. W. (1965). Ego distortion in terms of true and false self. In his *The maturational process and the facilitating environment: Studies in the theory of emotional development* (pp. 140–152). New York, NY: International Universities Press.

Wittgenstein, L. (1953). *Philosophical investigations.* New York, NY: Macmillan.

Word, C. O., Zanna, M. P., & Cooper, J. (1974). The nonverbal mediation of self-fulfilling prophecies on interracial interaction. *Journal of Experimental Social Psychology, 10*, 109–120.

Wrangham, R. (2009). *Catching fire: How cooking made us human.* New York, NY: Basic Books.

Wright, D. B., Self, G., & Justice, C. (2000). Memory conformity: Exploring the misinformation effects when presented by another person. *British Journal of Psychology, 91*, 189–202.

Wu, Z., & Su, Y. (2014). How do preschoolers' sharing behaviors relate to their theory of mind understanding? *Journal of Experimental Child Psychology, 120*, 73–86.

Yamagishi, T., Hashimoto, H., Cook, K. S., & Li, Y. (2012). Modesty in self-presentation: A comparison between the USA and Japan. *Asian Journal of Social Psychology, 15*, 60–68.

Youniss, J. (1980). *Parents and peers in social development.* Chicago, IL: University of Chicago Press.

Zahn-Waxler, C., Radke-Yamow, M., Wagner, E., & Chapman, M. (1992). Development of concern for others. *Developmental Psychology, 28*, 126–136.

Zajonc, R. B. (1960). The process of cognitive tuning and communication. *Journal of Abnormal and Social Psychology, 61*, 159–167.

Zeigarnik, B. (1938). On finished and unfinished tasks. In W. D. Ellis (Ed.), *A source book of gestalt psychology* (pp. 300–314). New York, NY: Harcourt, Brace, & World.

Zou, X., Scholer, A. A., & Higgins, E. T. (2014). In pursuit of progress: Promotion motivation and risk preference in the domain of gains. *Journal of Personality and Social Psychology, 106*, 183–201.

Index

Page numbers followed by *f* indicate figures; page numbers followed by *t* indicate tables.